Marxism
and Modernism

Marxism and Modernism

An Historical Study of Lukács, Brecht, Benjamin, and Adorno

Eugene Lunn

Verso

First published by
University of California Press
© 1982

Published 1985
Verso
15 Greek Street London W1V 5LF

**British Library
Cataloguing in Publication Data**

Lunn, Eugene
 Marxism and modernism: an historical study of
 Lukacs, Brecht, Benjamin and Adorno.
 1. Arts—Europe—Philosophy—History—20th
 century   2. Communist aesthetics—History—
 20th century.   3. Modernism (Aesthetics)—
 History—20th century
 I. Title
 700' .1   BH201

Printed in Great Britain by
Thetford Press Limited
Thetford, Norfolk

ISBN 0 86091 824 6

Contents

BIBLIOGRAPHY

To Donna, Rachel, and Benjamin

Acknowledgments

I should like to thank the following colleagues in the History Department at the University of California, Davis, for the helpful comments they made on earlier chapter drafts of this work: Ted Margadant, Bob Resch, Bill Hagen, and Roy Willis. At a later stage in the preparation of the manuscript, Russell Berman, Paul Thomas, and Mark Poster offered their knowledgeable support and a number of useful criticisms. My greatest intellectual debt, however, is to four persons in particular. My mentor in graduate school, Carl Schorske, showed me how the historian may interrelate ideas and social reality through the medium of intellectual biography. Martin Jay, who has written extensively on Western Marxism, read my manuscript with great care and provided me with numerous astute suggestions for its improvement. An earlier version of the sections on Brecht and Lukács received meticulous and perceptive attention from David Bathrick in his capacity as an editor of the journal *New German Critique*. Finally, my wife Donna Reed, who is a specialist in German and Comparative Literature, has been involved with this project from its inception a decade ago. Through the innumerable discussions we have had on modern European literature and aesthetics, many of the pivotal ideas of *Marxism and Modernism* were first given shape and direction.

Introduction

In the late 1960s, George Lichtheim, the discerning historian of Marxism and of twentieth-century Europe, wrote: "West Germany today, unlike its Eastern neighbor beyond the wall, provides a meeting place of Marxism and Modernism. Some such encounter had already begun in the later years of the Weimar Republic and, but for the catastrophic eruption of counter-revolution and war, might have set the tone for the intellectual élite in the country as a whole."[1] The book that follows is an inquiry into the historical sources and many-sided contours of this political-aesthetic "encounter." The focus will be upon the writings of its major articulators: Georg Lukács, Bertolt Brecht, Walter Benjamin, and Theodor Adorno. I have four major purposes in this study: (1) to contribute to a firmer understanding of the pivotal role of aesthetic modernism—its reception and critical analysis—within the renaissance of a dialectical "Western" Marxian theory since the 1920s; (2) to explore the varieties of European "avant-garde" culture of 1880–1930—the analysis of which has up to now been largely parceled out amongst critics of the various arts—as a subject of serious interest to intellectual historians of twentieth-century Europe; (3) to analyze four specific confrontations between Marxism and modernism which have served to benefit each of these traditions (one of the four writers, Lukács, allowed the critique to proceed in only one direction, and I have therefore been most critical of his approach); and (4) to contribute new

1. George Lichtheim, *From Marx to Hegel* (London, 1971), p. 130.

insights and perspectives (particularly of an historical nature) on the work of and interrelation between Brecht, Lukács, Benjamin, and Adorno, each of whom has come to be regarded as a major figure of European cultural and intellectual life in this century.

I have not attempted to deny or escape my own ambivalence toward both Marxism and modernism, though I judge each to be of vital concern to contemporary intellectuals. Instead, I have hoped to put to good use the potential strengths of this dual attitude. Let me briefly enumerate, prior to their fuller elaboration later on, some of the strengths and weaknesses of the two traditions which are pertinent to this study of their encounter. (This book is not an overall theoretical inquiry into the relation between these currents, but an examination of four historically specific forms of their interfacing; yet, it may be worthwhile, at the outset, to mention my own general attitudes toward Marxism and modernism.) At its best, Marxism contains penetrating, indispensable, historically defined criticisms of capitalist economy, society, and culture, and a powerful method of dialectical analysis. At the same time, these are often coupled (in Marx's own work and in much later "Marxism") with a dogmatic faith in historical inevitability, an exclusive focus upon the capitalist sources of modern oppression, and a tendency (in some of Marx's later writings, which was much accentuated by the "orthodoxy" which followed) toward a "copy" theory of consciousness as a "reflection" of so-called "objective" social processes. Modernist culture contains ingredients which may aid in the overcoming of these problems (ingredients which are latent in Marx's own work, as we shall see in Chapter 1, but very often absent from that of his "followers"), e.g., an intense concern with the mediation of "content" by form; use of synchronous montage as an alternative to merely linear additive time; techniques of "de-familiarizing" the object-world; cultivation of paradox and ambiguity as opposed to monolithic notions of a single objective reality; and exploration of the fragmented and alienated experience of individuals in modern urban and industrial societies (which may throw light on both capitalist and bureaucratic socialist worlds). Modernist art in some of its phases contains weaknesses of its own, however, which a culturally sensitive Marxism may historically clarify and fruitfully criticize—e.g., an aristocratic cult of hermetic art; a suggestion of an ahistorical and timeless "human condition," or an endlessly repetitive cycle of "mythical" recurrence; and a form of narrowly cultural revolt which facilitates the absorption of art, as fashion, into advertising or into "shocking" entertainment and new consumer products for the

well-to-do. (That Marxist understanding, however flexible and unorthodox, will not alone provide an adequate historical assessment of
modernist culture will be suggested by the approach of Chapter 2.
There I will attempt an historical overview and comparative analysis of
those modernist currents to be treated by the four writers; but I shall do
this with largely non-Marxist perspectives. In addition, Chapter 2 will
introduce the contrasting aesthetic sources of the thought of Lukács,
Brecht, Benjamin, and Adorno.)

Each of the four figures studied here developed different wide-
ranging historical frameworks for the analysis of modern art and culture. They did so, however, within a series of debates among themselves. It was through these confrontations (between Brecht and Lukács
on the one hand, and Benjamin and Adorno on the other) that a serious
and flexible Marxist aesthetics for the twentieth century began to
emerge for the first time. (Marx's own writings on art are suggestive on
this score, but fragmentary and thin, and not entirely equipped to address the problems of twentieth-century cultural life.) In this book, each
debate will be analyzed and amplified in terms of its roots in contrasting
personal biographies and historical experiences, and assessed in relation
to the variety of overall approaches to Marxism and modernism which
the four writers articulated. The emphasis throughout will be upon
comparative analysis. This procedure is not only appropriate to the mutually relational manner in which their thoughts were often formed and
crystalized (the multiple interactions amongst the four thinkers are a
fascinating aspect of this material); it is hoped that this method will also
clarify the very plurality of the Marxist-modernist "encounters" involved. Comparative treatment of the four writers will provide alternative vantages beyond the necessarily limited purview of each of them,
and will highlight the wide variety of plausible Marxist approaches
to modernist culture. These comparisons will often be elucidated, in
turn, through contrasts among the modernist movements themselves (in
particular, symbolism, cubism, and expressionism, and their later off-
shoots). All four writers came to Marxism only after having been
sophisticated critics or practitioners of the modern arts and after developing strong cultural, aesthetic, and social views, both of which experiences were to influence their various constructions of a Marxist aesthetics; they did not merely apply a preformed Marxism to the visual arts,
literature, or music. It will be a central concern of this study, in fact, to
carefully delineate the different strands of modernism to which each
was indebted, or toward which each turned his critical eye.

The book will concentrate on the period 1920–50, and especially 1928–40, for I am studying the formative years of these theoretical "encounters." (Actually, Benjamin died in 1940, and Brecht in 1956.) I have alluded to some of the major pertinent writings published by Adorno and Lukács after 1950: both were quite productive until their deaths in 1969 and 1971, respectively. But I have found the responses to modernism contained in this later work to be largely an extension of the positions and analyses developed in the years before 1950.

One other question of scope is worth clarifying at the outset. It could be argued that a fifth important Marxist intellectual, Ernst Bloch, deserves also to be considered here. Bloch was an important defender of expressionism against Lukács's strictures upon the movement in the 1930s, and his voluminous writings on aesthetics and literature were influenced by modernist premises. Yet, he did not concentrate his attention upon modernism or develop a sustained analysis of it. Rather, he sought in his work to elucidate utopian longings in an extremely wide range of world art from the last three millennia. Although I have made reference to relevant aspects of his work, I have chosen not to include him as a major focus—especially as I also needed to be carefully selective, given the already massive body of material on Marxism and modernism, and on the four chosen writers, which I decided to include.

In much of the immense literature which now exists on Lukács, Brecht, Benjamin, and Adorno, their theories and analyses have been treated with little attention to the concrete historical experiences out of which their respective work grew. This study, however, will emphasize the diverse, historically conditioned currents of aesthetics, philosophy, and political theory which they absorbed. It will examine the various urban settings which helped form each of them (e.g., Berlin, Moscow, Paris, or Vienna in the 1920s). In addition, their reactions to critical developments such as World War I, the Weimar Republic, Nazi Germany, and Stalinist Russia will be carefully analyzed. These historical currents, situations, or events, mediated through their own particular responses, are not merely a "background" or even "context" for their cultural and social ideas; they are contained within the inner structure and meaning of these ideas. To neglect the historical formation and options of the four writers would be to truncate and falsify their thought and render all the more difficult any judgment on the actual relation between this body of analysis and our own situation. It would also be a failure to apply to social and historical thinkers the approach via history which they encourage us to take to works of art. (This need not be the same approach, though, as theirs.) It is curious how often Marxist ideas have been treated in historically disembodied form.

A major historical situation, one of the origins of a serious Marxist confrontation with modernism beginning in the 1920s, is worth citing at the outset. The defeat of proletarian revolution in Central Europe (in the years 1918–23), and the victories of Fascism thereafter, both under presumably "advanced" "objective" economic and political conditions, brought a crisis upon traditional Marxian orthodoxy. These developments influenced the unprecedented turn of several independent Marxist thinkers toward questions of "consciousness" and culture as a vital but neglected part of an historical dialectic of society, and as a means of better understanding the stabilizing features of modern capitalism— e.g., Lukács's pioneering investigations of "reified" mental structures in a commodity society, the Frankfurt Institute's use of psychoanalytic theory, or Antonio Gramsci's attention to the cultural "hegemony" of the bourgeois class in the West. (Other examples could be adduced from the writings of Karl Korsch, Ernst Bloch, Wilhelm Reich, Max Horkheimer, Herbert Marcuse, or Brecht, Benjamin, and Adorno.) This was a major aspect of the "Western Marxist" current, as it has come to be called, which was at odds with both Social Democratic and Communist orthodoxy, and which was centered in Germany in the years 1923–33 and then among intellectual exiles from the Nazis. It was in this body of writings—little known until 1955 or 1960, but intensively studied thereafter—that a creative and undogmatic grappling with problems and inadequacies of classical Marxian theory was best carried out in the era of Hitler and Stalin.

One of the central foci of this strain of thought, and definitely one of its major accomplishments, was the analysis and reception of modern Western art and literature since the late nineteenth century. In his synoptic study of the whole movement, Perry Anderson has recently written: "The cultural and ideological focus of Western Marxism has . . . remained uniformly predominant from first to last. Aesthetics, since the Enlightenment the closest bridge of philosophy to the concrete world, has exercised an especial and constant attraction for its theorists. The great wealth and variety of the corpus of writing produced in this domain, far richer and subtler than anything within the classical heritage of historical materialism, may in the end prove to be the most permanent collective gain of this tradition."[2] Within this corpus, Anderson

---

2. Perry Anderson, *Considerations on Western Marxism* (London, 1976), p. 78.

cites the exchanges and relations between Lukács, Brecht, Benjamin, and Adorno as forming "one of the central debates in the cultural development of Western Marxism."[3] (I would contend, beyond this, that they are among the richest and most sophisticated in twentieth-century cultural thought as a whole.) One of the attractions of this body of ideas is stated by Henri Arvon: "Marxist Aesthetics remains all the more open to a total and ever-changing application of dialectics in that it is one of the rare branches of Marxist doctrine not to have been crushed and smothered beneath the weight of rigid dogma established once and for all and drummed into its proponents by an almost ritualistic recitation of magic formulas."[4] Arvon's comments serve well to introduce the following study of diverging confrontations between Marxism and modernism.

3. Ibid., p. 76.
4. Henri Arvon, *Marxist Esthetics* (Ithaca, N.Y., 1973), pp. 2–3.

PART ONE

Traditions

CHAPTER ONE

Art and Society in the Thought of Karl Marx

While emphasizing the central importance of the labor process, Marx viewed reality as a relational field comprising the totality of human experience. Hence, it is necessary to understand his interest in art, literature, and culture as dynamic elements which interact with the rest of his lifework. In this chapter, I shall attempt to describe not merely Marx's literary predilections, what he liked and why, but the "relational field" which he saw between art and other aspects of the whole social process. I shall also suggest the implications for aesthetic and cultural analysis of some of the main directions of his economic, social, and historical thought. My central concerns will be Marx's view of: the purposes of art; cultural production and human labor; alienation and commodity fetishism under capitalism; the dialectical course of historical development; the problem of ideology; and the question of literary realism. The chapter will conclude with a brief analysis of Marx's relation to major crosscurrents of European social and cultural theory in the eighteenth and nineteenth centuries. Only by posing the questions in such a broad manner is it possible to assess the Marxian legacy which was to be extended and reworked, within twentieth-century conditions, by Lukács, Brecht, Benjamin, and Adorno.

Marx never developed a systematic "aesthetics." Any description of his views of art and society must be a reconstruction of what are fragmentary and scattered passages whose implications Marx himself never fully worked out. Fortunately, we now have a number of sophisticated attempts to bring together the major aesthetic themes which Marx left in largely undeveloped form, and to relate them coherently to his wider thought.[1] Yet, it was the very possibility of varying interpretations of Marx's views, the fact that his lines of inquiry in the area of cultural activity may lead in different directions which he did not systematize, which helped stimulate the rich diversity of approaches between 1920 and 1950 which is the central subject of this book. Diversity of perspective was apparent, for example, in Marx's various comments on the essential purposes of art, a subject to which we shall now turn.

❖   ❖   ❖

Art, as a distinct part of human labor, is no mere "copy" or "reflection" of so-called external reality, according to Marx, but its infusing with human purposes. In the youthful *1844 Mss.*, Marx distinguished humans as natural beings who make their "life-activity the object of [their] consciousness."[2] In the process of labor, human beings develop both the world of nature *and* their own capacities. Although Marxism has often degenerated into a narrowly productivist and instrumental view of human beings (who are seen, as in the Soviet Union, simply as makers of material goods), and although Marx has been held accountable for facilitating this,[3] he usually understood labor and production in

1. S.S. Prawer, *Marx and World Literature* (Oxford, England, 1976); Peter Demetz, *Marx, Engels and the Poets* (Chicago, 1967); Mikhail Lifshitz, *The Philosophy of Art of Karl Marx* (London, 1973); the particularly incisive long introduction by Stefan Morawski to *Marx and Engels on Literature and Art*, ed. Lee Baxandall and Stefan Morawski (St. Louis, 1973), pp. 3–47; Adolfo Sanchez Vázquez, *Art and Society: Essays in Marxist Aesthetics* (New York, 1973); Henri Arvon, *Marxist Esthetics* (Ithaca, N.Y., 1973); Ernst Fischer, *The Necessity of Art: A Marxist Approach* (Baltimore, 1963); Istvan Mészáros, *Marx's Theory of Alienation* (London, 1970), chap. 7; Hans-Dietrich Sander, *Marxistische Ideologie und allgemeine Kunsttheorie* (Tübingen, 1970); Raymond Williams, *Marxism and Literature* (Oxford, England, 1977).

2. *The Marx-Engels Reader*, ed. Robert C. Tucker (New York, 1972), p. 62.

3. In the work of the Frankfurt School in the 1930s, especially that of Adorno and Horkheimer, there developed a criticism of "the ontological centrality of labor" in Marx's thought which was seen as narrowly instrumental and encouraging the development of technocratic societies. (See Martin Jay, *The Dialectical Imagination: A History of the Frankfurt School and the Institute for Social Research* [Boston, 1973], pp. 57–75 and 79.) The critique has been extended by Jürgen Habermas, who in the 1960s was the "heir apparent" of their work. Habermas has focused upon the need for alternative modes of understanding human self-constitution, most importantly symbolic, communicative interaction through language which is not aimed directly at the productive process. (See, for example, Jürgen Habermas, *Theory and Practice* [Boston, 1973], pp. 142–169; and Habermas, *Knowledge and Human Interests* [Boston, 1971], pp. 281–282.) The contention that Marx's view of labor and production excludes such considerations, and is narrowly instrumental and technocratic, is at least debatable and has been countered by Paul Thomas in "The Language of Real Life: Jürgen Habermas and the Distortion of Karl Marx," *Discourse: Berkeley Journal of Theoretical Studies in Media and Culture*, 1 (Fall 1979), 59–85.

wider terms: within a given natural and social environment, humans "produce" ideas, consciousness, language, and art, as well as instrumentally necessary goods.[4] "Conscious life-activity" is marked by what Marx, following Hegel, calls the *mediation* of the object by the subject and vice versa. "Labour is a process between man and nature," he writes in the first volume of *Capital*: "In this process man mediates, regulates and controls his material interchange with nature by means of his own activity. . . . [A]cting upon nature outside of him, and changing it, he changes his own nature also. The potentials that slumber within his nature are developed."[5]

Marx's observations on the origins of art reflected eighteenth-century traditions of German humanist aesthetics, albeit within a new materialist framework. While art developed, he speculated, out of the making of use-objects by primitive workers, it reveals human sensuous needs which go beyond physical necessity.[6] For both Engels and Marx, art never lost its connection with technical sophistication, the useful skills on which human culture rests. Yet, art is more than technical craft, more than the reproduction of external physical reality which makes possible the construction of, say, shelters, tools, etc. The category of the beautiful includes, for Marx, a classical sense of a work's symmetry, proportion, balance, and harmony, all of which attributes allow the construction of a coherent and attractive whole which rivals the shapes of material reality. The stress on such formal structures of art means that for Marx—and to a lesser degree for Engels also—art serves more than merely mimetic or directly utilitarian purposes. There is in art always an element of self-purpose in which the creation of formal attractiveness is an exercise of a human capacity for playful material activity[7] (the lack of which in modern capitalist labor is a prime measure of its alienation).

The appeal of art, for Marx, was to the eyes and ears, and not just to a philosophic, ethical, or political intelligence, or an abstract sense of form.[8] Closer here to the classical "paganism" of Goethe and Schiller than to Hegel—who saw art as an imperfect form of cognition to be surpassed by philosophy—Marx insisted on the continuing and lasting importance of aesthetic activity for the full education and emancipation of the human senses, a *Bildung* made all the more necessary by the capitalist debasement of human desires to the one of "possessing" or

---

4. Thomas, "Language of Real Life," pp. 71–72.
5. Baxandall and Morawski, *Marx and Engels on Literature and Art*, p. 53.
6. Ibid., p. 51.   7. Ibid., pp. 15–16.   8. Prawer, p. 207.

"having." [9] This points to one of the major issues, moreover, on which Marx was to break with Hegel's approach to contemporary reality: the subordination of art to conceptual thought was part of the idealist neglect of the material reality of working-class *sensual* deprivation and unhappiness.

If art is part of productive labor, while including formal and sensual enjoyment, it also becomes in the course of human evolution a form of contemplation, of consumption. As is shown by *The Grundrisse* (which did not appear in German until 1953), the pioneering efforts in the 1930s of Benjamin and Adorno and also of Brecht to develop a dialectical relation between cultural consumption and production had been suggested by Marx. Instead of seeing consumption as a passive given, unaltered by what is produced, Marx defined the active transformation of demand by what is aesthetically and economically supplied: "Does not the pianist as he produces music and satisfies our tonal sense, also produce that sense in some respects? The pianist stimulates production either by making us more active and lively individuals or . . . by arousing a new need. . . ." [10] "Production not only supplies a material for the need, but it also supplies a need for the material. . . . But consumption also mediates production . . . [in part because] consumption creates the need for new production." [11] *The Grundrisse* thus anticipates both the neo-Marxist stress on the alleged manufacture of "false needs" by an everexpanding consumer economy (the negative possibility), as well as Brecht's hopeful claim that the desire for good modern art can be aroused by its being produced. Marx's own awareness of the impact of expected reception on cultural creation, on the other hand, is strikingly evident in his one extended try at literary criticism: his 1845 critique of the immensely popular Eugène Sue novel *Les Mystères de Paris* stresses the influence upon the author of the ethical and political assumptions of its intended bourgeois public. [12]

With all the play of dialectical subtlety in Marx's discussion, it should not surprise us that he placed the primary stress on the role of production. This makes sense historically: nineteenth-century capital-

9. Baxandall and Morawski, *Marx and Engels on Literature and Art*, p. 69; "Economic and Philosophic Manuscripts of 1844," in *Marx-Engels Reader*, p. 73; see also the excellent discussion in Mészáros, *Marx's Theory of Alienation*, pp. 200–204.

10. *The Grundrisse*, ed. David McClellan (New York, 1971), p. 94.

11. Karl Marx, *The Grundrisse: Foundations of the Critique of Political Economy* (New York, 1973), p. 91. See the discussion of *The Grundrisse* in Ian Birchall, "The Total Marx and the Marxist Theory of Literature," in *Situating Marx*, ed. Paul Walton and Stuart Hall (London, 1972), pp. 131–132.

12. Prawer, *Marx and World Literature*, pp. 86 and 104.

ism developed far more by expanding the manufacture of goods for which there was already a demand than, as is the case today, by the encouragement of new needs. But what is produced by human manufacturing activity need not be merely commodities which diminish the laborer; production has historically developed, and can once again at a higher level develop, our aesthetic and other human needs in the very act of gratifying them. As against Feuerbach's contemplative materialism, Marx urged that we "conceive sensuousness as practical, human-sensuous activity." [13]

Art was of fundamental human *use* for Marx, although he rejected—as did many innovative writers and artists after 1850—narrow nineteenth-century bourgeois notions of utility. Marx means more than the specialized and formalized "*l'art pour l'art*" when he writes of medieval handicraft in *The Grundrisse* that "this work is still half artistic, it has still the aim in itself"; or when he speaks, in *Capital*, of the worker under modern capitalism as deprived of "enjoying that work as a play of his own mental and physical powers." [14] We may, in fact, isolate a number of different, although often related purposes of art in Marx's view, not the least of which would be its capacity to resist crude notions of utility. Of course, he did not dismiss the agitational value of art within the political struggles of the day, but this is only one—and far from the most emphasized—of its purposes. In addition to such directly political uses, Marx often viewed literature as an expression of ideological perspective, of social-class attitudes or habits of thought; or, alternatively, as in his frequent allusions to such masters as Aeschylus, Shakespeare, or Goethe, as a poetic embodiment of cognitive insight. Marx was sensitive to formal considerations which appeal directly to the senses and the emotions as well as to the intellect, even though in his writings—though not in his leisure [15]—he focused more on form as an expression of content. A careful reading of Marx's scattered comments on art and society would reveal, however, that of even greater significance to him was the fundamental human purpose of art as a measure of the emptiness or fullness of human life. [16]

13. *Marx-Engels Reader*, p. 108.
14. Baxandall and Morawski, *Marx and Engels on Literature and Art*, p. 16.
15. Prawer, *Marx and World Literature*, p. 415; Maynard Solomon, ed., *Marxism and Art: Essays Classic and Contemporary* (New York, 1973), p. 3.
16. This formulation of the various uses of art in Marx follows Morawski's "Introduction," in Baxandall and Morawski, *Marx and Engels on Literature and Art*, especially pp. 36–37. See also Thomas Metscher, "Aesthetik als Abbildtheorie: Erkenntnistheoretische Grundlagen der materialistischen Kunsttheorie und das Realismusproblem in den Literaturwissenschaften," *Argument*, 77 (December 1972), 969–974.

It has become a commonplace of scholarship on Marx and Engels to point out that, within their collaboration, Marx continued to stress Hegelian, classical, and German humanist motifs and concerns, while Engels was more enthusiastic about technological progress in social development, eighteenth-century materialism in epistemology, and literary realism in aesthetics.[17] It is not surprising, then, that it was Marx who emphasized more the transhistorical and fundamental humanizing value of art, and that in doing so he commented on the enduring importance of ancient Greek culture as in some respects a model for all later ages. (This, of course, was a common view of German intellectuals since Winckelmann and Goethe,[18] a perspective which could be used against modernist art, as Lukács was to do.)

Obviously, Marx was not suggesting the need to return to the past, even if that were possible. The classical component in his thought took form within an historical and dialectical framework where cultural decay is in tension with the very productive forces that may bring human advance. This is a feature of both his view of the decline of the ancient Greek world—his doctoral thesis of 1841 had stressed the historically useful innovations of the "egoistic" age of Epicurus[19]—and of the contemporary nineteenth-century situation. "There is one great fact . . . which no party can deny," he wrote of his own age. "On the one hand, there have started into life industrial and scientific forces, which no epoch of the former human history had ever suspected. On the other hand, there exist symptoms of decay, far surpassing the horrors of the latter times of the Roman Empire."[20] By placing his aesthetic observations within an historical counterpoint of decay *and* advance, Marx avoided any inducement to classical repose or any worship of the "eternal" truths of the ancient "model": in this way, the humanist and classical motifs in his thought became a further goad to action, coupled with concrete historical inquiry into the contradictions of historical development.

❖ ❖ ❖

17. See, for example, on the differences in philosophical framework and social thought, George Lichtheim's influential *Marxism: A Critical and Historical Study* (New York, 1961); and on the literary contrasts, see Demetz, *Marx, Engels and the Poets*, although he exaggerates the case.

18. See E.M. Butler, *The Tyranny of Greece over Germany* (Cambridge, England, 1935).

19. Lifschitz, *The Philosophy of Art of Karl Marx*, pp. 21–31.

20. Karl Marx, "Speech at the Anniversary of the Peoples' Paper," in *Marx-Engels Reader*, p. 427.

Under capitalist conditions, according to Marx, art has become, to an important degree, a form of alienated labor through its near reduction to commodity status in the marketplace. Marx included the production of art within his analysis of the reversal of purposes involved in all estranged labor under modern capitalist conditions: its creation has been transformed from a process in which the artist develops the self and humanizes nature into a means to his mere physical existence. Marx was well aware that the patronage system or other precapitalist forms of economic support were not free from alienating features for the artist, but he emphasized that the process was intensified by the spread of market conditions in the eighteenth and nineteenth centuries. Previously, at least there had been some degree of shared interests, tastes, values, and knowledge between artist and audience; now what connected the increasingly distant producer and consumer were the depersonalized market calculations of various cultural entrepreneurs. Pricing had become a competitive imperative which was often depreciative of the level and effort of workmanship. The competition for profits influenced the kind of cultural production that was marketable. While there was a kind of democratization of the audience in the nineteenth century, this was coupled with an increasing degree of homogenized merchandising in the very production of art and literature. As in all estranged labor, the worker had been alienated from the product of work. In the economic atmosphere of a "career open to talent," individual expression and freedom from immediate group restraint were more possible than they had been in the past, but they were often illusory, given the need to follow market calculations.[21] Marx followed Hegel's aesthetics here in seeing traits of bourgeois society—with all its progressive advance over "feudal" constrictions—as inimical to many forms of art (e.g., poetry), citing the increasing division of labor, the mechanization of many forms of human activity, and the predominance of quantitative over qualitative concerns.[22]

There was in this line of argument a sense of the violation of something sacred, a viewpoint developed in Marx's description of the contemporary demystifying of the exalted professions: "The bourgeoisie has stripped of its halo every occupation hitherto honored and looked

21. Morawski, "Introduction," in Baxandall and Morawski; *Marx and Engels on Literature and Art*, pp. 19–21.
22. Lifschitz, *The Philosophy of Art of Karl Marx*, pp. 13–14; Baxandall and Morawski, *Marx and Engels on Literature and Art*, p. 64.

up to with reverent awe. It has converted the physician, the lawyer, the priest, the poet, the man of science, into its paid wage laborers." [23]

But if one form of spiritualizing mystification has been eroded by the expansion of commerce—the romantic apotheosis of the arts as soaring above material reality—a new fetishism has replaced it: the fetishism of commodities. In *Capital*, the concept of human self-estrangement in the labor process was broadened into an attempt to solve the "mystery" of capitalism: the appearance that the world is governed by an objective process of laws which regulate the relations between things. As in all fetishized developments—in which "the productions of the human brain appear as independent beings endowed with life"—in a commodity "the social character of men's labour appears to them as an objective character stamped upon the product of that labour. . . . [A] definite social relation between men . . . assumes, in their eyes, the fantastic form of a relation between things." [24] That this is a new form of religious cult worship—which once again transforms humans from potential active makers of history into passive and frightened observers of inexorable forces—Marx suggests in the next sentence: "In order, therefore, to find an analogy, we must have recourse to the mist-enveloped regions of the religious world." [25] This critique was to prove a vital ingredient in all forms of "Western Marxism" after 1920, and particularly in cultural theory. But the full implications for the arts of the theory of commodity fetishism (developed by Lukács into the notion of "reification") were only fleetingly hinted at by either Marx or Engels. Later we shall see how ingeniously it was applied by all four of our major figures.

Whatever the implications of his argument concerning commodification, Marx did not view art, even in the nineteenth century, as entirely reduced to exchange-values which merely reflected the pervasive alienation. Even with its "halo" removed, art was capable of diagnosing, and pointing beyond, alienating social and economic conditions. For Marx the best art served the cognitive function of piercing through the ideological clouds which enshroud social realities. Moreover, by graphically embodying this relative freedom from the mere reflection of external circumstances, aesthetic creations could develop the desire for greater freedom from a dehumanized alienating society. All art has the capacity to create a *need* for aesthetic enjoyment and education which capitalist society cannot satisfy. Although coming increasingly under the influence of the marketplace, art is produced and consumed in relative au-

23. *Marx-Engels Reader*, p. 338.   24. Ibid., pp. 216–217.   25. Ibid.

tonomy and is not identical to factory work or to a pure commodity. No writer was more conscious of the monetary value of his craft than Balzac, and yet in Balzac's novels Marx and Engels saw the most accurate and historically rich portrait of French society of 1815–48.[26]

As intellectuals, artists and literati had some choice as to whether they would merely reflect the current alienation, encouraging adaptation, or help to transcend it. "Choice," Shlomo Avineri has written of Marx's view, "is the very embodiment of the intellectual's determined 'social being.'"[27] One of the important features of literature, however, which Lukács was to emphasize repeatedly, is that it may be cognitively valuable even where the author has not "chosen" to be committed to so-called "progressive" forces, as Engels wrote. The seriousness of Balzac's aesthetic craft compelled him to portray realistically the historical decline of the nobility he loved, although such sympathies no doubt helped distance him, to the benefit of that craft, from the ascending ideologies of the new commercial classes.[28]

Marx's observation that art may help create needs which capitalist society cannot satisfy raises a further issue—one which again points beyond art as alienated labor. Marx and Engels, as is well known, anticipated a utopian state beyond class society which was being prepared by historical developments in the present. Aesthetic and cultural considerations played an important role in their very brief suggestions of what such an unalienated society might be like. In this sense there is, properly qualified, a "utopian" value in art, although the differences in emphasis between Engels and Marx on this point are revealing. In Engels' writings, the focus is on a technically possible democratization of traditional culture through the expansion of leisure for all.[29] In Marx's writings, however, there is both a greater emphasis on the promise of future human fulfillment contained in the great works of past literature—what Adorno and Marcuse, following Stendhal, are to call a "Promesse de bonheur"—as well as an anticipation (or hope) that the character of *work itself* would become increasingly aesthetic in a future society. Not that Marx was not interested in the democratization of cultural activity. He even went so far as to hastily conclude, in the *German Ideology* (1846), that with a communist organization of society, painting as a

26. Baxandall and Morawski, *Marx and Engels on Literature and Art*, pp. 115–116, 148, and 150.

27. Schlomo Avineri, "Marx and the Intellectuals," *Journal of the History of Ideas*, 28 (1968), 277.

28. Baxandall and Morawski, *Marx and Engels on Literature and Art*, pp. 115–116.

29. Engels, "The Housing Question" (1872), in ibid., p. 73.

specialized professional activity would disappear as art was integrated into the variety of activities now available to many people.[30] But Marx also looked forward to the partial aestheticizing of the work process itself, a vital feature of the overcoming of alienation, in that labor would come to include a greater free play of physical and psychic faculties. Whereas present culture, "for the enormous majority, [is] a mere training to act as a machine," in a future communist society, genuine, free cultural life would develop in close touch with labor and modern technology; in this sense, the crippling division of labor between art and industry, and art and science, would be bridged without any Fourierist expectation of the transforming of all work into play.[31] With the democratized control of the means of production—that is, in an economy directed by social and not by private decisions—the "utopian" component of art as an enrichment of all human activities could come into its own.

❖   ❖   ❖

Much of what has become known as Marxist literary criticism has been an attempt to decipher the latent or manifest "ideological" content of literary works, their revelation of an underlying set of basic assumptions concerning human life in society, which is in turn said to be dependent upon the situation of a class in the social structure. In many cases, according to Marx and later Marxists, such ideological habits of thought help to strengthen the social and economic domination of ruling classes through their tendency to obsure the "real" historical forces at work. In this way, the expression "false consciousness" came to be used as a corollary of "ideology." Although many commentators in the West have charged Marx with ideological thinking—without clarifying how their own use of the word buries its original meaning and substitutes the notion of a knowledge which is politically committed—a more accurate critique would be to view Stalinism as an ideological use of Marx: what was once critical and subversive has deteriorated into an apologia of a massively powerful status quo.[32] In Marx's and Engels' original use, "ideology" was not understood in terms of a conscious and hypocritical manipulation of the public by a cynical bourgeois elite. Instead, those who chose to defend the reigning social system were viewed

30. Ibid. p. 71.
31. Ibid., pp. 22–24.
32. A particularly good discussion of this may be found in Iring Fetscher's *Marx and Marxism* (New York, 1971), pp. 148–181.

as necessarily neglectful of its own contradictory "grave-digging" elements and given to universal claims of its validity which function, in effect, to historically freeze the transiency of the present moment. "False consciousness," then, even when it is most obviously self-serving and self-justifying for the bourgeoisie—e.g., as in the assumption of the individual's moral responsibility for his or her poverty—is a form of historically understandable self-deception. In his analysis of the Eugène Sue novel *Les Mystères de Paris*, Marx sought to decode in this way the often unexamined premises of a reigning class's world-view. The richest of his discussions of aesthetically facilitated self-deceptions, of the ideological uses of literature, however, came six years later, in the brilliant opening pages of the *Eighteenth Brumaire of Louis Bonaparte*.

Using the categories of literary poetics directly in the construction of his historical argument, Marx begins with the famous statement that "all facts and personages of great importance in world history occur, as it were, twice, . . . the first time as tragedy, the second as farce." The ensuing overview of bourgeois political rhetoric from 1789 to 1851 in France is so tightly structured by this guiding literary metaphor that it has served as a compelling example for a number of critics who have emphasized the formal literary "strategies" in Marx's historical art.[33] Marx writes that the "traditions of all the dead generations weigh like a nightmare on the brain of the living," but that the use of heroic symbols of the past—the Roman Republic or Empire by the "conquering bourgeoisie" of 1789–1814, or the Napoleonic myth by the nephew—served vastly different purposes, depending upon whether or not the bourgeoisie welcomed basic social change or sought to prevent it. In the first case, during the Revolution of 1789, the Roman ghosts had "watched over the cradle" of modern bourgeois society, helping to delude the bourgeois revolutionaries about the social limitations of their own struggles. Analogously, the proclamation of universal rights of man was not manipulation or hypocrisy but a sincere self-deception which proved immensely useful in inspiring forceful actions beneficial not only to the bourgeoisie but also to the historical progress of capitalist society. Thus, the "awakening of the dead" in the Revolution of 1789, like the use of Old Testament metaphors in the Cromwellian upheaval before, "served

---

33. See Stanley E. Hyman, *The Tangled Bank: Darwin, Marx, Frazer and Freud as Imaginative Writers* (New York, 1962); Harold Rosenberg, "Politics as Illusion," in *Liberations: The Humanities in Revolution* (Wesleyan, Conn., 1972); Hayden White, *Metahistory: The Historical Imagination in Nineteenth-Century Europe* (Baltimore, 1974); and Jeffrey Mehlman, *Revolution and Repetition: Marx/Hugo/Balzac* (Berkeley, Calif., 1977).

the purpose of glorifying the new struggles, not of parodying the old; of magnifying the given tasks in imagination, not of taking flight from their solution in reality; of finding once more the spirit of revolution, not of making its ghost walk again." But in 1848–51, the bourgeois class, now frightened by continuing social revolution which threatened its own privileges, shrank back, and in its rhetoric "only the ghost of the old revolution walked." Soon the Napoleonic myth was also to be used, not to "magnify the given tasks in imagination," but to "take flight from their solution in reality." What was first a tragic poetics—the necessity for self-deception in an historical situation where the "rights of man" could still only benefit the few—had become the "farcical play" of "an adventurer (Napoleon III) who hides his trivially repulsive features under the iron death mask of Napoleon." [34]

Besides its analysis of ideology and the class reception of aesthetic styles, this long passage also suggests an historical basis for cultural formalism, the use of art and of "all the dead generations" as a surrogate for effective mastery of, and progressive innovation in, the social world. In comparing the poetics of bourgeois and proletarian revolutions, Marx emphasizes that "earlier revolutions required world-historical recollections in order to drug themselves concerning their own content. In order to arrive at its content, the revolution of the nineteenth century must let the dead bury the dead. There the phrase went beyond the content; here the content goes beyond the phrase." [35] For the development of a Marxist theory of aesthetic modernism, this is of real importance. Against the orthodox Communist charge that his modernist theatre represented an aestheticized formalism, Brecht answered—drawing out the implications of Marx's *Eighteenth Brumaire*, in effect—that formalism is present only where a solution is offered that is merely good on paper, or where there is a "holding fast to conventional forms while the changing social environment makes ever new demands upon art." [36] Walter Benjamin was to develop this argument further by shifting the charge of aestheticism from the avant-garde to the Nazis, whose substitution of "intoxicating" warfare for concrete social changes beneficial to the masses represented a kind of "aestheticizing of politics." [37] In

34. *Marx-Engels Reader*, pp. 437–438.
35. Ibid., p. 439.
36. Bertolt Brecht, "Die Expressionismus Debatte," in *Gesammelte Werke*, Vol. 19 (Frankfurt a.M., 1967), p. 291.
37. Walter Benjamin, "The Work of Art in the Age of Mechanical Reproduction," in *Illuminations*, ed. Hannah Arendt (New York, 1969), pp. 217–252.

such cases of aesthetics used for ideological purposes, a formalist situation of "the phrase [going] beyond the content" exists, an implicit avowal of the inability of a social system to solve its growing crises.

Marx and Engels were obviously not merely interested in studying hegemonic ideologies in literature. In line with the "Young German" literary movement of the 1830s and 1840s, they welcomed artistically accomplished writing which directly aided the struggle of the proletarian labor movement. It is important to emphasize again, however, in the light of later distortions, especially in Soviet culture, that this was only one, and not the most emphasized, of the purposes of art in their view. What is more, even in the cases where they praised the "tendentious" protest lyrics of a Heine, Freiligrath, or Weerth—three contemporaries whom they admired—they much appreciated the poet's independence of mind, innovations of language, and freedom from a simplistic didacticism. Marx and Engels also showed a lively interest in the emergence of genuine working-class cultural life.[38] (Marx, for example, drew upon the folk literature of chapbooks, songs, and jingles as an expression of plebeian wisdom and humor.)[39] Yet, although Marx stressed the necessity of a growth of genuine working-class consciousness in a deeply subjective sense for the final victory of socialism, and not merely the so-called objective working out of the capitalist economic process, it was left for later generations to develop the theory and practice of a working-class culture. While they disparaged all art which in its sophisticated aestheticism was intended for a highly restricted circle—by implication they would have deplored the aristocratic bearing of some modernist avant-gardes—Marx and Engels' attention was drawn to the value for all humanity of the best art which emerged from the upper classes, past and present.

Unlike many later "Marxist" literary critics, Marx and Engels themselves did not view most art and literature as simply a matter of class perspective or ideology. They recognized, of course, a literature of bourgeois apology, but many of their observations are grounded in a richer and more complex terrain: much of the most interesting art, far from being reducible to class origins or ideological outlook, heightens our sense of the ironies, complexities, and contradictions of the historical pressure upon cultural activity. Engels, in a fine passage, stressed, for example, Goethe's "double relation to his age," in which the "wretched-

38. Baxandall and Morawski, *Marx and Engels on Literature and Art*, pp. 33–35.
39. Prawer, *Marx and World Literature*, pp. 95–101 and 402.

ness" of German social and political conditions in the late eighteenth century alternatively mastered and then repelled the poet.[40] In the dialectic of art and history, moreover, there is not merely a "synchronic" relation of cultural activity to a contemporary society, but a "diachronic" indebtedness to prior historical developments, including those within the discipline, genre, or branch of art of a particular work. Although no area of intellectual or cultural history, such as philosophy or drama, has an autonomous history independent of the whole social process, the prior development of that field has a partial autonomy, is an element in its present creations, and leaves many "traces" upon it.

In the *Introduction to the Critique of Political Economy*, Marx commented on art and historical contradictions in a famous passage on ancient Greek art. Marx argued here that the greatly increased technical mastery which has been gained over natural forces since the time of the Greeks, the socially liberating potential of which seemed so evident to this radical offspring of the Enlightenment, had undercut the mythic bases of Greek arts, the finest aesthetic achievement in human history. Progress was to be understood, then, in dialectical and not simply linear terms. (Marx's Enlightenment, lest we forget, had been affected deeply by Hegel.) He writes:

Is the view of nature and of social relations which shaped Greek imagination and thus Greek mythology possible in the age of automatic machinery and railways and locomotives and electric telegraphs? Where does Vulcan come in as against Roberts and Co., Jupiter as against the lightning rod, and Hermes as against the Crédit Mobilier? All mythology masters and dominates and shapes the forces of nature in and through imagination; hence it disappears as soon as man gains mastery over the forces of nature. What becomes of the Goddess Fame side by side with Printing House Square? Or is the *Iliad* at all possible in a time of the hand-operated or the later steam press? Are not singing and reciting and the muse necessarily put out of existence by the printer's bar; and do not necessary prerequisites of epic poetry accordingly vanish?

Marx concludes by observing that the charm of Greek art "does not stand in contradiction with the undeveloped stage of the social order from which it had sprung. It is much more the result of the latter, and inseparably connected with the circumstance that the unripe social conditions under which the art arose and under which alone it could appear can never return." Using the romantic metaphor of society as a living organism, Marx stresses that the man who enjoys the "native ways

---

40. Engels, "German Socialism in Verse and Prose, II" (1847), in Baxandall and Morawski, *Marx and Engels on Literature and Art*, pp. 80–81.

of the child," and thus the Greek "childhood of humanity," "must strive to reproduce its truth at a higher stage." Technically advanced civilization has not made aesthetically rich culture impossible, merely the ancient Greek one.[41]

Marx's suggestions concerning the impact of technical change upon forms of imagination and art were to be much expanded by Brecht, Benjamin, and Adorno in their different ways. Lukács, who remained within the tradition of ideological decoding of literature, was to neglect one of the most fertile of Marx's various comments on art and society. But, once again, neither Marx nor Engels had pursued this very far. Neither gave much attention—understandably, given the cultural climate of their time—to changes in the technical production of artistic media themselves, i.e., the impact on aesthetic reception of new means of communication since the printing press, such as photography (then, of course, in its initial stages). The far greater visibility of these changes in the twentieth century (film, radio, television, etc.) was to aid in the emancipation of Marxist cultural theory from simply being a critique of ideology.

If art, then, is not reducible to class ideology, how is it related to historical development? Marxist cultural theory has often been simplified into a crude extension of the so-called "base-superstructure" notion, which received its most influential expression in the Preface to *A Contribution to the Critique of Political Economy* (1859). Instead of seeing how Marx usually developed a complex dialectic of social activity and consciousness in his actual historical and economic writings, many Marxists and commentators on Marx have followed his reductive programmatic view in this Preface that "the relations of production constitute the economic structure of society, the real foundation, on which rises a legal and political superstructure and to which correspond definite forms of social consciousness." This sentence and the rest of the famous passage seem to suggest that human consciousness and cultural activity are a so-called "superstructure" which reflects an economic foundation, the latter being an objective datum developing independently of human will.[42] Such, of course, was the one-sidedly objectivist conception developed by official Marxist parties in the Second International; this is a view which is also still widely associated with Marxism today. We have already seen, however, that this passive notion of human

41. Ibid., pp. 134–135.
42. *Marx-Engels Reader*, pp. 4–5.

conscious activity was what Marx saw as a major effect of the capitalist "fetishism of commodities," and thus as a mystification of history. There is now, moreover, a large literature in the West which has demonstrated the central importance of social praxis and the subject/object dialectic in both Marx's historical and theoretical writings. Shlomo Avineri, for example, has stressed, after an examination of Marx's indebtedness to Hegel, that for Marx "reality is not mere objective datum, external to man, but is shaped by him through consciousness," while the so-called "material base is not an objective, economic fact, but the organization of human consciousness and activity." In understanding cultural life, Avineri's next clarification is even more useful: "The distinction between 'material base' and 'superstructure' is not a distinction between 'matter' and 'spirit' . . . but between conscious human activity aimed at creation and preservation of the conditions of human life, and human consciousness, which furnishes reasons, rationalizations and modes of legitimation and moral justification for the specific forms that activity takes."[43] Extending this distinction, and remembering our earlier discussions of art and labor, we may then state that art may partake of not merely "base" or "superstructure," but both. Independent works of art may be either or both (1) a part of human conscious productive activity ("the base"), which would include the role of art in all physical and mental appropriation, and remaking, of the external world; or (2) an aspect of ideological "false consciousness" which is "superstructural."

In reacting against the deterioration of Marxist theory into a simple kind of "economic determinism," Lukács and still more the Frankfurt School were to stress the Hegelian view of the social whole as a seamless, constantly interacting "totality" in which production, philosophy, politics, etc. were all a part. But the "totality" model, although a necessary corrective, often tended to eclipse questions of determination which Marx's theory sought to answer. In understanding Marx's conception, it would be best to keep the "base-superstructure" model, but to conceive it very differently from its often abused usage. Raymond Williams, a leading Marxist cultural historian, has recently written of the model:

Each term of the proposition has to be revalued in a particular direction. We have to revalue determination towards the setting of limits and the exertion of

43. Schlomo Avineri, *The Social and Political Thought of Karl Marx* (Cambridge, England, 1968), pp. 65–77.

pressure, and away from a predicted, prefigured and controlled element. We have to revalue "superstructure" towards a related range of cultural practices, and away from a reflected, reproduced or specifically dependent content. And, crucially, we have to revalue "the base" away from the notion of a fixed economic and technological abstraction, and towards the specific activities of men in real social and economic relationships, containing fundamental contradictions and variations and therefore always in a state of dynamic process.[44]

❖   ❖   ❖

For Marx and Engels, there were a variety of ways in which an author's ideology might relate to the cognitive value of a work produced. A piece of literature may be entirely ideological, such as Eugène Sue's *Les Mystères de Paris* with its latent and manifest expressions of contemporary bourgeois prejudices and assumptions which mystify the social world. There may be a complex mixture, as Engels saw in Goethe, whose multiple relation to the various strata of German society is coupled with a tendency either to reflect, passively, the current provincialism of his environment, or to rise to an historically critical overview and mastery of it. Finally, there are cases, such as Balzac, where the ideological perspective (a reactionary royalist persuasion) in no way hinders the realistic presentation of historical evolution (French society in the early nineteenth century). The issue here is not ideological correctness but literary "realism," the meaning of which for Marx and Engels we need now to discuss.

Although Marx did not use the term "realism," his comments on the Sue novel, on Ferdinand Lassalle's play *Franz von Sickingen* (1859), and on contemporary British novelists demonstrate that he shared the conception which Engels developed in some letters in the 1880s. In their view, "realism" was not merely a current within mid-century European literature but an attribute of some of the best modern literature since Shakespeare; the great English dramatist is used by them as a model as much as is Balzac. As we shall see from their discussion, moreover, the criteria they use are both aesthetic and historical, for the cognitive value of a work will be lessened by poor formal construction. (Marx and Engels looked mainly to literature in their observations on realism, as was usual in their aesthetic thought, but a few of their rare remarks on painting continue a similar line of argument.)[45]

44. Raymond Williams, "'Base and Superstructure' in Marxist Cultural Theory," *New Left Review*, 82 (November–December 1973). This analysis has been expanded in Williams's *Marxism and Literature*, pp. 75–145.
45. Baxandall and Morawski, *Marx and Engels on Literature and Art*, p. 31.

In their praise of an authentic realism, Marx and Engels developed themes which were fairly common in European aesthetics in the mid-nineteenth century, especially in regard to English, French, and Russian novels. Reconstructing their suggestions, we may say that four criteria of realism are essential: (1) *Typicality*: representative and typical situations and characters need to be presented within a concrete and socially conditioning, as well as specific, historical environment. (2) *Individuality*: since the world is endlessly variegated and rich, and since neither historical situations nor human individuals are cast from the same mold, representative characters from the various social classes must be drawn with distinctive, unique, and individual qualities. In developing points 1 and 2, both Marx and Engels contrast Shakespeare's richly individualized characters, whose typicality is then all the more "real," with the "Schillerizing" tendency toward "making individuals into mere mouthpieces of their time," which they saw in Lassalle's Sickingen tragedy.[46] (3) *Organic plot construction*: the political "tendency" of the work, in Engels' words, "must spring forth from the situation and the action itself, without explicit attention called to it; the writer is not obliged to offer to the reader the future historical solution of the social conflicts he depicts."[47] (4) *The presentation of humans as subjects as well as objects of history*: although this criterion was stated in stronger terms by Marx than by Engels, it was Engels who wrote, in a letter to Margaret Harkness, the English novelist, that in her novel *City Girl*, "the working class figures as a passive mass, unable to help itself. . . . The rebellious reactions of the working class against the oppressive medium which surrounds them . . . belong to history and must therefore lay claim to a place in the domain of realism."[48] Without explicitly commenting on the matter, Engels was suggesting a contrast between Balzac's "realist" depiction of active humans making history within given situations and the naturalists' (e.g., Zola's) deterministic narrative of events. On this point, as well as on other questions of realism, Lukács was to embellish and elaborate exhaustively the few texts of Marx and Engels on the subject.

Before discussing the implications of this theory of realism, it should be emphasized that Marx and Engels had not offered it as a prescriptive aesthetic, as the theory was to later figure in Lukács's thought. Marx, as we have seen, loved and drew upon a wide variety of European literature, much of it antedating modern notions of historical realism.

46. Ibid., pp. 107 and 109.   47. Ibid., p. 113.   48. Ibid., pp. 114–115.

Even Engels, whose literary interests were more exclusively drawn to nineteenth-century works, read widely in the literature of German romanticism and particularly championed its politically inspired poetry in the 1840s.[49] More importantly, the various necessities of art—cognitive, political, sensuous, disalienating, "utopian," etc.—were far from exhausted by following the criteria of literary realism. While it is an important theme of their aesthetic thought, especially Engels', realism is only one kind of literature and art favored by the two.

The point needs to be stressed in this study of the Marxist response to modernist art and culture, because nineteenth-century realist aesthetics were so widely rejected by advanced artists and writers after 1880. When isolated from the themes of art as part of productive labor, as a component of the human conscious mediation of objects, or as a promise of a future more humane society, the realist theme appears to reduce aesthetic experience to the mirroring of social development. It is not sufficient to point out, as does Lukács, that Balzac actively "selected" typical situations and characters and did not seek, unlike the later naturalists, a photographic depiction of everyday life in its empirical immediacy.[50] This amounts only to the superiority of Balzac's *reflection* of the deeper historical evolution.

The problem may be seen in another way as a nineteenth-century confusion concerning the relation between "form" and "content" which, in their comments on literary realism, Marx and Engels were unable to escape. David Caute, a novelist and intellectual historian of socialism, has pointed out that within the tradition of Marxist aesthetics the historical and social "subject matter" of a literary work has been insufficiently distinguished from its "content." The content is not merely the subject matter "correctly" interpreted and given an attractive formal expression; it is the subject matter mediating and mediated by the artistic form employed. "This fact is grasped," Caute writes, "once we cease to identify content with the mimetic representation of a subject or theme." "The Anzin miners' strike of 1884 is the subject of Zola's novel *Germinal*; the content of the novel is what emerges through Zola's literary treatment of this subject."[51] Unlike Caute, I believe that it is possible to reconcile this point with Marx's general out-

49. Ibid.

50. Georg Lukács, "Narrate or Describe?" in *Writer and Critic and Other Essays*, ed. Arthur D. Kahn (New York, 1971).

51. David Caute, *The Illusion: An Essay on Politics, Theatre and the Novel* (New York, 1971), p. 151.

look; his emphasis, for example, upon the sensuous as well as the intellectual appropriation and transformation of the object world, and upon the importance of art in the human productive mediation of nature, defy the simple category of mimesis or reflection. But just as Marx himself after 1850 sometimes sounds like an objectivist—and did not contest the mechanistic materialism of some of Engels' late writings, such as the *Anti-Dühring*—so in his comments on nineteenth-century literature he did not clearly distinguish himself from the mimetic position of realism theory. In this, as in so much else in his thought, Marx showed that the vast synthesis of disparate philosophical, political, and aesthetic traditions which he had constructed was no simple organic unity but a field of tensions and some ambivalence.

❖   ❖   ❖

To complete this introductory chapter on Marx's aesthetics (in which I have stressed its connections with some of the essential directions of his general historical perspective), I should like to briefly situate his overall social outlook within some major currents of German and French thought in the century 1750–1850. As has been suggested, his views on art and society reworked and interlaced a wide variety of sometimes conflicting traditions, including German classical humanism, Hegelian philosophy, and French Enlightenment optimism concerning technical and social "progress." To more fully connect his fragmentary ideas on art with the shifting structures of his wider theoretical synthesis (from which larger framework, after all, later Marxist aesthetics drew, even if selectively), it is useful to present the divergent strands of thought which he attempted to synthesize.

We have seen repeatedly how Marx was indebted to German aesthetics and social philosophy of the period 1770–1815. Broadly speaking, it is possible to find a common aim among leading German Romantics, Idealists, and Humanists in these decades which succeeded the *Sturm und Drang* literary movement. Reacting against what they took to be the mechanistic, atomist, and utilitarian directions of Enlightenment thought in England and particularly France, Herder, Kant, Goethe, Schiller, Fichte, Hegel, and others insisted upon the moral autonomy, creative will, and self-expression of human beings. Instead of confronting the outer world as an objectified field for scientific calculation and instrumental technological use, they held that it must be conceived as the plane upon which humans express and realize their inner moral, aesthetic, and spiritual potentials. Freedom, in this view, was understood as the recognition by the "subject" that the world is constituted by its own expressive activity. Mind is not seen mechanically as a passive reflection of the "object," or in adversary relation to internal or external "nature" which it must dominate, but in creative interchange with both, and organically developing over time. Within this broad "expressivist" current, as it has recently been characterized by Charles Taylor,[52] there were divisions, of course. Romantics, for example, developed a culture of feeling and emotional spontaneity; they reacted, moreover, against all "rationalization of the world," to use Max Weber's later phrase, associating this pejoratively with bureaucratic absolutism or "Western" natural science.[53] Idealist philosophers such as Kant and Hegel, on the other hand, in whose work the German *Aufklärung* was culminated, sought to redefine and rescue "reason" and "progress" by connecting these with the role of the "subject" in cognition, creative expression in all understanding, and a state of law (*Rechtstaat*) in all political "advance." (Hegel clearly distinguished analytical *Verstand* from synthetic *Vernunft*, for example.) Yet, both currents stressed the need for organic temporal development, self-expression, and moral autonomy in their revolts against the French Enlightenment.

In eighteenth-century England and France, the use of "modern" procedures in the centralized state (which helped guarantee social peace) and among thriving business groups (which aided prosperity) helped dispose the intellectual classes, on the whole, toward "rationalizing" bureaucracy and a faith in progress via scientific and liberal institutional development. In this period of German thought, however, the autonomous and harmonious personality, drawn with allusions to ancient Greece, was counterposed to the desiccating and atomizing results of technical reason as defined by the French. The notions of an alienation of the self from one's social and political activity, and of the "reification" of the man-made modern world into a congealed, rigid, and distant mechanism, were already well developed within German humanist, idealist, and romantic thought in these decades.[54] Moreover, the French

52. Charles Taylor, *Hegel* (Cambridge, England, 1975). In this paragraph I have drawn particularly on Taylor's penetrating synoptic overview of German cultural aspiration in the decades 1770–1815, which appears on pp. 3–49 of his book. I have also found these useful: George Armstrong Kelly, *Politics, Idealism and History: Sources of Hegelian Thought* (London, 1969); and Herbert Marcuse, "Introduction," in *Reason and Revolution: Hegel and the Rise of Social Theory* (Boston, 1960).

53. Henri Brunschwig, *Enlightenment and Romanticism in Eighteenth-Century Prussia* (Chicago, 1974); Arthur Mitzman, "Anti-Progress: A Study in the Romantic Roots of German Sociology," *Social Research*, 33:1 (Spring 1966), 65–85.

54. Mitzman, "Anti-Progress."

Enlightenment's philosophic materialism, faith in "natural law," and optimistic belief in the social utility of technical and material "progress" were viewed as a threat to the already weak moral and intellectual autonomy, and self-determination, of the public.

There were, of course, exceptions to this pattern. For example, Rousseau was a major inspiration for the Germans[55]; there was obviously a French romantic movement after 1820 or so; and some major French political thinkers, such as DeMaistre and DeBonald, were strident reactionaries. On the whole, however, the distinction between two national currents of social theory before 1830 may stand: the French stress upon social progress through science and technology, and a remaking of the "objective" world of politics and economics; and the German concern for the "expressive" development of the creative "subject" in interchange with its enclosing natural and social order. It is in this context of social theory and social history that we should view the philosophical divergence between the more purely objectivist materialism of the French eighteenth century, which amounted to a view of the mind as a register of sensations or empirical data, and the German idealist emphasis on the role of the conscious reflective "subject" in cognitive perception and in the making of history. While Marx in the 1840s looked to France and England for guidance in the empirical reconstruction of the political world and in his hopes for potential progress through science and industry, as a German philosopher he resisted what he took to be the passive implications of a mechanical materialism and insisted on an Hegelian dialectic of active mind and objective reality.

By this time, the industrial revolution was of course beginning in Germany, although Marx's awareness of proletarian suffering derived more from reading about England and France. There had been among the "Young Germans" and young Hegelians, in addition, a reaction against romantic subjectivity and an interest in French political developments and philosophical materialism. Emerging at this juncture, Marx was to begin developing an attempted synthesis of German and French social thought in the years 1843–45. In his studies of labor, the role of aesthetics, the materialist philosophy of history, etc., there was a rich articulation of the dual response to capitalist modernity which many "free-lance" intellectuals were then feeling in still relatively "backward" Germany. For those Germans, many of them Jews, who were inspired by the hope for emancipation via political revolution on

55. See Kelly, *Politics, Idealism, and History,* pp. 25–77 and 89–99.

the French model and by the possibilities of material betterment for all through a democratic harnessing of modern technology, "modernization" appeared as *both* oppressive *and* hopeful, alternately alienating and liberating.[56] It has been suggested that such is the common experience of industrial capitalism in its first generation or so, when the earliest high hopes and high fears have not been eroded by a long experience of routine acquaintance and adjustment.[57] There is in such cases an ambivalent response, which will be given intellectual expression in ways depending upon the available constructs of social theory. The situation of relative "backwardness" in close proximity to more advanced societies could well encourage the hope that one's own nation might progress while avoiding the full strains and dehumanization of the modernizing process seen across the borders.

Some kind of process of thought like this occurred in Marx's mind when he developed the widely appealing perspective of present misery and potential liberation in his dialectical examination of capitalism. The present social organization of the forces of production, he was to argue over and over, obstructs their potential use for the elimination of poverty and inequality and for the full flowering of the creative human personality. Hegel's dialectical logic helped in such a way to articulate the contradictory experience of hope and dismay, ascent and decay, which Marx and others, particularly industrial workers and increasingly commodified intellectuals, felt in the face of modernizing capitalism. To repeat and present more fully Marx's succinct characterization of this experience:

On the one hand, there have started into life industrial and scientific forces, which no epoch of the former human history had ever suspected. On the other hand, there exist symptoms of decay, far surpassing the horrors of the Roman Empire. In our days everything seems pregnant with its contrary. Machinery, gifted with the wonderful power of shortening and fructifying human labour, we behold starving and overworking it. The new-fangled sources of wealth, by some strange weird spell, are turned into sources of want. The victories of art seem bought by the loss of character. . . . This antagonism between modern industry and science on the one hand, modern misery and dissolution on the other hand; this antagonism between the productive powers, and the social relations of our epoch, is a fact, palpable, overwhelming.[58]

56. On Marx's own ambivalence toward industrial capitalism, see Avineri, *The Social and Political Thought of Karl Marx*, p. 114.

57. See Adam Ulam, *The Unfinished Revolution: An Essay on the Sources of Influence of Marxism and Communism* (New York, 1960).

58. Karl Marx, "Speech at the Anniversary of the Peoples' Paper," in *Marx-Engels Reader*, p. 427.

In developing what he is to call the "dialectical contradictions" of the situation, Marx was to mediate the German traditions we have discussed (which focused upon "expressive" freedom and launched attacks upon a reified technical "reason") with the French-inspired materialist "science" which had been developed against the abuse of that heritage in the German 1840s and 1850s. In the years 1815–48, romantic and idealist thought was to be used to help defend and mystify the reconstituted old order of throne and altar. With this in mind, we can better understand Marx's welcoming of the demystifying effects of capitalism, with its pitiless exposure of the cash nexus and the commodification of exalted professions. After 1845, Marx was to throw himself into the study of the "objective" realities of French politics and British economics. In addition, he and Engels were to praise the realist social novels of England and France for their materialist outlook and mimetic aesthetic. In doing so, however, Marx did not merely adopt the "objectivist" perspectives of the French Enlightenment tradition. His dual response to capitalist modernization was developed through a "German-French" synthesis: on the one hand, present "decay" through perspectives on estranged labor and the reified "fetish of commodities," and, on the other hand, hope for (rationalized into a certainty of) "progress" and the overcoming of material want through the stress—stronger in Engels—on the productive capacities unleashed by capitalist development.[59] In this chapter, we have seen repeatedly how Marx interwove these currents in his remarks on art and society. In the rest of this book, we shall see how the Marxian amalgam of "subjective" and "objective" threads, and of alternating hope and dismay in the face of social "progress," was continued or disentangled within the variants of modernist culture and by the representatives of a neo-Marxist aesthetics after the First World War.

59. Other recent and similar attempts to clarify Marx's synthesis of French Enlightenment and German "Humanist" and "Idealist" currents may be found in Melvin Rader's *Marx's Interpretation of History* (Oxford, 1979), pp. 141–165; and in Taylor, *Hegel*, pp. 547–552.

CHAPTER TWO

Modernism in
Comparative Perspective

Modernism in the arts represents neither a unified vision nor a uniform aesthetic practice. This is a vital point for us to consider: as we shall see, Lukács, Brecht, Benjamin, and Adorno were not only at variance in their assessments of the diverse currents since symbolism and impressionism, but the last three contrasted with each other in their selective embraces of modernism. While Adorno defended Schoenberg's expressionist atonality against Stravinsky, Brecht followed in the cubist and constructivist footsteps of Meyerhold while attacking "psychological" authors such as Rilke and Dostoevsky. Benjamin embraced symbolist and surrealist poetics, but he and Lukács each disliked expressionism, although for different reasons. Lukács attacked Brecht, while identifying the roots of modernism in the naturalist era—against which Brechtian theatre had revolted.[1] The social and cultural theories of each of

1. For Adorno on Schoenberg, see *The Philosophy of Modern Music* (New York, 1973). On Brecht and Meyerhold, see Henri Arvon, *Marxist Esthetics* (Ithaca, N.Y., 1973), pp. 56–82. On Brecht's antipathy for Dostoevsky, as well as other psychologically oriented authors, see Walter Benjamin, *Understanding Brecht*, (London, 1973), p. 114. Lukács's analysis of naturalism may be seen in his essays, "The Intellectual Physiognomy of Literary Characters," in *Radical Perspectives in the Arts*, ed. Lee Baxandall (Baltimore, 1972), pp. 89–141, and "Narrate or Describe?" in *Writer and Critic and Other Essays*, ed. Arthur D. Kahn (New York, 1971), a collection of Lukács's pieces. Lukács's critique of expressionism is found in his "'Grösse und Verfall' des Expressionismus," in *Marxismus und Literatur: Eine Dokumentation in drei Bänden*, ed. Fritz Raddatz (Reinbeck bei Hamburg, 1969), Vol. 2, pp. 7–42, which is translated in his *Essays on Realism* (Cambridge, Mass., 1981). Benjamin's dislike of expressionism is discussed in Adorno, *Über Walter Benjamin* (Frankfurt a.M., 1970), pp. 96–97; his use of symbolist poetics is discussed in Charles Rosen, "The Origins of Walter Benjamin," *New York Review of Books*, November 10, 1977.

these writers represented a different path through, and interpretation of, the varied thicket of modern art. In order to grasp historically their reciprocal confronting of Marxism and modernism, and the richly textured debates to which this led, we need now to survey comparatively the multiple revolts against traditional realism and romanticism which were typical of advanced European culture in the decades between 1880 and 1930.

Let me emphasize at the outset that no attempt at comprehensiveness will be made here; not every one of the major figures or many new "avant-gardes" need be covered. Instead, I will attempt to distinguish between those modernist currents which were to be analyzed or developed (explicitly or implicitly) by our four neo-Marxists. In this chapter, the basic aesthetic and social postures of symbolism, cubism, and expressionism (and, to a lesser degree, naturalism, constructivism, and surrealism) will be explored. Then, in conclusion, I will briefly trace Marxist responses to modernism from the period of the Second International (1889–1914) to the reign of "socialist realism" in the Soviet 1930s.

❖   ❖   ❖

Before contrasting the variety of movements, it is well to consider some unifying aspects common, to a greater or lesser degree, within all of them. At the risk of being too schematic about such a complex and broad phenomenon, the following may be seen as major directions of aesthetic form and social perspective in modernism as a whole.

1. *Aesthetic Self-Consciousness or Self-Reflexiveness.* Modern artists, writers, and composers often draw attention to the media or materials with which they are working, the very processes of creation in their own craft. Novelists, for example, explore the problems of novel writing within their works (e.g., Joyce's *Ulysses* or Gide's *The Counterfeiters*); visual artists make the evocative or constructive function of colors a recurrent "subject matter" (e.g., Matisse, Nolde, or Kandinsky) or try to exploit the possibilities of a now acknowledged two-dimensional surface (e.g., Braque or Picasso). Symbolists and later poets demonstrate a heightened self-consciousness about the nature of poetic language and view words as objects in their own right (e.g., Mallarmé); playwrights intentionally reveal the theatrical constructions of their dramas (e.g., Meyerhold, Pirandello, Brecht). In doing so, modernists escape from the timeworn attempt, given new scientific pretensions in naturalist aesthetics, to make of art a transparent mere "reflection" or "representation"

of what is alleged to be "outer" reality. They also depart from the more direct expression of feeling favored by the romantics. The modernist work often willfully reveals its own reality as a construction or artifice, which may take the form of an hermetic and aristocratic mystique of creativity (as in much early symbolism); visual or linguistic distortion to convey intense subjective states of mind (strongest in expressionism); or suggestions that the wider social world is built and rebuilt by human beings and not "given" and unalterable (as in Bauhaus architecture or constructivist theatre).

2. *Simultaneity, Juxtaposition, or "Montage."* In much modernist art, narrative or temporal structure is weakened, or even disappears, in favor of an aesthetic ordering based on synchronicity, the logic of metaphor, or what is sometimes referred to as "spatial form." Instead of narrating outer sequential or additive time, modern novelists explore the simultaneity of experience in a moment of psychological time, in which are concentrated past, present, and future (e.g., Joyce, Woolf, and especially Proust). Things do not so much fall apart as fall together, reminding us of the derivation of the ubiquitous "symbol" from the Greek *symballein*, "to throw together." [2] Unity is often created from juxtaposing variant perspectives—of the eye, the feelings, the social class or culture, etc.—as in modern visual montage (e.g., Eisenstein, Grosz); metaphorical relationships suggested in modern poetry (e.g., Baudelaire); rhythmic and tonal simultaneity in music (e.g., Bartok or Stravinsky) [3]; or the multiple consciousnesses which intersect in a modern novel (e.g., Woolf's *To the Lighthouse*). Cyclical or mythical recurrence is frequently viewed as a deeper reality than the surfaces disclosed in temporally unfolding historical events, the frame of reference which is so prominent in the literature of nineteenth-century realism. Instead of a traditional art of transitions from one event, one sensation, one thing at a time, presented sequentially, modern art is often without apparent causal progression and completion. It is intended to exist within an open-ended and "continuous present" in which various experiences, past and present, inner and outer, of different persons are juxtaposed, their distances eclipsed as though on a flat surface. [4]

2. James McFarlane, "The Mind of Modernism," in *Modernism: 1890–1930*, ed. Malcolm Bradbury and James McFarlane (New York, 1976), p. 92. McFarlane writes: "The very vocabulary of chaos—disintegration, fragmentation, dislocation—implies a breaking away or a breaking apart. But the defining thing of the Modernist mode is not so much that things fall *apart* but that they fall *together*."
3. H.H. Stuckenschmidt, *Twentieth-Century Music* (New York, 1969), pp. 71–90.
4. See Roger Shattuck, *The Banquet Years: The Arts in France, 1885–1918* (New

Whether or not such a procedure shows an escape from historical thinking, or merely its purely linear evolutionary or additive forms, is a question that shall concern us later. For now it is enough to point out that in exploring simultaneity modernists were accepting the ephemeral and transitory present as the locus of art, the moment which is seen, in Ezra Pound's phrase, as a "brief gasp between one cliché and another."[5] At best, such an "aesthetic of the new" could freshen perceptions and cleanse the senses and language of routine, habitual, and automatic responses to the world, to "defamiliarize" the expected and ordinary connections between things in favor of new, and deeper, ones. Montage need not have such liberating functions, however, and could be readily applied in manipulative advertising and political propaganda, while the cult of novelty might easily degenerate into a worship of changing fashions.[6]

3. *Paradox, Ambiguity, and Uncertainty.* To confront the decline, by the late nineteenth century, of religious, philosophical, and scientific certainties (of God, objective truth, historical progress, etc.), as well as the very notion of a fixed viewpoint, modernists explore the paradoxical many-sidedness of the world. Alarmed at the spectre of nihilism, the loss of meaning in transcendent imperatives and firm secular values,[7] modernists view reality as necessarily constructed from relative perspectives, while they seek to exploit the aesthetic and ethical richness of ambiguous images, sounds, and authorial points of view. Many modernist works turn on ambiguous treatments of the contemporary city, the machine, or the "masses."[8] Modernists find aesthetic value in confronting urban experience, for example, from a variety of seemingly contradictory angles (the city as liberation from tradition and routine, but also as the locus of interpersonal estrangement and fragmented experience, as in the pioneering urban poems of Baudelaire).

Instead of an omniscient and reliable narrator, modern writers develop either single or multiple, but all limited and fallible, vantages from which to view events. Open-ended paradoxes may be structured in

---

York, 1958), pp. 331–360; and the pioneering study by Joseph Frank, first published in 1945, "Spatial Form in Modern Literature," in *The Widening Gyre* (New Brunswick, N.J., 1963), pp. 3–62.

5. Quoted in Renato Poggioli, *Theory of the Avant-Garde* (Cambridge, Mass., 1968), p. 82.

6. Ibid., pp. 79–84.

7. Irving Howe, "The Idea of the Modern," in *Literary Modernism*, ed. Irving Howe (New York, 1967), pp. 36–40.

8. See Peter Gay, *Art and Act: On Causes in History—Manet, Gropius, Mondrian* (New York, 1976), pp. 108–110.

such a manner as to suggest to the reader or audience how they may resolve the contradictions outside the intentionally unfinished work (as Brecht attempted to do), or provisionally synthesize the multiple perspectives (as cubist painters encourage their viewers). More radically, however, the paradoxes may be heightened to the point of apparent irresolution, confronting the reader or audience with a "Janus-faced" reality, impenetrable in its enigmas (e.g., Kafka or Beckett).

4. *"Dehumanization" and the Demise of the Integrated Individual Subject or Personality.* In both romantic and realist literature of the nineteenth century, individual characters are presented with highly structured personality features and develop their individuality through a life of social interaction. (We have seen the importance that Marx and Engels attached to this in their view of realism.) The narrator or playwright, through descriptions of conduct or psychic states, or through dramatic dialogue, endeavors to reveal integrated human characters in their process of more or less orderly formation and transformation. "Character, for modernists like Joyce, Woolf, Faulkner, however," Irving Howe has written, "is regarded not as a coherent, definable and well-structured entity, but as a psychic battlefield, or an insoluble puzzle, or the occasion for a flow of perceptions and sensations. This tendency to dissolve character into a stream of atomized experiences . . . gives way . . . to an opposite tendency . . . in which character is severed from psychology and confined to a sequence of severely objective events."[9] In modern painting, the human form is violently distorted by expressionists, decomposed and geometrically resynthesized by cubists, and disappears entirely, of course, in nonfigurative abstract art. We shall see repeatedly in this chapter and the ones that follow how impersonal poetics, dehumanization in the visual arts, collective or mass characters in theatre, and the fragmentation of personality in the novel are important features of the modern cultural landscape.[10] Yet, it will be necessary to show the widely contrasting manner in which this "crisis of individuality," so to speak, was handled within the variety of modernist currents.

In the sections which follow, an attempt will be made to historically situate the various seminal currents of modernism. For the moment, a few comments are in order concerning the general cultural and social

9. Howe, "Idea of the Modern," p. 34.
10. See, particularly, José Ortega y Gasset, *The Dehumanization of Art; and Other Essays on Art, Culture and Literature* (Princeton, N.J., 1968).

environment in which the overall "movement" developed. First, it is worth considering aspects of the broad sweep of European cultural and political life in the period. Aesthetic modernism developed in its initial stages within a wider context of declining religious faith among the educated population in the late nineteenth century, encouraging among artists, writers, and musicians an attitude toward art and its craft as, in a certain sense, a surrogate for religious certainties. The "revolt against positivism" in natural science and social thought, in addition, anticipated by Baudelaire and Nietzsche in the 1860s and 1870s, gained momentum by the 1890s and helped the spread of the pioneering symbolist revolt against mimetic aesthetics, while preparing some of the groundwork for later departures from nineteenth-century realism.[11] In a more specialized way, the very desire to simply reproduce or represent the natural or social world, as such, was undercut for many painters and novelists by the increasing importance of photography, on the one hand, and fact-finding social research, on the other, leaving them free to develop imaginative constructions or explore the peculiarities of their own aesthetic medium. (This was far from a universal conclusion; naturalism and symbolism coincided in time, after all, in their late nineteenth-century heyday.)

The threats to positivist science and secular optimism at the end of the nineteenth century were brought on, in part, by a political and intellectual crisis of liberalism, one from which the socialists of the Second International felt themselves immune. Middle-class radicalism of the 1789–1870 era had waned or become absorbed by the 1880s. The "heroic" and self-confident struggle against aristocratic absolutism had largely passed. (The French situation was something of an exception, with middle-class republicans fending off the monarchist right.) Traditional aristocratic, authoritarian, and military elites were now finding through such appeals as nationalism and imperialism the means to perpetuate their power into the modern world of industry, mass society, and parliamentary rule. The protracted depression of 1873–96, which saw governments turn away from free trade, caused many in the middle classes to fear that the economic system was running down; uncertainty about the future tended to replace earlier expectations of indefinite progress. The depression, as well as the recent democratic expansions of

11. For a general discussion of the "revolt against positivism," see H. Stuart Hughes, *Consciousness and Society: The Reconstruction of European Social Thought, 1890–1930* (New York, 1961), chap. 2. For its impact on aesthetic modernism, see McFarlane, "The Mind of Modernism," pp. 71–94.

the franchise, caused increasing electoral difficulties for liberal political parties. New mass movements, either socialist on their left or extreme nationalist on their right, were now causing considerable anxiety for the respectable bourgeois.[12] Many middle-class people still held to liberal assumptions, and the period 1896–1914 saw a return to prosperity and greater optimism, but the 1880s and 1890s saw the beginning of an intellectual bombardment of liberal certainties (which were also very much Marxist ones of the period). Notions of human rationality and secular progress through science and industry were now assaulted by thinkers such as Nietzsche, Pareto, Sorel, and Langbehn. Liberal intellectuals, in particular, feared for their future in mass society (Freud is an excellent example). At the same time, the addition of a pessimistic Darwinist-naturalist determinism to the Enlightenment tradition of critical rationality was laying the basis for later attacks upon the liberal creed.[13]

All of the major criteria of modernism that we have discussed—formal preoccupations, spatial montage, the cultivation of paradox, the demise of the individual subject—were influenced, in their origins, by this broad crisis of eighteenth- and nineteenth-century liberal thought. Stress upon simultaneity and a heightened "present consciousness," as opposed to temporal unfolding, resulted, in part, from a loss of belief in the beneficent course of linear historical development (although, as we shall see, the era 1905–25 saw a resurgence of historical hope now mixed also with dread, which was fueled by an opposition to notions of *automatic* progress). The "crisis of individuality" in modern art reflected the fears (or, in some cases, the hopes) of many intellectuals and artists concerning the coming of an age of "masses" and unprecedented technological power. Finally, paradoxical formulations and ambiguous images, as well as a concentration upon the formal craft of one's art, were all encouraged by the general loss of religious and secular certainties.[14] That much modernist culture grew out of such a weakening of liberal optimism helps to explain how it was not until the 1920s, and especially the 1930s, that a group of German Marxist intellectuals be-

12. David Landes, *The Unbound Prometheus: Technological Change and Industrial Development in Western Europe from 1750 to the Present* (Cambridge, England, 1969), pp. 231 and 240–246; Eric Hobsbawm, *The Age of Capital, 1848–1875* (New York, 1975), pp. 337–342.

13. George Lichtheim, *Europe in the Twentieth Century* (New York, 1972), pp. 209–220 and 243.

14. The most meticulous and sustained study of the relation between the crisis of liberalism and one case of the rise of aesthetic modernism is in Carl E. Schorske, *Fin de Siècle Vienna: Politics and Culture* (New York, 1980).

came sympathetic to the alternative culture of the modernists: now, particularly through the rise of fascism and the defeat of the German working class, they became aware that as socialists they were not immune, as the prewar Social Democrats had thought, to this sort of disillusionment.

Still another body of inherited belief that could no longer sustain the modernists was the conception of nature (developed by some of the romantics) as an effective counterfoil to modern urban and industrial society.[15] By the end of the nineteenth century, the increasingly visible extension of the constructed, urban, industrial, and scientific world had begun to remove the countryside as an available refuge and emotional inspiration for most of the literary and artistic avant-garde. This did not merely mean that nature diminished in importance as a subject of art and literature. The technical ability to master and control the given environment, the "humanization" of nature through the modern city and its various technological extensions, was also a source of the tendency since Baudelaire to view art and science as objects in their own right—as self-reflexive constructions, instead of as more or less direct expressions of feeling or as representations of outer or inner reality (as they had largely been seen in romantic aesthetics).[16] In modernist experience, "decadent" weariness with a "finished" or "completed" world (and its routine practices) alternates with hopes for a radical remaking of what has been humanly constructed (which can take right-wing or left-wing forms, e.g., D'Annunzio or Meyerhold). In this way, languid melancholia and revolutionary enthusiasm (the latter of which grew after 1905) may each be seen as a different response, in part, to the pervasive spread of a technological society.[17]

The influence of such broad cultural and political changes upon the modernists was mediated by their own particular social and economic

15. On this aspect of romanticism, see M.H. Abrams, *Natural Supernaturalism: Tradition and Revolution in Romantic Literature* (New York, 1973), especially pp. 88–116. Abrams warns against viewing the romantics as desiring a simple return to an easeful and undifferentiated nature; all the major writers, and especially Blake, he argues, "set as the goal of mankind the reachievement of a unity which has been earned by unceasing effort and which is . . . an equilibrium of opponent forces which preserves all the products and powers of intellection and culture" (p. 260).

16. See M.H. Abrams, *The Mirror and the Lamp: Romantic Theory and the Critical Tradition* (Oxford, England, 1953). For further contrasts between symbolism and romanticism, see Anna Balakian, *The Symbolist Movement: A Critical Appraisal* (New York, 1967), pp. 34–38.

17. On the influence of the technical "humanization of nature" upon modern writers and artists, I have found useful: Stephen Spender, *The Struggle of the Modern* (Berkeley, Calif., 1963), pp. 143–155; Fredric Jameson, "The Vanishing Mediator: Narrative Structure in Max Weber," *New German Critique*, 1 (Winter 1974); and Wylie Sypher, *Literature and Technology: The Alien Vision* (New York, 1968).

position, their new professional role as artists in an increasingly commercial society. Modernists were often members of defensive and belligerent coteries, circles, or self-proclaimed "avant-gardes." For such groups, the tyrannies of commercialization, conventional public opinion, and an innocuous and clichéd classical or romantic culture acted as an irritant and a provocation for revolt, but were exercised within limits that allowed the free play of scandal and experimentation (which themselves eventually could be absorbed and become a new cliché).[18] The military connotations of the phrase "avant-garde" suggest an embattled small community, desperately needing mutual support among themselves—encouraging an art for one's aesthetic peers, concerned with questions of craft and form[19]—so as to be able to launch "guerrilla raids" on the various cultural establishments.

By the last third of the nineteenth century, the professional position of the artist, writer, or musician (as a purveyor of cultural commodities on the market) also played a role in the growth of a modernist aesthetic and social outlook. The shift from patronage to market systems in the arts had begun in eighteenth-century England, and had antedated the modernists, on a wider scale, by at least a couple of generations, as César Graña has shown in his study of Parisian literati of 1830–60. By the mid-nineteenth century, the decline of the patronage system and the conditions of salability in a crowded, competitive market had placed a new emphasis upon originality and innovation and promised rapid fortune and fame as the reward for "creative" work; on the other hand, however, the uncertain response of a new, distant, mass middle-class public, and sheer dependence on impersonal business considerations, encouraged feelings of martyrdom among artists, writers, and musicians and rendered them impotent in a crass and hostile world.[20]

It was not, however, until the late nineteenth century that the full implications of the new market situation, taken together with the cultural changes discussed above, were to be felt in a radically altered aesthetic form and perspective: the modernist stress upon art as a self-referential construct instead of as a mirror of nature or society. Whereas earlier, among romantics and realists, feelings of isolation and the gulf between artist and public had not loomed quite so large—mitigated by the prevalence of integrative concepts such as those of a wider natural

18. Poggioli, *Theory of the Avant-Garde*, pp. 95–100 and 106–108.
19. Malcolm Bradbury, "The Cities of Modernism," in *Modernism*, p. 100.
20. César Graña, *Modernity and Its Discontents: French Society and the French Man of Letters in the Nineteenth Century* (New York, 1967), especially chap. 5.

environment or an encompassing social process—such sustaining beliefs were by now in decline. By the 1880s or 1890s, many writers and
artists, breaking fully from mimetic aesthetics, were more than ever
thrown back upon their own selves or their own craft as a central object
of their work, with only an "avant-garde" circle of initiates to share it
with. As with other groups of intellectuals by the last third of the century, they too were becoming "experts" within a delimited field. Championing their own special rights (e.g., "art for art's sake") as another
isolated "interest group," they were in this respect much like lawyers,
journalists, or professors, except that artists, writers, and musicians
were less comfortably self-employed, generally lacking a regular clientele.[21] It is easier to condemn this seemingly self-absorbed posture, as
many Marxists have done, and the often contemptuous and disdainful
aristocratic attitudes it undoubtedly spawned, than to recognize the
equally significant, but more promising, other result: a heightened attention to the ways in which all reality allegedly "pictured" in art is, in
fact, constructed by aesthetic activity, form, and materials.

❖   ❖   ❖

For reasons that have barely begun to be examined by scholars, literary and artistic modernism first developed in Paris during the Second
Empire and the early decades of the Third Republic in the twin guise of
impressionist painting and symbolist poetry. The first of these two
movements was, however, a transitional phenomenon. Attempting in an
ultra-positivist attitude to capture precisely what is seen in a fleeting in-
stant—inspired by the new photographic snapshot—many impressionists were driven (as is especially clear in Monet's later works) to explore
the very mechanisms and experience of seeing itself. By leaving
brushstroke traces of their work on the canvas, moreover, they began to
explore the material presence of the work of art itself, and to depart
from traditional illusionary realism, with its claim to have created a
translucent mirror through which to view so-called external reality.[22]
Yet, impressionist aesthetics, while they may point toward an overcom-

21. Poggioli, *Theory of the Avant-Garde*, pp. 112–114, where he writes that the artist
is led "to assume the fiction of being a self-employed professional, but in most cases he
lacks the doctor's, lawyer's and engineer's regular clientele." On the professionalization
process among intellectuals and artists, I have also drawn upon John R. Gillis, *The Devel-*
opment of European Society, 1770–1870 (Boston, 1977), pp. 271–274; and Wolfgang
Sauer, "Weimar Culture: Experiments in Modernism," *Social Research*, 39:2 (Summer
1972).
22. Alan Bowness, *Modern European Art* (London, 1972), chaps. 1 and 2; Wylie
Sypher, *From Rococo to Cubism in Art and Literature* (New York, 1960), last chapter.

ing of mimetic theory, are born of a positivist and naturalist attitude. The explicitness and sharpness of the break from tradition is greater in symbolism, according to many critics the richest source of modernism in the field of literature,[23] and, equally important for our purposes, the major aesthetic current in the work of Walter Benjamin.

For the symbolists, whose manifestoes appeared in the 1880s but whose practice developed from the earlier work of Baudelaire, Rimbaud, and Verlaine, poetic language must be removed as far as possible from its merely discursive, referential, or representational functions. A poem is an arrangement of words, and "the word 'rose,'" for example, "is an object as valid as the flower" whose image it conjures in the mind.[24] Although such use of language had often been exploited in literature, and most of all in poetry, it was the symbolists who, by concentrating upon the unique processes of their own poetic craft, insisted most strongly upon the metaphorical, and nonmimetic, function of words. Of course, realism too has its figurative mode. As Roman Jacobson observed, however, literary realists tended to use "metonymic" or "sequential" equivalences (e.g., "the White House considers a new policy"), developing the diachronic aspects of language by substituting "adjacent" or "contiguous" phrases; while symbolists, on the other hand, emphasized the highly associative metaphor (e.g., "the car beetled along"), exploiting the synchronic or "vertical" relations of language.[25]

For Baudelaire and the later symbolists, nature is no longer experienced as an independent reality existing in and for itself, the mind or imagination its discoverer or reflection; it is, rather, an "immense reservoir of [created] analogies," correspondences, and signs, a stimulant to the psychologically and musically resonant use of language. Art is not based upon nature but upon thought; thus, it is an artifice. The poet's craft is an evocative one, within which one voyages between the correspondences of the senses—as in Baudelaire's "conversing perfumes and colors and sounds"[26]—and things of the mind awaken analogous symbols in the world of images (or vice versa).[27]

23. An early influential treatment of symbolism as the major source of literary modernism in poetry and the novel is Edmund Wilson's *Axel's Castle* (London, 1961); a recent one is Stephen Spender's *The Struggle of the Modern*.

24. Poggioli, *Theory of the Avant-Garde*, pp. 196–199.

25. Roman Jacobson, "Two Aspects of Language: Metaphor and Metonymy," in *European Literary Theory and Practice*, ed. Vernon W. Gras (New York, 1973), pp. 119–129; Terence Hawkes, *Structuralism and Semiotics* (Berkeley, Calif., 1977), pp. 76–79.

26. Charles Baudelaire, *Flowers of Evil* (New York, 1962), p. 161.

27. Marcel Raymond, *From Baudelaire to Surrealism* (New York, 1950), pp. 15–19.

To find some anchor as artists within the new urban landscape, poets and novelists of symbolist inspiration built metaphorical bridges between ancient and modern myths (Joyce and Rilke are good examples), which by aesthetically clothing the naked objects and passing experiences of everyday life allowed the concentration to dwell upon them.[28] In a montage of spatialized experience—in which collective or personal memories, or far distant places, intermingle—the seeming pointlessness and ennui of sequential time is dissolved through a sensuous voyage in imagination. This is relatively accessible to poetry and painting. But spatializing even penetrated the more temporally organized arts of the novel (e.g., Proust) and music (e.g., Debussy and "musical impressionism").

The locus of this spatialized effect, cut off from the integrative creeds of the past and from the temporal unfolding of tradition, is the modern city—at first Paris of the late nineteenth century (later, Berlin, Dublin, New York, etc.), whose beauty and still largely preindustrial landscape helps explain the primacy of vision in this early symbolism. (Although it lacked large factories, Paris was a technically transformed city after the rapid work of urban renovation in the 1850s and 1860s, representing then a visibly man-made environment.)[29] Artists and writers delighted in observing the constantly shifting impermanence of crowds on the broad boulevards of Haussmann's metropolis. The urban perspective of the Parisian aesthetes went beyond simple positive or negative appraisals of the contemporary city. Instead of merely passing ethical or social judgments, they sought to fully experience the urban excess of stimuli, its confusions, transience, and lower depths within their own consciousness.[30] The contemporary city also stood revealed as a most compelling metaphor for all art in its very existence as a human construction.

That the Parisian aesthetes were not by any means entirely at home in this environment, or were sanguine about the future, is suggested by the need for aesthetic strategies of coping and survival, which did not always work. This can be seen as a matter of withdrawal and flight from social reality into an alternative mythical world constructed through the poetic transformation of what is seen or heard; it is easy to find many

28. Stephen Spender, in *The Struggle of the Modern*, stresses this attempt to live with the break in tradition by building poetic bridges backward while living fully in the present.
29. On the rapid transformation of Paris in this era, see David H. Pinkney, *Napoleon III and the Rebuilding of Paris* (Princeton, N.J., 1958).
30. Carl E. Schorske, "The Idea of the City in European Thought," in *The Historian and the City*, ed. Oscar Handlin (Cambridge, Mass., 1963), pp. 109–111.

cases of this in fin-de-siècle culture. At its most extreme, such withdrawal of energy from active engagement in the world took the form of
an obsession with decay and death (though aestheticized, and thereby
distanced, to some degree, from the direct confrontation of the terrors).
Both in France and later in fin-de-siècle Austria, symbolists (such as
Mallarmé or Hofmannsthal) cultivated a perverse enjoyment in seeing
themselves as a melancholy dying race and were eloquent purveyors of
the widespread myth of decadence in the late nineteenth century. The
sense of doom and the abyss was seen as a major source of new experience in a stale and tired world, a favorite word "*souffre*" ambiguously
meaning both the pit and the gateway to imagination.[31]

But the symbolists' art need not be seen only in terms of such seemingly perverse examples of aesthetic withdrawal. Their assault on the
language of conventional discourse and on the received liberal or other
assumptions of western European culture has another side. Symbolist
work was also an inspired and socially needed attack upon stale and
debased language in politics and commerce and its narrowing of experience. Symbolists insisted that "reality" is mediated by the language
through which we mentally construct it. Metaphor was not the only issue here. Mallarmé, for example, was not so much concerned with poetic correspondences as with creating a rich and enigmatic language of
ambiguous and multiple suggestiveness, freed from the limiting confines
of single and literal meanings.[32]

The symbolists were not simply rationalizing an escape from the
world, but were doing battle with more conventional "realists" and
"objectivists" over the meaning of so-called "reality." Charging the
symbolists with "escapism" does not adequately clarify a more pertinent problem of their work: late nineteenth-century symbolists often
used their formal technique in a way which reinforced a sense of social
impotence, as in the cultivation of an aesthetic of death. Much symbolist work of this period assumes and strengthens a fatalistic feeling of the
loss of mastery and control of a congealed and unyielding social mechanism. Thus, the early Yeats writes: "Every visionary knows that the

31. Balakian, *The Symbolist Movement*, pp. 65, 78, 143, 116 and 169. For a discussion of the Viennese case, which stresses the relation between obsessions with death and
the experience of evanescence and transience, see William M. Johnston, *The Austrian
Mind: An Intellectual and Social History, 1848–1938* (Berkeley, Calif., 1972), pp.
165–180.

32. Balakian, *The Symbolist Movement*, pp. 49 and 83–84. On the symbolist theory
of language, see A. G. Lehmann, *The Symbolist Aesthetic in France, 1885–1895* (Oxford,
England, 1968), pp. 129–193.

mind's eye soon comes to see a world which the will cannot shape or change, though it can call it up and banish it again."[33]

Such social pessimism and paralysis, surprisingly enough, links the French symbolists of the late nineteenth century with the contemporaneous literary movement of naturalism. Major naturalist writers such as Zola, Ibsen, and the early Hauptmann, by uncovering the disturbing "facts" of working-class poverty, or by exposing the cruel realities of the hallowed middle-class family, may have been attempting to politically activate their readers or audiences to support progressive causes. Yet, in naturalist work, social and hereditary pressures overpower human action and determine human character, and the social world is rendered as an independent mechanism out of control and a continuing source of anxiety. Symbolists of the period attempted in their art to poetically transform the way in which we think and imagine the world about us (and in this they were quite different from the naturalists), but they, too, fatalistically view that world as governed by forces over which they cannot exercise any control.[34] (A partial exception here are those symbolists who supported anarchist causes in the 1880s and 1890s; yet, there is little effect of such politics on their poetic, visual, or novelistic work.)[35]

It will be objected that symbolism is an extremely subjectivist art, while naturalists attempted objective distancing from their material. But this is to miss what is really new in the poetry of Baudelaire, Rimbaud, Mallarmé, and Eliot, the music of Debussy, and the novels of Proust, Joyce, and Woolf. Symbolists reacted against the view of art as romantic self-expression. In his late poems, Mallarmé, for example, sought to create impersonal works which suggest that the object-world, in all its poetic resonances and ambiguous meanings, leaves its traces in all of our thoughts.[36] For Mallarmé and the symbolists, the secret of poetic art lay in the "objective" independence of language (as a system handed down by tradition) from mere communicative, and thus intra-subjective, functions. (For this reason, it has been seen as a major source of recent French structuralist thought.)[37] "The pure work implies the elocutory disappearance of the poet," Mallarmé comments; "he

33. Quoted in Wilson, *Axel's Castle*, p. 42.
34. Balakian, *The Symbolist Movement*, pp. 138–139; and Balakian, *Surrealism: The Road to the Absolute* (New York, 1970), pp. 37–38.
35. See Eugenia W. Herbert, *The Artist and Social Reform: France and Belgium, 1885–1898* (New Haven, Conn., 1961), especially pp. 127–143, 179, and 211.
36. Raymond, *From Baudelaire to Surrealism*, p. 29.
37. See James A. Boon, *From Symbolism to Structuralism* (Oxford, England, 1972).

yields the initiative to the words, mobilized by the shock of their disparity; they light up with reciprocal reflections like a virtual trail of fire on precious stones: replacing the perceptible respiration of the old lyric afflatus or the enthusiastic personal direction of the sentence." [38] The hyperconscious symbolist poet, from Baudelaire to Eliot and Valéry, looks upon his own personality as an object, an "other"; he is a sensitive spectator to his own visions. [39] Not that the symbolists did not experience personal anguish, or rail against the crushing of the self in the modern world; rather, an impersonal poetics, focused on the mysteries of language, served as a release from such pains, as long as the "creative process" was in motion.

Much of French modernist literature, painting, and music (which has had very wide impact in the whole Western world) shows a tendency toward an impersonalizing aesthetic, a distancing from the ego through the play of language, sound, or sight. But this urge toward objective "distance" need not take the receptive, passive, and aestheticizing form that we have seen among the fin-de-siècle poets. The symbolism of T. S. Eliot, Paul Valéry, Joyce, Pound, or the later Yeats, in the decades after 1910, is not nearly so gripped by a languorous and melancholy frame of mind, or used as a withdrawal from more direct social observation and criticism. [40] Eliot, Pound, and Yeats, in fact, abandoning a pure aesthetic withdrawal, wedded their art at times to a manner of political suggestion which was in many ways decidedly reactionary. [41]

The major break from fin-de-siècle weariness and poetic lassitude, however, was in a new revolutionary formal departure, independent of symbolism and begun this time among the painters. In the years before World War I, the cubists were to develop an aggressive art which assaulted the seemingly immovable "facticity" and permanence of the object-world, while encouraging a more active sense of its human production and reproduction. With a burst of energy, they were to break from the melancholy mood often found in symbolist art and construct a more aggressive modernism, soon to be utilized politically in a left-wing manner in the turbulent environment of postrevolutionary Russia.

❖   ❖   ❖

38. Quoted in Rosen. "The Origins of Walter Benjamin."
39. Shattuck, *The Banquet Years*, p. 350; for further examples of this, see Arthur Rimbaud, *Complete Works* (New York, 1976), pp. 100–105.
40. Wilson, *Axel's Castle*, pp. 34–37, 55–56, and 80–110.
41. See John Harrison, *The Reactionaries: A Study of the Anti-Democratic Intelligentsia* (New York, 1967).

Whereas the cubists culminated impressionist and symbolist aesthetics—time expressed as simultaneity in space, aesthetic self-reflexiveness, etc.—they did so with an active sense of the human construction of nature and society. In cubism, objects do not evaporate into space once they have been metaphorically suggested, as in the tone colors of a Baudelaire, Monet, or Debussy. It is significant that colors are usually used by the cubists for architectural, not poetic or emotive, purposes. Human intelligence is not viewed as limited to the poetic metamorphosis, in imagination, of the world that is perceived, allowing art to be experienced as a compensating sanctuary; nor is outer reality seen to be necessarily determined by "reified" forces beyond our control.

With cubism, modern art and modern science—freed of nineteenth-century positivism—draw together. The cubist juxtaposition and dynamic collision of different angles and moments in space and time suggest, for one thing, the relativistic abandonment of the notion of fixed and absolute truths, or a monolithic objective order seen from a stationary point by an outside observer. In Gide's words, art becomes an "exploitation of an uncertainty." [42] In a major primary document of the movement, the artists Albert Gleizes and Jean Metsinger explained in 1912: "An object has not one absolute form—it has many; it has as many as there are planes in the region of perception." [43]

The object of research in modern science is not nature as such, but the human investigation of nature. "Natural science," writes Werner Heisenberg, "is part of the interplay between nature and ourselves; it describes nature as exposed to our method of questioning." [44] Similarly, in the pioneering work of Braque and Picasso of 1907–12, "all references to appearances are made as signs on the picture surface." Shorn of all the illusionary depth created by the traditions of Renaissance perspective, the painted canvas is now the "origin and sum of all that one sees." The multiple viewpoints that are juxtaposed in two-dimensional space, which force objects to be viewed in shifting relation to each other and in constant motion, are all presented in a "field of vision . . . which is the picture itself." [45]

But this is not merely a case of aesthetic self-consciousness, an awareness and flaunting by the painters, following the poets, of the pe-

42. Sypher, *From Rococo to Cubism*, p. 306.
43. Albert Gleizes and Jean Metzinger, "Cubism, 1912," in *Theories of Modern Art*, ed. Herschel B. Chipp (Berkeley, Calif., 1970), p. 214.
44. Werner Heisenberg, *Physics and Philosophy* (New York, 1958), p. 75.
45. John Berger, *The Moment of Cubism and Other Essays* (New York, 1969), pp. 20–22.

culiarities of their medium. The object-world, insofar as it has any meaning, is shown to be inseparable from the changing and multidimensional human perception of it. While the symbolists and impressionists had exploited metaphor and color to aestheticize reality, the cubists more directly assaulted the notion of art as leading an independent hermetic existence insulated from the outer visible world. At the same time, they sought to show through such means as incorporating "found objects" (e.g., news pages, pieces of cord or of wood) that art is not a window into the "external" world but an aspect of "reality" itself. In this view, "reality," inside and outside art, is an artifice and a "construction." [46]

In addition to this new confidence in penetrating and unsettling the allegedly fixed object-world, the cubists show a more hopeful, or at least open, attitude toward the *social* meaning of industrial society than did the symbolists. This is more explicit in variants or successors of the cubist impulse after 1917 (Russian and German constructivist painting, film, and theatre; *Neue Sachlichkeit*; "functional" architecture and music; the Bauhaus; etc.), in all of which art is enthusiastically conceived in relation to modern engineering. But this new hope, modernizing the dreams of the Enlightenment in the humane uses of the technical mastery of nature, was already implicit within the cubist movement. Guillaume Apollinaire, for example, an early literary articulator of cubist aesthetics and a central figure in French cultural life between 1905 and 1918, scorned the mere alchemy and musical resonance of words, as well as metaphorical bridges to the myths of the past, and sought to discover a new modernistic realism that would be enthusiastic about an industrial and urban future.[47] There is some parallel here with the simultaneous futurist movement. But in contrast with the Italian futurists (whose irrationally intoxicated identification with speed and machinery was a brutalizing aesthetic of modern war and destruction compatible with fascism), the cubists were far more rational, analytical, and constructive in both their artistic work and their social attitudes.

Strictly speaking, for Picasso and Braque conceptual experiments in "thinking the object" predominate; object choice is neutralized and varied, and includes people, natural scenes, tables, musical instruments, etc. The two great innovators, modern in their way of seeing, were less taken or absorbed with modern life as such. In the years 1911–25, however, Delauney, Léger, Apollinaire, and other French cubists, the cubist-

46. Sypher, *From Rococo to Cubism*, pp. 257–288 and 293.
47. Raymond, *From Baudelaire to Surrealism*, pp. 217–246.

inspired Russian constructivists (Tatlin, Gabo, Lissitzky, Meyerhold, Eisenstein, etc.), and the German Bauhaus school influenced by them clearly show a positive attitude toward the human potentials of advanced technology and mass production.[48] While this was not the only implication of the cubist current (another one was purely nonfigurative, abstract art), it was a major one, and of particular importance to many socially concerned artists, architects, filmmakers, and playwrights in the 1920s.

After 1911, cubist subject matter was often taken from the man-made constructions of the modern city: from the Eiffel tower (which fascinated many) to the ordinary objects of the modern every day, such as ashtrays or coffee cups. Generally speaking, the cubists pioneered the artistic acceptance of cheap, mass-produced objects, which they placed on their canvases and refused to see as inimical to "culture," but regarded as its modern redefinition.

Of the various modernisms, it was cubist work, significantly, which most clearly registered the technical innovations of cinematic montage, developed in Paris around 1900. Filmmaking, which has been seen as the quintessential twentieth-century art form in its technological construction and mass appeal, is a process of juxtaposing thousands of separate shots in a manner which (like our thought, according to the cubists) synchronizes the different spatial and temporal locations of an object. Many directors were to use montage in a linear or lyrical way, creating the illusion of steady, uninterrupted flow by the quick succession of minutely different shots. Eisenstein, however, with cubist and Marxist inspiration, used cinema to reveal social reality as a changeable construction of variant and conflicting viewpoints and objects (the film is "built" in the editing room, not merely received by our mind's eye). In doing so, he helped reveal the cinematic inspirations of cubism, though even his startling montage did not create/describe the world in as radically simultaneous a manner as the painters had done.[49] Cinema also helped the cubists in their study of the "silent, dynamic power" of objects. In the 1920s, Fernand Léger wrote: "Before the invention of the moving-picture, no one knew the possibilities latent in a foot—a hand—a hat."[50]

48. Werner Haftmann, *Painting in the Twentieth Century* (New York, 1965), pp. 98–101, 115–116, 193–195, and 235–238.

49. Sypher, *From Rococo to Cubism*, pp. 274–276; Arnold Hauser, *The Social History of Art* (New York, 1958), Vol. 4, p. 239.

50. Chipp, *Theories of Modern Art*, pp. 279–280. See also John Berger, "Fernand

Léger's remark suggests a further issue. Turning away from psychological portraiture, the cubists sought to reveal the ambiguities in our perception of the physical human figure and face, which they rendered as an organization of planes and geometric structures to be faceted on the picture surface. As in scientific theorizing, to help master the immense complexity of the world with an eye toward reconstructing it, they simplified all human and physical forms down to their basic shapes, taking apart a machine in order to rebuild it.[51] It may be hard for us, who are so familiar with the often dehumanizing uses of our own technology, to view this depersonalizing perspective as a potentially hopeful one. Yet, for the cubists, the mechanical focus provided a means of getting rid of the idea of the artist as an isolated genius, a hero figure, cut off from modern industrial society and cultivating his or her own personality.[52] Their acceptance of technological society and its culture was within a French intellectual climate which had long been more hospitable to science, urban life, machinery, etc., than was the case, for example, in more rapidly industrializing England of the nineteenth century, or in Germany, 1870–1945.

We have said that modernism is related to the multiple blows to political and intellectual liberalism sustained by 1900. This would seem to be contradicted by the cubist assertion of analytical intelligence, sense of social mastery, and scientific and industrial hope. Yet, cubist confidence is not that of the liberal (and social democratic) outlook: traditional empiricism and trust in slow, linear, evolutionary progress has been overtaken by the cubists' revolutionary assault on the seeming stability of objects, which are taken apart, brought into collision, and reassembled on the picture surface, one possible construction among many. Each moment of time is made up of such contingent syntheses by which human activity and perception remake the world. The new "Enlightenment" was that, in effect, of modern physics.

Seen from another vantage, cubist beginnings (1907–14) coincided with a new socialist militancy in Europe, as French Syndicalists, German Left Social Democrats, and Russian Bolsheviks broke with the evolutionary and parliamentary versions of Marxism that had been influential in the Second International. The cubist painters did not themselves,

---

Léger," in *Selected Essays and Articles: The Look of Things* (New York, 1972), pp. 107–121.

51. John Berger, *Success and Failure of Picasso* (London, England, 1965), pp. 56–57.

52. Bowness, *Modern European Art*, p. 127.

of course, make such connections in these prewar years. It was their followers after 1917, including Russian and German constructivists, German dadaists, and French surrealists, who developed radical political
implications from cubist procedures. In these movements, it was also
the case, as with symbolism, that modernist aesthetics grew out of a crisis of liberal politics and intellectual assumptions. But what developed
here, instead of political withdrawal and aestheticism, was a new revolutionary urgency, a sense that social progress was not simply assured—
especially given the various conservative habits of thought ingrained in
the population—but could be actively furthered by attacking these habits head-on with modernist cultural tactics, such as those implicit in the
language of cubism.

It is well to begin a survey of this Marxist modernism of the 1920s
with the Soviet Union. In the decade after 1917, Russian painters, poets,
architects, and theatre and film directors produced a whole series of
models for modern leftist art which ultimately derive from cubism. This
was the period of Anatoly Lunacharsky's enlightened tenure as education minister, and in which the party leadership was relatively indulgent
toward cultural experimentation; Trotsky's *Literature and Revolution*
was written in this spirit in 1922. While the great majority of Russian
writers (symbolist or realist) opposed the revolution (the futurists are a
major exception) and went into exile, many visual artists rallied to the
victorious Communists in hopes of a new liberated culture and society
based on industrialism.[53] For them, as for the governing Communists,
"the idea of industrialization had acquired a lyrical power, for it seemed
to offer a way of avoiding, instead of suffering and enduring, a whole
phase of history."[54] Thus, the often utopian (and sometimes naive) celebration of the machine and material production in postrevolutionary
Russian art was doubtless related to the country's grinding poverty and
economic backwardness as compared with western Europe, and to the
hopes of many of its westernized intellectuals for an alternative (socialist) route to modernity.

Italian futurism (shorn of its more destructive frenzies) and French
cubism had both been felt in Russian painting and poetry just before
World War I. After 1917, such artists as Lissitsky, Eisenstein, Tatlin,

53. Gleb Struve, *Russian Literature under Lenin and Stalin, 1917–1953* (Norman,
Okla., 1971), p. 5; Camilia Gray, *The Great Experiment: Russian Art, 1863–1922* (London, 1962), p. 215.
54. John Berger, *Art and Revolution: Ernst Neizvestny and the Role of the Artist in
the USSR* (New York, 1969), p. 216.

Mayakovsky, Rodchenko, Meyerhold, and others sought to extend this work in a politically and socially revolutionary manner. In the experimental theatre, film, geometric typography, or architectural plans of these years (which were generally called "constructivist"), the machine became the model, or metaphor, for artistic creation itself. In a constructivist manifesto of 1923, the following appeared: "The material formation of the object is to be substituted for its aesthetic combination. The object is to be treated as a whole, and thus will be of no discernible style, but simply a product of an industrial order like a car, an aeroplane and such like."[55] The artist became a prophet of a collectively directed technology, as in, for example, Tatlin's famous "Monument to the Third International" or Naum Gabo's "Project for a Radio Station."[56] Architecture, the most natural field for the constructivists' grandiose attempt to integrate art, industry, and social life, was largely foreclosed to them, however; as with other visions, the Tatlin and Gabo designs were never built, which was largely due to the economic distress of the country in the first fifteen years after 1917. When building became economically feasible again, by 1932, socialist realism had been established as the official style.[57]

It was in theatre and film, instead, that constructivism was most fully realized. In the plays directed by Vsevolod Meyerhold in the 1920s, whose impact upon Brecht is unmistakable,[58] traditional illusionist conventions of the stage were done away with entirely. Instead of a curtain or naturalist props, there were nothing but "constructions," such as scaffoldings, cubes, and arches. These and other dynamic geometric objects were very much part of the action of the plays. Actors and objects were in almost continual motion, while the drama was repeatedly "interrupted" by spotlights, projected film sequences, and an irregular musical accompaniment of a usually popular variety (accordion or jazz tunes). The acting, based on what Meyerhold called "biomechanics," directly assaulted the naturalist procedures developed by Stanislavsky, and took the form of depersonalized, stylized, and symbolic gestures (often from gymnastics), each signifying, but not imitating, a different emotion. Radically breaking from individualized characters, Meyerhold distinguished his actors according to their economic class: certain physical movements symbolized one class or another. To enhance the popu-

55. Gray, *The Great Experiment*, pp. 249–250.
56. Berger, *Art and Revolution*, pp. 37–46.
57. Gray, *The Great Experiment*, p. 251.
58. John Willett, *The Theatre of Bertolt Brecht* (New York, 1968), p. 208.

lar appeal of his theatre and assault the conservative traditions of high art, Meyerhold introduced court jesters, circus acrobats and clowns, or commedia dell'arte figures. The performance was not a finished product, but an open-ended creation of actors and audience alike, the spectators actively contributing to its construction.[59] While the settings and movements suggested the contemporary industrial world, they did not merely "represent" them; the audience was never allowed to forget that it was in a theatrical workshop which was a productive force in its own right.

Marxist constructivism of a similar kind was evident in the cinematic work of Sergei Eisenstein, who had worked with Meyerhold. We have already cited his cubistic montage techniques, through which he sought to demonstrate the architectural construction involved in film editing ("built," not "shot") and the dialectical collision of economic classes and productive forces in the social process. Eisenstein shared Meyerhold's utopian stress on collective human types, heroic masses, and industrial machines. But the heart of his procedures and social outlook was discontinuity, the collision of images, objects, and social forces, which he explicitly contrasted in his writings with the more continuous, evolutionary "linkage of pieces" which he found in most other cinema. For Eisenstein, montage could best be "compared to the series of explosions of an internal combustion engine, driving forward its automobile or tractor."[60] He intentionally sought to jar his audiences loose from the usual passive consumption of an easily digested linear narrative. Instead, he constructed startling juxtapositions of shots, and symbolic allusions, which forced the viewer to be alert and to interrelate images or events in an active manner. In concentrating his camera upon selected physical details, Eisenstein did not merely shoot close-ups (e.g., the doctor's glasses in *Potemkin*) but carefully composed symbolic cross-references, which depended for their effect on the audience's intelligent participation.[61]

Modernist Marxism, utilizing means ultimately derivative from cubism, was also evident in Germany in the 1920s. Dadaist montage was elsewhere associated with intentional nihilistic nonsense, the random and absurdist protest against respectable logic and reason (rendered

59. *Meyerhold on Theatre*, ed. Edward Braun (New York, 1969), pp. 159–166 and 183–203; Henri Arvon, *Marxist Esthetics*, pp. 60–64.
60. Sergei Eisenstein, *Film Form and Film Sense* (New York, 1957), p. 38.
61. Thorold Dickinson, *A Discovery of Cinema* (Oxford, England, 1971), p. 24.

bankrupt by the mechanized horrors of the World War).[62] In Berlin, however, it was closely allied with Communist sympathies by 1919 and developed as an art of embittered—but decidedly clear—social criticism. In particular, such artists as Richard Huelsenbeck, John Heartfield, and most importantly George Grosz (who were all acutely conscious of Soviet developments) used montage on canvas or through juxtaposed photos to launch savage attacks on the German ruling classes and the militarist ethos.[63] On another front, Erwin Piscator, the experimental theatre director and theoretician who had been allied with Dada, transmitted Meyerhold's ideas to Germany. Piscator subordinated individuals entirely to their "epic" roles in the class struggle, and used modern technical media such as multiple and simultaneous film projections, newspaper headlines, and moving platforms both to define the historical era of that struggle and to "interrupt" the action so as to reveal its constructed and nonlinear quality. As with Meyerhold who preceded and Brecht who followed, such "constructivist" methods were used in order to rouse his audiences to collective action.[64]

Less specifically Marxist, yet committed to developing an egalitarian art based on constructivism, was the work of the famous Bauhaus architectural school founded in 1919. (The school had first been much influenced by German expressionism, but drew upon constructivist attitudes and designs increasingly after 1922.) Bauhaus co-workers sought modern means toward a socially democratic end by returning the artist to industrial production. "Using the machine as another kind of tool," as Walter Gropius, the guiding spirit of the school, wrote, the artist "could 'bring art back to the people' through the mass production of beautiful things."[65] Modern geometric and functional design was related to a conception of art as a craft, a form of "hand-labor" produced by the collective efforts of various "artist-workmen."[66]

These examples of artistic activity in Germany and Russia in the 1920s illustrate the wide range of politically left-wing (usually Marxist)

62. Raymond, *From Baudelaire to Surrealism*, p. 203; Berger, *The Moment of Cubism*, pp. 29–31; Tristan Tzara, "Dada Manifesto," in *Paths to the Present*, ed. Eugen Weber (New York, 1960), pp. 247–253.

63. Beth Irwin Lewis, *George Grosz: Art and Politics in the Weimar Republic* (Madison, Wisc., 1971), pp. 52–61; Donald Drew Egbert, *Social Radicalism and the Arts: Western Europe* (New York, 1970), pp. 632–637.

64. Jürgen Rühle, *Theater und Revolution* (München, 1963), pp. 132–158.

65. Quoted in Barbara M. Lane, *Architecture and Politics in Germany, 1918–1945* (Cambridge, Mass., 1968), p. 67.

66. Ibid., pp. 50–51 and 57.

cubist derivatives. The major French post-cubist movement of the period, however, surrealism, presents a more complex and ambivalent case. From one perspective, surrealism represented an alternative to cubist aesthetics, inasmuch as the cubists sought to penetrate and restructure the world's objects, while the surrealists endeavored to liberate their own fantasy life. Yet, the surrealists revealed certain cubist approaches to the imagination. Drawing on Freudian psychology and earlier Parisian avant-gardes (especially the symbolists), they sought to surrender to dream logic in their "automatic writing" and "free association," but in their art and literature they presented this material as startling pictorial juxtapositions of radically disassociated images. Thus, the nineteenth-century poet Lautréamont, a major influence,[67] had constructed this favorite surrealist image: "He is as handsome . . . as the fortuitous encounter on a dissecting table of a sewing machine and an umbrella."[68] "The spirit is marvelously prompt to seize the faintest rapport that exists between two objects selected by chance," wrote André Breton, "and the poets know that they can always, without fear of deceit, say that one is like the other."[69] Instead of the chaotic spontaneity of dadaist anti-logic, however, the surrealists cultivated a notion of "objective chance," the simultaneous existence of the contradictory principles of randomness and hidden order. Thus, Aragon and Breton, in their narratives of Parisian daily life, searched for the "casual facticity of the coincidence (the necessary *and* chance encounter, for example) without any attempt to transpose the quotidian into fiction."[70] Suggesting his method, Aragon wrote in Le Paysan de Paris: "Reality is the apparent absence of contradiction. The wondrous is contradiction appearing in the real."[71]

Surrealists depicted simultaneous and mutually confronting inner and outer experiences, rendered in extreme naturalist detail, as in the paintings of Dali, Tanguy, and Ernst, which seem to be photographs of their fantasies. This montage was often intended to help remake the social world on the model of the life of dreams. Following the symbolists, they rejected romantic self-expression in presenting the traces and im-

---

67. Maurice Nadeau, *The History of Surrealism* (New York, 1965), pp. 75–76.

68. Quoted in Roger Shattuck, "Surrealism Reappraised," in *The History of Surrealism*, by Maurice Nadeau, p. 25.

69. Quoted in Roger Short, "Dada and Surrealism," in *Modernism*, ed. Bradbury and McFarlane, p. 303.

70. Shattuck, "Surrealism Reappraised," p. 20; see also the excellent discussion in Peter Bürger, *Theorie der Avant-Garde* (Frankfurt a.M., 1972), pp. 87–92.

71. Louis Aragon, *The Nightwalker*, trans. Frederick Brown (Englewood Cliffs, N.J., 1970), p. 166. This is the English edition of *Le Paysan de Paris*.

ages of the world of objects which are left in the mind as reverberations. This "objectivity" took linguistic and imagistic forms: "One evening in particular, as I was about to fall asleep," Breton wrote, "I became aware of a sentence . . . that knocked at the window." [72] As successors to the cubists, however, the surrealists offered these images in dynamic collision and radical montage, but with a more pointed intent to "deepen the foundations of the real" by shocking their audiences from habituated isolating of experiences, especially those of waking and dreaming.[73] Seemingly "free" associations, then, were far more "constructed" than passively "received," even if Breton urged that the mind be divested of its critical faculty and become a "silent receptacle of so many echoes, modest registering machines." [74]

Engaged in a very delicate juggling act, the surrealists sought with great difficulty to balance and connect "surrender to the unconscious" and psychic automatism with social revolution. Many were drawn toward Communism after 1927 or so, and thereafter invoked Marxist materialism in their war against idealist aesthetics and bourgeois culture. But in attempting to build bridges to Marxist philosophy and political action, the surrealists were thwarted by the mechanical materialism and dictatorial behavior of official Communism, which by the late 1920s was increasingly subordinated to Stalinist control.[75] Yet, Communist commitments may have functioned in part as a defense against their acceptance as an enjoyable scandal by the bourgeois public, or absorption by the Paris literary world, the fate of so many avant-gardes, particularly after 1950.[76] This is not necessarily a purely aesthetic posture, of course, but a political distancing act in defense of a self-proclaimed cultural indigestibility. Seen from this angle, such commitments had some success for a while.

In the late 1930s, Benjamin and Adorno disputed whether surrealists merely mirror the experience of a reified world out of control (to which they surrender in its domination of the data of the "unconscious") or seriously and effectively counter that world (through shocks to habitual

72. André Breton, "What Is Surrealism?" in *Paths to the Present*, ed. Eugen Weber, p. 261.
73. André Breton, "First Surrealist Manifesto," in *Surrealism*, by Patrick Waldberg (London, 1965), pp. 66–75; Breton, "What Is Surrealism?" pp. 253–279.
74. Breton, "What Is Surrealism?" p. 264.
75. Balakian, *Surrealism*, pp. 135–139; Ferdinand Alquié, *The Philosophy of Surrealism* (Ann Arbor, Mich., 1965), pp. 56–67; Herbert Gershman, *The Surrealist Revolution in France* (Ann Arbor, Mich., 1969), pp. 86–116.
76. Roger Short, "The Politics of Surrealism," in *Left-Wing Intellectuals Between the Wars, 1919–39*, ed. Walter Laqueur and George L. Mosse (New York, 1966), p. 23.

logic and mental associations). To this we shall return in a later chapter. At this point, it is sufficient to note how ambivalent surrealism appears: alternatively active and passive, hopeful and despairing, the master and the register of postwar confusions in western and central Europe which contrasted with the buoyant utopian mood of early Russian constructivism.

What the surrealists and constructivists shared was the continuation and development of French modernist aesthetics: a rejection not merely of realist "mimesis" but also of romantic self-expression, a focus on objectifying and depersonalizing functions of language, image, and sound. This direction taken by French modernists will become clearer in a further comparative focus, a glance at the expressionist avant-gardes of Germany and Austria in the years surrounding World War I.

❖ ❖ ❖

A languorous aestheticism (influenced by currents from France) marked the first wave of artistic modernity in Vienna, a culture of political despair mounted by the postliberal intelligentsia after 1890.[77] In the more expressionist decade before the war, however, a heightened urgent communication of anguish and dread was voiced in the arts (e.g., the path from Klimt to Schiele and Kokoschka).[78] In Germany, in contrast, the rhetorical intensity and violent visual distortions of the expressionists grew in reaction against the emotional inexpressiveness they felt in naturalist literature, the avant-garde of 1890s Berlin. Whatever the immediate background of expressionism in various locales, however, this movement of 1905–20 first provided the German-speaking world with its own distinctive modernist arts. In the nervous, agitated, and suffering paintings, dramas, and poems of this generation, Austrian and German artists projected their inner turmoils upon all that felt alien and oppressive: the machine, the city, the family, the "masses." In these years, the cubists were confidently analyzing and reassembling the world's objects; the expressionists, in a spirit of primitive and anguished religiosity, sought desperately to expel inner torments from their prison within the self.

Expressionist writers often sought through their work to overcome feelings of self-contempt, guilt, and unworthiness. As sensitive artists and overcerebral intellectuals, feeling that they were unable to function

77. See Carl E. Schorske, *Fin de Siècle Vienna.*
78. On this shift, see ibid., final chapter; and Johnston, *The Austrian Mind,* pp. 143–147.

in the social world—unlike the practical, sober bourgeois whom they often envied (frequently their own fathers)—they sought to relate to "humanity" by revealing a suffering and a longing for regeneration which all share.[79] The creations which resulted show a "common determination to subordinate form and nature to emotional and visionary experience." Edvard Munch, a major influence, had "felt a scream pass through nature" and had placed this anguish on a canvas.[80] Expressionist painters violently and aggressively distorted the human figure, drawing upon German Gothic and Reformation depictions of Christ's torment, or the stylizations of primitive sculpture.[81] Kandinsky explained their affinity with primitive art in this way: "Like ourselves, these pure artists sought to express only inner and essential feelings in their works; in this process they ignored as a matter of course the fortuitous."[82] Expressionist writers, in order to force language to convey psychically urgent outbursts, constructed chopped-up, telescoped, or inverted sentences, monosyllabic shrieks, or furious hyperboles. Their purposes—as modern as their work appears aesthetically—were ethical, spiritual, or "political," the communication of intense pains to help build a community of the sufferers. On another level, much of this activity, whatever its intended goals, seems to serve a largely therapeutic function: its "anguish appears to be not so much reflected in the art as released through it."[83]

In expressionism, violent denunciations and pleas for love and brotherhood often stand side by side. The vocabulary of a tormented and apocalyptic religiosity abounds in the frequent usage of words like "abyss," "darkness," "cry," "goodness," "soul," "love," "spirit," etc. The paintings of Nolde and the sculpture of Barlach provide visual examples of a longing for spiritual innocence; but in the years before World War I, there are clear anticipations (fearful? hopeful?) of the coming Armageddon. The intensity of erotic and violent instincts unleashed in this art is obvious and has been related to a more general middle-class cultural revolt in Germany and Austria, in the years be-

79. Walter H. Sokel, *The Writer in Extremis: Expressionism in Twentieth-Century German Literature* (Palo Alto, Calif., 1959), especially chaps. 4 and 5.

80. Victor H. Miesel, ed., *Voices of German Expressionism* (Englewood Cliffs, N.J., 1970), p. 1.

81. Peter Selz, *German Expressionist Painting* (Berkeley, Calif., 1957), pp. 12–19. On "aggressive deformation" in expressionist literature and painting, see Richard Hamann and Jost Hermand, *Expressionismus* (München, 1976), pp. 44–57.

82. Wassily Kandinsky, "Concerning the Spiritual in Art," in *Paths to the Present*, ed. Eugen Weber, pp. 211–212 and 220.

83. Rosen, *Arnold Schoenberg* (New York, 1975), p. 15.

tween 1905 and 1920, against the puritan asceticism and repressiveness of the nineteenth-century Victorian cultural superego.[84]

In the best expressionist work—in Kafka, Schoenberg, and Beckmann, for example—strength lies precisely in the refusal of resolution, harmony, or easy comfort (a point Adorno was to emphasize in his praise of Schoenberg):[85] e.g., Kafka's paradoxes or the floating musical tonalities of an "emancipated dissonance." Schoenberg's determination not to resolve dissonant chords with consonant ones was a rejection of the tradition of the harmonic cadence, the quieting of tension in the direction of repose, which had been fundamental to centuries of music.[86] In the works of Schoenberg, Kafka or Beckmann, the agonies of the artist might be communicated with new formal means, but could not be easily mollified. Thus, the expressionist dream is a "nightmare" which is the world out there; there is little of the symbolist or surrealist interest in actual dreams as a higher revelation or an enriching of experience.[87]

But the new formal methods of Kafka and Schoenberg were not typical of all varieties of expressionism. The major distinction within the movement was not so much between its "religious" and its "political" wings—both of which were fueled by psychic and spiritual hungers—as between its heavily rhetorical and its objectifying methods of artistic construction. The more naive and aesthetically more traditional expressionists (like Johst, Ehrenstein, Rubiner, and often Toller) simply declaim and shriek out their feelings, failing to give them an independent formal intensity which would command attention to the fullest. Much that was ephemeral in the movement was of this kind—objectionable on both aesthetic and political grounds. Those who expressed extreme states of mind more effectively did so through various means of formalized objectification: the concentrated and provocative cynicism of Wedekind and Sternheim; the personified embodiment of emotions in Barlach's sculpture; the extended aphoristic parables of Georg Kaiser's dramas (whose epic qualities influenced Brecht); the spare linguistic condensation and abstractions of the "Sturm poets"; the strict formal reorganization in Schoenberg's serial music; and, most of all, the decep-

84. Arthur Mitzman, *The Iron Cage: An Interpretation of Max Weber* (New York, 1969), p. 251. See also his "Anarchism, Expressionism and Psychoanalysis," *New German Critique*, 11 (Winter 1977); and Roy Pascal, *From Naturalism to Expressionism: German Literature and Society, 1880–1918* (London, 1973), pp. 229–255.

85. See, for example, Adorno, *The Philosophy of Modern Music*, pp. 39–40.

86. Rosen, *Arnold Schoenberg*, p. 26.

87. Sokel, *The Writer in Extremis*, pp. 37–38.

tively simple classical prose and condensed parabolic form of Kafka's dreamlike visualizations.[88]

Expressionist objectification was markedly different from symbolist or cubist varieties, however, as Schoenberg's devotee Theodor Adorno was to suggest. French forms of modernism revealed either a welcome depersonalizing surrender to the objectifying qualities of language, sight, and sound (as in symbolism or surrealism) or a "scientific" study of the object world, promising its intellectual or physical reconstruction (cubism). The most effective art of the expressionists, however, objectified as a means of intensifying their personal projections, as in the terrifying vision of Gregor Samsa's metamorphosis. In France, modernists often reacted strongly against romantic personalized subjectivity. But if German expressionist work showed a liquidation of the autonomous psychological self, this had been for the expressionists a painful experience of ego dissolution demanding to be communicated, not a welcome release from "romantic" individuality.[89] "If the contemplation of self provides no solace because one is no longer even sure what or where the self is," Anna Balakian has written of the expressionists, "the cult of language, which was such a boon for the symbolists, no longer offers any comfort, or any power to assuage the desolation of the human spirit."[90] The clarification is vital in order to understand the contrasting forms of "dehumanization" and "stylization" in modernist culture, and is especially central to our concerns. Such distinctions will help to illuminate the conflicts between our four major figures, two of whom embraced the "end of subjectivity" in the new collectivist and technological age (Brecht and Benjamin, drawing on Russian or French sources in their different ways), and two of whom, in the German or Austrian tradition, sought to combat it (Lukács and Adorno, the first with classical nostalgia, the second with modernist stoicism).

We have seen in the previous chapter how common it was in German romantic social thought to warn of the threats to personal development posed by modern social life. With the rapid traumatic impact of urban and industrial growth in Germany from 1870 to 1914, this concern was intensified among German middle classes, professors, intellectuals, and

88. Ibid., pp. 50–51, 106–113, and 161.
89. An excellent illustration of this is the continued romantic presence, although radically redirected toward anguished dissonance and fragmentation, in Schoenberg's music to the end of his life: e.g., the "rise and fall of melodies [which] imply the tonal oscillation from agitation to stability," and the fact that no melodic lines are "expressively neutral." Rosen, *Arnold Schoenberg*, pp. 45–46.
90. Balakian, *The Symbolist Movement*, p. 195.

artists.[91] Many expressionist poems, plays, films, and paintings show revulsion for the impersonal, mechanical, routinized, and authoritarian
aspects of modern factory and urban life, continuing with a new urgency a main tendency of romantic social thought (Kaiser's *Gas* and
Fritz Lang's *Metropolis* are two well-known examples.)[92] The vision of
the demonic technological city introduced new formal elements into
German poetry of this period, whose disassociated and violently clash-
ing images and meanings puncture the ideal of the integrated human
"subject."[93] The bleak, heavily industrial, and militarized Berlin was the
city of many expressionists, so different from the still spacious, visually
appealing, and only slowly industrializing Paris. Unlike the montage
technique developed by the French, the juxtaposing of cacophonous experiences was presented by the expressionists as a protest and an ominous warning; it did not suggest a social or aesthetic acclimation to, or
validation of, the new metropolis.

Protest directed against the alleged loss of selfhood in modern society is clearest in the depiction of the collective "mass," reduced in
many expressionist plays and films to faceless automatons acting irrationally upon demagogic suggestion. Constructivists and Marxists in
theatre and film in the 1920s (such as Meyerhold, Eisenstein, Piscator,
and Brecht) openly embraced the tendency toward collectivization in
modern society when they substituted social "types" (such as the industrialist, the worker, or the soldier) for traditional individuated characters. The expressionist plays which preceded their work, however, show
the subordination of person to social role (i.e., "father," "son," "mass,"
etc.) in a spirit of profound pessimistic disillusionment, as in Ernst
Toller's *Man and the Masses* (1919).[94] In such cases, experiences are na-
ively and rhetorically presented that receive much more compelling
treatment in Kafka's novels and stories, which subtly present the insid-
ious demise of all hope for the autonomy of the subject in the face of
pervasive and *internalized* social and bureaucratic controls.

In his aesthetic and social analyses, Theodor Adorno, drawing upon
Freud as much as Marx, was to mournfully stress the radical expres-

91. See George L. Mosse, *The Crisis of German Ideology* (New York, 1964); Fritz
Stern, *The Politics of Cultural Despair* (Berkeley, Calif., 1961); and Fritz Ringer, *The Decline of the German Mandarins: The German Academic Community, 1890–1933* (Cambridge, Mass., 1969).
92. Sokel, *The Writer in Extremis*, p. 195.
93. Pascal, *From Naturalism to Expressionism*, pp. 143–180.
94. Ibid., pp. 148–149.

sionist thesis of the willing "dissolution of the subject" in what he called the "totally administered society" of the late bourgeois era.[95] By stressing "alienation" and "reification," Marxist writers (e.g., Adorno) were able to treat such issues with greater subtlety than in the often simplistic and frankly elitist handling of the expressionists: in many of the works of the latter, intellectuals, somehow capable of autonomous choice and assertive will, are contrasted with the robotized "masses."[96] (Traces of this elitism are evident in Adorno and other Frankfurt Marxists, but only within an assessment of the position of the intelligentsia which was much more searching and many-sided than that offered by the expressionists.)

Many expressionists sought release from the burdens of personal isolation by integrating in a new self-determining collective "subject": a spiritually transformed "community" of one kind or another. The hope for an emergence of such an alternative to individual impotence or mass automatism—which amounted to another version of the German middle-class longing for rooted *Gemeinschaft* in place of modern atomized *Gesellschaft*[97]—was greatest toward the end of the World War. Thus, Ernst Toller longed, through political action, "to find man in the mass; to free community in the mass."[98] In the years 1917–19, many expressionists became politically intoxicated, feverishly hoping for a renewal or *Wandlung* whose outlines were left in spiritualizing vagueness. Their vacuous and abstract language ("the new man," "the revolution of the spirit") suggests something of the immense distance of these intellectuals from the broad social strata of German society, but also reflects the chiliastic atmosphere of the period, symbolized so well in the title of a major expressionist anthology of 1919, *Menschheitsdämmerung*, with its evocatively ambiguous meaning of both "twilight" and "dawn" for humanity.[99] The immediate postwar period brought forth many such ambivalent expressions of "utopia" and "apocalypse," extreme hope

95. See, for example, Theodor Adorno, *Minima Moralia* (London, 1974), pp. 15–18 and many other passages.

96. Pascal, *From Naturalism to Expressionism*, pp. 148–149.

97. The terms, though long contrasted in Germanic romantic social thought, were classically defined around 1890 in Ferdinand Tönnies' famous sociological study, *Gemeinschaft und Gesellschaft*.

98. Ernst Toller, "Man and the Masses," in *Avant-Garde Drama: Major Plays and Documents, Post-World War One*, ed. Bernard F. Dukore and David C. Gerould (New York, 1969), p. 162.

99. Sokel, *The Writer in Extremis*, pp. 164–169. For expressionistic pronouncements of the period of World War I, the November Revolution of 1918, and after, see Miesel, *Voices of German Expressionism*, pp. 151–188.

and dread[100] (though not always taking expressionist form), an attitude which was to continue throughout the interwar years and may be seen, in different ways, among all four of our Marxist figures of "Weimar Culture." In Vienna, postwar agonies of famine, unemployment, and bureaucratic collapse served to continue its intellectuals in their world-weary diagnosis of the slow lingering death of their society[101]—the kind of apolitical cultural modernist attitude which was strongest in Austria, and which Adorno absorbed while in Vienna in the 1920s.[102] Many German expressionists, however, turned their spiritual hungers in a millenarian direction during and after the German Revolution of 1918–19.

The disillusionments which followed the failure of radical socialist hopes in that revolution were bitter indeed; for most expressionists, the bourgeois parliamentary compromise of the new Weimar Republic seemed little different from the old monarchic order. By 1921 and 1922, the breakup of the movement in various political directions, left and right, became clear, soon to be followed by the repudiation by many former expressionists of the whole intensely subjective approach.[103] Yet, the current did not simply die in the early 1920s. It filtered, for example, into the seemingly disengaged *Neue Sachlichkeit* style of the late 1920s,[104] was absorbed and turned in conservative directions within the German film industry,[105] and later provided anti-fascists like Picasso and the Mexican muralists with the pictorial style they needed to release their anguished political protests in the 1930s.[106] Other examples of a continuing and contrasting expressionist presence could be adduced in Western cultural life since the early 1920s. Yet, the moment of greatest influence and visibility, the years surrounding World War I, had passed.

100. See Ivo Frenzel, "Utopia and Apocalypse in German Literature," *Social Research*, 39:2 (Summer 1972), 314.

101. Johnston, *The Austrian Mind*, pp. 73–75 and 165–180.

102. Adorno's years in Vienna from 1925 to 1926 and their impact on his outlook are discussed by Martin Jay, *The Dialectical Imagination: A History of the Frankfurt School and the Institute for Social Research* (Boston, 1973), pp. 22–23, and, more extensively, by Susan Buck-Morss, *The Origin of Negative Dialectics: Theodor W. Adorno, Walter Benjamin and the Frankfurt Institute* (New York, 1977), pp. 11–17. This pivotal phase of his career will also be analyzed in Chapter 7 of the present study.

103. Sokel, *The Writer in Extremis*, pp. 192–226; John Willett, *Expressionism* (New York, 1970), pp. 185–195.

104. Helmut Gruber, "The German Writer as Social Critic, 1927 to 1933," *Studi Germanici*, 7:2/3 (1969), 258–286.

105. See Siegfried Kracauer, *From Caligari to Hitler* (Princeton, N.J., 1960); and Lotte Eisner, *The Haunted Screen* (Berkeley, Calif., 1969).

106. Willett, *Expressionism*, pp. 210–216.

❖ ❖ ❖

In Parts Two and Three of this book, we will study how diverse features of the movements we have just surveyed either fertilized or were criticized within the writings of Lukács, Brecht, Benjamin, and Adorno. In completing Part One, however, we need to briefly examine the history of Marxist responses to modernism, up to the promulgation of official socialist realism in the 1930s.

It is easy to state how incompatible the modernist abandonment of evolutionary sequence and formal stylization appears to the "rationalist optimism" and realist aesthetics which are usually seen as the major hallmarks of Marx's approach. Marx believed in progress, so it is said, while modernist art is decidedly pessimistic. But this is an inadequate formulation on both sides. Neglecting Marx's critique of nineteenth-century liberal notions of continuous linear advance, such an approach disregards his ambivalent and dialectical response to industrial capitalist society and technological "improvement," which we discussed in Chapter 1.[107] On the other hand, modernists show more than social despair. More common, especially in the decades 1905–30, are various mixtures of hope and anxiety, depending upon the modernist current, geographical location, or moment in time involved.

Marx did, of course, share with bourgeois liberals certain rationalist and confident assumptions about the course of history which became far more difficult for many Western intellectuals to hold after 1880, and especially after 1914. Yet, the version of Marxism disseminated by the Second International and later by the Communist movement represented a caricature of Marx's thought as a set of predetermined scientific laws, mechanical economic explanations of history, a theory of steady and ineluctable historical advance, and a cult of industrial productivity.[108] From such a vantage point, modernist aesthetic concerns—e.g., dissatisfaction with sequential linear time, exploration of simultaneity, "psychological" time, or "spatial" time—would necessarily appear irresponsible, self-indulgent, and wrongheaded. No doubt, Marx-

107. This is the case even among otherwise well-informed commentators on this subject, who fail to distinguish sufficiently between Marx and his widely received caricature. A recent example, which contains a spirited and imaginative defense of modernism from a generally left-wing point of view, is David Caute's *The Illusion* (New York, 1971).

108. Excellent accounts of the Marxism of the Second International, and especially its leading party, the SPD, are contained in George Lichtheim, *Marxism: A Critical and Historical Study* (New York, 1961), pp. 203–351; Andrew Arato, "Reexamining the Second International," *Telos*, 18 (Winter 1973–74), 2–52; and Lucio Coletti, "The Marxism of the Second International," *Telos*, 8 (Summer 1971).

ists, including those sympathetic to the avant-garde, have things to criticize in modernist culture. (We shall discuss many of those offered by Brecht, Benjamin, and Adorno.) However, an objectivist epistemology and dogmatic historical optimism were to help insulate "orthodox" Marxists entirely from the cultural innovations of the avant-garde and prevent a more fruitful confronting of modernist experience.

As for matters of aesthetic and literary form, an exclusive focus on certain directions in Marx's thought has frequently led to an erroneously prescriptive, narrowly utilitarian, realist aesthetic among Marxists. This makes them bristle at aesthetic stylizations and any abandonment of the traditional customs of formal representation, especially those of the nineteenth century. We might reiterate here that: (1) Marx saw a wide variety of possible "uses" for art, one of which is its relative autonomy from immediate economic or political needs, and the self-purpose it contains in defiance of a society based on alienated and commercially instrumentalized labor; and (2) Marx viewed art, as he did other forms of conscious labor activity, as part of the human productive mediation of the objective world, not its mere reflection or mimetic representation.

It is quite true that Marx's private aesthetic sensitivities to formal questions are not entirely revealed in the "content" analyses upon which he concentrated his published remarks on literature. More seriously, it is also true that the element of humanist classicism in Marx's outlook might well be used (as Lukács was to do) against modernist fragmentation and the disjunctions (instead of dialectical interplay) between subject and object. No doubt, he would have been alarmed by the demise of the integrated subjective self in modernism. Yet, Marx's theories of "alienation" and "reification" provide powerful suggestions for the sympathetic historical interpretation of the "end of subjectivity" in the modernist arts. On this point, a crucial question may be whether a work of art need be finished and complete, with an omniscient author who presents an implicit framework to answer the social problems which have been suggested in the work (Lukács's perspective); or whether (as Benjamin and Adorno alleged) the critic might find *unintended* and fragmentary historical "truth" in avant-garde art, and enjoin the artist, under modern conditions of ambiguity and contingency, to create open-ended works which raise compelling questions to be pondered by the audience (as Brecht, at his best, was able to do). Important aspects of modernist culture—as Brecht, Benjamin, and Adorno were to argue with different cases in mind—might well contain new formal strategies for the resistance to, and overcoming of, social paralysis and reified consciousness: e.g., by "distancing" techniques, metaphorical assaults upon linear time, the countering of routinized language, or atomized experiences. With such a view it would be possible to develop in a twentieth-century context Marx's dialectical approach to the best art of his time as both a product of art's commodified status and a promise of disalienation.

Whatever the potentials of Marx's own views, modernists and Marxists were worlds apart in the three decades before World War I (though not always in the 1920s, as we have seen). In understanding the earlier period, let us note the bohemian or aristocratic bearing of much of the cultural avant-garde in these years, which often precluded any wide interest in an alliance with a proletarian mass movement (a posture influenced, in part, by the writer's or artist's position in the new marketplace). If there was any avant-garde politics, it was often of an extreme libertarian and anarchist variety, as, for example, among neo-impressionists and symbolists in the 1880s and 1890s, and among some cubists, expressionists, and futurists in the years 1907–14.[109] On the other hand, the official socialist parties within the Second International (1889–1914), given their rigidly deterministic and optimistic outlook, could not help showing contempt for anything that might reveal traits of social pessimism or acute aesthetic self-consciousness.

The discussion in the 1890s within the German Social Democratic Party on naturalist literature provides a compelling example of socialist intellectual insularity in the period. (We may use this case because still more modernist schools did not receive nearly as much attention, and, in any event, the naturalists were attacked for features of their work which were even more pronounced among symbolists, expressionists, etc.) In the *Neue Zeit* in 1890 and 1891, Wilhelm Liebknecht, a founder of the German Marxist movement, and Robert Schweichel, an aging socialist poet and dramatist, each charged that the literary avant-garde of the naturalists was little more than a pessimistic expression of a bourgeois culture on its way out, the literary refuse of a class in decay. Although some younger members of the party showed more sympathy

---

109. See Poggioli, *Theory of the Avant-Garde*, pp. 94–101; Egbert, *Social Radicalism and the Arts*, pp. 237–326; Herbert, *The Artist and Social Reform*; and Helmut Kreutzer, *Die Boheme: Analyse und Dokumentation der intellektuellen Subkultur vom 19. Jahrhundert bis zur Gegenwart* (Stuttgart, 1971).

with new cultural forms, these individuals were of little real influence. In the *Freie Volksbühne*, the Social Democrats' attempt at working-class "education" through theatrical performances, the party wanted the audiences to get at least an indirect socialist message. As for formal questions, in an actual party debate on naturalism and aesthetic theory, at Gotha in 1896, August Bebel himself warned that literature and art in a socialist movement should not flagrantly disturb the conservative tastes in these matters of most of its members, though he cautioned also against favoring exclusively traditional artistic styles.[110] The *SPD*, of course, was a massively growing institution by the mid-1890s; rooted in the expanding trade union movement, it was the most powerful wing of the Second International and within fifteen years was to become the largest single party in the Reichstag. Its historical optimism and trust in evolutionary advance, though shortsighted and intellectually rigid, is understandable. But what is more germane is that *SPD* and trade union leaders felt that the "scientific" expectation of victory which they offered to otherwise dispirited working people was a major appeal of socialism. Given this perspective and their often intense suspicion of the thought-world of independent intellectuals, it is not surprising that, anticipating "socialist realism," they wanted a clearly "positive," not "negative," literature. At the 1896 conference, one party official commented: "The worker who must struggle against poverty, who in times of unemployment is already disposed to a certain mood of depression, is not able to enjoy art when misery is depicted repeatedly in the most blatant colors."[111] (From this perspective it would be hard to defend the disturbing and demanding cubists, for example, whatever the social potentials envisioned by their art.)

There were, of course, more sophisticated treatments of literary and aesthetic theory in the period of the Second International—notably the work of Franz Mehring and Georgi Plekhanov—but these, too, reflected a vulgarized deformation of Marxism and failed to provide adequate bases for an evaluation of the potentials of modernism. For Plekhanov, who was a major influence upon Lenin and all later Russian Marxists, art represented "the class or stratum whose tastes it expresses." Seeking the sociological "laws" which give rise to art in various historical periods, he highly accentuated and overemphasized the deter-

110. Vernon L. Lidtke, "Naturalism and Socialism in Germany," *American Historical Review*, 79:1 (February 1974), 14–37.
111. Ibid.

ministic components in Marxism. Plekhanov viewed cultural history simply as the "reflection of the history of its classes, of their struggle, one with the other." Most western European literature after about 1850 is reduced in his perspective to bourgeois apologetics.[112]

In the work of Franz Mehring, the most highly respected intellectual of the *SPD*, Marx's German classical interests in particular were continued; these, however, were made the basis of a one-sidedly pejorative analysis of modernism which Lukács was to inherit and elaborate on a new philosophical basis after 1930. As was common among the other party leaders, Mehring attacked the pessimistic outlook in the recent naturalist literature. German workers preferred the classics of the late eighteenth century—Schiller, Lessing, Goethe, etc.—to the "decadent" modernists, Mehring asserted, because they sensed a parallel between their own outlook and the literature of the bourgeoisie in its period of revolutionary confidence and historical ascent.[113] The theory was an example of Mehring's crudely reductionist historical methods, in which art is explained as a reflection of class ideology at a particular time. Elsewhere in his writings, a mechanical materialism prevails, as when he analyzes Lessing's literary formation as a mirror of economic and social facts, such as those obtaining in eighteenth-century Saxony, Lessing's native region.[114]

Thus, Marxists of the Second International failed to adequately confront the developing modernist directions around them. It was only in the 1920s that a Marxist culture drawing on modernist procedures was to emerge. We have surveyed this conjuncture of political and cultural rebellion in the constructivist and surrealist currents, where, significantly, it was modernists who moved toward Marxism, and not vice versa (as we shall also note in the cases of Brecht, Benjamin, and Adorno). But the various attempts to use modernist aesthetics for Marxist ends was short-lived: in Germany, the Nazis put an end, after 1933, to all varieties of cultural experiment, while at the same time the Communist policy of socialist realism was being developed, which still reigns in the Soviet orbit and is the culmination and nadir of pseudo-Marxist aesthetics.

10 yrs.

The consolidation of Stalin's rule in the Soviet Union, the decreasing

112. Maynard Solomon, ed., *Marxism and Art: Essays Classic and Contemporary* (New York, 1973), pp. 119–121; Diana Laurenson and Alan Swingewood, *The Sociology of Literature* (London, 1972), pp. 51–53.
113. Lidtke, "Naturalism and Socialism in Germany."
114. Peter Demetz, *Marx, Engels and the Poets* (Chicago, 1967), pp. 186–187.

role of the older Europeanized intelligentsia and the rise of many ex-peasants in the Soviet Communist Party by 1930, and the mobilization of the whole country for rapid industrialization after 1928 all contrib-uted to the end of the relatively open and intensely experimental post-revolutionary period in the arts. But the doctrine of "socialist realism," announced in 1934 and rigidly enforced thereafter, meant more than a dictatorial evaluation of works of art in terms of their conveying the current political line. With a decidedly mechanistic Marxism as its phil-osophical premise, and with the "education" of the masses as its alleged end, the new cultural orthodoxy enforced a sentimentalized and conser-vative naturalism as the only correct formal procedure. Historical "truth" was said to emerge through the accurate "reflection" of society in works of art. The central stress on creating optimistic, healthy, posi-tive "heroes" suggested, however, that instead of continuing the tradi-tion of nineteenth-century realism—with its uncovering of disturbing aspects of social reality in a critical and ironic manner—"socialist real-ism" refurbished the stabilizing intents of Victorian middle-class moral-izing. The prescribed literary and pictorial language was a mixture of an inflated, "heroic," pseudoclassical style with prosaic naturalist descrip-tions of ordinary, everyday life, all in the name of the "truthful histor-ically concrete representation of reality in its revolutionary develop-ment." In effect, this meant an aesthetic as well as political valorizing of the immediate status quo, interpreted by the party as a stable, harmo-nized, socialist industrial order.[115]

All formal methods associated with Western modernism were at-tacked as "decadent" or "formalist," and proscribed as such. Writers such as Shakespeare, Balzac, and Stendhal were held up (at least before the intensification of Russian nationalism in the late 1930s) as models of "realism" from the past. As "gentry" or "bourgeois" realists, however, these old masters, it was argued, had to be negative and critical of their age, unlike current Soviet writers. Having the advantage of living in a classless society (sic!), the latter should be affirmative and positive.[116] Zhdanov, soon to become Stalin's literary czar, promulgated in the 1930s and 1940s an extreme economic determinist view of art as a su-perstructural reflection of the ruling class: thus, he spoke of the "dec-

115. Abram Tertz, The Trial Begins and On Socialist Realism (New York, 1960), pp. 189–218; Berger, Art and Revolution, pp. 47–63; Boris Thomson, The Premature Revolution: Russian Literature and Society, 1917–1946 (London, 1972), pp. 223–234.
116. Hermann Ermolaev, Soviet Literary Theories, 1917–1939: The Genesis of So-cialist Realism (Berkeley, Calif., 1963), pp. 184–203.

adence and disintegration of bourgeois literature, resulting from the collapse and decay of the capitalist system. . . . Now everything is degenerating—themes, talents, authors, heroes." The term "decadence" was used indiscriminately to apply to all forms of modern cultural experiment (and not merely those which perversely aestheticized death and violence); in this deployment, Communist cultural theory was analogous to the writings of social darwinists, racists, and fascists of the early twentieth century.[117]

"Socialist realism" and other conservative aspects of official Soviet cultural and social policy after 1930 represented the final deterioration of a critical method of social analysis (Marxism) into a facile, mechanistic ideology and world-view supportive of a powerful bureaucratic establishment, ruthless in its suppression of all "deviance."[118] This is not the place to enter the complex historical debates on the sources of Stalinism as a system of rule. This brief glance at Soviet cultural policy between the wars merely concludes, on an unhappy note, our survey of attitudes toward art (particularly modern art) within Marxist political movements up to 1940. The incomprehension and violent dismissal of modernist currents in the name of Marxism had reached a peak in the policy of "socialist realism," just a few years after the promising experiments on the cultural left in the previous decade (both in artistic practice and critical historical analysis). Both of these developments—the postwar beginnings of a Marxist reception of modernism and the straitjacketing of Communist culture which followed—were part of the background of the immensely fruitful aesthetic debates among German exile intellectuals after 1933. The most important of these widely ramifying confrontations—those between Lukács and Brecht, on the one hand, and Benjamin and Adorno, on the other—are the subject of the rest of this study.

117. Solomon, *Marxism and Art*, pp. 237–238.
118. Fetscher, *Marx and Marxism* (New York, 1971), pp. 148–181.

PART TWO

Lukács and Brecht

CHAPTER THREE

A Debate on Realism and Modernism

During the 1930s, the dramatist Bertolt Brecht and the literary and political critic Georg Lukács developed independent Marxist perspectives on modern art and cultural life which differed in fundamental ways. Each was a well-known intellectual exile from fascism and allied (albeit critically) with the Communist movement. Their contrasting Marxist aesthetics were directed in part toward the question of which literary traditions could best be utilized and reworked in the anti-fascist struggle: nineteenth-century realism or twentieth-century modernist forms. For purposes of analysis, our treatment of Lukács and Brecht will be divided up in the following way. First, in this chapter, the explicitly disputed literary issues of the 1930s will be explored, one of the richest controversies in the history of Marxist aesthetics, and one especially germane to the question of modernism. In Chapters 4 and 5, the roots of aesthetic divergence will be studied in the intellectual and political biographies of Lukács and Brecht up to the 1940s: how each drew upon contrasting aspects of Marx's work, represented varying cultural and historical sensibilities, and evaluated differently the events of the inter-war years. As we shall see, at the core of Lukács's work was a traditional ethical and aesthetic humanism, drawn with patrician and idealist strokes (which mediated his uses of Marxian analysis), and deeply committed to the continuity of European classical culture. Brecht, on the other hand, attempted to apply notions of scientific experimentation and economic production in search of a modernist aesthetic attuned to the technical and collectivist twentieth century. Though both men drew upon Marx's work, they used characteristically different components of the master's broad synthesis.

In 1938 and 1939, Brecht wrote, but did not publish, a number of essays in which he criticized Lukács's more traditionalist literary canons. Not published until 1966, after which they were widely discussed, particularly in Germany,[1] Brecht's essays were partly occasioned by a heated controversy about the relation between expressionism and Nazism then being carried out in the Moscow journal *Das Wort*, a forum for anti-Nazi German exile intellectuals.[2] (That Brecht did not publish these articles may well have been due to his view of this whole debate as harmful to a united front of left intellectuals against fascism.)[3] Lukács had himself contributed to the origin of this debate in 1934 with an article in *Das Wort* entitled "'Grösse und Verfall' des Expressionismus,"[4] in which he alleged that the expressionist movement had unwittingly contributed to the spread of the kind of mystical irrationalism on which

1. As a result of the publication of these essays in 1966, in *Schriften zur Literatur und Kunst*, 3 vols. (Frankfurt a.M.), republished in Vol. 19 of the *Gesammelte Werke* (hereafter *GW*) in 1967, there have been a number of attempts to compare Brecht's literary views with those of Lukács. None of these analyses, however, have dealt sufficiently with Brecht's and Lukács's full aesthetic and social theories; the connection of these with the prior development of Marxist and modernist aesthetics; Brecht's and Lukács's intellectual and political biographies up to 1940; and their responses to Nazism and Stalinism. The major studies are Klaus Völker, "Brecht und Lukács: Analyse einer Meinungsverschiedenheit," *Kursbuch*, 7 (1966), 80–101; Werner Mittenzwei, "Marxismus und Realismus: Die Brecht-Lukács Debatte," *Das Argument*, 46 (March 1968), 12–43, which has been translated in *Preserve and Create: Essays in Marxist Literary Criticism*, ed. (New York, 1973); Viktor Zmegač, *Kunst und Wirklichkeit: Zur Literaturtheorie bei Brecht, Lukács und Broch* (Bad Homburg, 1969), pp. 9–41; Helga Gallas, *Marxistische Literaturtheorie: Kontroversen im Bund proletarisch-revolutionärer Schriftsteller* (Neuwied und Berlin, 1971), especially pp. 11–30 and 135–178; Fritz Raddatz, *Lukács* (Reinbek bei Hamburg, 1972), pp. 82–91; Henri Arvon, *Marxist Esthetics* (Ithaca, N.Y., 1973), pp. 100–112; Klaus L. Berghahn, "Volksthümlichkeit und Realismus: Nochmals zur Brecht-Lukács Debatte," *Basis*, 4 (1973), 7–37. My own comparative analysis of Brecht and Lukács in this book is a revision and enrichment of my article "Marxism and Art in the Era of Stalin and Hitler: The Brecht-Lukács Debate," *New German Critique*, 3 (Fall, 1974), 12–44.
2. On the expressionism debate in *Das Wort*, see the introduction and reprints in Hans-Jürgen Schmitt, ed., *Die Expressionismusdebatte: Materialien zu einer marxistische Realismus-Konzeption* (Frankfurt a.M., 1973); David R. Bathrick, "Moderne Kunst und Klassenkampf: Der Expressionismus Debatte in der Exilzeitschrift *Das Wort*," *Exil und innere Emigration*, edited by Reinhold Grimm and Jost Hermand (Frankfurt a.M., 1973), pp. 89–109; and Franz Schonauer, "Expressionismus und Faschismus: Eine Diskussion aus dem Jahre 1938," *Literatur und Kritik*, 1:7–8 (1966).
3. Mittenzwei, "Marxismus und Realismus," p. 15. We do not actually know whether they were submitted to *Das Wort* and rejected, or whether Brecht decided against sending them. (See "Presentation II," *Aesthetics and Politics*, ed. Perry Anderson et al. [London, 1977], p. 62. This short introduction precedes an English translation of four of the most important of Brecht's critiques of Lukács.)
4. Reprinted in *Marxismus und Literatur*, Vol. 2, and translated in Georg Lukács, *Essays on Realism* (Cambridge, Mass., 1981).

Nazism thrived. But Brecht was responding not merely to the dispute over expressionism, but to the whole of Lukács's literary criticism in this decade, in which a most powerfully sustained attack on aesthetic modernism had been articulated with the use of Marxist analyses. Since, however, in certain ways Lukács's outlook resembled, and provided philosophical underpinning for, Soviet cultural policy (if not for the actually dismal practice of socialist realism), Brecht, by formulating his own response to this body of work, was defending experimentation against current official orthodoxies and developing an important theoretical basis for the Marxist reception of modernism.

Before examining their positions, however, a few words of caution are in order. Although the contrasts between Brecht's and Lukács's views of realism and modernism offer real insight into the rich variety of a possible twentieth-century Marxist aesthetics, the tendencies to divide the field up between them and to see the two positions as antithetical and mutually exclusive are real errors, ones made frequently in the many attempts to reconstruct their "debate" as a means of championing Brecht's contributions.[5] The work of Walter Benjamin and Theodor Adorno, which will be examined later, highlight some of the inadequacies and narrowness of *both* Lukács's *and* Brecht's outlooks, while showing, by contrast, how much the separate dyads held in common. Both Lukács and Brecht were more or less within the Leninist orbit and equivocated in their critiques of Stalinism as a political and social system, a stance which obviously affected their views of art: "Thus Lukács and Brecht represent both inside and outside the socialist camp a theoretical justification for existing policies *as well as* methodological starting points for major alternatives."[6] Their dispute remained, with all its freedom from Stalinist crudities, within the parameters of Communist cultural discussion and political militancy. Benjamin and Adorno, on the other hand, were institutionally related (the latter far more so) to the independent, but politically quietist, Institute of Social Research. Their aesthetic debates—more distant from the Communist movement—were focused on the significance of avant-garde and commercial art under Western capitalism.

In addition to the shared space of Lukács's and Brecht's political positions, it is significant that while Brecht defended the socialist uses of

5. This is true of my article of 1974 on the debate, but even more so of the accounts of Völker, Mittenzwei and Gallas.

6. David Bathrick, "The Dialectics of Legitimation: Brecht in the GDR," *New German Critique*, 2 (Spring, 1974), 97.

certain modernist aesthetic techniques (e.g., distancing and montage), he shared Lukács's antipathy to much other modernist work, e.g., abstract art and writers such as Baudelaire, Rilke, Dostoevsky, and (on the whole) Kafka. While brilliantly developing the activist potentials of constructivist aesthetics, Brecht's utilitarian urgency placed him out of sympathy with many other significant currents of modern cultural experience. His critique of Lukács's more classical theories was searching and important, but ultimately not really adequate as an alternative view of twentieth-century Western art.[7] For this reason also, we will need to turn for other perspectives to the work of Benjamin and Adorno. But that must await the concluding chapters.

❖   ❖   ❖

During the decade of the 1930s, Lukács had developed a carefully delineated polemical theory of modern European literature based largely on a distinction between realism and naturalism. In the period 1789–1848, in which, according to Lukács, the bourgeoisie of Europe fought heroically, optimistically, and conclusively against political absolutism and aristocratic society, a rich culture of literary realism flourished which was heir to the great classical and humanist traditions of the West. While showing aesthetic continuities from Shakespeare and Cervantes to the early nineteenth century, Lukács concentrated his attention in his discussion of realism upon the nineteenth-century novels of Scott, Stendhal, Goethe, and Dickens, but especially Tolstoi and Balzac. Lukács defined realism as a literary mode in which the lives of individual characters were portrayed as part of a narrative which situated them within the entire historical dynamics of their society. Through the retrospective voice, great realist novels contain an epic hierarchy of events and objects, and reveal what is essential and significant in the historically conditioned transformation of individual character. Drawing repeatedly upon Engels' and Marx's comments on realism, Lukács emphasized both the depiction of full individuality *and* historical typicality. Viewed from the standpoint of participants and yet structured by the omniscient historical understanding of the author, the best realist novels presented general historical reality as a process revealed in concrete, individual experience, mediated by particular groups, institutions, classes, etc. While the reader experiences how and why individuals actively contribute to their own "fates"—and are thus not simply

---

7. "Presentation II," *Aesthetics and Politics*, pp. 64–65. Zimmerman, "Brecht's Aesthetics of Production," *Praxis* 3 (1976), notes on pp. 133–134.

passive reflections of allegedly determining "facts"—such characters are seen as both unique *and* representative manifestations of wider historical currents.[8]

Thus, in a Balzac novel, Lukács emphasized, characters are not abstract personifications of historical trends (what Marx had dubbed "Schillerizing," and Lukács was later to attack in modernist allegories), but living, rounded, full personalities in their own right. In his later *Aesthetics* (published in 1962), Lukács was to elaborate this point exhaustively in his stress upon *Besonderheit* ("speciality") as the central category of art, by which he meant a mediated particularity in the classical sense of a "symbol": what is generally "signified" as well as the unique living person or object which is the "signifier."[9] On the other hand, the mediating events, trends, and social situations are not presented as part of the "dull fortuitousness of everyday life"—the merely surface "phenomena"—but as examples of what is essential in an historical period, the crucial currents helping to shape the present and the future.

The key to this ability to interrelate individuals and social development, to present humans as both objects and creative subjects of history, lay in the author's capacity to "present social institutions as human relationships and social objects as the vehicles of such relationships."[10] In this way, Lukács imaginatively applied Marx's critique of capitalist "reification" to literary realism: in the narrative voice lay the cognitive ability to uncover the construction of economic and social life through human interaction. It was one of Lukács's major contentions that this capacity, soon to be lost in the more fully evolved and "finished" capitalism of the era of Zola, was objectively possible for a Balzac who was fortunate to be "contemporary with a social transformation which permitted him to see objects not as completed material substances but as they issued from human work; to have been able to apprehend social change as a network of individual stories."[11] That such an ideologically reactionary writer as the royalist Balzac had this

8. The theory appeared in most of Lukács' prolific work of the period, but was expressed most clearly and searchingly in "The Intellectual Physiognomy of Literary Characters," translated in *Radical Perspectives in the Arts*, ed. Lee Baxandall (Baltimore, 1972), and "Narrate or Describe?," translated in *Writer and Critic and Other Essays*, ed. Arthur D. Kahn (New York, 1971).

9. Béla Királyfalvi, *The Aesthetics of György Lukács* (Princeton, N.J., 1975), pp. 73–77.

10. Georg Lukács, *Studies in European Realism* (New York, 1964), pp. 92–93.

11. Fredric Jameson, *Marxism and Form: Twentieth Century Dialectical Theories of Literature* (Princeton, N.J., 1971), p. 203.

cognitive insight, and the requisite plastic imagination to embody it in
living images, provided Lukács—as it had Engels—with his major
counter to those who would reduce literature to the personal politics of
the author. Balzac could compose his realist narratives, in touch with
the living processes of history despite his ideological biases, because of
both the objective possibilities of his situation and the fact that he actively participated in the life of his age and was able to feel palpably
(and not abstractly) its social forces as they crisscrossed within his life.
"Thus realism is dependent on the possibility of access to the forces of
change in a given moment of history," as Fredric Jameson has written of
Lukács's view.[12]

It is precisely this access that has been lacking, according to Lukács,
in the new literary movements since the naturalist novels of Flaubert
and Zola after 1850. If the outer world is experienced increasingly as a
succession of completed material substances, seemingly operating
through automatic mechanisms—a reflection of the full maturity of
capitalist mystification—then the writer will tend toward the merely
factual description of objective reality and lose the capacity to create
truly realist narratives. Reflecting the writer's more passive relation to
the social forces of the age, he/she becomes a mere observer of scenes.
Realists had presented everyday details of psychic mood or social fact as
part of their character's life experience and development and in relation
to the historical "totality." Naturalists, on the other hand, present immediate empirical reality as an objectified "given," abstracted from
individual and historical change. Events are merely presented as a
"setting" or "background." The "treatment does not arise out of the
subjective importance of the events" in an "organic" manner, but from
the "artifice in the formal stylization." To compensate for the gulf between sensate appearance and historical essence in the novel, metaphors
and symbols are utilized, according to Lukács, in an arbitrary and fortuitous manner to encompass and integrate the social totality. In the
end, the richly defined, "harmonious," and active personalities of realism have given way to the "finished products" of naturalism. The world
appears "alien" because it is not viewed as changeable through purposive human action, while the reader—instead of emotionally participat-
ing in a dramatic narrative—is reduced to a passive observer of mechanically ordered occurrences.[13]

12. Ibid., p. 204.
13. Lukács, "Narrate or Describe?," pp. 115, 139.

The comprehensive vision and omniscience of the realist author is lost in naturalism. Without any real sense of the causality of events, the naturalistic author's voice is relativized to the various psychologies of his characters. Static situations with fetishized objects are described, alternating with isolated, fleeting, subjective impressions—an abstract objectivity alternating with a false subjectivity. Given this pendulum effect, we can see how Lukács might argue, as he did, that naturalism became the prototype of all modernist writing. In all of the various modernist movements, reality is perceived merely in its factual immediacy, divorced from "those mediations which connect experiences with the objective reality of society." [14] The mechanical split between subject and object, between immediate phenomena and historical essence—instead of their actual dialectical interplay—was the thread uniting the whole variety of modernist experiment since Flaubert and Baudelaire. Thus "vulgar" materialist naturalism and extreme subjectivist expressionism each extract immediate experience, portrayed as "objects" or as fervent emotion, from the historically changing social totality. [15] To give a further example, Lukács argued that "Neue Sachlichkeit" (or reportorial) German novels of the late 1920s showed the familiar pendulum swing from the other, equally mechanical extreme of "psychological novels," such as those of Dostoevsky, Hamsun, or Huysmans: instead of the isolation of individual feelings and moods from the wider social realities, we now have the isolation of "objective facts" from concrete personal experience. [16] The extreme chasm between subject and object was also evident in symbolist work, although Lukács was less concerned with this current in the 1930s. Early in his career, in *Soul and Form* around 1910, he had objected to the impressionistic and fragmented immediacies of the symbolist exploration of psychic mood, comparing it with naturalist treatment of social facts [17]; while in his late *Aesthetics* (1962), he criticized the excessively allegorical results: the abstract,

[margin note: CF. CRITICISM OF POST MODERN]

14. Lukács, "Es geht um den Realismus," *Marxismus und Literatur*, Vol. 2, ed. Fritz Raddatz, pp. 67–68. This essay has been translated in *Aesthetics and Politics*, pp. 28–59.
15. Ibid., pp. 67–70. In the 1930s Lukács stressed the relation of all modernisms to naturalist reification. Later, as in a work of 1955 translated as *Realism in Our Time* (New York, 1971), Lukács would attack aesthetic modernism for depriving humans of their social and historical connectedness, "throwing" them as isolated atoms into the world—as do existential philosophers fashionable in the 1940s and 1950s in the West. The continuity of essential argument was, however, still evident.
16. Lukács, "Reportage oder Gestaltung?," *Marxismus und Literatur*, Vol. 2, p. 150. This essay has been translated in *Essays on Realism*, pp. 45–75.
17. Lukács, *Soul and Form* (Cambridge, Mass., 1971), pp. 72–74. This is discussed in Istvan Mészáros, *Lukács' Concept of the Dialectic* (London, 1972), pp. 65–66.

mystical, and contentless nature of its symbols, in which the concrete, individual, and unique dissolve.[18] In all of these variations, modernism for Lukács displayed a fetishized immediacy which on a few occasions he identified with the fundamental formal principle of montage, for him the "sticking together of disconnected facts."[19] The flattened juxtaposition of disparate images typified the loss of realism in modern Western culture, as did the "formalistic" obsession with technical experiments, an art which drew attention self-reflexively to its own procedures.

Conditioned by the extreme division of labor in advanced capitalism, and by the resultant preoccupation of writers and artists with their craft as a specialized technical skill, modernists are out of contact with the social experience of the "broad masses," Lukács argued. The overwhelming majority has little access to, and even less interest in, such avant-garde art. While the great humanist and realist literature of the past provided wide numbers of readers with insight into their own life experiences—as do the inheritors of that tradition, e.g., Romain Rolland, Thomas Mann, and Maxim Gorki—"the broad masses can learn nothing from avant-garde literature, for its view of reality is so subjective, confused and disfigured."[20] Failing to note how the Nazis were then manipulating the term and arrogating it for their own repressive purposes, Lukács insisted on a necessary *Volksthumlichkeit* ("popularity," or "closeness to the people") of all worthwhile art, the most common of all traditional left-wing denunciations of culturally avant-garde movements. Such a capacity of literature to find wide resonance in the population requires writers to evolve in their work from the humanistic cultural continuum of the past (especially realism, with its rich and concrete depictions of popular life), instead of radically breaking from these traditions, as do the modernists. Only in this way may there develop a truly "popular front" culture, of such burning concern to anti-Nazi intellectuals in the late 1930s. Here Lukács approached the question of popular accessibility and broad social and educational impact, not in terms of the changing historical problems of aesthetic reception, but as a matter of retaining realist forms.[21]

18. Karályfalvi, *The Aesthetics of György Lukács*, pp. 97–98.
19. Lukács, *The Historical Novel* (New York, 1966), p. 252. Lukács' opposition to montage is emphasized in Laszlo Illés, "Die Freiheit der kunstlerischen Richtungen und das Zeitgemässe," in *Littérature et Réalité*, ed. B. Köpeczi and P. Juhász (Budapest, 1966).
20. Lukács, "Es geht um den Realismus," *Marxismus und Literatur*, Vol. 2, pp. 84–86. On the contended issue of accessibility and "popularity," see Berghahn, "Volksthümlichkeit und Realismus."
21. Berghahn, "Volksthümlichkeit und Realismus," p. 21.

Lukács was well aware of the defense which runs: "Does not modernism show how twentieth-century capitalism transforms humans into appurtenances of things?" His response was to charge the modernists with failure to go beyond the seeming "facts," with uncritically reflecting the immediate experience of chaos, dehumanization, and alienation in advanced capitalist society, instead of carefully indicating their deeper sources and the historical forces working towards overcoming them.[22] Such a procedure would be available if contemporary writers learned from the practices of "bourgeois realism," which reflected neither the surface phenomena of its age nor the immediate beliefs of its creators. Realist works dramatized the deeper currents of history at a time when the bourgeoisie was still in some sense a progressive force, rationalist in outlook and confident of the future. Thus, for writers who seek to advance the cause of "revolutionary democracy" (the popular-front term which Lukács repeatedly used in these years), Lukács prescribed that they build upon nineteenth-century realism, while becoming at least open to socialist solutions without necessarily having to affirm them. (His major example for this "critical" realism was Thomas Mann, and for "socialist realism," Maxim Gorki.) In this way, such writers might avoid the widespread tendency of Western intellectuals, in despair at the course of events in the twentieth century, to escape from reason and historical modes of understanding as they gaze fatalistically at the increasing decay around them. The depth of realist art, and its broad relevance, would be served not through any tendentious or merely agitational intent, Lukács insisted (continuing Marx and Engels, and indirectly attacking official "socialist realism" on this score), but through the organic emergence of the "tendency" from a concrete and rich historical presentation.[23]

Lukács's theory of realism rested on a correlation of cultural health with the historical rise of social classes. If there is to be a meaningful "proletarian culture," Lukács argued, it must build upon the literary forms created in the optimistic and humanistic period of bourgeois ideology, and not those resulting from the spreading bourgeois disbelief in any rational and progressive meaning of history. The cultural life of the age of bourgeois ascent—developed by Goethe and Balzac, for example—gave voice to progressive and humanist perspectives appropriate

22. Lukács, "Narrate or Describe?," pp. 144–146.
23. Lukács, "Tendenz oder Parteilichkeit," *Marxismus und Literatur*, Vol. 2, pp. 139–149. This essay has been translated in *Essays on Realism*, pp. 33–44.

to a popular-front battle against fascism; modernist literary forms since naturalism mirror and are tied to the irrationalist subjectivism or mechanical positivism of "bourgeois decay." As such, they can only feed, rather than be used against, fascist ideology.

In the 1930s, Lukács's primary attack upon such alleged intellectual "precursors" of German fascism was aimed at the expressionist movement in literature. In a piece which he wrote soon after Hitler came to power, Lukács began preparatory work on a massive history of "irrationalist" philosophy and its connection with the radical right, *Die Zerstörung der Vernunft*, which was published in 1954 and is one of his weakest books.[24] In the 1934 article, Lukács excoriated the political and social attitudes of expressionist writers, which he saw as unintentionally mirroring the mystical irrationalism of imperialist ideology in the years 1905–20. In their seeming revolt against German society, he argued, these writers developed a species of romantic anti-capitalism which only mystified the world by proclaiming a knowledge based on inner experience. Concrete individuals disappeared in favor of allegorical and thus dehumanized abstractions in expressionist dramas. An ideology of extreme subjectivism underlay the literary techniques, which, by merely projecting inner anguish, dissolved the real social relations between people into a pathetic and abstract bathos of emotion. Solipsism and extreme distance from the working masses, Lukács further contended, made many expressionists into advocates of a "spiritual" or intellectual elite, a stance that was easily transferable to fascism. Thus, although a number of expressionists viewed themselves as politically left-wing, the basic thrust of their work only helped to aid those reactionary forces which made a mystique of *Geist*, will, and chaos, while obscuring class issues and the rational mastery of historical change.[25]

By failing to go beyond their own immediate emotional experiences in what Lukács regarded simply as the institutions of advanced capitalism, the expressionists merely eternalized the chaos and inhumanity they saw, only inviting further decay or "barbarism." In this vulgar Marxist characterization of the relation between expressionist literature and Wilhelmian society, Lukács did little to clarify the actual German social environment (which contained, relevantly for the expressionists, far more precapitalist and traditional authoritarian institutions than the more purely business society of the U.S.A., for example). At the

24. See *Die Zerstörung der Vernunft* (East Berlin, 1954).
25. Lukács, "'Grösse und Verfall' des Expressionismus," *Marxismus und Literatur*, Vol. 2, pp. 7–42.

same time, he reduced works of art (including literary techniques) to reflexes of class ideology. Where Balzac's or Tolstoi's narrative methods were eminently serviceable for current progressive uses, despite the authors' own reactionary tendencies, modernist forms such as those of expressionism were apparently tied indissolubly to late bourgeois ideological decay and thus could not be transformed to serve other purposes, a point which Brecht contended.

It was not that the expressionists did not specifically support the industrial proletariat in the Marxist manner, for Lukács was almost as harsh with the Marxist avant-garde of the 1920s and early 1930s, much of which developed activist potentials of cubist aesthetics, as we saw earlier. He objected in 1932, for example, to attempts to create a modernist "proletarian literature" during the Weimar Republic, and cited Brecht's plays and dramatic theory as the most developed of these tendencies. Seeing in Brecht an extreme example of "Proletcult" rejection of the bourgeois literary past, Lukács attacked Brecht's didactic *Lehrstücke* (teaching plays), in particular, as utterly failing to provide the basis of a true socialist realism. Instead of creating representative, yet individualized, characters in psychological conflict and in relation to the wider social dynamics, Brecht's figures merely symbolized abstract functions in the class struggle as they spoke in a montage of disembodied argument and purely agitational dialogues. The attempt to create a kind of scientific laboratory for political education and action—one of the premises of these *Lehrstücke*, and a common feature of constructivist drama—was seen by Lukács as a substituting of tendentiousness for realism, and an unwarranted intrusion of scientific paradigms upon literary work. The means by which Brecht sought to distance his audience from simple empathy with his characters and encourage them to think critically upon the action, especially his "estrangement" devices, Lukács attacked as merely formalistic techniques, artificially imposed upon the material, a charge he was to repeat in later assessments of Brecht.[26]

Having surveyed Lukács's sometimes searching, sometimes crude

26. Lukács, "Reportage oder Gestaltung?" and "Aus der Not eine Tugend," *Marxismus und Literatur*, Vol. 2, pp. 150–158 and 166–177. These originally appeared in the KPD journal *Linkskurve* and are carefully analyzed in Gallas, *Marxistische Literaturtheorie*, pp. 139–141, and Russell Berman, "Lukács' Critique of Bredel and Ottwalt: A Political Account of an Aesthetic Debate of 1931–32," *New German Critique*, 10 (Winter, 1977), 155–178. Beginning with *Realism in Our Time* (first published in 1955), and continuing in *Aesthetik* (1962), Lukács tempered his attack on Brecht, especially as he viewed Brecht's plays of 1938–45—e.g., *Mother Courage, Galileo*—as far greater works of literary realism than the more purely agitational plays of 1930–32.

critiques of the 1930s, we may turn to Brecht's unpublished responses of 1938–39. In these, Brecht repeatedly stressed the necessity for artistic experiment in all socialist movements, and deplored the attempts of critics like Lukács and other Moscow-based arbiters of literary form to tie the hands of practicing artists and writers. The vicious attacks upon the expressionists (of whose emotional self-indulgence Brecht was himself highly critical) by the actual or potential cultural bureaucrats of the Soviet Union and Nazi Germany showed a fear of uncontrollable "libertarian sentiments" of many kinds. "Acts of liberation are being suppressed for their own sake—self-liberation from constricting rules, old regulations, which have become fetters." [27] Of such critics as Lukács, Brecht commented acidly to Walter Benjamin, in a conversation of July 1938: "They are, to put it bluntly, enemies of production. Production makes them uncomfortable. You never know what's coming out. And they themselves don't want to produce. They want to play the apparatchik and exercise control over other people. Every one of their criticisms contains a threat." [28] Thus, the attack upon modernism revealed a fear of its lack of piety toward tradition and authority, as well as its open-endedness, contingent attitudes, and experimental procedures.

More particularly, Brecht strenuously opposed the prohibitive narrowness of Lukács's view of realism. He did not object very much to Lukács's characterization of nineteenth-century literature, but to the construction of a restrictive realist "model" which was based entirely on a limited range of formal examples from one historical period and which excluded the potential realist possibilities in modern art. What was needed, instead, was a wider concept of realism as a confronting of a many-sided, contradictory (and often hidden) historical reality, whatever the formal means which facilitated this. "Realism is not a matter of form. . . . Literary forms have to be checked against reality, not against aesthetics—even realist aesthetics. There are many ways of suppressing truth and many ways of stating it." [29] To emphasize the formal and historical breadth of his definition, Brecht argued that writers as diverse as Hašek (the creator of the *Good Soldier Schweik*) and Shelley, Swift and Grimmelshausen, as well as Balzac, were great realists. All of them had

---

27. Bertolt Brecht, "Über den formalistischen Charakter der Realismustheorie," *GW*, Vol. 19, pp. 298–307. This piece, as well as three other related ones published in his collected works, "Volksthümlichkeit und Realismus," "Die Essays von Georg Lukács," and "Bemerkungen zu einem Aufsatz," are translated in *Aesthetics and Politics*, pp. 68–85. Brecht wrote a number of other articles on this subject in 1938 and 1939, which are also published in Vol. 19 of the collected works, and which remain untranslated.

28. Walter Benjamin, *Understanding Brecht* (London, 1973), p. 118.

29. Brecht, "Weite und Vielfalt der realistischen Schreibweise," *GW*, Vol. 19, p. 149.

used multiple means, including wild fantasy, the grotesque, parable, allegory, typifying of individuals, etc., for realistic purposes. Those writers experimenting with new formal means to reveal a constantly changing social reality—now more necessary than ever—were not the real
formalists, Brecht slyly insisted; "formalism," he threw back at Lukács,
is the attempt to "hold fast to conventional forms while the changing
social environment makes ever new demands upon art." [30] The question
of which stylistic techniques to use was a practical matter to be solved in
individual cases by artists sensitive to problems of audience response
within a fast-changing historical world. [31] Literary forms have varying
social functions over time. What was once revealing about Balzac's narrative technique may not be so today. Such a question, however, cannot
be settled on an a priori basis, but needs to be answered by experimentation with a variety of means.

Lukács's argument had stressed the continuity of classical bourgeois
realism and the needs of an emergent socialist literature. In response,
Brecht emphasized the disparities between the social content of Balzac's
work—tied to a social structure rooted in family property and defined
by the individual competition of a still nascent capitalism—and the collectivist realities of the twentieth century. Whereas Lukács's "realism"
assumed that individuals had access, through their own personal experience, to the social whole, modern technical and collective life—the
complex of massive and sprawling corporate activities, scientific, military, and industrial bureaucracies, etc.—can be comprehended only
through abstractions from the individual's vantage point. Such a reality
may need to be "built up" through a montage of carefully and purposefully juxtaposed nonlinear images if we are to suggest anything
of its "totality." [32] For this reason alone, one might justify on realist
grounds the formal self-consciousness of the modernists and their rejection of mimetic pretensions: by showing how a montage of images is
being created, the process of "artificially" reconstructing the social
whole will be bared. (Without acknowledging this, Brecht had here
drawn not upon modernist aesthetics as such, but specifically upon directions within the cubist current.)

Brecht stressed that since we share the same historical world with the

30. Brecht, "Die Expressionismus Debatte," GW, Vol. 19, p. 291.
31. Brecht, "Praktisches zur Expressionismus," GW, Vol. 19, pp. 292–296.
32. Brecht, "Bemerkungen zu einem Aufsatz," GW, Vol. 19, pp. 309–312, and
"Übergang vom bürgerlichen zum sozialistischen Realismus," GW, Vol. 19, pp. 376–378.
Brecht had previously developed the point in his long essay of 1932, "Die Dreigroschenprozess," republished in GW, Vol. 18. It appears most directly on pp. 161–162.

modernists and not with authors such as Goethe, Balzac, and Tolstoi, we can turn modernist literary techniques (developed in response to twentieth-century conditions) more readily to our own purposes.[33] Literary forms, like other "forces of production," are separable from their class or ideological uses within the current "relations of production," Brecht argued, using the familiar Marxian formula of capitalist contradictions, and can thus be transformed to serve other, more progressive purposes. These productive forces—e.g., oil trusts, steam engines, film industries, literary techniques, etc.—need to be more than appropriated, however; they must be transformed in their function. Thus, in deploying inner monologue, montage, or *Verfremdung* (distancing), for example, socialist writers would want to use them to undercut the despairing or mythmaking outlooks to which they were tied in a Joyce, Kafka, Dos Passos, or Döblin. While open apologists for fascism might be called "decadent," the term is in general too monolithic; it denies the historical contradictions in the contemporary situation, and fails to note the mutual existence of "decline" and "rise" in many of the same works.[34] "The techniques of Joyce and Döblin . . . are not merely products of decay; to exclude oneself from influence by them, in order to modify them, leaves one open to the influence of the epigoni, namely the Hemingways. The works of Joyce and Döblin exhibit the world historical contradiction between the productive forces and the relations of production. In their works productive forces are represented. The socialist writer can learn in these documents of *Ausweglosigkeit* [literally, "no-way-out-ness"] worthwhile highly developed technical elements: these will see the way out."[35]

Lukács had argued that modernist art expressed the views only of avant-garde cliques and was disbarred from broad appeal to the mass of the population. Without denying that this was often the case, particularly within the conditions of cultural production and distribution in the West, Brecht objected to the fatalistic implication of the charge. Referring to his own experiences and those of Piscator, he argued that working-class audiences, while rejecting theatricality for its own sake, usually support and understand any innovations, even the most audacious, so long as they help reveal the "real mechanisms of society."

33. Brecht, "Über den formalistischen Charakter der Realismustheorie," *GW*, Vol. 19, pp. 303–306.
34. Brecht, *Arbeitsjournal, 1938–1955*, Vol. 1, (Frankfurt a.M.; 1973), pp. 12–14, 28–29; Mittenzwei, "Marxismus und Realismus," pp. 26–28.
35. Brecht, "Notizen über realistischen Schreibweise," *GW*, Vol. 19, pp. 359–361.

"Popularity," in any case, should not be limited to immediate accessibility and communication. Fresh means of all kinds must be found—not only new literary forms and methods, but new technical media such as radio and film—to broaden and enrich artistic traditions which have been genuine expressions of the common people in the past; but these may not be instantly understood. To develop the expressive possibilities of working-class culture, Brecht argued, requires an educational process that goes both ways, a mutual and ongoing exchange of views between practicing artists and workers.[36] Much of the best realist art, in any case, was not popular to begin with: "The comprehensibility of a literary work is not merely assured when it is written exactly like other works which were understood in their time. These other works, which were understood in their time, were not always written like the works before them. Steps had been taken to make them comprehensible. In the same way, we must do something for the comprehensibility of new works today. There is not only such a thing as *being popular*, there is also the process of *becoming popular*."[37]

These were the major points which Brecht made explicitly but privately against Lukács's analyses of realism and modernism. In the chapters that follow, we shall explore how such conflicting views were part of a wider disparity—of intellectual and political orientations, historical outlook, and applications of Marxism to art. But implied in the arguments we have already surveyed was a disagreement concerning the essential purposes of art, one of the premises which lay beneath Brecht's and Lukács's critical judgments. For Lukács, all great art presents a social "totality" in which the merely apparent contradiction between immediate experience and historical development is overcome, that is, in which "the opposition of individual case and historical law is dissolved."[38] Through the reception of this "totality," the reader vicariously experiences the reintegration of a seemingly fragmented, dehumanized world. In his *Aesthetics* (1962), Lukács was to argue at length that such an experience of reintegrated totality, as well as the exposure to "all-sided social-human personalities," would help in morally readying its recipients for active progressive participation in the world.[39] Brecht insisted, however, that a response to contemporary dehumanization

36. Brecht, "Volksthümlichkeit und Realismus," *GW*, Vol. 19, pp. 322–331. See also Berghahn's article of the same name.
37. Ibid, p. 331. The translation is taken from *Aesthetics and Politics*, p. 85.
38. Quoted in Mittenzwei, "Marxismus und Realismus," p. 29.
39. Királyfalvi, *The Aesthetics of György Lukács*, pp. 117–122, 143.

which treated men and women as "rounded," "harmonic," and integrated personalities was merely a solution on paper.[40] A harmoniously structured reconciliation of contradictions facilitated, moreover, a sense of cathartic fulfillment within the audience and made political action appear unnecessary. By accentuating the conflict between everyday appearance and what is historically realizable, often through showing the "strangeness" of the "normal," Brecht hoped to galvanize his audience into action outside the theatre. Art needed to be "open-ended," to be completed by the audience, and not "closed" by the author's reconciliation of contradictions.[41]

Differences of genre no doubt contributed to the contrasts here: Lukács focused upon the broadly conceived, privately read "contemplative" novel form; Brecht directed his attention to the public and potentially more "activating" drama. But these literary choices, as well as the more fundamental contrast between Lukács's classical humanism and Brecht's "production aesthetics," were themselves deeply influenced by their intellectual and political formations, to which we shall now turn.

40. Brecht, "Bemerkungen zum Formalismus," *GW*, Vol. 19, p. 316.
41. Mittenzwei, "Marxismus und Realismus," pp. 29–32; Gallas, *Marxistische Literaturtheorie*, pp. 167–168.

CHAPTER FOUR

Paths Toward a
Marxist Aesthetics

Lukács grew up in Budapest in a rich Jewish family with important ties to the Hungarian aristocracy, as was common among wealthier Hungarian Jews. He was the son of the director of Hungary's leading bank, the Budapest *Kreditanstalt*. His father, originally named Joseph Löwinger, was given the name Lukács in 1890 (when Georg was five) and ennobled in 1901. His mother, manager of the patrician house, was born into the nobility. As late as the age of twenty-six, Lukács was known by the name Georg von Lukács. The later admirer of Goethean classicism and nineteenth-century humanist high culture thus had his roots in the patrician wing of the *haute bourgeoisie*. This should be borne in mind when one considers his lifelong attempt to rescue the essentials of classical culture in its contemporary age of decline. The Jewish background, on the other hand, may have played a role in the humanist Marxism and rationalist optimism with which he was to interpret the meaning of that classical heritage. His close relation to the "mandarins" of German academic and literary life before 1914—the strong influence of Weber and Simmel, and his early interest in Mann, for example—also played its part in encouraging a patrician interpretation of the prewar crisis of bourgeois culture.[1]

The pattern of adolescent rebellion against parental authority often

1. See Morris Watnick, "Georg Lukács: or Aesthetics and Communism," *Survey*, 23 (January–March, 1958), 60–66 and Raddatz, *Lukács*, pp. 13–25. For the patrician orientation of Weber, Simmel and much prewar German sociology, see Ringer, *The Decline of the German Mandarins*, and Arthur Mitzman, *The Iron Cage: A Study of Max Weber* (New York, 1969), pp. 187–191, 242–245, 256–270.

[91

anticipates later forms of revolt. It is therefore significant that Lukács rejected a banking future desired by his father, turning instead to his uncle as a counter-model: a man who had withdrawn from the "vulgar" details of "everyday life" and devoted himself to the "higher" pursuits of meditation and Talmudic study.[2] In the years before 1914, Lukács hoped that the "inward" realms of art and philosophy would provide an escape from the social dehumanization which he saw in advanced bourgeois civilization.[3] "What appalled him most," Morris Watnick has written, "was the despoiled culture of modern industrial society, aesthetic ugliness and human uprootedness. The greatest influence here was Simmel, whose *Philosophie des Geldes* (1900) played a considerable part in his intellectual development. This was a romantic anticapitalist use of 'alienation' which, pessimistically, saw material progress per se as a threat to cultural values."[4]

As Michael Löwy has shown in his excellent study of Lukács's early development, "romantic anti-capitalism" was a tendency which the Hungarian thinker shared with many leading German and Hungarian bourgeois intellectuals before World War I, e.g., Mann, George, Tönnies, Simmel, Bloch, the Hungarians Ady and Szabó, etc.[5] In many ways, this outlook was a "tragic" one. In *Soul and Form* (1910), for example, Lukács repeatedly emphasized the necessary conflict and unbridgeable distinction between "authentic life" and empirical reality.[6] Against the inescapable human isolation and fragmented experience of the present, the early Lukács held up counter-images of classical organic harmony, the "whole man" fully alive in a unified community and natural world, as in the dramatic opening passage of *Theory of the Novel* (1914), which introduced a discussion of ancient Greek epic literature in this way:

Happy are those ages when the starry sky is the map of all possible paths—ages whose paths are illuminated by the light of the stars. Everything in such ages is new and yet familiar, full of adventure and yet their own. The world is wide and yet is like a home, for the fire that burns in the soul is of the same essential nature as the stars; the world and the self, the light and the fire, are sharply

2. Raddatz, *Lukács*, pp. 7–8.

3. Andrew Arato, "Georg Lukács: The Search for a Revolutionary Subject," *The Unknown Dimension: European Marxism Since Lenin* (New York, 1972), p. 83.

4. Watnick, "Georg Lukács," p. 65.

5. Michael Löwy, *Georg Lukács: From Romanticism to Bolshevism* (London, 1979), pp. 22–90. A fine survey of the many recent investigations of Lukács' complex early intellectual development is Paul Breines, "Young Lukács, Old Lukács, New Lukács," *Journal of Modern History*, 51:7 (September 1979), 533–546.

6. Lukács, *Soul and Form* (Cambridge, Mass., 1978), pp. 34–35, 100–101, 153–154.

distinct, yet they never become permanent strangers to one another, for fire is the soul of all light and all fire clothes itself in light.[7]

As early as 1905, at the age of twenty, Lukács immersed himself in the study of German idealist philosophy and the art of the *Goethezeit*,[8] through which sources he absorbed an idealized picture of the ancient Greek polis as a paradigm of ethical and political "wholeness." In a long study entitled *The History of the Development of Modern Drama*, written in Hungarian in the years 1906–09, Lukács juxtaposed the allegedly "organic" society of classical Greece with the mechanistic, atomized, and depersonalized world of bourgeois society,[9] a contrast which also underlay the better-known *Theory of the Novel*.

In many of his early works, Lukács drew upon a pessimistic version of alienation theory which had originated in the humanist and idealist age of Goethe and Hegel and had been more fully developed in prewar German sociology. This was a nonsocialist criticism of the desiccating and dehumanizing tendencies of the modern bourgeois industrial world. In Georg Simmel's view of modern society, for example, humans are said to lose control of the products of their creation, which become "objectified" to such a degree that they become independent of their creators; thus, people experience the world as alien objects unresponsive to human needs.[10] In his study of modern drama, Lukács argued that in the plays of Ibsen, Strindberg, and others the personality turns inward as the outer environment is felt as an alien intersection point of great objective forces out of control. Humans become lonely and isolated from each other, while the language expressing this is increasingly "fragmented, allusive and impressionistic in form." In a world painfully split between subject and object, the individual character appears to be reduced to the symptoms of personal pathology.[11] In *Theory of the Novel*, Lukács stressed what he called the experience of "transcendental homelessness" in the novel form, the loss of a sense of harmonious, inte-

7. Lukács, *Theory of the Novel* (Cambridge, Mass., 1971), p. 29.

8. Andrew Arato and Paul Breines, *The Young Lukács and the Origins of Western Marxism* (New York, 1979), pp. 7–10.

9. György Markus, "The Soul and Life: The Young Lukács and the Problem of Culture," *Telos*, 32 (Summer, 1977), 110–113. The original Hungarian edition is the only complete one: *A modern dráma fejlödésének története*, 2 vols. (Budapest: Franklin, 1911). The second chapter of vol. 1 appeared in German in 1914, from which a selection was translated into English and is available as "The Theory of Modern Drama," in Eric Bentley, ed., *The Theory of the Modern Stage* (Baltimore, Md., 1965), pp. 425–450.

10. See the first (!) English translation of this major work: Georg Simmel, *The Philosophy of Money*, trans. Tom Bottomore and David Frisby (London, 1978).

11. Lukács, "The Sociology of Modern Drama," pp. 425–450.

grated, and soulful connection of humans with their world, which had been central to classical epic literature. Humans are "simply existent" in a world of mere "convention," the embodiment of regular, senseless necessities; they obey strict mechanical laws which have neither meaning nor "sensuous immediacy" for the active subject. This is no mere "estrangement from nature," but an alienation from a "second," manmade "nature," an environment experienced "as a prison instead of as a parental home." [12] While the values of the self seem to "draw their justification only from the fact of having been subjectively experienced," the price of "this immoderate elevation of the subject" is the "abandonment of any claim to participation in the shaping of the outside world." [13]

This analysis, which was later to be developed with the aid of an historical optimism based upon Marxist convictions (an optimism that stressed a "socialist" solution), had not been intended in these youthful works as an indictment of literary modernism. Lukács was here exploring his own feelings of a ubiquitous and largely inescapable cultural decay. Yet, important aspects of the later defense of "realist" against "modernist" literature are anticipated in Lukács's early writings. In an essay contained in *Soul and Form*, Lukács praised elements of a renewed epic in the writings of the nineteenth-century German realist Theodor Storm. Lukács saw a unity in Storm's work between interiority and external events, in contrast to the isolating of impressionistic psychological moods or a naturalistically disembodied outer world, as in more recent literature. He also stressed that Storm's art was based on the specific, "vividly seen" pictures from which the typical and general was constructed.[14] (Thomas Mann, whom Lukács would later champion as the greatest contemporary literary realist, wrote in 1918 that his own work, especially *Buddenbrooks* [1901], had influenced Lukács's Storm essay.[15]) In a chapter on tragedy, Lukács further revealed the classical frame of his later theory of realism by citing, in contrast to Ibsen's naturalist dramas, Sophocles' method of grounding the universal in the concretely individual while going beyond "ordinary life" (mere factual existence) to the "true, concealed essence of life." [16] In *Theory of the Novel*, Lukács, now under the influence of Hegel, referred specifically to the "concrete totality" of the ancient Greek community, in which individual physiognomy and organic whole mutually determine one another,

12. Lukács, *Theory of the Novel*, pp. 60–66, 70–93.
13. Ibid., p. 117.
14. Lukács, *Soul and Form*, pp. 62–67, 74–77.
15. Löwy, *Georg Lukács*, p. 36.
16. Ibid., pp. 162–167.

a "totality" which is expressible through the narration of events.[17] Finally, in the same work, he discussed the humanistic tradition of the *Bildungsroman* (beginning with Goethe's *Wilhelm Meister*) as a problematic but partially successful attempt, under bourgeois conditions, to represent personal interiority and outer social reality as reconcilable through the intervention of active men. The given world is not presented as organic; this was possible only in the older epics. Individuals are still "transcendentally homeless." But "the social world is partially open to penetration by living meaning."[18]

However, the major glimmer of hope in *Theory of the Novel* involved less a theory of "realism" (for Lukács before 1917, such a frame of reference would have implied too much a reconciliation with the historical decline he saw all around) than an example of utopian longing for a world beyond the constricting confines of the presently "real." At the end of the study, the Russians Tolstoi and Dostoevsky (significantly, writers apart from the modern West) provided Lukács with different modes of a utopian and antinomian "community of feeling among simple human beings," freed from all "disruptive" objective structures.[19] In the years 1910–16, Lukács was occupied at different times with a socially messianic interpretation (which he never completed) of Dostoevsky's work. To Lukács, Dostoevsky drew upon images of ancient social and natural harmony for projections of a liberated future.[20] Yet, this was only part of a series of utopian suggestions which punctuated Lukács's writings in these early years; it is clear, at least with hindsight, that he was by no means content to settle forever within a pessimistic or tragic outlook.[21]

Besides utopian aspects, there were also elements of a Marxist sociological approach, and potential bridges to a revolutionary Marxist politics, in his early thought. In his first book, *History of the Development of Modern Drama*, Lukács was indebted to Simmel where the latter was closest to Marx. In this work Lukács interpreted alienation—in

17. Lukács, *Theory of the Novel*, pp. 56–61, 66–67.
18. Ibid., pp. 132–143.
19. Ibid., pp. 144–152.
20. Löwy, *Georg Lukács*, pp. 52–56, 93. As Löwy points out, Lukács shared this interest in Russian mysticism with many German "romantic anti-capitalists" in these years, but the socially utopian form his interest took was closest to that of Ernst Bloch. Lukács and Bloch were close friends in the years 1912–18. The latter's adoption of Leninism by 1918 paralleled Lukács' own. Unlike Lukács, however, Bloch was to retain a revolutionary utopianism to the end of his life, a difference which was clear in their debate on expressionism in the 1930s.
21. Arato and Breines, *The Young Lukács*, pp. 69–71, 107; Löwy, *Georg Lukács*, pp. 110, 116–121.

an extended and detailed treatment—in specific and many-sided relation to the modern division of labor under capitalism.[22] Although he did
not embrace a socialist alternative (socialism was associated with the
prewar Hungarian and German Social Democrats, whose accommodations with bourgeois parliamentary order he despised), there were
vaguely collectivist and revolutionary democratic components in Lukács's early writings, which formed a counterpoint to his patrician perspectives. Lukács had been much affected by the radical anti-absolutist
left intelligentsia in Hungary, especially the Jacobin poet Endre Ady and
the syndicalist Ervin Szabó, who were influential leftist critics of the
temporizing and legalistic Hungarian Social Democrats.[23] In political as
well as cultural matters, Lukács's early position represented a totalistic
refusal to reconcile himself to existing realities. The first years of his
Communist politics were to continue the pattern, in part, through an
ultra-left "revolutionary romanticism."[24] But within the context of his
Communist commitment after 1917, Lukács would find various means
of mediating between the patrician and "revolutionary democratic" aspects of his outlook (e.g., by emphasizing the democratization, in communist society, of the high classical humanist culture of the past).[25]
   Lukács experienced the first years of the World War in "despair over
the state of the world." The "present appeared . . . as a condition of
total degradation," he later wrote of the period. Vaguely democratic in
sentiment, he could not help siding against the central European monar-
chies, but an anticipated Anglo-French victory provided little solace for
such a foe of the culture of industrial society: "Who was to save us from
Western civilization?"[26] The war itself was experienced at a distance,
since he was declared unfit for military service.[27] Twenty-five years old
in 1914, Lukács had already developed deep roots in nineteenth-century
idealist culture in the period before the war. His despair during the early

22. Arato and Breines, *The Young Lukács*, pp. 14–26; Markus, "The Soul and Life,"
pp. 110–114.
23. Löwy, *Georg Lukács*, pp. 71–90.
24. Ibid., pp. 145–167.
25. Lukács, "The Old Culture and the New Culture" (1920), in *Marxism and Human
Liberation*, edited by E. San Juan, Jr. (New York, 1973), p. 4.
26. Lukács, *Theory of the Novel*, pp. 11–12 (this is part of the 1962 Preface to a new
edition of the book); "Preface to New Edition (1967)," *History and Class Consciousness*
(Cambridge, Mass., 1971), p. xi. For more on Lukács' reactions to the war in relation to
his early intellectual development, see Ferenc Fehér, "The Last Phase of Romantic Anti-
Capitalism: Lukács' Response to the War," *New German Critique*, 10 (Winter 1977),
139–154.
27. G.H.R. Parkinson, "Introduction," *Georg Lukács: The Man, His Work, His
Ideas* (New York, 1970), p. 6.

war years included a profound concern for the threatened continuity of European humanist traditions. The year 1917, however, provided a release. The Russian Revolution finally gave Lukács some real hope: in his view, it constructed a bridge into the future which would eventually rescue Europe from its own decay.[28] By 1920, he was writing of the proletariat's mission for the future as a re-creation of the Greek epic community—the purpose of politics was, in his view, the renewal of a holistic culture.[29] Embracing Marxism, Lukács was to interpret it, and in part revitalize it, with perspectives drawn from the humanism and idealism of his own youthful development before 1917.

In certain important ways, Lukács's Marxist humanism, as well as his training in German idealist philosophy, enabled him to recapture some of the essential directions of Marx's thought, long hidden in the late nineteenth and early twentieth centuries by the accretions of scientism and positivism. In the essay collection *History and Class Consciousness* (1923), his most widely discussed work in the West, Lukács used perspectives derived from Simmel, Weber, and, most of all, Hegel to powerfully criticize the deterioration of Marxism into a system of natural laws of economic motion, thereby losing the dimension of human active self-emancipation in history. In this immensely influential work, Lukács began the long reassessment of Marxism necessitated in the West by successive defeats of working-class revolutions under presumably "advanced" economic and political conditions (as in Germany, 1918–19).

In *History and Class Consciousness*, he repeatedly stressed the baleful pacifying effects of a mechanical economic determinist position which he identified with Engels' outlook and which encouraged a contemplative faith in objective necessity. What was needed was a reassertion of the active subject's (the proletariat's, he insisted) creation of the historical world as part of a true dialectic of object and subject. If the proletariat is subjectively unprepared to build socialism—in part because of a consciousness formed by "bourgeois" ideologies which isolate "facts" as objective data—the current crisis of capitalist society could lead to a long period of civil and imperial wars eventuating in a new barbarism.[30] The heart of the philosophically rich argument was a

28. Lukács, "Preface to New Edition (1967)," *History and Class Consciousness*, p. xi.
29. Lukács, "The Old Culture and the New Culture"; Löwy, *Georg Lukács*, pp. 142, 166–167; Arato and Breines, *The Young Lukács*, p. 80.
30. Lukács, *History and Class Consciousness*, pp. 208–209, 306–311.

brilliant re-creation and expansion of Marx's theory of alienation from the chapter on the "fetishism of commodities" in *Das Kapital*. (The 1844 Manuscripts were as yet still unavailable.) Whereas in early capitalism the "personal nature of economic relations was still understood" (which made possible, Lukács was to argue in the 1930s, the creations of literary realism), as the process grew more complex and indirect it became more difficult to penetrate the "veil of reification," the illusory appearance of commodities and social life as a "phantom objectivity," a web formed by the impersonal relations between things. Human activity is felt as though "estranged," as is public life from the private self. Only through a unity of philosophically aware theory—as opposed to an habituated and distorting empiricism—and politically active proletarian struggle will it be possible to experience the world as a creation of human, socially interactive labor, and not preexistent automatic laws.

Instead of the ideological distortions caused by bourgeois society, which lead to the extreme separations of subjectivity and objectivity, isolated fact and abstract laws, Marxism is a method of analysis based on the dialectic of subject and object and the point of view of "concrete totality," the awareness of the historically *mediated* quality of all particulars by the whole. Thus, it provides the necessary corrective to all methods which focus on crude immediacies and reified laws abstracted from them, the "second nature" of an advanced and congealed capitalist society.[31] It was in this way, in the early 1920s, that Lukács reinterpreted Marxism with the aid of his own prewar humanism and idealism. Thus, modern "homelessness" in a world of alien objects was now seen as changeable, not merely because it was tied to the specific workings of capitalist social and ideological life (he had argued that as early as 1906–09), but because the proletariat could realize the classical heritage of the "whole man" in a new socialist society.

Brecht came from a different sector of the increasingly differentiated bourgeoisie, and soon developed a social outlook which contrasted with that of Lukács. Both of Brecht's parents came from Achern, in the Black Forest, where the family had owned a tobacco store. His father was employed in a paper factory by the time of Bertolt's birth in 1898, and by 1914 had become its director.[32] By this time, he was a fairly well-to-do burgher. But the formation of this upwardly mobile middle-

31. This brief summary of the philosophical argument (the political one will follow later) is based particularly on the central long chapter on "Reification and the Consciousness of the Proletariat," on pp. 83–222.

32. Frederic Ewen, *Bertolt Brecht: His Life, His Art and His Times* (New York, 1967), p. 55.

class life did not proceed that simply: the coefficient of the son's revolt against respectable bourgeois society, an allegiance to plebeian traditions against the rich, was partly rooted in the family's history. Brecht's ancestors "had been shrewd, hard headed peasants from Baden" before the family's tobacco shop had "lifted" them into the ranks of the *Kleinbürgertum* (petty bourgeoisie). An early model for the boy seems to have been a 72-year-old grandmother who "suddenly shocked the family by abandoning the dull, cramped conventions of petty bourgeois gentility and consorting with all sorts of queer and not quite respectable people."[33] Brecht's later Schweikian insistence on the practical and down-to-earth material needs of survival, his admiration for the sly wisdom of anti-heroic cowardice, and his distrust of high-flown sentiments and "Kultur" find some roots in this available plebeian alternative to the family's increasing social status. When he "left his own class," Brecht later wrote of himself, he "joined the common people."[34] Literal truthfulness here is less important than the social orientation it reveals: his was not the revolt of a patrician aesthete, but of a self-proclaimed "man of the masses." Even if such a posture was partly one of Brecht's masks, it left a deep imprint upon his work. Impatient with idealism, Brecht's pivotal emphasis upon the uses of scientific knowledge and upon art as an aspect of human technical production and labor was strongly conditioned by this commitment to the practical needs of the "plebeian" classes.[35]

Prevented by class background as well as by age from forming any deep roots in prewar German culture of whatever variety, Brecht responded quite differently from Lukács to the horrors of war. Drafted at sixteen as a medical orderly, he came in direct contact with the results of the slaughter, and his postwar poetry was "haunted by images of dismembered bodies."[36] Brecht experienced the agonizing horror of a broken world, an experience which lent to his nihilistic early plays and

33. Martin Esslin, *Brecht: The Man and His Work*, 2nd edition (New York, 1971), p. 5.
34. Brecht, "Svendborger Gedichte," *GW*, Vol. 9, p. 721.
35. I have chosen here to use the term "plebeian"—and not the more sociologically distinct "proletarian" or "petty bourgeois"—because it seems closest to Brecht's own self-interpretation and expresses best the social-ethical outlook of much of his work, even though his theoretical and political writings often rely upon stricter Marxist categories. I am following the usage of the term in an early, excellent discussion of Brecht's plays by Hans Mayer, "Bertolt Brecht oder die plebejische Tradition," *Literatur der Übergangszeit: Essays* (Wiesbaden, n.d. [though probably 1949]), pp. 225–238. In his powerful critique of Brecht in 1962, Adorno was to berate the dramatist for dishonest posing as a "man of the masses." See "On Commitment," *Aesthetics and Politics*, pp. 177–195.
36. Esslin, pp. 7–8.

poems a brutal expressionist realism comparable to that of Grosz and Beckmann. In contrast to Lukács, it was the war and not the relatively stable and comfortably prosperous years of 1900–14, that served as Brecht's initiation into the world. Such a formative experience permanently frustrated any return to a prewar normalcy only dimly remembered at best. The world appeared to Brecht as though "swept clean" by destruction; and although widely differing possibilities for a new postwar culture and society of course existed, the reestablishment of continuity with the old was not likely to be a goal. The breakdown of tradition was simply an accomplished fact.[37]

Brecht's early poems and pre-Marxist plays, written during six years he spent in Munich (1918–24), reflect his adaptation to the intense social dislocations of the postwar years. Besides violent and biting satire on respectable hypocrisies and values, there was a fascination with (and sympathy for) aimlessly desperate outcasts—crooks, beggars, whores— and with the latest fashions of newly urbanized popular culture: jazz, boxing, pop music, and American sounds. The pessimism was neither traditionalist nor sentimental, but was expressed through the direct discourse of hard, cold statement. His first work for the theatre, *Baal*, was a savage satire on the vapid sentimentality of many expressionist plays then being performed (1918–19). Instead of depicting his artist-protagonist as a sensitive, lonely, and martyred genius, Brecht created in Baal (the name was taken from a Syrian pagan earth-god) an amoral Dionysiac force of nature, who ravenously devours life, unmoved by the harm he does to others or himself.[38] Baal embodies the "purposelessness of a universe in which nothing lasts."[39] "Like the dadaists of the same period, whom war had shocked into 'coolness' and 'nihilism,'" Walter Sokel has written, Brecht "could not stomach the naive dreams of grandeur and lachrymose self-pity of many expressionists."[40] The vitalistic urges and riotous, chopped imagery of the play have connections with expressionism (as is the case with much of his early work), but Brecht separated these entirely from all trace of self-dramatized emotionality, Christian spirituality, and sentimental idealism.[41]

In his early poems and plays, Brecht was influenced by the vagrant

37. Hannah Arendt, *Men in Dark Times* (New York, 1968), pp. 218–228.
38. Brecht, "Baal," in Walter Sokel, ed., *An Anthology of German Expressionist Drama* (New York, 1963), pp. 305–366.
39. Walter Sokel, "Introduction," *Anthology of German Expressionist Drama*, p. xxviii.
40. Ibid., p. xxvi.
41. Ibid., pp. xxix–xxxii; Esslin, *Brecht*, p. 117.

and rebellious lyricism of Villon and Rimbaud, as well as by the cynical, tough, and materialistic form of pre-expressionism in Büchner and Wedekind.[42] Drawing upon such literary sources, as well as his own experience of postwar Germany, Brecht offered a nihilistic portrayal of a desacralized nature, perhaps the most fundamental feature of his work before 1924. Instead of the nature which Rousseau and the romantics conceived, or which Goethe described as the "living garment of the divinity," the natural world was seen by Brecht as a hostile environment, cruelly indifferent to human suffering and senselessly destructive.[43] This was a Darwinian schema, but one presented with a nihilism far outdistancing the sad shocks with which the genial biologist read the ruthless biological struggle. "Baal's sky is filled with vultures that wait to eat him, unless he manages to eat them first."[44] Unlike Lukács, moreover, Brecht presented no counter-images of harmony and organic beauty against which to compare the present brutality and chaos.

Brecht was looking in the early 1920s for a stage that would be less egotistical than that of the expressionists and as tough and impersonal as the modern newspapers and machines so visible in the urban world of the Weimar Republic. Soon after moving to Berlin in 1924, he began to find the ingredients for such a theatre. Arriving in the German metropolis just when the cultural scene was undergoing a shift from expressionism to what was soon called *Neue Sachlichkeit* ("New Objectivity"), Brecht quickly absorbed a number of pivotal cubist and constructivist influences which were to bear fruit in his own "epic" drama and his later Marxist "production aesthetics."

Brecht worked in the mid-1920s with Erwin Piscator in the Berliner Volksbühne, where simultaneity, cinematic cutting, and "proletarian," "collectivist" rejection of individual heroes paralleled, and was partly indebted to, Meyerhold's theatre.[45] (It should be said, however, that Brecht's own plays were less reportorial and documentary, more parabolic and lyrical, than Piscator's.) The links between the German and Soviet avant-gardes, notably in drama and the visual arts, were very close at this time, as John Willet has documented in detail in his recent study of the "new sobriety" in Weimar culture.[46] Postwar German dada-

42. John Willett, *The Theatre of Bertolt Brecht* (New York, 1959), pp. 105–109; Ewen, p. 65.

43. Keith A. Dickson, *Towards Utopia: A Study of Brecht* (Oxford, England, 1980), pp. 15–17; Sokel, "Introduction," p. xxviii.

44. Sokel, "Introduction," p. xxviii.

45. Willett, *Theatre of Bertolt Brecht*, pp. 109–110; Ewen, *Brecht*, pp. 146–159.

46. John Willett, *Art and Politics in the Weimar Period, 1917–1933: The New So-*

ists had been much influenced in the years 1918–20 by Soviet visual experiments. Constructivist painters came to Berlin in 1922 and were avidly followed, later making a significant impact on the Bauhaus.[47] A number of constructivist theatrical troupes visited Berlin from 1922 to 1930, including those of Tairov and Meyerhold,[48] the latter of which Brecht explicitly praised in the spring of 1930.[49] In 1926, Eisenstein's *Potemkin* was shown in Berlin. Brecht was among those who responded most enthusiastically to its radical montage methods of cinematic construction.[50] Brecht learned of the new Moscow theatre, art, and cinema directly through such sources,[51] and through his daily work with Piscator, but also indirectly from friends he knew in the years after 1924: George Grosz and John Heartfield, whose politically revolutionary forms of visual montage drew upon Soviet constructivists such as Tatlin[52]; Asja Lacis, a Latvian Communist and a leader of Soviet experimental children's theatre, with whom Brecht worked in his production of *Edward the Second* (1924) and whom he plied with questions about Meyerhold, Tairov, Majakovsky, and Tretjakov[53]; Walter Benjamin, who visited Moscow in 1926–27 and befriended Brecht in 1928[54]; and Sergei Tretjakov himself, a playwright and cultural thinker for *Novy Lef* who was developing (with Boris Arvatov and others) an aesthetics of "production" from which Brecht would learn in formulating his own Marxist cultural theories in the 1930s. Brecht and Tretjakov became good friends after the Soviet writer visited Berlin in 1931.[55]

---

briety (New York, 1978). This is an invaluable guide to the international links (particularly between Berlin and Moscow) of a machine-minded culture of 1924–29. It is a superb source for situating Brecht within those particular modernist strains to which his work is most related after 1924.

47. Ibid., pp. 50–54, 74–82.

48. Lew Kopelew, "Brecht und die Russische Theaterrevolution," *Brecht Heute*, 3 (1973), 27.

49. Brecht, "Sowjettheater und proletarisches Theater," *GW*, Vol. 15, pp. 204–205. In a talk "Über experimentelles Theater," in 1939, by which time Meyerhold had disappeared in the midst of the purges, Brecht again spoke enthusiastically about the Soviet director, referring to his "radical constructivist" theatre. *GW*, Vol. 15, pp. 285–286.

50. Willett, *Art and Politics in the Weimar Period*, p. 143; see also Brecht, *GW*, Vol. 20, p. 46, where he refers to "the enormous impact that the great films of Eisenstein had upon me."

51. Willett, *Theatre of Bertolt Brecht*, p. 111.

52. Kopelew, "Brecht und die Russische Theaterrevolution," p. 34; Ewen, p. 159.

53. Asja Lacis, *Revolutionär im Beruf: Berichte uber proletarisches Theater, über Meyerhold, Brecht, Benjamin und Piscator* (München, 1972), pp. 37, 54, 58; Kopelew, pp. 33–34.

54. Bernd Witte, *Walter Benjamin—Der Intellektuelle als Kritiker: Untersuchungen zu seinem Frühwerk* (Stuttgart, 1976), pp. 173–175.

55. Marjorie L. Hoover. "Brecht's Soviet Connection, Tretjakov." *Brecht Heute*, 3 (1973), 41; David Bathrick "Affirmative and Negative Culture: The Avant-Garde under

The impact on Brecht of these diverse figures and currents was, first, upon his dramatic practice beginning in the mid-1920s, and then, more gradually, upon his theoretical writings on theatre and culture after 1929. As early as *Mann ist Mann* (1926), Brecht's theatre became an experimental self-reflexive workshop in which humans and social reality were shown to be constructions capable of being "reassembled" (*ummontiert*). His new episodic drama (which he would soon describe as "epic theatre") attempted to dispel the naturalist illusions of art as "reflection" while developing cubist and constructivist means of politically activating his audience. Using various methods to interrupt the linear dramatic flow (e.g., through a montage of discontinuous scenes, interpolations of cinema, formal songs, informational signposts, etc.), Brecht sought now to encourage his audiences to question in a rational manner the necessity, and experience the "strangeness," of the "normal" and "familiar" course of things, such as the self-destructive effects of "ethical behavior" for the poor. In addition, he attempted to prevent his audiences from emotionally identifying with individual characters by making his actors and actresses move in and out of their roles, playfully revealing the process of their own theatrical art (a technique which he learned not only from Soviet sources, but also from the cubistic drama of Pirandello).[56]

Soon after working out the rudiments of a new theatre, Brecht began to develop (after 1928) a conception of "production aesthetics," which he formed with a Marxism filtered through constructivist lenses: e.g., he viewed art as an aspect of material labor; as a construction based on the formative principles of technological modes of production, such as montage; and as an activity which was tied to new mechanical media, such as film and radio. Brecht's Marxist approach to modernism showed the imprint of aesthetic sources which antedated his first serious engagement with Marxist politics or methods of social analysis. In his case, these traditions placed the emphasis upon the positive potentials of the depersonalized, urban, machine age, in strong contrast to Lukács's early classical humanist rejection of this world.

One might argue that in his epic theatre, his production aesthetics, and, after 1928, his Leninist politics, Brecht was at war with any "gen-

---

'Actually Existing Socialism' —The Case of the *GDR*," *Social Research*, 47:1 (Spring 1980), 174–178.

56. Willett, *Theatre of Bertolt Brecht*, pp. 112–113. The evolving theory of epic drama after 1926 may be studied in the fine collection *Brecht on Theatre*, ed. by John Willett (New York, 1964). See, especially pp. 33–52, which contain the earliest systematic formulations, from 1930–31.

tle," "romantic," or "soft" qualities he found in himself. His intense dislike of compassion and idealistic sentiment, while on the one hand directed effectively against the often unproductive results of such feelings, at times seemed to suggest an anxious attempt to exorcise them from his own personality. Brecht's fascination with America in the 1920s included, for example, a considerable enjoyment of the very chaos, brutality, and unscrupulous commercial vitality which his plays also satirized, a feature evident in addition in the dubious analogy between fascists, businessmen, and criminals which was to be present in some of his work in the 1930s.[57] As a boy, Brecht was a sensitive outsider and somewhat frail and sickly; to compensate for this, his mother provided him with considerable emotional protection, which he was to remember with great thankfulness. This maternal care was ridiculed by his classmates, however, who saw Brecht arriving at school accompanied by his mother.[58] Later he was beaten up a number of times by German army veterans because of his outspoken pacifism. Very early, he attempted to prove his hardness and "masculinity" in the violent world of postwar Germany with slyness and icy wit. While it would be psychologically reductionist to interpret Brecht's work primarily as a defense against what is stereotypically called his "feminine" side, he does give the impression sometimes of trying hard to be cold, ruthless, and "supermasculine," in part identifying with the aggression which might be aimed against his own frailty. In his critique of Brecht, written in 1962, Theodor Adorno commented: "Already the exaggerated adolescent virility of the young Brecht betrayed the borrowed courage of the intellectual who, in despair at violence, suddenly hastens towards a violent practice which he has every reason to fear."[59] Thus, Brecht's hard-nosed "vulgarity," plebeian "realism," and advocacy of industrial productivity and scientific thinking, which were aimed against all traces of a sentimental "humanistic" outlook, might be seen in part as serving these needs of his personality. At the same time, however, such a perspective—while it partially constricted the breadth of his vision and the range of his sympathy, and could even help justify the industrializing

57. Iring Fetscher, "Bertolt Brecht and America," *Salmagundi* 10–11 (Fall, 1969–Winter 1970), 250–255.

58. Klaus Völker, *Bertolt Brecht: Eine Biographie* (München, 1976), p. 12.

59. Adorno, "On Commitment," *Aesthetics and Politics*, p. 187. Analogously, Richard Hofstadter, in his superb *Anti-Intellectualism in American Life* (New York, 1962), pp. 291–295, discusses the contempt felt by many American middle class Communists in the 1930s for soft, aesthetically minded, intellectuals, attempting through such means to declass themselves and become "masculine," "practical" proletarians.

Stalinist dictatorship[60]—provided the basis of much of his power as a thinker and artist. As we shall see in a fuller study of his "production aesthetics," Brecht's strengths and weaknesses were often directly related to various attempts at liquidating the German heritage of aristocratic and romantic subjectivity.

Born into a world of war and revolution, Brecht stressed the necessity to start afresh, the imperative to radically transform traditional culture. Insisting (when becoming a Marxist) that an emergent collectivist and proletarian world would have to make major departures from the nineteenth-century bourgeois heritage, Brecht developed a sharply leftist perspective by the early 1930s, focusing upon class struggle. By this time, however, Lukács had begun to de-emphasize class struggle in favor of a continuity of proletarian culture with bourgeois classical humanism, the intellectual basis for his anti-fascist popular-front posture. Such political differences were to be very much a part of their aesthetic "debates."

At first, Lukács began his Marxist political career with connections to the Communist libertarian left wing, although he managed in *History and Class Consciousness* to build more than enough bridges to an orthodox Leninist position. The book clearly echoed not only Lukács's immersion in German idealism but the political critiques launched by Council Communists, Luxemburgists, and anarcho-syndicalists in the years 1912–19 against Social Democratic and Bolshevik orthodoxies, the latter of which treated the working classes as the object of historical necessities working through party directives. These critiques (which were to bear major intellectual fruit in the renaissance of a dialectical and Hegelian Marxism in the hands of Lukács, Korsch, Bloch, and Gramsci in the early 1920s) all stressed (1) a view of the working class as potential self-emancipating subject of historical change, and (2) the necessity for the ideological, as well as economic, liberation of the working class from bourgeois cultural "hegemony." Abandoning the later Marx's and the Second International's dogma of a necessary progress toward socialism, all of these Central European thinkers stressed in the early fascist era that such a development is by no means automatic but

---

60. David Bathrick has shrewdly pointed out ("Affirmative and Negative Culture," pp. 181–183) how the kind of "production aesthetics" which Brecht shared with much of the Soviet avant-garde of the 1920s could become a defense of an industrializing, technical "domination of nature" of the Stalinist variety, even though it also contained strong libertarian and democratic elements. Chapter five of this book will explore Brecht's and Lukács' ambivalent, and partly legitimating, responses to Stalinism.

requires a subjectively rich emergence of true proletarian class (and therefore also cultural) consciousness. Yet, the postwar revolutionary wave had receded by 1923, and although working-class defeats encouraged an even greater stress upon emancipating the proletariat from bourgeois "consciousness" as these figures saw it, the stress in Lukács's book was decidedly philosophical, a reexamination of the question of consciousness in the Marxian dialectic.[61] The historical situation seemed to justify a long-neglected attention to epistemological and cultural questions, one major reason for the renewed discussion of a Marxist aesthetics which was to follow.

Yet, *History and Class Consciousness* shows Lukács in transit from a vaguely syndicalist decisionism, with traces of Erwin Szabó, Georges Sorel, and Rosa Luxemburg, to Leninist party orthodoxy.[62] In the essays at the end of the book, written last, the view of the working class as the self-determining "subject" of modern history is increasingly attenuated as Lukács emphasizes the pivotal role of a highly disciplined Communist party—albeit in close touch with the masses—in helping to form "true" proletarian class consciousness, as distinct from the merely empirical awareness of a "spontaneous instinctive movement," unable to see beyond the directly immediate.[63] In this way, Lukács attempted to unite his philosophical renewal of Marxian dialectics with the Leninist party. In the course of doing so, however, he was to provide both a more sophisticated intellectual basis for communism than Lenin ever managed, as well as methodological departures for later, more democratic critiques of orthodox communism.

It is no wonder that the work was condemned in Moscow in 1924, and that Lukács, to remain within the party, was forced to make his first of a number of recantations. Yet, this first volte-face was more sincere than later ones. By early 1924, Lukács had disowned the "ultra-leftism" still evident in *History and Class Consciousness*, for, like Stalin, he had come to see Western capitalism as essentially stabilized.[64] Lukács was responding most here to the ebb of the postwar revolutionary wave in

61. On the historical origins and major directions of this school of thought, now often called simply "Western Marxism," see the favorable accounts in Dick Howard and Karl Klare, eds., *The Unknown Dimension: European Marxism Since Lenin* (New York, 1972), especially pp. 3–80, and Russell Jacoby, "The Critique of Automatic Marxism," *Telos*, 10 (Winter, 1971–2); and the critical one in Perry Anderson, *Considerations on Western Marxism* (London, 1977).

62. George Lichtheim, *Georg Lukács* (New York, 1970), p. 36.

63. Lukács, *History and Class Consciousness*, last essay, and especially pp. 314–339.

64. Paul Breines, "Praxis and Its Theorists: The Impact of Lukács and Korsch in the 1920s," *Telos*, 11 (Spring, 1972), 87.

Germany, as well as to the situation faced by the Hungarian Communist Party. A major figure in the Hungarian Party since 1919 (he was Minister of Education in the short-lived Hungarian Soviet Republic), by 1924 he had sided with the so-called Landler faction against Bela Kun. This faction defined the struggle against the extreme right-wing authoritarian Horthy regime in terms of the need for a broadly-based democratic republic, instead of a socialist revolution.[65]

Hungary, of course, was not a modern capitalist nation, but "still semifeudal in its pattern of landholding and society and guided by its regent, Admiral Nicholas Horthy, in the closest possible conformity to the spirit of the Old Régime."[66] In a pamphlet which came to be called the *Blum Theses* (1928), and which contained the political outlook underlying much of his later work,[67] Lukács argued that within this overwhelmingly peasant society, the working classes were socially dependent on the agricultural poor and politically dependent on the bourgeoisie and the Social Democrats. A broad "democratic" front was therefore needed to bring down the Horthy regime and realize the full potential of bourgeois reforms.[68] To distinguish his proposal from a simple appeal for capitalist democracy, Lukács stressed that a democracy was required in which the bourgeoisie "has ceded at least parts of its power to the broad masses of the workers."[69]

Lukács was now fully and (at least until 1968) permanently reversed from his earlier stance, viewing his new popular-front gradualism as a "realistic" assessment of the objective state of things, in contrast to his earlier utopian intemperance. Significantly, in a work of 1926, he detected in Hegel not the dialectical analyst of subject/object relations so much as the mature realist, "reconciling" himself with reality and eschewing all utopias.[70] A contemplative and "reflectionist" side of Lukács's sensibility was now coming to the fore. After the rejection of

65. Rodney Livingston, "Introduction" to Georg Lukács, *Political Writings, 1919–1929* (London, 1972).

66. H.S. Hughes, *Contemporary Europe: A History* (Englewood Cliffs, N.J., 1961), p. 336.

67. See "Preface to New Edition (1967)," *History and Class Consciousness*, p. xxx, where Lukács speaks of the Blum Theses as containing the outlook which "determined from now on all my theoretical and practical activities."

68. Georg Lukács, "Blum Theses," in *Political Writings, 1919–1929*, pp. 229–253; Peter Ludz, "Der Begriff der 'demokratischen Diktatur' in der politischen Philosophie von Georg Lukács," *Festschrift zum achtzigsten Geburtstag von Georg Lukács*, edited by Frank Benseler (Neuwied and Berlin, 1965), pp. 63–64.

69. Lukács, "Blum Theses," p. 243.

70. Michael Löwy, "Lukács and Stalinism," *New Left Review*, 91 (May–June, 1975), 25–27.

the *Blum Theses* by the Hungarian party, he decided to leave active politics and return to theory. If he was right about the historical analysis contained therein, Lukács concluded, and yet had failed to persuade his colleagues, he must be lacking in the requisite political capacities.[71] For twenty-eight years after 1928, including the whole Stalin era, Lukács was to concentrate on his literary and philosophical studies, which contained the general political stance implicit in the *Blum Theses*.

Lukács's belief in the necessity for a popular front of the liberal bourgeoisie and workers was reinforced through his direct experience of Nazism in Germany during his short stay in Berlin between 1931 and 1932.[72] In certain important ways, however, Brecht's political path was different. His first Marxist teacher, the sociologist Fritz Sternberg, followed Rosa Luxemburg's, and not Lenin's, ideas in his work on imperialism, published in 1926. Brecht admired Luxemburg and, unlike Lukács, continued to take her penetrating critique of Lenin's view of party organization very seriously when he planned a play in her honor.[73] The figure who most influenced his Marxism, however, was Karl Korsch, a close intellectual friend of Brecht's by 1928.[74] In contrast to Lukács, whose *History and Class Consciousness* paralleled his own *Marxism and Philosophy* (1923), Korsch did not shift from his earlier leftist position, resisted the Bolshevization of the KPD and the Comintern, and was finally expelled from the party in 1926. His attacks on the Comintern as an instrument of Russian foreign policy repudiated the theory of capitalist "stabilization" as a reflection of "the needs of a defensive state trying to form an alliance with world capitalism." Even before the Great Depression, Korsch had argued that "all the objective requirements for concrete revolutionary politics" existed in Germany.[75] Although, as we shall see, Brecht never fully embraced Korsch's leftist critique of dictatorial and bureaucratic rule in Stalinist Russia, he continued to entertain such an independent perspective while remaining within the general confines of political Leninism.

But the major difference between Brecht's and Lukács's politics was

71. G.H.R. Parkinson, *Georg Lukács* (London, 1977), p. 12; Lukács, "An Unofficial Interview," *New Left Review*, 68 (July–August 1971), 57–58.
72. Helga Gallas' analysis of his work from this period (in *Marxistische Literaturtheorie*) provides ample evidence for this, though not always explicitly.
73. Klaus-Detlev Müller, *Die Funktion der Geschichte im Werk Bertolt Brechts: Studien zum Verhältnis von Marxismus und Aesthetik* (Tübingen, 1967), pp. 23–26.
74. Wolfdietrich Rasch, "Bertolt Brechts Marxistischer Lehrer," *Merkur*, 17 (1963), 1003.
75. Fred Halliday, "Karl Korsch: An Introduction," *Marxism and Philosophy* (New York, 1970), pp. 17–20.

over the issue of class struggle, which Lukács had come to deemphasize. Brecht neither accepted official Bolshevik discipline nor looked favorably upon "bourgeois democracy" as a necessary expedient. More institutionally independent of Stalinism than Lukács (he never joined the party), Brecht's Marxism focused early on class struggle categories, which the depression only intensified. In the crisis years of the Weimar Republic, 1929–32, Brecht developed a form of theatre (*Lehrstücke*, or learning plays) in which working-class people explored vital political issues by alternating in their own performance of different social roles and tactical positions. Such works (e.g., *The Measures Taken*), designed to be performed only by and for proletarian audiences, were intended to estrange them from the influence of "bourgeois" moralistic and idealistic thought, including classical notions of art.[76] But this was no sectarian posture in the Stalinist sense; Brecht opposed the disastrous war on Social Democrats being waged by the German Communists in the critical years 1929–1932. Although he was not public about it, Brecht strongly felt that all workers—SPD and KPD—must unite against Nazism;[77] this alone would implement a class conflict politics, unlike Lukács's "popular front" with the liberal bourgeoisie. Thus, while Lukács's most lasting political development occurred in the relatively stable period between 1924 and 1928, and was mediated particularly by Hungarian and Soviet conditions, Brecht's coincided with the accentuated class struggles within advanced German capitalism after 1928, with Korsch providing a link to the experiences of 1918–19.

For political reasons, then, as well as others, Brecht objected to a simple continuation of the heritage of bourgeois humanism and classical realism, which he saw as tied to socially individualist and largely pretechnical cultural conditions, which "bourgeois art" hoped to perpetuate. Instead, he favored a combative and activist modern culture, drawing from many different traditions, but one which would highlight, among other things, the vast differences between the classes. Only this would serve the cultural production developed by and for a twentieth-century proletariat, mindful of its collectivist and technical interests. Yet, such political differences were only part of the contrast between Brecht's Marxism and that of Lukács.

❖   ❖   ❖

76. Ewen, pp. 235–256; Willett, *Theatre of Bertolt Brecht*, pp. 74–79.
77. Fritz Sternberg, *Der Dichter und die Ratio: Erinnerungen an Bertolt Brecht* (Göttingen, 1963), p. 207.

Throughout his career, Lukács criticized capitalism largely from the perspective of an aesthetic and ethical humanism and idealism, rather than in terms of social and economic inequalities or the political power of corporate wealth. For him capitalism represented the "enslavement and fragmentation of the individual and of the horrifying ugliness of life which inevitably and increasingly accompanies this development." Under this social system, "all human aspirations toward a beautiful and harmonious existence are inexorably crushed by society."[78] One of the primary attractions of Marxism to Lukács was its potential as an historical theory for overcoming materialist concerns. It is significant that he conceived of true art under capitalism as essentially free of the apparatus of economic production. In 1920, he defined culture as "the ensemble of valuable products and abilities which are dispensable in relation to the immediate maintenance of life." From such a perspective, the "liberation from capitalism" was envisioned as a "liberation from the rule of the economy,"[79] a view which Lukács later formally disavowed but retained in practice. Moreover, he repeatedly cited the division of labor under capitalism as a source of the fragmentation of the human essence and personality. In his view, capitalism was inherently hostile to art and culture, and this "disintegration of the concrete totality into abstract specializations"[80] was a major cause.

In his interpretation of Marxist humanism by the 1930s, Lukács saw Marx and Engels urging "the writers of their time to . . . grasp man in his essence and totality."[81] He now came close to creating an "essentialist" ontology of "anthropological man," interpreting "the course of history as a battle between human wholeness and the successive modes of alienation introduced by the different divisions of labor."[82] Humanism was interpreted as a critique of the "subjugation" of "man's nature" under capitalism.[83] A profound involvement with Hegel had led Lukács to conceive of history as the "realization" and "fulfillment" of the totality

78. Lukács, "The Ideal of the Harmonious Man in Bourgeois Aesthetics," *Writer and Critic*, p. 92.
79. "The Old Culture and the New Culture," *Marxism and Human Liberation*, p. 4.
80. Lukács, "Marx and Engels on Aesthetics," *Writer and Critic*, p. 70.
81. Ibid.
82. Stanley Mitchell, "An Extended Note to Ian Birchall's Paper," in *Situating Marx* (London, 1972), p. 149. Earlier, in *History and Class Consciousness*, pp. 186–194, Lukács had been well aware of the dangers of an unhistorical ontology of "man," as in the anthropological humanism of Feuerbach. Later, in *Realism in Our Time* (1955) he scored the literary modernists repeatedly for substituting an abstract "human condition" for historically specific processes.
83. Lukács, "Preface to New Edition (1967)," p. xxiv.

of human attributes.[84] In the *Holy Family* (1845), however, Marx had distinguished himself from an ontological reading of the theory of alienation and had "challenged the static implications of Feuerbach's anthropology by making de-alienated man an historical potentiality rather than an inherent reality."[85] Lukács's "humanism" overplayed the classical idealist elements of the youthful Marx's synthesis and, in so doing, neglected their later grounding in a history of social production, a major change between the early Marx and *Kapital*.

In Moscow in 1931, Lukács had enthusiastically examined the newly discovered *Economic and Philosophical Manuscripts of 1844*, which further helped him to see Marx's writings from the perspective of his youthful indebtedness to Goethean humanism as well as Hegelian idealism. Lukács's works of the mid-1930s on Hegel and Goethe illustrate this well.[86] His critique of all crudely unmediated "facts" and his view of art as a "totalizing" perspective, as a reconciliation of the opposition of historical essence and sensate appearance, derives, of course, from an Hegelian reading of Marx.[87] Behind his term "realism" lay Hegel's aesthetics—with its praise of "visible-concrete" as against "conceptual-abstract" means of representation—as well as Goethe's poetic method of perceiving the general in the individually specific.[88] Lukács's insistence that realist literature depict harmonious, many-sided, creatively developed individual personalities owes much to both the aesthetic humanism of the young Marx and to Weimar classicism. Significantly, and in the tradition of German idealism, Lukács sharply divided scientific from artistic modes of perception. Art, he wrote in his *Aesthetics* (1962), is "anthropomorphic," always containing images of the human personality; science, however, seeks consciously to eliminate the subjective element from the results.[89]

Brecht, on the other hand, searching for the contemporary functions of cultural models, regarded German classical and idealist culture as an ideological prop of the ruling classes of early twentieth-century Germany. Whatever initial role Faustian heroics or Schillerian pathos may

84. Silvia Federici, "Notes on Lukács' Aesthetics," *Telos*," (Spring, 1972), 147; and Stanley Mitchell, "Extended Note to Ian Birchall's Paper," p. 149.
85. Martin Jay, "The Frankfurt School's Critique of Marxist Humanism," *Social Research*, 39:2 (Summer, 1972), 292.
86. Lukács, *Der junge Hegel* (Zürich, 1948); and *Goethe und seine Zeit* (Berlin, 1946), which appeared in English as *Goethe and His Age* (New York, 1969).
87. Mittenzwei, "Marxismus und Realismus," pp. 29–31.
88. Gallas, *Marxistische Literaturtheorie*, p. 170.
89. Királyfalvi, *The Aesthetics of György Lukács*, pp. 36, 51.

have performed in the 1790s, they had been emptied of this meaning and turned to manipulative advantage in the language of contemporary domination. In *Saint Joan of the Stockyards*, written at the beginning of the depression, Brecht parodied the social functions of lofty classical language by having the industrialist Pierpont Mauler repeatedly use it in his apostrophes to money and power. This was Brecht's view of the real "vulgarity" of his culture, what Fritz Stern has aptly described as the "vulgar idealism" of the German upper middle classes after 1870.[90]

As for Hegelian idealism, while Brecht's Marxism focused on the dialectical interaction of object and subject, he tended to distinguish the Marxist from the Hegelian dialectic. In this he may well have been influenced by Korsch's development after 1930. Korsch's *Karl Marx* (which Brecht admired greatly, and which he and Korsch discussed at length in Svendborg, Denmark, in 1933–36, while the book was still a manuscript) viewed Marx as having advanced from Hegelian philosophy to materialist science.[91]

Instead of linking Marxism with Hegel and Goethe, Brecht emphasized the indebtedness of Marxist critical rationalism to the radical materialists of the French Enlightenment, and in particular to Denis Diderot. Building upon Diderot, the philosopher of theatre, and upon Enlightenment aesthetics in general, Brecht asked from the actor "that his tears flow from the brain,"[92] and that art combine entertainment and education concerning the nature of a changing social reality. Instead of rounded aesthetic "experience," which was Lukács's concern, the focus in both Brecht and Diderot was upon the intellectually cognitive and politically useful function of art.[93] The central figure of the *Encyclopedia*, himself endeavoring to evade the censors, would have greatly appreciated Brecht's use of *Sklavensprache* (the speech of slaves) as the art of the possible, avoiding suicidal heroics in its communication of useful truths.[94] Finally, like the cubists and the constructivist Russian avant-garde of the 1920s, Brecht strongly rejected the nineteenth-century idealist redefinition of art as an imaginative pursuit higher than "mere" craft or technical skill; instead, it was his intention to forge, in

90. Fritz Stern, "The Political Consequences of the Unpolitical German," *The Failure of Illiberalism* (New York, 1972).

91. Rasch, "Bertolt Brechts Marxistischer Lehrer," p. 1004; Karl Korsch, *Karl Marx* (New York, 1963), p. 169.

92. Darko Suvin, "The Mirror and the Dynamo," *Radical Perspectives in the Arts*, ed. Lee Baxandall (Baltimore, 1972), p. 83.

93. Müller, *Geschichte im Werke Bertolt Brechts*, pp. 172–174.

94. Theo Buck, *Brecht und Diderot: Über Schwierigkeiten der Rationalität in Deutschland* (Tübingen, 1971), pp. 64–65.

materialist terms, a link between art and the constructive, mechanical, and useful skills, such as the "art of directing, of teaching, of machine building and of flying." In this respect, Brecht came particularly close to seventeenth- and eighteenth-century French and English philosophy in linking art, science, production, and social praxis,[95] and it is not surprising, therefore, that he emphasized Marx's relation to this tradition.[96]

Brecht saw Marxism as a materialist and scientific method able to undermine the idealist culture and ethics which kept the "common people" in their place. Long before he read Marx, his works revealed a suspicion of merely emotive, idealistic, or religious responses to social realities. In viewing art as a demythologizing tool, he used skeptical scientific thinking as a model.[97] His purpose was not merely to produce the joys of satirical exposure, though these are not to be minimized; it was to develop a *modus operandi* for radical social change. In this sense, utility was the guiding thread: if moral idealism was to serve rather than hinder the transformation of society, then compassion would have to be made truly functional.

Before his acquaintance with Marxist theory, Brecht had been both fascinated and horrified by the stock exchange[98]; he first studied *Kapital* in 1926, he tells us, to comprehend the dynamics of the grain market for the play he was then writing (later integrated into *Saint Joan of the Stockyards*).[99] Regarding this "cold" study of Marx, Brecht later claimed that his training in the natural sciences (as a medical student) may have immunized him against strong emotional influences and conditioned his more scientific interest in Marxism.[100] This, of course, was another Brechtian mask: an attempted pragmatic and productive response to his own pain at socially-caused suffering, and a steeling of himself, especially in the crisis years 1929–32, against all "softness." Yet, as *Galileo* illustrates, he believed that only a critical and scientific approach to social issues could serve the cause of the plebeian poor and oppressed. Whereas Lukács's work is associated with the attack on

95. Besides Diderot, Brecht drew upon Francis Bacon's concept of an inductive, experimental and socially emancipatory science. See "Notizen über realistische Schreibweise," *GW*, Vol. 19, pp. 367–369 and Heinz Brüggemann, *Literarische Technik und Soziale Revolution: Versuche über das Verhältnis von Kunstproduktion, Marxismus und literarischer Tradition in den theoretischen Schriften Bertolt Brechts* (Reinbek bei Hamburg, 1973), p. 256.
96. Brüggemann, *Literarische Technik und Soziale Revolution*, pp. 255–256.
97. Willett, *Theatre of Bertolt Brecht*, pp. 78–79.
98. Hans Mayer, "Bertolt Brecht and the Tradition," in *Steppenwolf and Everyman: Outsiders and Conformists in Contemporary Literature* (New York, 1971), p. 102.
99. Brecht, "Marxistische Studien," *GW*, Vol. 20, p. 46.
100. Ibid., p. 96.

positivist and merely economist Marxism, Brecht criticized those sentimental humanists who were suspicious of useful scientific and economic
knowledge. "They think that truth is only what sounds nice," he wrote.
"If truth should prove to be something statistical, dry or factual, something difficult to find and requiring study, they do not recognize it as
truth; it does not intoxicate them." [101] Two years after the Nazi takeover,
he wrote: "Times of extreme oppression are usually times when there is
much talk about high and lofty matters. At such times it takes courage
to write of low and ignoble matters such as food and shelter for workers; when all sorts of honors are showered upon the peasants it takes
courage to speak of machines and good stock feeds which would lighten
their honorable labors." [102]

Yet, the distinction between Brecht's advocacy of an anti-psychological, technically minded, materialist science and Lukács's Hegelian and
humanist Marxism should not be overdrawn. Although Brecht had been
affected, for example, by the new enthusiasm for American technology
which played a part in the literature of "New Objectivity" in the late
1920s, he was not an idolator of technical progress as such, and stressed
the need for a "functional transformation" of new productive methods
in a socialist direction. [103] In addition, Brecht directed his "estrangement" devices against a merely empirical perception of contemporary
reality. Like Marx, he understood science as a process of inquiry into
historical structures not always revealed in the immediate "facts."
Whether or not Marx's work is to be judged strictly as "scientific,"
Brecht's own view of science was developed in terms of Marx's practice
of a critical, dialectical, and historical method very different from its
later positivist reading. Here there is a similarity with the earlier Lukács
of *History and Class Consciousness*, the critic of the mechanistic orthodoxies of the Second International.

The central essay of that book had been the discussion of "reification," Lukács's term for the phenomenon of commodity fetishism in
capitalist society which Marx had described. Productive life, "definite
social relations between men," Marx wrote of capitalism, "assumes, in
their [men's] eyes, the fantastic form of a relation between things." [104]

101. Brecht, "Writing the Truth: Five Difficulties," in *Galileo* (New York, 1966),
p. 135.

102. Ibid., p. 134.

103. See Helmut Lethen, *Neue Sachlichkeit, 1924–1932: Studien zur Literatur des
"Weissen Sozialismus"* (Stuttgart, 1970), pp. 114–126; Klaus Völker, *Bertolt Brecht: Eine
Biographie*, p. 127.

104. *Marx-Engels Reader*, p. 217.

Since Brecht and Lukács both rely heavily upon this analysis, it is worth comparing their applications of it.

We have seen how, in the 1930s, Lukács drew on the theory of reification in his literary studies when he criticized naturalist and modernist literature for failing to go beyond the apparent split between personal action and objective history in modern capitalist society. Brecht, too, sought to attack contemporary reification, although the devices of "estrangement" used for that purpose needed the viewer to complete the demystifying process through political action. Ernst Bloch has shown the various ways in which Brecht attempted to shock his audiences out of their involuntary adjustment to lives "reified into things"; these techniques constitute the so-called *Verfremdung* ("estrangement") effects, which were designed to actively overcome *Entfremdung* ("alienation").[105] If, as Brecht believed, capitalist "normality" numbs the perception of history as endless change and human construction, and veils the contradictions between professed values and social realities, then the "customary" must be seen as strange and unexpected, thus awakening the dreamer from a "reified" sleep.

Yet, with all this apparent similarity, Lukács and Brecht did not see alienation in the same way. Lukács was acutely troubled by what he saw as the "degradation and destruction of the individual under capitalism," and insisted that a contemporary realist literature must reassert the "noble" resistance of individuals against their environment, portrayed in the great novels of the nineteenth century.[106] For him, alienation derived from the capitalist division of labor, in which the individual worker's experience of a unified and "self-contained" process was destroyed.[107] Hence, his concept of realism called for a social totality not abstracted from personal, individual experience—which would only mirror the process of alienation—but concretely revealed through inner character development as well as external, and individualized, human interaction. In this way, the reader's experience of art would counteract the social experience of dehumanization and help him/her to realize individuality.

For Brecht, however, such traditional humanist attitudes obscured collective realities of modern social production and failed to grasp the extent of contemporary reified consciousness. As we saw earlier, Brecht

105. Ernst Bloch, "Entfremdung, Verfremdung: Alienation, Estrangement," in *Brecht*, ed., Erika Munk (New York, 1972), pp. 7–11.
106. Lukács, "The Ideal of the Harmonious Man in Bourgeois Aesthetics," p. 98.
107. Lukács, "The Old Culture and the New Culture," pp. 6–7.

argued that one can no longer expect private everyday life to provide access to general historical dynamics. The functioning reality of a large corporation, for example, cannot be understood from individual personal experience.[108] To encompass the full social totality required a constructivist montage of shifting multiple viewpoints. An art was needed, Brecht claimed, which flaunted its own reality as an imaginative "artifice" or rational "construction" in order to pierce the illusory cognitive claims of private experience. Aesthetic antidotes to historical development could not be effective. Instead of seeking "typical" harmonious individualities as concretized historical forces or providing individualized "catharsis" for the emotionally involved reader, Brecht attempted to reveal the contemporary dynamics of collective social structures hidden from normal personal experiences.

Reacting against the inward focus of much German cultural tradition, Brecht avoided individual psychological portraiture by focusing upon his character's active social behavior. This did not always mean attempting to extinguish all traces of personal uniqueness, the extreme collectivizing procedure followed in the *Lehrstücke* of 1929–32. With the securing of the Nazi dictatorship by 1936, and the end of any hopes of immediate political struggle against it, Brecht's Marxism developed greater breadth in the late 1930s, becoming a widening concern for critical scientific inquiry and the often subtle shifts in human conduct brought about by class society and historical change. In this period, his finest plays were begun (*Mother Courage, The Good Person of Setzuan, Galileo*, and *The Caucasian Chalk Circle*), in all of which there is a deeply humane interest in creating sharply defined, unheroic, plebeian figures who are not merely abstract embodiments of social phenomena.[109] At the same time, he began to characterize the *Verfremdungseffekt* by distinguishing "catharsis" from emotional responses that are conducive to critical thought, e.g., moral outrage at social injustice, or sorrow (which we observe in ourselves) at the course of the dramatic action.[110] As before, however, he sought every means to prevent simple audience "identification" with individual characters. As we have seen, Lukács strongly criticized this. The disagreement stemmed, in part, from Brecht's view that only an activist and collectivist value

108. Brecht, "Der Dreigroschenprozess," *GW*, Vol. 18, pp. 161–162.
109. The theoretical basis for this shift was provided in the so-called *Messingkauf Dialogues*, written largely from 1938–42, where Brecht emphasized, for example, that the influence of class should be shown as "applying differently to different peasants." (*Messingkauf Dialogues* [London, 1965], p. 80).
110. Ibid., p. 47; and *Brecht on Theatre*, ed. John Willett (New York, 1964), p. 227.

structure would help emancipate the lower classes, whereas for Lukács the "destruction of the individual" was at the heart of capitalist alienation and must be resisted in art.[111] Beyond this, however, Brecht had attempted to apply Marx's analysis of "reification" to twentieth-century collective and "mass society," where technologized social engineering exceeded Marx's experience, as well as the experience of his favorite "realist" writer, Balzac.

In Brecht's 1926 play *Mann ist Mann*, Galy Gay is so insistently and repeatedly transformed from one persona to another by the forces of his environment that it would be anachronistic to see him as alienated from himself in these roles: his "self" is in each of the transformations.[112] Such a viewpoint, which received ambivalent expression in this early play, provided, of course, its own solution: total changeability encourages the hope that things can be very different. The issue for Brecht was not any inevitable psychic depersonalization in the modern, collectivist age—a common traditionalist reading of the theory of alienation—but the question of how technology is used and to whose advantage. In his plays, Brecht observed present emancipatory possibilities from the vantage of their fuller realization in a potential future.[113] He saw all human life as a process of continual historical change,[114] and not the realization of some "essence," as in Lukács's teleological view. Brecht's modernist "humanism" contrasted in this way from Lukács's classical version.

In recent years, Lukács's literary studies of the 1930s have been praised by some of his analysts as the work of a subtle dialectical Marxist and criticized by others as either mechanistically materialist or subjectively idealist. In fact, although Lukács viewed his work as a return to dialectical methods, he is more correctly seen in terms of all three postures, depending upon which aspect of his aesthetics one examines: his content analysis of realism, his view of the historical sources of literary representation, or his discussion of the social reception of art.

In his theory of realism, Lukács argued for a dialectical treatment in

111. For a lengthier analysis of "individual character" in Brecht's work—and the difference here from Lukács—see Klaus Detlev Müller, *Geschichte im Werk Bertolt Brechts*, pp. 148–167.

112. Brecht, "Mann ist Mann," *GW*, Vol. 1, pp. 297–377. See also his thoughts on modern depersonalized collective life in the "Vorrede zu 'Mann ist Mann,' April, 1927," *GW*, Vol. 17, pp. 976–978.

113. Suvin, "The Mirror and the Dynamo," p. 88.

114. Müller, *Geschichte im Werk Bertolt Brechts*, p. 52; Brüggemann, *Literarische Technik und Soziale Revolution*, pp. 90–95.

which "typical" subjective personalities pursued their goals in actions
continually mediated by larger elements of the objective historical process. According to Lukács the author should create characters whose
active role in the transforming of objective conditions was part of
an endless interaction of consciousness and social being. But Lukács
concentrated his own dialectical methods entirely upon a content aesthetic *within* the novel. In the years 1928–56, decades in which he was
reduced to political impotence, Lukács continued the strong evolutionary focus of his view of capitalist stabilization. By the early 1930s, he
separated literary dialectics from political praxis and fell back upon a
"copy" theory of artistic representation which essentially denied the
novelist the productive power of consciousness. "Any apprehension of
the external world," he wrote in 1934 in a revealing essay entitled "Art
and Objective Truth," is "nothing more than a reflection in consciousness of the world that exists independently of consciousness." [115] Here
Lukács reproduced the deterministic Marxism which marked the passivity and reactive politics of the Second International as well as of Soviet Russia after 1930.

Lukács followed Marx and Engels in strongly opposing the reductionist view that an author's class or conscious ideology simply dictated
the meaning of his/her work, although he did not always apply this
caution to literature he disliked. Nevertheless, his historical analysis of
the social sources of literature does indeed *reduce* literature to a mere
repetition of an era's characteristic ideological positions, which it derives from the historical position of the dominant social class. Hence,
while Balzac, in spite of his aristocratic royalism, revealed in his narratives the rational and historically optimistic ideology of the emergent
bourgeoisie, expressionism simply mirrored the mystical irrationalism
of "bourgeois decay." While this avoids crude economic determinism,
passive reflection of historical ideologies was no real alternative to a
mechanistic aesthetics: the realist artist ends up reproducing cognitively
the objective historical essence contained behind merely sensate appearances. There is no mediation of the social relations by the forces of
production of which literary techniques are a part. Form is merely an
expression of objective content. In epistemological as well as productive
terms, the artist's work is superfluous. [116]

If Lukács's conception of the origins of literature made peace with

---

115. Lukács, "Art and Objective Truth," *Writer and Critic*, p. 25.
116. See the excellent discussion in Thomas Metscher's philosophically articulate
"Aesthetik als Abbildtheorie: Erkenntnistheoretische Grundlagen der materialistischen

the rigidly objectivist Marxism of Communist orthodoxy, his aesthetic idealism found expression in the dimension of literary response. For Lukács the work of art, a reflection of reality, was actually an "illusion" of a self-contained historical totality (although the two positions would appear to be in contradiction, he held to both simultaneously). To achieve artistic effect—the cathartic immersion and surrender of the reader to the fictional momentum—the writer must be able to create a fully believable "illusion" of life, to make this created "world" emerge as the reflection of life in its total motion. While the work "by its very nature offers a truer, more complete, more vivid and more dynamic reflection of reality than the recipient otherwise possesses," a work of art becomes such only "by possessing this self-containment, this capacity to achieve its effect on its own." [117] Thus, Lukács had managed to keep alive his youthful desire for creative works which liberate the recipient from dehumanized specialization and permit the experience of final truths. [118] Although by 1930 the ultimate "essence" for Lukács had become historical change, the notion of the privileged autonomy of art remained.

Brecht's plays, on the other hand, sought to demystify the notion of art as an autonomous and privileged "illusion" of life's integration by repeatedly exposing their own workings as changeable constructions. In his theoretical writings from 1928 to 1940, Brecht criticized the approach which regarded art as a special form of the cognitive "reflection" of reality. Whereas Lukács viewed realist literature as an objective "picture" (*Abbild*) of historical change, Brecht challenged such undialectical materialism and viewed representation as including "both the model to be represented and the ways of representing it." [119] He firmly rejected the reductionist and reified usage of "superstructure" implicit in the views of art and consciousness as mere passive "reflexes" of a socioeconomic base, and saw literary activity, instead, as part of a "transforming praxis" similar to other forms of productive consciousness. "Should we not simply say," Brecht asked, "that we are not able to perceive anything that we are not able to change, even that which does not change us?" [120] Following Marx's critique of Feuerbach's materialism, Brecht viewed art not merely as a reflection of economic relations

Kunsttheorie und das Realismusproblem in den Literaturwissenschaften," *Argument*, 77 (December 1972), 919–976.

117. Lukács, "Art and Objective Truth," pp. 36–40.
118. Georg Lichtheim, *Georg Lukács*, p. 5.
119. Suvin, "The Mirror and the Dynamo," p. 82.
120. Brecht, "Marxistische Studien," *GW*, Vol. 20, p. 140.

but as itself a "practical building element of this reality, a constitutive part of the productive activity of the societal individual."[121] The dramatist's literary theory and practice was closely related to Marx's concept of knowledge as critique. Art, in this view, is not merely mimetic but anticipatory. Insisting on the relative autonomy of intellectual praxis, Brecht held that art could aid in the transformation of the given reality through its ability to anticipate an alternative and realizable socioeconomic system.[122]

The ability of art to help in changing the given social relations derived, for Brecht, not from any allegedly privileged position "above" the tumult of the everyday world, but from the opposite: art's position as part of the productive forces of society. In this view, art as production was linked not merely with "superstructural" elements such as cognitive abstraction, but with those technical forces of collective production fettered, and contradicted, by social relations based upon private accumulation. With this "production aesthetics," drawn from Marx's "classical" analysis of the political economy of capitalism, Brecht offered an alternative to the exclusive focus upon ideological social content in art, the narrow way in which Marx's aesthetic views had generally been developed since his death.

In reply to Lukács's attack on modernist literary techniques, as we have seen, Brecht pointed to the contradiction, to be resolved by historical praxis, between the potential emancipatory use of montage, Joycean inner monologue, and Kafkaesque distancing, for example, and the social relations to which they have been previously connected. These formal means are not inevitably tied to their current social or ideological uses any more than advanced industrial production is wedded to the social relations which originally engendered them.[123] The relative "autonomy" of literary techniques and forms from social and ideological history was, for Brecht, that of all technological means of production. Here was a flexible position which allowed the reworking of many

121. Brüggemann, *Literarische Technik und Soziale Revolution*, p. 84.
122. Brecht, "Marxistische Studien," *GW*, Vol. 20, pp. 76–78.
123. Brecht, "Notizen über realistische Schreibweise," *GW*, Vol. 19, pp. 360–361; Brüggemann, *Literarische Technik und Soziale Revolution*, pp. 173–177. A similar perspective on formal innovations in art as fettered technical means of production was developed during the expressionism debate, and used against Lukács, by Ernst Bloch, and Brecht's musical collaborator and friend, Hans Eisler. See Bloch/Eisler, "Die Kunst zu erben," in *Marxismus und Literatur*, Vol. 2, pp. 105–109. Also close to Brecht was Eisler-Bloch's defense of new cultural media such as records, radio, film, etc. on this basis. On Eisler's theories, which were developed particularly in relation to music, see Gallas, *Marxistische Literaturtheorie*, pp. 174–178, and, especially, Gunther Mayer, "Zur Dialektik des musikalischen Materials," *Alternative*, 69 (December 1969).

different aesthetic forms, especially modernist ones which have arisen in response to twentieth-century conditions. Yet, while Brecht's work combined a great variety of forms and influences which he made his own—ranging from Chinese acting techniques to the Bible, from the poetry of Villon to that of Kipling—there is a central drift to his aesthetic thought, a set of unifying bases into which the eclectic borrowings were fit. Of great importance in understanding Brecht's Marxist aesthetics is that much of his theory and practice is not simply "modernist," but shows, generally speaking, an imaginative adaptation of specifically cubist and constructivist strains, as opposed to currents which derived from symbolism or expressionism. While his language shows traces of Rimbaud,[124] Brecht could not abide any merely metaphorical and poeticized transformation of physical and social reality, as in symbolist aesthetics. The semimusical dissolution of the solid material world was too melancholic and passive for the hardy realist in Brecht, although it proved a heady temptation to his friend Walter Benjamin. The tough, quick-firing style of Büchner and Wedekind influenced him, but the later full-fledged expressionism which claimed these earlier dramatists as sources was far too solipsistic, emotional, and egotistical for him, too abstractly idealist and "incapable of shedding light on the world as an object of human activity."[125] Even the most objectifying of expressionists, Kafka, while in certain ways historically prophetic and technically fruitful in his uses of parable and emotional distancing, was, for Brecht, too much of a mystifying visionary, eternalizing his own pessimistic obsessions.[126] Although Brecht welcomed and cultivated the aesthetic pleasures of wit and humor in the theatre, especially if they served the purposes of developing dialectical thinking or revealing social realities, he was deeply suspicious of all art which "merely" liberated and refreshed the senses, e.g., wildly colorful nonobjective painting, which he crudely saw as politically reactionary in effect, since it obscured the real world and its material problems.[127] He repeatedly criticized writers who concentrated upon personal psychological analyses without raising issues of historical causality. While his own plays, and especially his poems, reveal a gifted lyricist, Brecht was

124. Willett, *Theatre of Bertolt Brecht*, pp. 88–89.
125. Ibid., p. 105. See also Walter Sokel, "Brecht und Expressionismus," in *Die sogenannten Zwanziger Jahre*, ed. Reinhold Grimm and Jost Hermand (Frankfurt a.M., 1970).
126. See Benjamin, *Understanding Brecht* (London, 1973), pp. 107–112.
127. Brecht, "On Non-Objective Painting," in *Marxism and Art*, ed. Berel Lang and Forest Williams (New York, 1972), pp. 423–425.

impatient with beauty experienced as such, refusing to see any social uses in such seeming inutility. He claimed to Walter Benjamin, half in jest, that as a boy "a prolonged illness . . . had begun when a school-fellow had played Chopin to him on the piano and he had not the strength to protest." [128]

Many of these damning judgments Brecht shared with his fellow Leninist Lukács, but not, as we shall see, with other less utilitarian and productivist critics such as Benjamin and Adorno. The Marxism which Brecht "applied" to cultural experience—unlike Lukács's, however—was itself mediated by Brecht's essentially cubistic modernism, traits of which were in evidence before his Marxist education. Instead of a da-daist or surrealist montage—"shock for entertainment's sake" with "objects which do not return from the estrangement," [129] according to Brecht—his montage is cubistic: i.e., it is intellectually designed to reveal a knowable, but shifting, multifaceted and contradictory outer reality, estranging his audiences from habituated mental assumptions so that they may be able to truly master the social world. His anti-psychological, plebeian, and pro-industrial attitudes—all of which con-tributed to his "production aesthetics"—are in the cubist tradition in-augurated in prewar Paris. His estrangement devices share the cubists' "scientific" desire to analytically decompose, aggressively rearrange, and then restructure the object world. Brecht's technique, in which, as he wrote, "an estranging representation is one which allows the ob-ject to be recognized, yet at the same time makes it seem strange," at-tempted, in effect, to give a socialist direction to Braque's aesthetic: "It is always desirable to have two notions—one to demolish the other." [130] A jagged discontinuity and interrupted quality in Brecht's plays is in-tended to encourage an attitude of rational and urgent intervention in the world, in contrast to the pacifying effects of the smooth and organic linear narratives of much traditional literary art. At the same time, the individual temporal moment, the point at which the cubistically inter-faced views clash, is radically historicized and relativized; Brecht clearly intends here to reorient, to "functionally transform," the tendency in much prewar modernism to eschew historical development in favor of cyclical myth or the eternalizing of the presently immediate. His es-tranging methods develop the artistic "self-reflexiveness" which we saw

128. Benjamin, *Understanding Brecht*, p. 114.
129. Brecht, "Notizen über V-Effekte," *GW*, Vol. 15, p. 364; *Messingkauf Dialogues*, pp. 77–78.
130. See Suvin, "The Mirror and the Dynamo," p. 84.

at its height in cubism; hence, they preclude the "documentary montage" of Piscator's epic theatre. Piscator's concentration upon current political events and his usage of contemporary newsreels and newspapers, for example, were techniques which Brecht found too immediate and direct, a poetically impoverished, mimetic reproducing of the outer world, instead of its parabolic reconstruction in the theatre.[131]

Verfremdungseffekt and montage were interrelated and easily accessible aspects of every human being's life, means through which the world is experienced afresh: "To see one's mother as a man's wife," Brecht wrote, "one needs a V-effekt; this is provided, for instance, when one acquires a stepfather."[132] The discontinuous cutting of his cinematically inspired theatrical construction, and the music of many of his plays, are other cases in point. His musical collaborators after 1928 (Hindemith, Eisler, Dessau, and Weill) were all indebted to the "cubist" movement in Parisian music of the 1920s, the light, mechanically spirited, and jazz-influenced montages of the anti-romantics, Satie, Stravinsky, and Milhaud.[133] Still more broadly, cubist montage was the very technique which Brecht chose to reassemble and refunction the traditions of the cultural past: instead of linear continuity and simple "growth"—Lukács's sense of tradition and that of all classicists— Brecht saw a wealth of possible rearranged combinations of widely scattered cultural fragments whose purposes have changed over time.[134]

But the road from Picasso to Brecht had to pass through the Russian Marxist avant-garde of the 1920s, the more direct source of Brecht's modernism. We have already seen various ways in which Brecht's theatrical practice and "production aesthetics" drew upon figures and currents in Russian futurism and constructivism. In the constructivist journals *Lef* and *Novy Lef* of the 1920s, writers such as Mayakowsky, Boris Arvatov, Sergei Tretjakov, and the formalist critic Viktor Shklovsky developed the concept of art as a defamiliarizing, estranging, and renewing experience in a political context, as a part of industrial production and as a potential aspect of the self-emancipation of the working masses.[135] As we saw, Brecht's friendships with Asja Lacis, Erwin Pisca-

131. Völker, *Bertolt Brecht: Eine Biographie*, pp. 128–131.
132. *Brecht on Theatre*, p. 144.
133. Willett, *Theatre of Bertolt Brecht*, pp. 125–133.
134. Rainer Friedrich, "Brecht and Eisenstein," *Telos*, 31 (Spring 1977); Burckhardt Lindner, "Brecht/Benjamin/Adorno—Über Veränderungen der Kunstproduktion im wissenschaftlich-technischen Zeitalter," *Bertolt Brecht I*, Sonderband aus der Reihe Text und Kritik (München, 1972), pp. 18–20.
135. Stanley Mitchell, "From Shklovsky to Brecht: Some Preliminary Remarks To-

tor, Walter Benjamin, and Sergei Tretjakov provided him with important contacts to this body of work. Tretjakov, in particular, had argued
in *Novy Lef* against a simple embellishing of traditions, such as that of
Tolstoyan realism, and had hoped for a new culture to emerge from the
interaction, for example, of newspaper people, writers, and "worker
correspondents" who would learn to "literarize" their industrial experiences, while all authors grew to see themselves as cultural producers. It
was with such suggestions in mind that Tretjakov and his associates
hoped to stem the drift in Soviet cultural policy by the early 1930s toward bureaucratic control and the use of cultural forms for "mass hyp-
nosis" and ideological manipulation.[136] It is clear how related these concepts are to Brecht's aesthetic thought. As for his theatrical practice, we
have already seen how Meyerhold and Eisenstein had developed a
Marxist constructivism in drama and film of which Brecht was well
aware by the mid-1920s and which he was to extend in his own unique
ways: anti-illusionist theatre as artifice, discontinuous cutting, pro-
industrial content, class characters, etc.[137] Thus, in his battle with German cultural traditions, and especially their romantic, idealist, and inward focus, Brecht was to draw inspiration from early Soviet Moscow
and, more distantly, prewar Paris.

A fascination (following the cubists) with urban modernity and its
technical experiments, had caused Brecht to concentrate upon the human potentials of technology, and, at times, to neglect the problems resulting from industrial modernization, which Lukács's approach emphasized. Such enthusiasm was sorely tried by the lawsuit he lost in
1931 concerning the changes made in the filming of *The Threepenny
Opera*. The long essay he wrote in response to this experience helped,

---

wards a History of the Politicization of Russian Formalism," *Screen*, 15:2 (Summer
1974), 74–80; Brüggemann, *Literarische Technik und Soziale Revolution*, pp. 102–103,
139–164.

136. Brüggemann, *Literarische Technik und Soziale Revolution*, pp. 190–194; see
also the analysis of the Brecht-Tretjakov correspondence of 1933–37 in Marjorie Hoover,
"Brecht's Soviet Connection, Tretjakov," *Brecht Heute*, 3 (1973), 39–56. Walter Benjamin, in particular, was to develop this argument further, in his most "Brechtian" of articles, "The Author as Producer" (1934), translated in *Understanding Brecht*; and "The
Work of Art in the Age of Mechanical Reproduction," which first appeared in English in
Illuminations (New York, 1969).

137. For a fine comparative analysis of Eisenstein's and Brecht's montage, see Rainer
Friedrich, "Brecht and Eisenstein." On Brecht's relation to Meyerhold, see Lew Kopelev,
"Brecht und die Russische Theaterrevolution," *Brecht Heute*, 3 (1973), 19–38. Further
information on Brecht's relation to the Russian avant-garde, focusing on Brecht's reaction
to its dire fate in the late 1930s, is found in John Fuegi, "The Soviet Union and Brecht: The
Exile's Choice," *Brecht Heute*, 2 (1972).

however, to clarify his thoughts on contemporary artistic production and the uses of new technical media. Against traditional humanists, Brecht argued that cinema as mass entertainment need not be seen as an inferior art form. (The problem of the masses, in any case, is not its "lack of taste," but its "lack of power." [138]) If it were functionally redirected by progressive cultural workers, Brecht argued, film would be able to expand the perceptual functions of art by its graphic focus on the external dynamics of social interaction, superseding the introspective psychology of old "untechnical" narrative art.[139] The collective and unmistakably technological production of cinema could then provide the coup de grace to illusionist aesthetics, demystifying the reverence of art as a higher reality with a religious "glow." [140]

The experience of the film industry in 1930 and 1931 accentuated Brecht's view of the proletarianization of the modern intellectual and artist. Instead of occupying a privileged position as a seer above the fray, the artist, Brecht argued (without fully demonstrating it), was a brain worker in a position analogous to, though not identical with, that of factory workers. For an artist to romantically insist upon autonomy from the cultural productive apparatus in the hope of avoiding the commodification of his/her "creative product"—the advice which critics of liberal persuasion gave to Brecht after he lost his lawsuit—is similar, according to Brecht, to an industrial worker exercising his/her ostensible "freedom" not to work for industrialists.[141] (This aloofness would also confirm the right of the cultural entrepreneurs to do bad work.) If art reveals the experience of alienated production under capitalism, it does so not as a mere "reflection" of a society presumed to be external to the art work, but as a consequence of the alienation of intellectual workers from the products of their labor. The industrialization of art and artists, in Brecht's view, was inescapable and had considerable human potential. In the struggles for a true democratization of the cultural means of production, artistic work would lose its quality of alienated labor by being consciously directed toward collective human ends, instead of toward profit. But the very experience of commodified art is

138. Helmut Lethen, *Neue Sachlichkeit*, p. 120.
139. Brecht, "Dreigroschenprozess," *GW*, Vol. 18, pp. 156–159.
140. Ibid., p. 158. It should be noted that Brecht showed more care here than Walter Benjamin did later in avoiding the implication of an inherently progressive function of the new media. See Benjamin's "The Work of Art in the Age of Mechanical Reproduction," *Illuminations*, pp. 217–251.
141. Brecht, "Die Dreigroschenprozess," pp. 156–159.

useful, and should not be avoided; it helps to undermine the myth of art as "personal expression," and shows artists their situation as workers and producers.[142]

Brecht's view of the emancipatory potentials of a redirected modern technology was related to his critique of art as the "closed" creation of an omniscient author "distributing" his/her finished cultural products to an audience. This implicitly elitist concept had been continued in Lukács's view that the reader "experiences" the author's "totalizing" integration of reality. Culture was not seen by Lukács as qualitatively redefined by self-determining, collectivist production, but as the passive quantitative *distribution* of the given traditional literary forms.[143] In praising the "popularity" of Maxim Gorki, Roman Rolland, Anatole France, and Thomas Mann, for example, as opposed to the inaccessibility of modernist writers, Lukács had argued that their work had truly "penetrated into the mass."[144] Brecht, on the other hand, had very early broken from the patronizing concept of "laying on" an artistically closed "experience," an approach which merely reinforced the pervasive social training in passive consumption.[145] A modernist insistence upon leaving his dramatic works "open-ended," with contradictions to be resolved by an intellectually aroused audience, was related to the most strongly libertarian and radically democratic components of Brecht's complex political makeup.

Brecht envisioned modern media, if functionally reutilized, working against traditional elitist practices. As in other aspects of his Marxist aesthetics, he argued for going further than questions of altered distribution to a view of culture as interacting production by all. In a series of notes about radio, written in 1932, Brecht spelled out one set of possibilities for the new medium. If each radio were able to receive *and* transmit, allowing the listener to speak as well as to hear, it would be a "vast network of pipes," making producers of all its users and bringing them all "into a relationship instead of isolating them." To give a truly public character to "public occasions," the radio could provide means for the ruled to question the rulers, opening the communication process into a complex network of open challenge, debate, and exchange. To

142. Lethen, *Neue Sachlichkeit*, p. 122. Lethen examines Brecht's "Dreigroschenprozess" in detail on pp. 117–122. The impact of film on Brecht's epic theatre is discussed in Lindner, "Brecht/Benjamin/Adorno," pp. 18–20.
143. This view pervades the 1920 essay, "The Old Culture and the New Culture," and is implicit in many of Lukács's later literary studies.
144. Lukács, "Es geht um den Realismus," p. 82.
145. Walter Sokel, "Brecht und Expressionismus," pp. 72–73.

underline how such a democratically controlled technology could dissolve the previously closed processes of social and cultural transmission from "on high," Brecht emphasized that the prime objective could be that of "turning the audience not only into pupils but into teachers." If such a libertarian and democratic use of modern technical production appeared "utopian," Brecht concluded, "then I would ask you to consider why it is utopian." [146]

146. Bertolt Brecht, "Der Rundfunk als Kommunikationsapparat," GW, Vol. 18, pp. 129–131. See Hans Magnus Enzensberger, "The Consciousness Industry: Constituents of a Theory of Media," New Left Review, 64 (November–December, 1970) for an extrapolation from Brecht's suggestions. There is a full examination of Brecht's thoughts on the implications of radio transmission in Peter Groth and Manfred Voigts, "Die Entwicklung der Brechtschen Radiotheorie, 1927–1932," Brecht Jahrbuch, 1976 (Frankfurt a.M., 1977).

CHAPTER 5

Stalinism, Nazism, and History

The Marxist aesthetics of Brecht and Lukács in the 1930s were developed in counterpoint with major political upheavals of these tumultuous years in Germany and Russia, the twin poles of concern for such communist anti-fascists. Aesthetic theory and historical experience mediated one another: Nazism and Stalinism helped to condition their cultural postures, but these realities, in turn, were interpreted through contrasting theoretical lenses, as were the "popular fronts" which each favored. Brecht, for one thing, used his "production aesthetics" as the basis of some searching unpublished critiques of Stalinist society. Both Brecht and Lukács, however, shared a public allegiance and primary orientation (however "independent" in tone) to the communist movement—a pattern that was to be continued by each until their deaths, respectively, in 1956 in East Germany, and in 1971 in Hungary. Both men made their various, sometimes shabby accommodations with a system of bureaucratic and dictatorial rule very far removed indeed from the Marxist program of working-class self-emancipation and radically democratic socialism, which became increasingly excluded from the growing communist monolith. (If anything, it was Lukács, more than Brecht, who actively worked to democratize communism in the 1950s, through his courageous participation in the Hungarian Revolution, so different from Brecht's ambivalent and hedged responses to the workers' uprising in East Germany in June 1953.)[1] While their

---

1. This account is largely limited to their political-cultural thought of 1928–40, since that is the period of the "debate" on modernism and the development of their contrasting Marxist aesthetics. There is no need to treat the post-war years in detail. On Lukács's

responses to Nazi Germany were dramatically different—reflecting contrasts between Lukács's patrician idealism and Brecht's insistence upon class struggles in favor of all the poor—their approaches to Soviet Russia revealed disparities, but within a common Leninist framework. Brecht's private doubts about Stalinism, however, made clear from posthumously published works, went much further than Lukács's, as far as we may judge, and were consistent conclusions from his more libertarian side, the emphasis in his modernist aesthetics. But the issues are more complex than this and need now to be explored, not least for their connection with the variant *cultural* politics of the two figures in the 1930s.

Since 1917, Lukács had been buoyantly optimistic concerning the Bolshevik Revolution, which he saw as a cultural "salvation from abroad." In Morris Watnick's words: "Since the capitalist west, in his view, already found itself in a quagmire of cultural decadence, the Soviet Union stood as the sole remaining hope for nourishing and transmitting that culture to the future." [2] After 1924, political solidarity with Soviet Russia was smoothed, as Lukács moved away from the critical and heretical left Communist perspectives of *History and Class Consciousness*, with its at least potentially democratic stress upon the need for a working class as the creative, self-determining subject in history. If Brecht's choice of Denmark after 1933 was part of a pattern of distance which he wanted to maintain from Soviet Communist discipline, especially on cultural questions, the Hungarian critic's greater accommodation to Stalinism in these years was symbolized and accentuated by his Moscow exile after 1932.

It was not merely because of his proximity to the Stalinist machine of repression in the 1930s that Lukács was to write, sounding almost official, of "the living heroes who really liberated mankind, the heroes of the great October Revolution." [3] In his literary writings of the period, Lukács made it clear that he regarded Soviet society as having "realized" socialism, [4] a position which lent a retrospective, teleological opti-

---

political career and thinking after 1945 see Michael Löwy, "Lukács and Stalinism," *New Left Review*, 91, (May–June 1975), reprinted in Löwy, *Georg Lukács*; on Brecht's attitudes toward, and behavior in, the *DDR*., see especially Peter Bormans, "Brecht und der Stalinismus," *Brecht Jahrbuch, 1974*, (Frankfurt a.M., 1975) pp. 53–76, which is carefully researched, as is Helmut Dahmer, "Bertolt Brecht and Stalinism," *Telos*, 22 (Winter, 1974–75).

2. Watnick, "Georg Lukács," p. 57.
3. Georg Lukács, *Studies in European Realism* (New York, 1964), p. 241.
4. Ibid.

mism to his view of the historical process. Because of his identification
of Soviet Russia with the cause of socialism and the fight against fascism, Lukács engaged in the self-abasing recantations which allowed
him to remain within the Communist fold and avoid Korsch's political
isolation. Even in his heretical *History and Class Consciousness*, Lukács
had insisted upon the strictest party discipline, continuing Lenin's policy of elevating the intellectual vanguard "to the role of an independent
historical entity which alone embodied the true consciousness of revolution," against Marx's insistence upon the *self-emancipation* of the
working class.[5] Such a view of the party "vanguard" helps to explain
how Lukács managed to wed an elevated, culturally "humanist" Marxism to Stalinist politics. This, however, was not entirely clear until 1935
when Stalin adopted the "popular front" with liberal bourgeois elements which Lukács had wanted since 1928 and had defended indirectly in his literary studies.

Particularly germane to our discussion is Lukács's relation to "socialist realism" in the Soviet Union. Enforcing a literature of sentimentalized "positive heroes," "socialist realism" was part of a broad
Stalinist policy which facilitated official denials of continued social contradictions and struggles; justified the return of social hierarchy and
privilege tied to an "heroically" monumentalist culture; and aided in
the rise of a new uncritical technical and managerial "intelligentsia."[6]
In the era of limited destalinization in the 1960s, Lukács was to claim
that, thirty years before, he had attempted to fight against "socialist realist" policies by implicitly comparing its simplistic propaganda with
the classical realist achievements of Balzac, Tolstoi, and Goethe.[7] It is
true that his critique of a literature produced by party order and judged
for its immediate agitational value, as well as his opposition to a vulgar
Marxist reduction of literature to its class origins, had been aimed

5. Lichtheim, *Georg Lukács*, p. 47. See also the excellent discussion of Lukács's politics after 1928 in Istvan Mészáros, *Lukács' Concept of the Dialectic*, pp. 76–84.

6. Isaac Deutscher, *Stalin: A Political Biography* (New York, 1960), pp. 337–342;
John Berger, *Art and Revolution: Ernest Neizvestny and the Role of the Artist in the
USSR* (New York, 1969), pp. 60–63.

7. Georg Lukács, "Preface," *Writer and Critic*, p. 7. George Steiner ("Georg Lukács
and His Devil's Pact," *Language and Silence* [Middlesex, England, 1969], pp. 291–306)
among older liberal critics, has defended Lukács along these lines. Younger German critics, such as Helga Gallas and Klaus Völker, have claimed, on the other hand, that Lukács
was a major influence upon Zhdanovite policies with which his literary critical work was
entirely consistent. (See Gallas, *Marxistische Literaturtheorie*, and Völker, "Brecht und
Lukács.") The two contrasting interpretations are defended, significantly, by reference to
different aspects of Lukács's work, e.g., his critique of propagandistic art, or his attacks
on western "decadence."

squarely at officially sanctioned practice in Russia, and that these positions often placed Lukács in great danger.[8] Equally significant, however, was that the critic's narrow championing of the classical realist tradition and his virulent rejection of modernist "decadence" provided shreds of intellectual respectability for the literal liquidation of modernist experiment and experimenters. Furthermore, although Lukács may have seen his Balzac model as an implicit critique of the trivialities of current "socialist realism," his own argument for a reassuring plot outline, with positively portrayed individual heroes, was eminently consistent with the official theory, even if its practitioners failed to present Lukács's desired "social totality" in their works.[9] In this, Lukács's position came close to a dignified, sophisticated version of Soviet party doctrine. The underlying structural similarity lay in his continued use of a fixed and static notion of "culture," the democratization of which amounted merely to its increased "distribution" among the masses, a goal which Soviet authorities could accommodate without relinquishing their power. Significantly, Lukács had written in 1920: "Communism aims at creating a social order in which everyone is able to live in a way that in precapitalist eras was possible only for the ruling class."[10]

Brecht shared much with Lukács in his attitude toward the Soviet Union in the 1930s. Unlike his Marxist teachers, Korsch and Sternberg, Brecht refused to break with Soviet Russia despite a growing skepticism, or at least ambivalence, toward Stalin's rule. To abandon official communism, especially at a time when he felt that it alone represented the defense of Europe against fascism, would be a grave mistake; it would also mean "isolating oneself from the masses."[11] Faced with the same dilemma as many other leftist intellectuals in the period—how to reconcile moral and political scruples, i.e., misgivings about Stalinism, with effective action in a critical situation—Brecht chose the "useful," as he saw it, while being "positively critical."[12] Skeptical of Stalinism within a general stance of support, his criticisms were mental reservations which allowed dialectical approaches to political issues and an ongoing questioning of events with the posing of alternative explanations. In his many private writings on developments within the Com-

8. Hans-Dietrich Sander, *Marxistische Ideologie und Allgemeine Kunsttheorie*, pp. 220–229; Hans-Jürgen Schmitt, ed., *Die Expressionismusdebatte: Materialien zu einer marxistischen Realismus-Konzeption* (Frankfurt a.M., 1973), p. 10.
9. Lukács, "The Intellectual Physiognomy of Literary Characters," p. 125.
10. Lukács, "The Old Culture of the New Culture," p. 5.
11. Völker, *Bertolt Brecht; Eine Biographie*, p. 182.
12. Brecht, *Arbeitsjournal, 1938–1955*, Vol. 1, p. 36 (entry for Jan. 19, 1939).

munist movement and the Soviet Union, Brecht gave vent to his playful
and suspicious instincts by simultaneously juxtaposing arguments for
and against official policies, often with the aid of the penetrating critiques of Korsch and Fritz Sternberg, friends and teachers whom he
continued to cultivate. Yet, these contradictory and sometimes unresolved experiments were a private mental dialectic. Publicly, such as in
his speeches to groups of anti-fascist writers in 1935 and 1936, he un-
equivocally supported Soviet internal policies,[13] and he finally settled, of
course, in Stalinist East Germany after World War II.

However strong his equivocations and ambivalence, Brecht sought to
discipline his personal responses as a political actor, the darker side of
that attempted liquidation of ego and subjectivity which we have seen in
many aspects of his work. In *The Measures Taken* (1931), Brecht presented this Leninist subordination of self to party decision and discipline in an exploratory manner, creating a situation in which such actions were neither "humanistic" nor easy, but painful and uncertain,
while he accentuated the agonizing contradictions of a real situation.[14]
It was an exercise in quieting his own doubts about absolute group
commitment and the necessity of force and violence for social change in
certain historical situations. His avoidance here of the comforting sim-
plicities of the more sentimental Gorki works admired by Lukács, in
which questionable actions were performed only by the ruling classes,
won Brecht Moscow's embarrassed strictures upon the play.[15] Yet, although he may have provided aesthetic interest and realist candor in
such works, they suggest his adoption of the fundamentals of a Leninist
politics which he continued to hold until his death. (Brecht was, of
course, in disagreement with Lenin's philosophical position, his crude
theory of reflection, and his cultural traditionalism.) Brecht's Leninism
was as enlightened, democratic, and humane as was possible within
such a species of authoritarian praxis: stressing the need for a critical-
minded Marxism; the diffusion of social and cultural experiment; the
active participation of the *whole* party, in contact with the working
masses, in major decisions, etc. He *was* drawn, however, to the cunning
practicality of Lenin's thought and action, which contrasted sharply
with sentimentalized humanism,[16] and probably a little also to the

13. Brecht, "Aufsätze über den Faschismus," *GW*, Vol. 20, p. 245.
14. Brecht, "The Measures Taken," pp. 75–108 of *The Jewish Wife and Other Short
Plays* (New York, 1965).
15. Esslin, *Brecht*, pp. 163–164.
16. David Bathrick, "The Dialectics of Legitimation," pp. 101–102. According to

cold, stereotypically "masculine" ruthlessness which he could never quite achieve himself. His political relation to Leninism was perhaps best shown in a statement he made to Walter Benjamin in 1938: "In Russia a dictatorship rules over the proletariat. One should avoid as long as possible cutting oneself off from it insofar as this dictatorship still performs practical tasks for the proletariat . . . ."[17] Shortly before his death in 1956, Brecht wrote: "The liquidation of Stalinism can only succeed through a gigantic mobilization of the wisdom of the masses by the party."[18] This is not quite the naive notion of bureaucratic self-reform; the emphasis upon mass input is significant. Yet, Brecht fundamentally failed to oppose a self-perpetuating elite, viewing mass action as productive and purposive only through being directed by the party. On the early months of the German Democratic Republic, he even wrote in his journal: "There were tasks which, under the given circumstances, had to be carried out without support, indeed with the resistance of the workers."[19]

With a full play of contradictory argument for and against, Brecht sought in the end to defend the dictatorial Stalinist bureaucracy by stressing its alleged necessity for rapidly expanding economic production, which was needed in turn to equalize the conditions of life for the various social strata.[20] Later in the decade, he emphasized the necessities of military production to defend against Nazi Germany.[21] Both arguments, of course, were familiar forms of Stalinist apologia, rendered somewhat plausible because the economic and international situation would, in any case, have made the implementation of a truly democratic and free society very difficult even if there had been the political will to do so. But such arguments also suggested the legitimating aspects of Brecht's "production aesthetics," which could imply a technical and industrial "domination of nature" (both of the outer environment and the human being) which was being realized in Stalinist societies.[22]

Brecht's criticism of the purges, significantly, was limited to the lack

Tretjakov, Brecht studied and quoted Lenin "as a great thinker," and possessed many of his works in his library. See Hubert Witt, ed., *Brecht as They Knew Him* (New York, 1974), p. 77.

17. Benjamin, *Understanding Brecht*, p. 121.
18. Brecht, "Vorschläge für den Frieden," *GW*, Vol. 20, pp. 325–326.
19. Brecht, *Arbeitsjournal, 1938–1955*, Vol. 2, p. 1009.
20. Brecht, "Marxistische Studien," *GW*, Vol. 20, pp. 66, 101–107; Bormans, "Brecht und der Stalinismus," p. 65.
21. Brecht, "Marxistische Studien," *GW*, Vol. 20, pp. 104–105.
22. David Bathrick, "Affirmative and Negative Culture," pp. 181–183. The critique

of proofs of guilt which had been advanced, and did not address the
political and ideological premises of the purges.[23] (Like everyone else in
the West, Brecht was, of course, ignorant of the sheer extent of the
purges, which involved millions of persons beyond the party.)[24] In all
this, Brecht attempted desperately to retain hope in this one concrete
alternative to Western capitalism and fascism, feeling, no doubt, that
the abandonment of this commitment would mean a return to the aimless and chaotic nihilism and pessimism that he felt in the early 1920s,
for him a political and cultural dead end. There was much here that
Brecht shared with Lukács, however more dialectically open-ended and
"modern" Brecht's optimism may have been. A productivist focus on
scientific and technological "progress," no less than a "humanist" one
emphasizing the continuity of classical culture, could provide an apologia for Stalinism. But Brecht's "production aesthetics," as we saw in the
previous chapter, also had a sharp critical edge which could be aimed
against the undemocratic and authoritarian nature of an industrializing
Soviet Russia.

The depth of Brecht's doubts about Soviet society, his entertaining of
theoretical perspectives from the Western left opposition to Stalinism,
and particularly the way in which he developed Marxist cultural theory
as a critique of Soviet political economy (and not merely as a narrowly
ideological or aesthetic matter) led to more searching critiques of Stalinism in the 1930s than Lukács advanced. Many of Brecht's legitimating
arguments, at least when presented to friends or in his private writings,
were treated tentatively, within a counterpoint of defense *and* critique, a
symptom of his ambivalence, no doubt, but also of his intellectual independence. His opting for exile in Denmark is significant. (That Brecht
did not choose the Soviet Union is attributable in part, of course, to his
awareness of the fate of Russian avant-garde artists under the Stalinist
liquidation of cultural experiment in the 1930s.[25] The concrete physical
danger was quite real, should he emigrate East.)

Brecht's questioning of Soviet cultural policy in the 1930s extended,
however, to frequent critical observations on the social, political, and
ideological *roots* of the artistic straitjacketing there. He was appalled
by the deterioration of Marxism in Russia into a closed, ideological,

---

of all technocratic instrumentalizing of outer and inner nature was made by Adorno and
Horkheimer in *Dialectic of Enlightenment* (New York, 1972), first published in 1947.
    23. Ibid., pp. 111–116; Bormans, "Brecht und der Stalinismus," pp. 63–65.
    24. See especially Roy Medvedev, *Let History Judge: The Origins and Consequences
of Stalinism* (New York, 1971).
    25. See John Fuegi, "The Soviet Union and Brecht."

self-justifying system, controlled by a "clerical camarilla" and transformed into a static and uncritical *Weltanschauung*.[26] He strongly criticized the subordination of Western Communist parties to Stalin's view
of Russia's needs, and he deplored the resultant decay of critical intelligence within party ranks.[27] We have already cited his attempts to
defend the Stalinist bureaucracy in terms of economic and military necessities. Yet, he also took very seriously the most thoroughgoing of critiques. "Only blockheads can deny," he said to Walter Benjamin in
1938, that "Russia is now under personal rule."[28] More fundamentally,
he was well aware of Korsch's attack on the Soviet bureaucratic apparatus, and he himself frequently questioned Soviet claims that the
bureaucracy was serving the interests of the working masses instead
of its own political rule.[29] With Walter Benjamin as his audience, he
impersonated the Soviet State and slyly pouted: "I know I *ought* to
wither away."[30] In letters to Korsch in 1939 and 1941, he asked the anti-
Stalinist heretic to provide a dialectical analysis of the problems of economic growth in the Soviet Union and their relations to the destruction
of independent working-class organizations, and he commented skep-
tically on the alleged historical justification for the elimination of the
Soviets.[31]

By remaining outside the Stalinist orbit (in exile first in Denmark,
then in Sweden, Finland, and the U.S.), it may be that Brecht was able to
produce his finest work free from official discipline in the late 1930s and
early 1940s, and from the sorry spectacle of an actually functioning Stalinist society, an independence which he lost in adopting East Germany
in 1948.[32] His more directly political pronouncements or dramas (*Arturo Ui*, *The Roundheads and the Peakheads*, etc.), however, do not always show the insight and lively imagination which he generally managed to keep intact in the years of exile. Brecht's libertarian, playful,
and skeptical side was primarily channeled, it appears, into his aesthetic
theories and those plays and poems whose connection with politics was

26. Brecht to Korsch, letters of 1937 and February, 1939, held at International Institute of Social History, Amsterdam. The letters are numbered 1386/27 and 210/02. Benjamin, *Understanding Brecht*, pp. 114–115.
27. Brecht, "Me-ti. Buch der Wendungen," *GW*, Vol. 12, p. 539.
28. Benjamin, *Understanding Brecht*, p. 117.
29. Brecht, "Me-ti. Buch der Wendungen," *GW*, Vol. 12, p. 537.
30. Benjamin, *Understanding Brecht*, p. 115.
31. Brecht to Korsch, letter of February, 1939, 210/02; Rasch, "Bertolt Brechts Marxistischer Lehrer," pp. 998–1000.
32. See, for example, Hannah Arendt, "Bert Brecht, 1898–1956," *Men in Dark
Times* (New York, 1968), pp. 212–216, and Lichtheim, *Europe in the Twentieth Century*,
p. 144.

more indirect (*Galileo, The Caucasian Chalk Circle*, etc.) In a sense, then, Brecht's art and his Marxist aesthetics contained—in sublimated form—the critical social and political perspectives which his overt Leninist politics only weakly provided.

His dispute with Soviet aesthetics, for example, was widely framed and included in its range of criticism some of the main directions of Soviet society. He did not merely charge that realist literature must serve a critical function in relation to developing social reality, that the cheery positivism of so-called "socialist realism" utterly failed in this regard,[33] and that the Soviet's attacks on Western modernist "decadence" resembled a similar pseudoclassicism of the Nazi regime.[34] His critique of Soviet cultural life went further and embodied the most democratic and libertarian aspects of his "production aesthetics": measured against the standard of an emancipating social production, Soviet art merely continued the alienated pseudo-autonomy of passively received art "objects." Just as the replacement of privately concentrated property by state control did not ensure that alienated factory labor would be overcome—since it was yet to be controlled by the producers themselves in the Soviet Union—so the mere *appropriation* of traditional cultural production had not put an end to the reified concept and experience of art.[35] But this restriction of literature simply translated a wider failure: instead of qualitatively emancipating social labor, the Stalinist regime focused entirely on quantitatively increased production.[36] In both the party-controlled economy and the traditionalist restriction of realist literary techniques, "the new humanity of the class-conscious proletariat"—of both factory and intellectual laborers—was not being permitted "to form itself."[37]

❖   ❖   ❖

Of even greater immediate importance than the assessment of Soviet development in the 1930s was the need to fight the Nazi regime in Germany. For Lukács, as George Lichtheim has written, "the decisive battle

33. Brecht, "Aufsätze zur Literatur," *GW*, Vol. 19, pp. 445–446.
34. Brecht, *Arbeitsjournal, 1938–1955*, Vol. 1, pp. 13–14. The context of Brecht's comparison of Nazi and Stalinist cultural policy was a critique of Lukács in his private journal. The point had been made more publicly, and in the expressionism debate, by Ernst Bloch and Hans Eisler, in "Die Kunst zu Erben," reprinted in *Marxismus und Literatur*, Vol 2, pp. 105–109.
35. Brecht, "Marxistische Studien," *GW*, Vol. 20, p. 120; Brüggemann, *Literarische Technik und Soziale Revolution*, pp. 104–115.
36. Brüggemann, *Literarische Technik und Soziale Revolution*, pp. 104–115.
37. Brecht, "Bemerkungen zum Formalismus," *GW*, Vol. 19, p. 316.

had to be fought out at the level of conscious choice between the two basic currents within German culture: rationalism and humanism on the one hand, irrationalism and barbarism on the other. In political terms, the intelligentsia had to be converted." Germany's classical tradition—in which Hegel and Marx were linked with the humanist Weimar of Goethe and Schiller—needed to be restored "before it was over-whelmed by the romantic flood and the latter's catastrophic outcome."[38] This perspective was to dominate Lukács's later attempt to trace the alleged "intellectual origins" of Nazism in *Zerstörung der Vernunft* (Destruction of Reason, 1954).

Similarly, Lukács viewed the expressionists, as we have seen, as romantic anti-capitalists whose implicit ideological position—whatever their conscious motives—linked them with the irrationalist mysticism of Wilhelminian philosophy, ostensibly one of the central sources of Nazi belief.[39] Whatever its merits as an interpretation of the literary movement, and these were not very great, the approach failed to go beyond Nazi ideology in interpreting Hitler's regime. With "culture" discussed in terms of historically "progressive" ideologies, and decadence seen as resulting from their overthrow, Lukács neglected a social and political analysis of Nazism, as a movement and as a regime, in its concrete relation to traditional elites and to the hard-pressed lower middle classes. It seemed at times, as the writer Anna Seghers expressed to Lukács in an exchange of letters in 1938, that Lukács was fighting "decadence" more than fascism.[40]

The social implications of Lukács's own position were close to those of patrician anti-fascists, whose leading spokesman, Thomas Mann, provided Lukács with his primary example of contemporary cultural resistance. Neglecting in Mann what was closest to himself, Lukács failed to see that the impulse which moved the novelist "into opposition and exile was not just 'progressive antifascism'; . . . it was rather the antagonism of the cultivated patrician bourgeois to the savage plebeians, the *Kleinbürger and Lumpenproletariat* who were running amok in the shadow of the swastika."[41] Denouncing as "petty bourgeois" such im-

38. Lichtheim, *Georg Lukács*, pp. 85–86.
39. Lukács, "'Grösse und Verfall' des Expressionismus," pp. 11–17. This essay is translated in Lukács, *Essays on Realism*, pp. 76–113.
40. "Ein Briefwechsel zwischen Anna Seghers und Georg Lukács," in *Marxismus und Literatur*, Vol. 2, pp. 129–130. This has also been translated in Lukács, *Essays on Realism*, pp. 167–197.
41. Isaac Deutscher, "Georg Lukács and Critical Realism," *Marxism in Our Time* (Berkeley, Calif., 1972), p. 285.

mature and "irrational" forms of rebellion as expressionism,[42] Lukács sought to fight Nazism by invoking the patrician respectability of earlier bourgeois high culture. His neglect of the material and social needs of the bulk of the German population and his stress on the ideological conflict derived partly from the claim that the intelligentsia occupied a pivotal position and needed to be converted to a "progressive" humanist perspective;[43] but it may also have resulted from Lukács's own concern to allay guilt for his "irrationalist" and "romantic anti-capitalist" youth.

Instead of a struggle between humanist "culture" and fascist "barbarism," Brecht saw the Nazi movement and regime in the much stricter Marxist sense of a conflict between capitalist and proletarian classes. At times he indulged in a common vulgar Marxist identification of fascism with capitalism in crisis. Western European and American capitalism, he argued, had not yet found it necessary to overthrow democratic restraints in their protection of property, as had the German and Italian rich, but their time would soon come.[44] While Lukács avoided *any* class analysis of fascism, Brecht overlooked, as had almost all Marxists of the period, the importance of traditional military, bureaucratic, and aristocratic elites in the victory of Central European fascism, the still very powerful residue of precapitalist social structures. In his plays, his speeches, and his theoretical writings, Brecht's responses to Nazism suffered from other major weaknesses. He never understood the role of the state in smoothing social contradictions, minimizing workers' grievances, and reducing business competition in twentieth-century capitalism, and he thus misleadingly saw fascism as a heightened extension of a long gone "anarchy of production."[45] In *The Resistible Rise of Arturo Ui* and elsewhere, a related crude and obsessive fascination with an analogy between business machinations and anarchic crime made him dangerously trivialize the Nazi juggernaut as a ring of petty gangsters.[46] He was no less blind on the issue of anti-Semitism. As a symptom of an all too orthodox Marxism on this score, where a healthy "revisionism" was sorely needed, often Brecht mechanically reduced "racial" to class

---

42. Lukács, "'Grösse und Verfall' des Expressionismus," p. 39.
43. This defense of Lukács's approach to Nazism in the 1930s, though not his later *Zerstörung der Vernunft*, is made by Lichtheim, *Georg Lukács*, pp. 85–86.
44. Brecht, "Aufsätze über den Faschismus," *GW*, Vol. 20, pp. 188, 239–242.
45. Lethen, *Neue Sachlichkeit*, pp. 124–126; Fetscher, "Bertolt Brecht and America," p. 264.
46. Adorno, "On Commitment," p. 184. More extensively: Müller, *Geschichte im Werk Bertolt Brechts*, pp. 72–76.

issues. (Even the more unorthodox Frankfurt school, Adorno included, did much the same until the mid-1940s.)[47] He even went so far as to predict, in effect (in *The Roundheads and the Peakheads*, 1936), that rich Jews would eventually side with Nazism against poor "Aryans" and poor Jews[48]—as if they would ever have been given the option to do so.

In other ways, Brecht avoided a vulgar Marxist appraisal of Nazism and addressed critical social and ideological issues unseen by Lukács. He gave considerable attention, for example, to the pivotal appeals of Nazism to the lower middle classes, as did other independent Marxists such as Siegfried Kracauer and Ernst Bloch, thus voiding the conspiratorial implications of many a crude Marxist analysis at the time.[49] He recognized full well that Nazism had mass support far beyond the socially privileged. Brecht saw the vaunted *Volksgemeinschaft* as an attempt to obfuscate the class divisions not only between proletarian and capitalist, but between *Mittelstand* small business, white-collar elements and the economic elites.[50] In *Mother Courage*, begun in the late 1930s, he showed an impoverished small trader who in attempting to profit from war merely suffered from the slaughter. Brecht's plays were often concerned with such examples of "false consciousness" among the lower middle classes. He correctly noted, moreover, how ideological manipulation would merely result in the sacrifice of *Kleinhandel* (small trade) to the expanding big business war economy.[51]

47. See Martin Jay, "The Jews and the Frankfurt School: Critical Theory's Analysis of anti-Semitism," *New German Critique*, 19 (Winter 1981).

48. Ewen, *Brecht*, pp. 307–311. See also Brecht, "Aufsätze über den Faschismus," *GW*, Vol. 20, p. 248, where he argues that the essence of the Nazi persecution of the Jews was that Jews and workers were together hounded as part of the class struggle. In *The Jewish Wife*, another short play on racism, he showed somewhat more sensitivity to the particular plight of the Jews. See Brecht, *The Jewish Wife and Other Short Plays* (New York, 1965).

49. Franz Norbert Mennemeier, "Bertolt Brechts Faschismus-Theorie und einige Folgen für die literarische Praxis," in Arntzen, Helmut, et al., eds., *Literaturwissenschaft und Geschichtsphilosophie: Festschrift für Wilhelm Emrich* (Bertlin, 1975), pp. 564–567. Kracauer's *Die Angestellten* (1930) was a pioneering study of the easily manipulated situation of the lower middle classes, a study which was unique in criticizing the Marxist view of an eventual joining of the proletariat by the *Mittelstand*. (See Martin Jay, "The Extraterritorial Life of Siegfried Kracauer," *Salmagundi*, 31/32 [Fall 1975–Winter 1976], 56–57.) Ernst Bloch's *Die Erbschaft dieser Zeit* (1935) was more othodox in its assessment.

50. Brecht, "Aufsätze über den Faschismus," *GW*, Vol. 20, pp. 237–238; Fritz Sternberg, *Der Dichter und die Ratio*, pp. 18–19; Müller, *Geschichte im Werk Bertolt Brechts*, pp. 76–82.

51. On this historical trend after 1933, see David Schoenbaum, *Hitler's Social Revolution* (New York, 1966), pp. 113–151. On the economic and social sources of the plight of the *Mittelstand* in the Weimar Republic, see Chapters 1 and 2 of Hermann Lebovics, *Social Conservatism and the German Middle Classes, 1914–1933* (Princeton, N.J., 1968).

Instead of seeing the ideological struggle between romantic irrationalism and a classical humanism revamped for twentieth-century
usage, the view which brought Lukács in line with liberal anti-fascists,
Brecht concentrated on Nazi idealist rhetoric and its capacity to obscure
the material problems of the masses, especially the lower middle classes.
He pointed out, for example, how idealistic self-sacrifice for *Volk*, soil,
and race was officially enjoined for the unpolitical and economically in-
secure *Kleinbürger* and passionately embraced by them.[52] In Brecht's
eyes, an elevated idealist humanism was an unproductive response to
such mythologizing heroic rhetoric, since this merely continued the
struggle at a level of reified abstraction which favored the Nazi ability to
hide the real world. What was needed, instead of talk about defending
"Kultur," was a literature of plain-speaking plebeian realism. This
Brecht attempted to present in works such as *Schweik in the Second
World War*, whose "idiotic" little "hero" subverts, out of practical op-
portunism, the heroic poses of those in power. If culture is to be defended, Brecht argued further, it needs to be seen in relation to the entire productive activity of the masses.[53]

The experience of Nazism heightened Brecht's desire for a realist literature which would reveal a material reality hidden by official culture.[54] In this art, no period or literary style had a monopoly, although
certain modernist techniques possessed advantages over more classical
procedures. Explicitly countering Lukács, Brecht defended modernist
experiment where it had exposed a reality opaque to everyday or individual "experience," and cited Nazi manipulation of language and visual image as the real formalism. His suspicion of the aesthetics of catharsis had been accentuated by an observation of Nazi theatricality, the
deliberate Wagnerian construction of an illusionary reality with which
spectators would passionately identify.[55] A sharp rejection of vicariously
fulfilling emotionality and insistence upon critical observation and intelligence, moreover, were closely connected with an awareness of the
manipulated psychodrama of Nazi political culture.[56] To paraphrase

52. Brecht, "Aufsätze über den Faschismus," *GW*, Vol. 20, p. 182.
53. Ibid., p. 249.
54. Brecht, "Praktisches zur Expressionismus debatte," *GW*, Vol. 19, pp. 292–296.
55. Brecht, "Radiotheorie, 1927–1932," *GW*, Vol. 18, p. 132; "Bemerkungen zum
Formalismus," *GW*, Vol. 19, pp. 313–319. For an excellent discussion of this aspect of
Nazi culture see Siegfried Kracauer, *From Caligari to Hitler: A Psychological History of
the German Film* (Princeton, 1960), pp. 300–303, where the Nazi film *Triumph des
Willens* is analyzed.
56. *Brecht on Theatre*, p. 145; Ewen, *Bertolt Brecht*, pp. 217–218.

Walter Benjamin, Brecht's politicizing of art intended to challenge the aestheticized politics of the Nazis.[57]

Like Lukács after 1928 and official Communist policy after 1934, Brecht also favored a popular front against Nazism. But whereas Lukács sought bourgeois liberal allies for the working classes and accentuated the classical patrician strand of the literary heritage, Brecht worked for a united front from below, one made up of workers, the lower middle classes, peasants, and the alienated intelligentsia against the economic and political elites, either old or new. His criterion for inclusion was that all those should unite together who lacked control over their means of production, although—in orthodox fashion—he assumed a central position for the industrial proletariat.[58] This class, however, was not to be approached simply as a passive object of party policy: his hope for a popular front of the SPD and KPD against the Nazis, which Stalin had effectively opposed in the critical years 1930–33, had been for a common effort of rank-and-file workers, and not simply for alliances of parliamentarians, trade union bureaucrats, and Communist officials.[59]

❖ ❖ ❖

In their responses to Stalinism and Nazism, Brecht and Lukács revealed different views of the modern historical process. Laboring under the strain of his own extremely pessimistic view of Western society and culture before and during World War I, Lukács moved in the late 1920s and the 1930s, after abandoning the more open-ended historical perspectives of *History and Class Consciousness*, toward a compensatory, opposite pole—a sanitized Marxism with history conceived as inevitable stages of progress. His portrayal of Nazism as "barbaric" and "decadent" denuded the contemporary world of its real contradictions and terrors as he set "heroic" Soviet "progress" in a contrasting positive light. The latter would bypass the "decay" and "sickness" of advanced capitalist society and continue the progressive culture of an earlier

57. The formulation is used in Walter Benjamin's "The Work of Art in the Age of Mechanical Reproduction," p. 242.

58. Brecht, "Aufsätze über den Faschismus," *GW*, Vol. 20, pp. 259–260; and "Writing the Truth: Five Difficulties," p. 150.

59. Fritz Sternberg, *Der Dichter und die Ratio*, pp. 26–27. In the Comintern's policy of 1921–8 there were stronger elements of a popular front "from below" (including, some felt, lower middle classes) than after 1934. See Helmut Gruber, *International Communism in the Era of Lenin; A Documentary History* (New York, 1967), pp. 359–371, 411, 491–498.

bourgeois humanism. In a manner very similar to Stalinist polemics, Lukács's now deterministic view of history allowed him to view modern Western art as "objectively" reactionary.

For one who had contrived to believe in a closed historical process of progressive stages known in advance, Western modernist pessimism was to be repressed in favor of the implicitly progressive perspectives found in a Balzac or Goethe, or the "enthusiastic certainty of victory" which the critic found in Gorki.[60] What Lukács demanded of literature, in effect, and what Kafka, Joyce, and Toller did not provide, was a continuous reassurance that this road to progress was inevitably proceeding in spite of capitalist "decay," world war, and fascism (and often in spite of the author's own political sympathies). His adoption of an Hegelian teleology of history's "cunning" and immanent rationality, as well as his passive aesthetics of reflection, are to be seen in this light: if art helps, through a positive resolution of contradictions, to convince one of inexorable progress toward human fulfillment, then there remains little urgency to intervene actively for its success.

Lukács's optimism needed constant protection against the painful doubts raised by contemporary European and particularly German experience. This helps to explain the frantic tone of his one-sided attacks on all deviations from nineteenth-century historical rationalism. The experience of fascism was thereby prevented from influencing the simple faith in progress, reason, and humanity cultivated by Lukács since the early 1920s. One of the central building blocks for this evasion of the troubling realities of contemporary history was the extreme geographical split within his perceptions, which separated a sanitized, young, and fresh Soviet Russia from the "decaying" West of advanced capitalism. In the 1930s, neither area received from Lukács the kind of critical analysis which was needed. Instead, he largely identified himself with Stalinist Russia and read the Western cultural tradition with a retrospective optimism, condemning the modernists for their despairing abandonment of the faith in history.

Brecht did not embrace such a pacified optimism (though some of his comments concerning Soviet industrial "progress" came close to this). Instead, Marxist perspectives after 1928 provided him with "seedlings of hope" which he planted in a ground of historical pessimism and skepticism framed by experiences of war, fascism, and Stalinism. One of the recurrent motifs of all his poetry and drama is the imagery of the

60. Lukács, "The Ideal of the Harmonious Man in Bourgeois Aesthetics," p. 99.

"dark times" in which we live (as in his poem "To Posterity").[61] Refusing to turn his back on the palpable experience of despair which his early plays and poems reveal, Brecht feared that Nazism might usher in a "new dark age." By the late 1930s, he was thinking beyond the immediate conflicts to "encompass all the social struggles of humanity, where qualities like cunning and endurance are more important than heroism." Instead of the well-rounded individuals of Lukács's liking, Brecht's wise "sages" were anonymous, resourceful, and resilient men or women of the masses—Galy Gay, Herr Keuner, Azdak, or Schweik—who ask questions "even from under the wheels," as he wrote of Kafka's characters.[62]

Critics have often failed to see that Brecht's Marxism, instead of being a compensatory optimistic facade which fails to hide a "basically pessimistic" outlook,[63] was deeply enriched by this experience. Like Antonio Gramsci and Walter Benjamin, Brecht avoided the truly pessimistic "optimism" of the official Communist faith in historical inevitability—that disastrous assumption which had inhibited the KPD from effectively resisting the Nazi seizure of power. Brecht managed to live and work in the tension between despair and hope, emphasizing the contradictory nature of every historical moment. This was a major reason for his use of a modernist aesthetics of contingency and uncertainty, which derived from the experience of being poised in a situation fraught simultaneously with great danger and great possibility. History is not an objectively guaranteed march toward a goal already known in advance. Rather, it is a project, mediated by given social realities, but proceeding from the concrete transforming praxis of human beings.[64] The experience of present despair shown in his plays is not denied or evaded by being contrasted with a *potentially* more just future.

Refusing to evade many of the troubling realities of his time through recourse to a comforting faith in inevitable progress, Brecht's art aimed to assault his audience's passive and fatalistic inertia, its adjustment to the "course of things." The shocks of "estrangement" from "normal" perceptions were urgently needed to encourage active intervention into

---

61. This poem is contained in *Selected Poems of Bertolt Brecht*, trans. H.R. Hays (New York, 1959), pp. 173–177.

62. Stanley Mitchell, "Introduction to Benjamin and Brecht," *New Left Review*, 77 (January–February, 1973), 3–4.

63. This view, associated in the United States with the work of Martin Esslin and Robert Brustein, is developed at length in the study of Qayum Qureshi, *Pessimismus und Fortschrittsglaube bei Brecht* (Köln, 1971).

64. Brüggemann, *Literarische Technik und Soziale Revolution*, pp. 90–91.

the historical process. Lukács's retrospective sociology of literary reflections, on the other hand, contained little of this urgency. The critic's carefully preserved belief in the inexorable upward march of history encouraged a contemplative aesthetic whose critical edge was aimed at pessimistic art works which might shake the faith.

Brecht was far more open to the fragmented and contradictory moods of contemporary literature. Works of very different implicit ideological persuasion might well contain "moments" of real experience upon which the reader or audience needed to reflect. Although he viewed Kafka's extreme historical pessimism critically—stressing the different uses to which his literary techniques might be applied—Brecht could also learn from him concerning the resistible dangers of contemporary history, such as alienating bureaucracy, urban life, etc., or prophetic anticipations of a Nazi or Soviet secret police.[65] Literature, in any case, helps to make us aware not of reassuring answers, but of problems to be resolved outside it. Lukács had segregated processes of decay and ascent, compartmentalized them into different historical periods and geographical locations; early bourgeois Europe and contemporary Russia were judged to be "progressive," whereas late bourgeois society was condemned as "decadent." Ernst Bloch wrote, however, in response to Lukács's attack on expressionism: "Aren't there any dialectical relations between decay and ascent? . . . Aren't there here also materials of transition from the old to the new?"[66]

Brecht's art and thought were directed toward problems of contemporary advanced industrial society, from which Lukács sought to escape. Lukács never lost his early revulsion toward twentieth-century culture and the social confusions it revealed. As late as 1970, one year before his death, he wrote: "With its forms of organization, its science and its techniques of manipulation, modern life moves relentlessly toward reducing the word to the mechanical simplicity of a mere sign. That means a radical departure from life."[67] Significantly, his literary taste was for works which reveal the *emergence* of modern social classes (e.g., the French bourgeoisie in Balzac, the Russian proletariat in Gorki), and not the problems of a mature industrial society.[68] His construction

---

65. As in his conversation with Benjamin, p. 108–111 of *Understanding Brecht*.

66. Ernst Bloch, "Diskussionen über Expressionismus," *Marxismus und Literatur*, Vol. 2, p. 56. This essay is translated in *Aesthetics and Politics*, pp. 16–27. Brecht made the same point in his *Arbeitsjournal, 1935–1955*, Vol. 1, pp. 28–29.

67. Lukács, "Preface (1970)," *Writer and Critic*, p. 11.

68. See pp. 207–211, from the chapter on Gorki, in *Studies in European Realism* (New York, 1964).

of a Marxist aesthetics is related to these historical persuasions, especially the traditionalist manner in which he conceived of both realism and humanism.

Brecht's work, on the other hand, was a product of the new, urban, technological society of the Weimar Republic. Very early, he simply accepted this world as his milieu, not bemoaning the passing of classical cultures, but seeking instead to create an art attuned to the new age. In his experimentalism, intentionally open-ended dramas, and brand of Marxist aesthetics, he shared the perspectives of the modernists, especially those who developed cubistic montage and welcomed the twentieth-century world of technology and mass society. Instead of being based on what he saw, on occasion, as the "backward" directions in Stalinist Russia,[69] his Marxism was a response to reified experiences under advanced capitalist conditions in the West. Here, in the asphalt cities of modernity, he sought to redirect its tendencies, saying, in essence, as in one of his critiques of Lukács: "There is no way back. It's a matter not of the good old, but the bad new. Not the dismantling of technology, but its build-up. We will not be human again by leaving the masses, but only through going into them . . . but not in the sense that we were human earlier."[70]

69. Benjamin, *Understanding Brecht*, pp. 116–117.
70. Brecht, "Die Essays von Georg Lukács," *GW*, Vol. 19, p. 298.

PART THREE

Benjamin and Adorno

CHAPTER SIX

Avant-Garde and Culture Industry

Largely independent of Communist politics and the realism issue over which Brecht and Lukács contended, Theodor Adorno and Walter Benjamin were also to confront one another with alternative configurations of Marxism and modernism in the 1930s.[1] (Actually, Adorno was to continue to draw upon Benjamin, as well as to counter his friend's provocative theses, for decades after the latter's death in 1940.) Benjamin and Adorno were both intensely modernist in outlook. The confrontation which we shall construct between their perspectives (for an actual "debate" occurred even less here; Adorno alone took the offensive) centered not on modernism as such, but on the historical meanings to be attached to avant-garde and commercialized "mass" art in capitalist society. Benjamin and Adorno each developed rich and penetrating dialectical readings of the modernist experience since Baudelaire which

---

1. The *Gesammelte Schriften* [hereafter *GS*] of Benjamin and Adorno are in the process of being published by Suhrkamp Verlag, Frankfurt a.M., in 6 vols., 1972– and 23 vols., 1970– , respectively. In the period 1967–73 a virulent controversy (fueled by the events of 1967–68) raged between certain German New Left intellectuals, who favored Benjamin, and followers of the Frankfurt based Institute for Social Research, who sided with Adorno's critiques of Benjamin's Marxism. The issue behind the debate (apart from controversy about the Institute's handling of Benjamin's writings) was the question of how much to revise Marxism, with the Benjamin devotees towing a fairly orthodox line often by sidestepping the eclectic complexities of Benjamin's actual thought. A summary of the debate may be found in "Marxistischer Rabbi," *Der Spiegel*, 22, 16 (April 15, 1968). Both of the thinkers were distorted in the dispute. Since 1973, however, there has been more judicious, extensive and careful consideration of the two, which was especially needed in the case of Benjamin's work. My own research has benefited much from this interpretive work of the last decade, even if I have often found myself differing from specific analyses; the notes that follow should suggest the specifics.

showed a wider grasp and sympathy than either Brecht or Lukács. But these interpretations, in turn, were contrasting ones: Benjamin, as we shall see, was particularly drawn to the spatializing, metaphorical, and depersonalized literature of modern Paris (though also, in time, to Brechtian and Russian constructivist art). Adorno's analyses, on the other hand, were indebted to Austro-German musical and philosophical traditions and to the crisis of subjectivity registered in the Viennese modernism of Freud and Schoenberg. These two axes were to profoundly affect their contrasting assessments of technically reproduced art (what Adorno was to call, pejoratively, the "culture industry" of film, "pop" music, etc.). The "Marxism" with which they interpreted avant-garde and "popular" art was, in both cases, more unorthodox and idiosyncratic than that of either Brecht or Lukács (or almost any other kind of Marxism, for that matter) and was continuously being cross-fertilized by their variant aesthetic sensibilities; such seemingly incompatible currents as psychoanalysis (Adorno) or Jewish mystical theology (Benjamin); as well as a profound historical pessimism which came to dominate Adorno's work and was to remain a major component in Benjamin's ambivalent outlook throughout his life. The differences in their uses of Marxian analysis were also to influence their contrasting orientations toward modern culture. In Chapters 7 and 8, the intellectual biographies of Benjamin and Adorno and the unusually open and supple Marxisms they developed will be studied in order to illuminate their critical work on avant-garde and "mass" culture, which will then be surveyed in Chapter 9. To begin, however, we need once again to lay out the areas of most explicit dispute, or rather Adorno's response in the late 1930s and early 1940s to Benjamin's defense of the film medium and interrelated study of Baudelaire and nineteenth-century Paris.

❖ ❖ ❖

Benjamin (1892–1940) and Adorno (1903–1969) had known each other since 1923, and Adorno had been profoundly impressed and influenced by the older man's pre-Marxist writings published before 1928.[2] By the mid-1930s, however, Benjamin's surrealist tendencies and, more important, his contacts with a Brechtian Marxism which Adorno felt to be a crude species of vulgar materialism caused Adorno to write a series

---

2. Susan Buck-Morss, *The Origin of Negative Dialectics: Theodor W. Adorno, Walter Benjamin and the Frankfurt Institute* (New York, 1977), pp. 20–25, 69–110.

of letters to him which strongly objected to the shift in his outlook. He criticized, in particular, Benjamin's positive views of the new mass media and the undialectical approaches he found in Benjamin's materialist study of Baudelaire and his Paris. A number of Adorno's most important essays written from 1936 to 1945 (studies of radio, film, jazz, and popular music) were attempts, among other things, to refute Benjamin's analyses of the "popular" arts. Later we shall integrate this confrontation into the respective bodies of work which each man produced. (In Benjamin's case, this will reveal the studied ambivalence that his work *as a whole* shows toward the crisis of traditional culture which Brecht had seen simply as a hopeful opportunity.) For the moment, we shall concentrate on those of Benjamin's essays which drew Adorno's fire and on the various responses Benjamin made to these criticisms, a political-aesthetic encounter about which a great deal has been written in the past decade.[3]

In 1936, Benjamin published a now famous essay entitled "The Work of Art in the Age of Mechanical Reproduction," which was strongly influenced by Brechtian themes. The essay concentrated upon defining the "aura" of traditional art before the twentieth century, and analyzed its decay under the impact of new cultural technologies. Cinema, in particular, he argued, tended to dispel the "auratic" traces left upon art through its successive historical functions as part of magic and ritual, religious worship, and the secular cult of beauty since the Renaissance. Now, with the final decay of its auratic spell as an object of cultic reverence, art was a potential instrument in the emancipation of the

3. I am speaking here less of the specific controversies of 1967–73 than of various broader attempts to compare the basic structure of Adorno's and Benjamin's thought in considerations which seek to throw light in this way on Adorno's letters of the 1930s. The two major studies in English are Martin Jay, *The Dialectical Imagination*, pp. 173–218, and Susan Buck-Morss, *The Origin of Negative Dialectics*, especially chapters 8–11. Both writers side with Adorno's positions and treat his thought in greater detail than Benjamin's. Philip Slater, *The Origin and Significance of the Frankfurt School: A Marxist Perspective* (London 1977), pp. 119–148, and Zienhard Wawrzyn, *Walter Benjamin's Kunsttheorie: Kritik einer Rezeption* (Darmstadt, 1973) are very hostile toward Adorno within the context of an orthodox Marxist reading of Benjamin. A number of shorter comparative treatments distribute their critical comments toward both: Helmut Pfotenhauer, *Aesthetische Erfahrung und gesellschaftliche System: Untersuchungen zum Spätwerk Walter Benjamin* (Stuttgart, 1975), pp. 44–52, 84–102; Michael T. Jones, "Constellations of Modernity: The Literary Essays of Theodor W. Adorno," Doctoral dissertation, Yale University, 1978, pp. 180–202; Andrew Arato, "Esthetic Theory and Cultural Criticism," in the *Essential Frankfurt School Reader*, ed. Andrew Arato and Eike Gebhardt (New York, 1979), pp. 207–219; "Presentation III," in *Aesthetics and Politics* (London, 1977), pp. 100–109; and Burckhardt Lindner, "Herrschaft als Trauma: Adorno's Gesellschaftstheorie zwischen Marx und Benjamin," *Text und Kritik*, 56 (1977), 72–91.

masses. Thus, the historical trajectory of art passed from religion to politics.[4] Appearing to draw on Weber's notion of the inexorable *Entzauberung* (literally, "demagification") of the modern world, Benjamin read it, in effect, with the more optimistic Enlightenment perspective of the *Communist Manifesto*: capitalism, in this view, had stripped the idealistic and theological "halo" away from our perceptions of human relationships.[5]

Emphasizing that the historical meaning of art changes with the character of its technical production, Benjamin suggested that the reproducibility of photos, prints, and, most of all, film destroyed the sense of uniqueness, unapproachability, authenticity, and rootedness in cultural tradition of "auratic" art. Late-nineteenth-century aesthetes had attempted to salvage this secularized "theology" of autonomous culture in the face of the increasingly profitable exhibition value of art and the advent of new technical media such as photography. However, the social advance of the masses and the invention of media such as film, which depends upon distribution to the masses, had led to the inexorable "decay of aura" in the twentieth century.[6] This meant that all attempts to create self-contained, unique, and autonomous art and literature were both hopeless and anachronistic.

Defining "aura," at one point, as uniqueness and the "phenomena of distance, however close [an object] may be," Benjamin singled out two circumstances which led to its present decay: the "desire of contemporary masses to bring things closer spatially and humanly," and their "just as ardent . . . bent toward overcoming the uniqueness of every reality by accepting its reproduction." Thus, the social basis of the decay of aura was, in his view, the "sense of the universal equality of things" which imbued the contemporary masses. Montage and radical juxtapositions—in both technically reproducible art and the work of dadaists and surrealists—were historically conditioned by the masses' attempt to overcome spatial, temporal, and social distances, such as those between high and low (economically and culturally), past and present, there and here.[7]

4. Benjamin, *Illuminations*, pp. 217–252.

5. Arato, "Esthetic Theory and Cultural Criticism," p. 209; Irving Wohlfahrt, "'The Smallest Guarantee, the Straw at Which the Drowning Man Clutches': On the Messianic Structure of Walter Benjamin's Last Reflections," *Glyph*, 3 (1978), 192.

6. Benjamin, *Illuminations*, pp. 217–228.

7. Ibid., p. 223. For a fuller discussion of Benjamin's concept of aura and its decay, see Wawrzyn, *Walter Benjamins Kunsttheorie*, pp. 25–40, and Heinz Paetzold, "Walter Benjamin's Theory of the End of Art," in *International Journal of Sociology*, 7 (1977), 25–75.

Although Benjamin was composing, almost simultaneously, other essays which suggested the irreplaceable losses to human experience in the destruction of the auratic tradition, here in the "Work of Art" essay he saw only positive results from the disintegrating process. This was clearest in his one-sided estimation of the tendencies of cinematic art. The very mechanism of film production, he was suggesting, is inherently progressive, though this effect is thwarted by the subordination of cinema in capitalist society to the interests of the moviemakers' capital. For one thing (this was one of the most dubious of Benjamin's overoptimistic judgments), the elimination of the actual unique presence of the actor (as distinguished from theatre) and the discontinuous montage of performances which make up the edited and constructed film "role" (disallowing identification of the actor with his character) lead to the vanishing of his own "aura." Here Benjamin acknowledged that the movie industry resisted this by building up the star "personality" artificially outside the studio, but he insisted that this was an attempt to resist the implications of their own mode of production.[8] As for the reception of film, Benjamin emphasized the positive value of the less concentrated and more distracted state of mind with which the mass audiences viewed cinema, as compared with the more individualized experience of paintings or novels. The mastery of skills and the tactile appropriation of the world cannot be accomplished largely through contemplation, he argued; noticing the object in incidental fashion, in an almost absentminded state of distraction, the public could tactile appropriate the material as a matter of habit.[9] Rather than creating an absence of knowledgeable understanding, this was a new form of "expertise" in which critical and receptive attitudes of the public coincide. As with sports, which lead to such "expert" discussions of a bicycle race as that among a "group of newspaper boys leaning on their bicycles," Benjamin alleged that a similar active awareness fuses with visual and emotional enjoyment in the moviegoing public when seeing, for example, a Chaplin film. This unity, he emphasized, is what makes an artistic reception a "progressive" one. This process is most advanced in Russia, Benjamin argued, citing the experiments of "worker correspondents" in the press, a literary acknowledgment of the technical expertise of the readers-turned-writers. In Russian film, analogously, workers are not so much actors as people who portray themselves in their work process. All these interlocking changes heralded the eclipse of "distance" in the

8. Benjamin, *Illuminations*, pp. 229–231.
9. Ibid., pp. 231–235.

production and reception of art and its transformation from an unap-
proachable and unique object of worship (facilitating submission to authority, Benjamin implied) to an agent of collective self-emancipation.[10]

Although he did not at all make this clear, Benjamin was doubtless
constructing what he felt at the time to be an historically plausible
(though, for all that, no less utopian) scenario. The vulnerability of the
essay (besides the fact that it had not caught up with Soviet realities of
the 1930s) lay in his apparent insistence that all these changes were not
so much potential uses as *inherent* implications of the new media. What
prevented their immediate realization, in his view, was the dialectic of
productive modes and productive relations in capitalist society, the contradictions most extreme in the Nazi subversion of the emancipating
implications both of technology and modern collective society. Fascism
and Nazism, he emphasized, preserve the property system by giving the
"masses not their right, but instead a chance to express themselves."
Similarly, technology is violated in the glorification of an aestheticized
modern violence which is the culmination of "l'art pour l'art." Citing
Marinetti's futurist celebration of the "beauties" of mechanized warfare
(enriching a "flowery meadow with the fiery orchids of machine guns"),
Benjamin argued that fascism "expects war to supply the artistic grati-
fication of a sense perception that has been changed by technology."
The self-alienation of mankind, Benjamin commented, "has reached
such a degree that it can experience its own destruction as an aesthetic
pleasure of the first order." "This is the situation of politics which fascism is rendering aesthetic," Benjamin concluded; "Communism," on
the other hand, "responds by politicizing art."[11]

Without addressing himself specifically to the issue of fascism,
Adorno responded to Benjamin's essay with a strong dissent from many
of its major theses. In a letter of March 1936 to Benjamin, he agreed
that the "aural element of the work of art is declining," but he objected
to the "sublimated remnant of certain Brechtian motifs" which he
found in Benjamin's interpretation of that decline. The avant-garde "autonomous work of art," which Benjamin appeared to view as illusionary, magical, and auratic (and therefore counterrevolutionary), Adorno
described as decreasingly so as a result of the technical self-liquidation
of its aura through the immanent development of its own "formal
laws." Citing Kafka and particularly Schoenberg, he stressed how art-

10. Ibid., pp. 234–241.
11. Ibid., pp. 241–242.

ists working on the problems of this seemingly hermetic art were chang-ing it into a technically planned work, and that it was this immanent process which was diminishing the mythical, fetishized qualities of avant-garde production. Isolated and reified as it may be by the alien-ated division of labor in capitalist culture (which creates a chasm be-tween "serious" and "popular" art), "autonomous" art dialectically juxtaposes this magical element with what approximates a "state of freedom," in which a product reveals how it is "consciously produced and made." To politicize this art in a Brechtian sense, to place it in the service of immediate use-values, is to destroy this transcending and truly progressive component.[12]

Over thirty years later, in his last major work, *Aesthetische Theorie*, Adorno was to continue this line of argument in a focus on the process of de-aestheticization (*Entkunstung*) in modern avant-garde art, the consciously executed destruction of aura.[13] This did not mean the end of traditional art through the extrinsic intervention of machine technol-ogy or the masses (Benjamin's argument), but rather its immanent tech-nical development in which auratic qualities are eroded from within. In the face of a Brechtian politicized art or the affirmative "culture indus-try," this process kept alive the primary function of art as a negation of a completely instrumentalized world:[14] only "where art observes its im-manence does it convince practical reason of its absurdity."[15] In a truly free society, such negative "autonomous" art might not be necessary, but today the danger, according to Adorno, is its premature func-tionalized reconciliation with a repressive world: "It is not unthinkable that humanity, once it has attained realization, no longer needs a closed, immanent culture; [however,] today a false abolition of culture, a vehi-cle of barbarism, threatens."[16]

Adorno charged in his letter to Benjamin that his friend had overesti-mated the technicality of "dependent art" while underestimating that of autonomous art. Montage and other advanced techniques are very little used in film; "rather, reality is everywhere constructed with an infantile mimetism and then 'photographed.'" If anything has an "auratic" char-

12. Adorno to Benjamin, 18 March 1976, in *Aesthetics and Politics*, pp. 120–126.
13. Adorno, *Ästhetische Theorie* (Frankfurt a.M., 1970), p. 123.
14. Ibid., p. 336.
15. Ibid., p. 475.
16. Ibid., p. 424. For fuller discussions of this last work of Adorno's on aesthetics, see Gerhard Kaiser, *Benjamin, Adorno: Zwei Studien* (Frankfurt a.M., 1974), pp. 79–168, and Burckhardt Lindner und W. Martin Lüdke, eds., *Materialien zur ästhetischen Theorie Theodor W. Adornos* (Frankfurt a.M., 1979).

acter, it is film, Adorno wrote, and has it "to an extreme and highly suspect degree." As for its reception, the laughter of the audience at a cinema is "full of the worst bourgeois sadism." The theory of distraction, although a seductive one, Adorno found particularly unconvincing. "In a communist society work will be organized in such a way," he wrote, "that people will no longer need to be so tired and so stultified that they need distraction." (Here, as elsewhere in these letters, Adorno may have been attempting to counteract Brecht's influence upon Benjamin by taking a more revolutionary tone than he otherwise showed.) [17] In an article of 1940 on "popular" music, Adorno wrote that commercial entertainment in capitalist society is the correlate of the mechanized and rationalized labor process: a "fully concentrated and conscious experience of art" is not possible for those who seek in leisure a "relief from both boredom and effort simultaneously." [18] The notions of "expertise" and "distraction" Adorno found as romanticized in Benjamin's account as his appeal "to the actual consciousness of actual workers who have absolutely no advantage over the bourgeois except their interest in revolution, but otherwise bear all the marks of mutilation of the typical bourgeois character." Disregarding how Brecht attempted to rectify such "mutilation" with the distancing techniques of his epic theatre, Adorno urged Benjamin to completely "liquidate" such allegedly Brechtian motifs as the assumption of a clear-sighted and "spontaneous power of the proletariat in the historical process."

In the radical sundering of advanced from mass art, Adorno argued, Schoenberg and the American film both disclose the "stigmata" of capitalism in the twentieth century, for avant-garde and popular art "are torn halves of an integral freedom, to which however they do not add up." [19] What is needed, instead of sacrificing one to the other, is to analyze how each suffers from the chasm between challenging sophistication and broad appeal. Adorno's approach was less this evenhanded

---

17. *Aesthetics and Politics*, p. 102.

18. Adorno, "On Popular Music," *Studies in Philosophy and Social Science*, 9:1 (1941), 38. Rolf Tiedemann, a student of Adorno's, argued in his *Studien zur Philosophie Walter Benjamins* (Frankfurt, 1965), p. 92, that some of Benjamin's theses concerning "distracted" collective reception show an affinity with the "totalitarian" art policy of the Nazi state, where individuals are manipulated in a mass and there is a loss of autonomous thought. Whether justifiably or not, however, Benjamin implicitly dismissed such manipulations and affirmed the critical functions of the kind of "distracted" state he described. Helmut Lethen, a fairly orthodox Marxist, has defended Benjamin's theory of mass reception against Adorno and conservative cultural critics. In doing so he distorts Adorno's critique by simply assimilating it to the conservative position (Heidegger's, for example). See Lethen, *Neue Sachlichkeit*, pp. 134–135.

19. Adorno to Benjamin, March 18, 1936, in *Aesthetics and Politics*, pp. 123–125.

treatment, however, than a tireless attempt to reveal the "progressive" features in selected works of hermetic modernism while exposing what he felt to be the truly repressive characteristics hidden behind the democratic facades of "popular" art. In the same letter to Benjamin in which he debated the "Work of Art" piece, Adorno cited his own recent essay on jazz which began his extended assaults upon the "culture industry": "It arrives at a complete verdict on jazz, in particular by revealing its 'progressive' elements (semblance of montage, collective work, primacy of reproduction over production) as facades of something that is in truth quite reactionary." [20]

Adorno attempted in his 1936 essay "Über Jazz," as well as in his later critiques of "popular" culture, to decode the ideological significance of the art both from the inner structural principles of its construction and from the manner of its reception. For example, the improvisational "breaks" of the seemingly free and spontaneous jazz soloist or "subject," who appears to be freed from the choruslike repetitions of the music, have merely ornamental significance. Instead of having a constructive and constitutive value in relation to the development of the whole, they go nowhere and merely confirm the sacrifice of the individual to an abstractly preformed collective. This "virtuosity of adapting" occurs also in the syncopation of the rhythms.[21] Unlike Beethoven's syncopation, which gives voice to the historical "subject" through its power to produce new law from out of its revolt against old, jazz syncopation is purposeless and arbitrarily revoked,[22] the reflection and reinforcement of the pseudofreedoms of impotent individuals in late capitalist society. The claims for jazz's primitive "naturalness," as a protest against mechanized and decadent civilization, are equally spurious. What appears to be a liberating harnessing of the archaic is in fact its subordination to modern commercial logic: the apparently wild agitation, feigning the unexpected, is rooted in a rigid and timeless immobility, the repetitive sameness of the exchangeable commodity form which must appear always to be new.[23] Thus, "nature" returned—after having been repressed, but only in a repressive form—the ritualistic sacrifice of the individual to the collective; the substitution of spatialized, static, and mythic repetition for real historical development in music. (The two were connected for Adorno, since temporality was a crucial

20. Ibid., p. 125.
21. Adorno, "Über Jazz," *Zeitschrift für Sozialforschung*, 5:2 (1936), pp. 242–243, 252–256.
22. Ibid., p. 255. Buck-Morss, *Origin of Negative Dialectics*, p. 105.
23. Adorno, "Über Jazz," *Zeitschrift für Sozialforschung*, pp. 242–243.

aspect of individual experience.) [24] Thus, archaic and modern features dialectically revealed the other in Adorno's double-edged critique of jazz's "primitivist" and "progressive" defenders. [25] While jazz's rhythmic resemblance to military march facilitates its uses by fascism (even if jazz was then banned in Germany), its claims of free collectivity reveal, upon inspection, an even closer similarity, a "fictive Gemeinschaft . . . of co-ordinated atoms under a force being acted out upon them." [26]

Even in its origins, jazz was less the expression of primitive and archaic needs than the music of slaves showing sadomasochistic features. [27] (Here Adorno introduced Freudian motifs, reinterpreted by Erich Fromm, to underpin his view of the liquidation of the subject in his/her submission to authority.) The sexual liberation promised by "hot" jazz hides an actual fear of castration which is implicit in the soloist's performance, the threat of impotence which brings identification with the collective which one fears. [28] A similar masochistic passivity is induced, finally, in the receiver of the music. Instead of encouraging active listening, as does a Beethoven sonata, jazz discourages listening in favor of dancing. Faced with the loss of the music's power if one were actually to listen, the dancer prefers the "false consciousness of dreaming what you don't dare to think." [29]

As must be evident from this exposition, Adorno's perceptions of mass culture, however acute in many places, were blurred by an ethno-centric provincialism of one reared within the traditions of European high culture and unable to see much beyond it. This may in turn have contributed to his failure to make the necessary distinction between commercial jazz and the forms which were more genuinely rooted in black culture. [30] His second major assault upon mass culture, "On the Fetish Character of Music and the Regression of Hearing," published in 1938, continued the monolithic pessimism but was more squarely aimed. The article was marked by Adorno's critical responses to Benjamin's "Work of Art" piece, and by an extension of the Freudo-Marxist interpretations of the earlier jazz essay. In exile now in the United

24. Jay, *Dialectical Imagination*, p. 187.
25. Buck-Morss, *Origin of Negative Dialectics*, p. 264.
26. Adorno, "Über Jazz," *Zeitschrift für Sozialforschung*, p. 250.
27. Ibid., pp. 242–243. In a later piece of 1953, translated as "Perennial fashion-Jazz," in *Prisms* (New York, 1967), pp. 119–132, Adorno extended the Freudian components of his analysis.
28. Ibid., p. 256.
29. Adorno, "Über Jazz," *Moments Musicaux* (Frankfurt a.M., 1964), pp. 119–120.
30. Jay, *Dialectical Imagination*, pp. 186–187.

States, Adorno began a polemical barrage upon the American cultural environment within which he felt so alien.

The production and reception of both so-called "serious" and "light" music are today dominated by the exchange values of contemporary marketing, he charged, which serve up the music as a fetishized culinary object to be easily digested. The structural understanding of the whole in its temporal development was sacrificed in contemporary musical life to the various gimmicks used to sell the works as commodities to vast audiences which have learned to crave them. To illustrate his point, Adorno cited the attention paid to performances and arrangements over actual compositions; obsession with "stars" (such as Toscanini) in both classical and popular music; frequent impressionistic color effects; standardized hit tunes; atomized listening to romantic climaxes or to melodies ripped out of their constructive contexts; etc.[31] In the face of such soothing pleasantries which make for "easy listening," Adorno affirmed the "sign of advanced art" in the ascetic exclusion "of all culinary delights which seek to be consumed immediately for their own sake."[32] Adorno's models here, significantly, were the first and second Vienna "schools": "the coloristic parsimony of Haydn or Beethoven, . . . the predominance of the principle of construction over the melodic particular springing . . . out of the dynamic unity"[33]; and the difficult, anxious music of Schoenberg and Webern, which gives voice to the terror felt in the face of the crisis of individuality, a terror which is ordinarily evaded.[34]

One attempt to evade such anxieties, according to Adorno, was through the various forms of psychological regression in mass culture. With "nothing left for the consciousness but to capitulate before the superior power of the advertised stuff," the audience seeks to "purchase spiritual peace by making the imposed goods literally its own thing."[35] This is then called individual "taste," denying the evident passive dependency involved in identifying oneself with what has been "palmed off" on one. What is musically prepared and enjoyed is a child's diet of formulaic sounds whose sure sign is the "arrogantly ignorant rejection of everything unfamiliar" in favor of the endless repetition of the "most comfortable and fluent" sugary resolutions. The behavioral outline of

31. Adorno, "On the Fetish-Character in Music and the Regression of Listening," in *The Essential Frankfurt School Reader*, pp. 270–299; Jay, *Dialectical Imagination*, pp. 189–190.

32. Adorno, "Fetish-Character in Music," p. 274.

33. Ibid., p. 282.   34. Ibid., pp. 298–299.   35. Ibid., p. 287.

the culture consumer combines the masochistic features of one who "loves his own cell, . . . the sacrifice of individuality," and sadistically shows intense rage, following the fashions, toward what yesterday he was intoxicated with, "as if in retrospect to revenge himself for the fact that the ecstasy was not actually such." [36]

Much of this analysis of mass culture Adorno continued in the "Culture Industry" chapter of the book *Dialectic of Enlightenment*, which he wrote in 1944 and 1945 with Max Horkheimer, his closest associate in the Frankfurt Institute for Social Research, which Adorno had joined in 1938 (and which we shall examine in later chapters). The book was already being discussed by Adorno and Horkheimer, however, at the time of Adorno's critique of Benjamin in the late 1930s.[37] In their most pessimistic assessment of the course of Western historical development, Horkheimer and Adorno indicted the "culture industry" (they rejected the term "mass culture" as an illusory suggestion of spontaneous popularity)[38] for its aid to the allegedly totalitarian directions of modern capitalist society. Without attempting to summarize the lengthy and extremely provocative discussion, much of which repeated Adorno's earlier treatments of the contemporary musical scene, it is worth citing some emphases which were new in his developing critique.

Continuous with his earlier studies, Adorno stressed here, too, the so-called "liquidation of the individual" in contemporary Western society, though in this work he related this "liquidation" more to the "pseudodemocratic" pre-arranged harmonizing of the collective whole and particular persons.[39] The "administered" system of late capitalism, in which nineteenth-century contradictions between proletariat and capital, individual and society, and high and low culture appeared to be smoothed out, functioned less on the basis of the "cunning of the authorities" (in the corporate and governmental bureaucracies) than as a result of "the misplaced love of the common people for the wrong which is done them."[40] Modern industrial society presented the picture of an homogenized whole, a seamless web of interconnected pieces. As a result of the apparent identity of exchangeable persons, classes, com-

36. Ibid., pp. 286–290, 296.
37. Adorno to Benjamin, Nov. 10, 1938, in Adorno, *Über Walter Benjamin* (Frankfurt a.M., 1970), p. 143.
38. Adorno, "Culture Industry Reconsidered," *New German Critique*, 6 (Fall 1975), 12, 19.
39. Adorno and Max Horkheimer, *The Dialectic of Enlightenment* (New York, 1972), p. 121.
40. Ibid., p. 133.

modities, popular songs, and films, the last remaining "negative" and partially autonomous spaces (which had previously been possible because of the "contradictions") were disappearing—just those pockets of resistance within which works of a critically minded art might be created. Philosophically speaking, the dialectical mediation of opposites (subject and object; art and society; etc.) was giving way to a near total "identity" between them. In the face of a pervasive monolithic domination of "instrumental reason," which eschewed the rational scrutiny of substantive social ends while manipulating and exploiting nature without and within, the possibilities of structural change and transcendence of the given world were becoming more and more remote. For Adorno and Horkheimer, the "culture industry" existed to help smooth the functioning of just such a "rationalized" world. Whereas nineteenth-century high culture and contemporary avant-gardes honestly protested (by means of artistic sublimations) the emotional poverty of their societies, the "culture industry" dispensed pseudosatisfactions which directly enticed but did not fulfill: "Works of art are ascetic and unashamed; the culture industry is pornographic and prudish." [41] As a result of such illusory pleasures which destroy the mediated ones of true art, the clear perception of injustice is eroded and the consumer population is tied ever closer, through its instinctual needs, to the administering apparatus.

In the perspective of these intellectual exiles from Nazi Germany, the American "culture industry" closely resembled the coordinated *Volksgemeinschaft* of fascism, whose social-psychological bases were tirelessly analyzed by members of the Institute for Social Research in the 1930s and 1940s.[42] In this way, the failure to distinguish liberal capitalism from fascism often weakened the Institute's work and Adorno's own analyses of modern society and "mass culture." Adorno and Horkheimer wrote, for example: "In America radio . . . has acquired the illusory form of disinterested, unbiased authority which suits fascism admirably. The radio becomes the universal mouthpiece of the Führer. . . . The inherent tendency of radio is to make the speaker's word, the false commandment, absolute." [43] While Benjamin had come very close to unhistorically hypostasizing the technology of film, while acknowledging how it was being abused, Adorno went all the way in that direction at times (as he did with respect to radio) and seemed to preclude any but

41. Ibid., p. 140.
42. See Jay, *Dialectical Imagination*, chs. 3, 4, 5 and 7.
43. Adorno and Horkheimer, *Dialectic of Enlightenment*, p. 159.

the most pernicious uses. Adorno understood well the fallacy in any appeals to a nineteenth-century "autonomous" bourgeois subject: "individuality" is always mediated by the whole social process, and its nineteenth-century form is historically irretrievable in any case. Yet, Jürgen Habermas has seen flaws in Adorno's excessively "defensive" *Kulturkritik* which resemble those which Brecht had cited in Lukács's: "Adorno's theses can be proven with examples from literature and music, only as long as they remain dependent on reproductive techniques that prescribe isolated reading and contemplative listening, i.e., a mode of reception that leads down the royal road to bourgeois individuation." [44] Here was a case (there were others) in which the one-sidedness of the actual exchange between Benjamin and Adorno (with Benjamin never taking the offensive) left important issues more unresolved than they might otherwise have been.

Adorno's other critique of Benjamin's work in the 1930s concerned the first two completed parts of Benjamin's study of nineteenth-century Paris, the so-called *Passagenarbeit.* The first part was an extraordinarily cryptic overview of the whole project, an exposé completed in 1935, which Benjamin entitled "Paris, the Capital of the Nineteenth Century," providing a characteristically spatial metaphor for a period of time. With a blazing speed afforded by his analogical method, Benjamin constructed a montage which radically juxtaposed aspects of the commercialized culture of Baudelaire's metropolis.

Revealing a fascination with the first appearance of new technologies such as the iron-supported commercial arcades, gas lighting, and the daguerreotype in mid-nineteenth-century Paris, Benjamin counters this impulse by viewing novelty as the "quintessence of false consciousness" under capitalism, "of which fashion is the tireless agent." Doubting their own function, artists, for example, are forced to make *nouveauté* their highest value. But there is a collective desire to transcend the "deficiencies of the social order of production," Benjamin emphasizes, a desire to go beyond a social system which defeats the promise of the "new" by turning it immediately into a salable commodity. This desire takes the form of "images of the collective consciousness" in which memory of the very ancient past releases hope for a utopian future: "In the dream in which every epoch sees in images the epoch which is to succeed it, the latter appears coupled with elements of prehistory—that

44. Jürgen Habermas, "Consciousness Raising or Redemptive Criticism," *New German Critique*, 17 (Spring 1979), 43.

is to say, of a classless society." [45] Benjamin suggests that such a utopian possibility existed in the Fourierist phalanstery, which, he argues, took its "architectonic canon" from the arcades, and its highly complicated social organization from the new machinery. The ambiguous images of prehistory and transfigured present appear also in the lyric tones of Baudelaire, who conjures up the chthonic elements of Paris's topographical formation, even as he—with the whole bohemian strata— goes into the marketplace to find a buyer for his poetic wares. [46]

The popularity of World Exhibitions provides Benjamin with a key to his examination of the cultural commodity form in mid-nineteenth-century Paris. Taking his cue from Marx's notion of the "theological capers" of the commodity, the fetishistic worship of objects which have been alienated from their social production and usage, Benjamin develops an interlocking picture of the aestheticized deathliness of glorified exchange value:

> Fashion prescribed the ritual by which the fetish commodity wished to be worshipped, and Grandville [the Exhibition entrepreneur] extended the sway of fashion over the objects of daily use as much as over the cosmos. In pursuing it to its extremes, he revealed its nature. It stands in opposition to the organic. It prostitutes a living body to the inorganic world. In relation to the living it represents the rights of the corpse. Fetishism, which succumbs to the sex-appeal of the inorganic, is its vital nerve; and the cult of the commodity recruits this to its service. [47]

Such consumer "festivals" anticipated the entertainment industry of today, Benjamin remarks, revealing the critical side of his response to technically reproducible art under capitalism. More important, he concludes the précis of his project by suggesting that the wars and fascism of the twentieth century had "turned the wish-symbols of the previous century into rubble." Viewing the incipient misdirection of modern technical advances from his vantage point in the 1930s, Benjamin writes, in his last line: "With the upheaval of the market economy, we begin to recognize the monuments of the bourgeoisie as ruins even before they have crumbled." [48]

In the extended essay "The Paris of the Second Empire in Baudelaire," completed in 1938, Benjamin began to flesh out such themes with an immense amount of material data, constructing correspondences

---

45. Benjamin, *Charles Baudelaire: A Lyric Poet in the Age of High Capitalism* (London, 1973), pp. 159–160.
46. Ibid., pp. 170–172.   47. Ibid., pp. 164–166.   48. Ibid., p. 176.

and metaphorical relations between Baudelaire's poetry and his political, social, and economic milieu.[49] Now it became clear that for Benjamin, the poet did not merely sell his wares, but actually empathized with the inorganic commodity's "experience" of the metropolitan crowds; thus, Baudelaire registers the "shocks" felt when surrendering to the transient swarm of his "buyers." The poet abandons himself, in "holy prostitution of his soul," to the intoxication which he feels in having "stimulated" his potential mass of customers.[50] As seller of himself, he has no personality or convictions, but assumes many masks—ragpicker, strolling flâneur, apache, and dandy are a few—while all along preserving his incognito, a task which is facilitated by his metamorphoses of language.[51]

One purpose of Benjamin's approach was to counteract the alluring appeals of late-nineteenth-century aestheticism by subjecting Baudelaire's poetry to materialist analysis. Yet, Benjamin's construction of a web of metaphorical comparisons seemed to embody Baudelaire's own imagination, while extending it in the direction of surrealist montage (which intends to create shock from unexpected fusion effects). The hallmark of this method was the eclipse of the aura of "distance" (spatial and temporal, as well as between art and material existence), which, Benjamin had argued, is a basic desire of the metropolitan masses. (That such images or metaphors could create their own magical aura, Benjamin did not see; or did he?) Baudelaire's technique, especially his surprising connections between antiquity and the most banal and everyday modern (a favorite symbolist device which freezes time), was then, in turn, made a part of Benjamin's own "correspondences": such "flash-like appearances" are those of a literary "putschist," the counterpart to a Blanqui who perpetrates political shocks.[52] (Benjamin had prepared this analogy with a section at the beginning of the essay comparing

49. Benjamin, *Charles Baudelaire*, pp. 9–101. In April and September 1938 (*Briefe*, Vol. 2, edited by Theodor W. Adorno and Gershom Scholem [Frankfurt a.M., 1966], pp. 750–752 and 774–775), Benjamin wrote to Max Horkheimer that this essay was only part two of a triptych: part one, never completed, was to treat Baudelaire's allegories; part two, the social constellations in his work (the two completed essays, "Paris of the Second Empire" and "Some Motifs in Baudelaire" were different versions of this); part three, also never completed, a theoretical synthesis, with its own circle of themes, especially the commodity as a poetic object. This whole triptych was to be a miniature model of the *Passagenarbeit* whose outlines were suggested in the *précis* of 1935, "Paris, Capital of the Nineteenth Century."

50. Benjamin, *Charles Baudelaire*, pp. 55–61. See Pfotenhauer, *Aesthetische Erfahrung*, pp. 59–66, on the whole question of Benjamin's use of the notion of commodity fetishism in the *Arcades* study.

51. Benjamin, *Charles Baudelaire*, pp. 80, 97–98.

52. Ibid., pp. 99–100.

Baudelaire with the world of the professional conspirators.)[53] Throughout the text, Benjamin underpinned such startling constellations with meticulously assembled factual documentation on Parisian topography, ragpickers, conspirators, gas lanterns, urban detectives, feuilleton journalism, the wine tax of the Second Republic, etc., each of which was intended to illuminate, as social motifs, the material residues left in Baudelaire's lyrics. In this way, as well as the myriad ways in which a central interpretive thread was woven from the concept of commodity fetishism,[54] Benjamin mutually interfaced French modernist aesthetics and Marxist materialism in a manner which modified the meaning of each of them. (We shall later note a further major component, the tradition of Jewish messianic longing, which helped form Benjamin's anti-evolutionary notion of time as well as his "redemptive" literary exegesis.)

Let us now turn to Adorno's responses to Benjamin's *Arcades* study. In a letter of August 1935, Adorno criticized the configuration of ancient past and utopian future in the Paris exposé essay. Instead of decoding the primitive archaic hidden within the bourgeois modern as a rebuttal to the "progressive" apologists of the latest fashion (Adorno's own method, as we have seen), Benjamin had construed "the relationship between the oldest and the newest" as "one of utopian reference to a 'classless society.'" The "modern archaic" should be seen as a "catastrophe," but Benjamin had valorized it as a golden age.[55] "Your uncritical acceptance of the first appearance of technology," Adorno wrote, "is connected with your over-valuation of the archaic as such."[56] Furthermore, the historical "subject" which seeks to transcend the capitalist present—a "subject" which Adorno, given his views of the proletariat, did not have much hope for—appeared in Benjamin's draft essay as the "dream" of a "collective consciousness," a psychologizing category for Adorno, dangerously similar to reactionary Jungian thinking. Instead of seeing the fetish of commodities as a material reality which "produces consciousness," Benjamin had unwarrantably subjectivized it as an immediate "fact of consciousness" present in an "archaic collective ego."[57]

No doubt the Jungian-sounding language, which Benjamin never

53. Ibid., pp. 11–20.
54. To Gershom Scholem, Benjamin wrote that the "fetishism of commodites" was the central issue of the entire *Arcades* project. Benjamin, *Briefe*, Vol. 2, p. 654.
55. Adorno to Benjamin, August 2, 1935, in *Aesthetics and Politics*, p. 112.
56. Ibid., p. 116. In a letter to Benjamin of December 1934, Adorno had similarly criticized his friend's fascination (in an essay on Kafka) with the archaic and the modern, without dialectically mediating them. See Adorno, *Über Walter Benjamin*, pp. 103–105.
57. Adorno to Benjamin, August 2, 1935, in *Aesthetics and Politics*, pp. 111, 113.

used again, was unfortunate and misleading.[58] But having made this point, Adorno erred in failing to note the metaphorical tone of Benjamin's language, which may have been inspired by Marx's remark: "The world long possesses the dream of something before the consciousness to be able to truly possess it."[59] Apart from that, however, and more seriously, Adorno dissented from Benjamin's apparent assumption of the direct developmental emergence of transcendent utopian possibilities within capitalist society, possibilities which are thwarted by the present class relations.[60] If there were any utopian elements, these must be seen immanently, within works of art, Adorno held, and these would exist as moments of critical *negation* of capitalist development. This difference was implicit in Adorno's critique, and helps to explain why he missed in the Paris exposé a greater focus on the "dialectical image of the nineteenth century as Hell," and not merely as utopia (an emphasis which Benjamin had apparently made more explicit in an earlier draft essay on the *Arcades* project, which Adorno saw but which has been lost).[61] In fact, it would be hard to find a more "hellish" description of mid-nineteenth-century bourgeois society than Benjamin's central reference, in the second draft, to the worship of the dead commodity object as a succumbing to the "sex-appeal of the inorganic," the "corpse."

The real issue here, however, as Susan Buck-Morss has shown, was a political one: the implicit affirmation by Benjamin of the Marxist notion that commodity fetishism of this kind might be (Marx had said *will be*) transcended by the working class, the collective, revolutionary "subject." Instead of such revolutionary *affirmation* (which actually could not have been more muted and distanced than it was in the Paris study), Adorno insisted upon critical *negation* all along the line.[62] In rejecting the notion of collective consciousness, he emphasized that he was not invoking some allegedly self-contained and atomized "bourgeois individual," abstracted from the "real social process." Yet, he wrote, "the 'individual' is a dialectical instrument of transition that must not be

---

58. Carl Rudbeck, on pp. 173–177 of his dissertation, "The Literary Criticism of Walter Benjamin," Doctoral dissertation, State University of New York at Binghamton, 1976, effectively distinguishes Benjamin's usage of dream images from Jung's unhistorical, backward-looking and anti-rationalist "collective archetypes."

59. Hildegaard Brenner, "Die Lesbarkeit der Bilder: Skizzen zur Passagenentwurf," *Alternative*, 59/60 (April–June 1968), 48–61.

60. Buck-Morss, *Origin of Negative Dialectics*, p. 145.

61. Adorno to Benjamin, August 2, 1935, in *Aesthetics and Politics*, p. 111.

62. Buck-Morss, *Origin of Negative Dialectics*, p. 145.

mythicized away, but can only be superseded," [63] without making clear whether, or how, such supersession might take other than the "totalitarian" form bemoaned in *Dialectic of Enlightenment*.

Adorno's response (of November 1938) to Benjamin's "The Paris of the Second Empire in Baudelaire" was even harsher. Taking Benjamin to task for relating "the pragmatic contents of Baudelaire's work directly to adjacent features in the social history of his time, preferably economic features," Adorno urged him to produce a revised version in which cultural traits would be materialistically determined only by being "mediated through the *total social process*." In desisting from a truly "mediated" analysis in the present essay, in relating "superstructural" elements "immediately and perhaps even causally to corresponding features of the infrastructure," Adorno detected a marked reluctance on Benjamin's part to theoretically intervene in presenting his materials. These theoretical omissions lent to Benjamin's empirical evidence—the wine tax, the Paris streets, the feuilletonists—a mystified quality of material enumeration which Adorno found at the "crossroads of magic and positivism": the metaphorical relations which Benjamin's montage suggested created an artful spell which resisted historical and philosophical illumination. Instead, Adorno wrote, "panorama and 'traces,' flâneur and arcades, modernism and the unchanging, *without* a theoretical interpretation—is this a 'material' which can patiently await interpretation without being consumed by its own aura?" [64] To Adorno his older friend had not only surrendered to the myths of technology and the proletariat, but had underpinned this abdication by eliminating "the role of the active, critically reflective subject in the cognitive process." [65] Benjamin's pre-Marxist studies of Goethe and the German baroque, Adorno commented, were better Marxism than such current work.

Fearing that the Institute of Social Research would desert him in his financial straits (he was then eking out a precarious living in Paris), Benjamin had reason to be pliant toward Adorno's criticisms. [66] With evident dismay, Benjamin replied in December 1938. Lamely defending his philological method, "the examination of a text which proceeds by details and so magically fixates the reader on it," Benjamin failed to clarify how he had "read" the wider historical reality, which was to dispel "the

63. *Aesthetics and Politics*, p. 119.　　　64. Ibid. pp. 126–133.
65. Buck-Morss, *Origin of Negative Dialectics*, p. 171.
66. Benjamin, *Briefe*, Vol. 2, pp. 683, 839, 890.

appearance of closed facticity" as a kind of "social text." He was saving
the full theoretical analysis, however, for as yet uncompleted sections of
the *Passagenarbeit*.[67] What he was in no position to defend in 1938 was
his actual aversion to systematic and discursive philosophical argument.
Although interested as a student in neo-Kantian currents, Benjamin had
very early rejected Hegelian thought,[68] the major source of Adorno's
and Horkheimer's stress on theoretically "mediated" categories. He had
written to Horkheimer that he regarded philosophical jargon as the
"chatter of pimps," and was attempting to free himself from it.[69] Instead of making a "direct inference from the wine duty to Baudelaire's
'L'Ame du Vin'," for example, he wrote to Adorno, he was reading an
historical constellation, philologically, within the poem. He understood
well that the wine tax was mediated by "the significance of intoxication
for Baudelaire," but such interpretations, upon which he would be concentrating, must succeed, but not disturb, the process by which the
poem is allowed to "come into its own."[70] Be that as it may, Adorno
may not have been wrong in "detecting a deeper aversion in Benjamin
to systematic theoretical exposition as such, an innate reluctance to de-
cant the mysterious elixir of the world into any translucent vessel of ordered discourse."[71] The intervention of the analyst lay properly not in
discursive theory but in the "construction" of historical constellations,
so that poetic product and material existence, nineteenth-century Paris
and 1930s Europe, mutually interpenetrate one another: the theoretical
meanings were to emerge from such constructions. If such a procedure
differed from his earlier work on Goethe and the German baroque
(completed in 1923–24), Benjamin commented, then this resulted from
a "solidarity with the experiences which all of us have shared in the past
15 years."[72]

Benjamin concluded his letter by commenting on the disagreements
concerning the "popular arts." The essay "On the Fetish Character of
Music" was more pessimistic than his own assessments, he wrote, but
this may have resulted from "our viewing the matter" from "apparently
different but equally acceptable angles." The "Work of Art in the Age of
Mechanical Reproduction," in attempting "to articulate positive mo-

67. Benjamin to Adorno, November 9, 1938, in *Aesthetics and Politics*, pp. 134–136.
68. Benjamin, *Briefe*, Vol. 1, p. 166.
69. Jay, *Dialectical Imagination*, p. 169.
70. *Aesthetics and Politics*, p. 137.
71. "Presentation III," *Aesthetics and Politics*, p. 104.
72. *Aesthetics and Politics*, p. 136.

ments as clearly as you managed to articulate negative ones," has weaknesses where there are "strengths in your study." The sound film, for example, Benjamin now wrote, was successfully redirecting the cinematic potentials of silent cinema into regressive channels.[73]

Such comments appear to have been conciliatory ones. Yet, they also suggested the ambiguity and ambivalence in Benjamin's views which he always enigmatically desisted from clarifying. *Throughout* the period 1928–40, the years of his "Marxism" (such as it was), he entertained alternative, if not entirely contradictory, views of the modern historical process and the place of art and mass culture within it. After receiving Adorno's critique of the completed sections of the *Arcades* study, he set about composing a very different analysis which revealed the impact of some of Adorno's criticisms, especially of his analytical methods. Yet, the new work was less an acknowledgment of Adorno's position than an airing of the antithetical side of his own. Entitled "On Some Motifs in Baudelaire," this new essay approached the decline of aura, tradition, and integrated reflective experience as critically as the "Work of Art" piece had celebrated it. In the "shocks" of the new mass urban environment, Benjamin now argued, the human perceptual apparatus is continually bombarded with sensations and stimuli which it cannot integrate in a coherent manner. Mere existence (*Erlebnis*) increasingly replaced thoughtful ongoing experience (*Erfahrung*). To illustrate this, Benjamin referred to concepts in the work of Proust, Bergson, Simmel, and Freud, and, sociologically, to "collisions" in the urban mass, to the reified industrial labor process, and to the atomized presentation of information dispensed by the press. The conscious self-emancipating collective of proletarian "class" is replaced, in pessimistic fashion, by the manipulable and amorphous "mass." Baudelaire's poetry, in this light, is seen as an early attempt to parry unassimilable modern "happenings" and random stimuli by means of the "correspondences"—which seek to harness the rituals of memory against the empty passage of meaningless seconds—and "spleen," which exposes that passage in all its nakedness.[74] But to little avail. Baudelaire "indicated the price for which the sensation of the modern age may be had: the disintegration of the aura in the experience of shock." [75]

What a reversal! In this essay, aura is conceived as a complex of im-

73. Ibid., pp. 139–140.
74. Benjamin, *Illuminations*, pp. 180–185.
75. Ibid., p. 197.

mensely valuable human experiences (such as a sense of ritual, community, and the meaningful transmission of tradition) which is being lamentably eroded in modern (including, by implication, Soviet) society. Apart from its relation to tradition, the experience of aura is now defined as "the transposition of a response common in human relationships to the relationship between the inanimate or natural object and man. The person we look at, or who feels he is being looked at, looks at us in return. To perceive the aura of an object we look at means to invest it with the ability to look at us in turn."[76] In response to this essay (which he received with great enthusiasm, as it came much closer to his own analysis), Adorno commented that the new usage of "aura" was related to the *Erfahrung* which was in eclipse in industrial society and to the Marxian concept of the sedimented labor in humanly constructed objects; the decay of aura meant the reified alienating of those objects from their creators, the loss of the "human trace" in them.[77]

Benjamin followed the second Baudelaire essay a year later, 1940, with an extraordinary series of notes, "Theses on the Philosophy of History." In these notes Benjamin savaged the bourgeois, Social Democratic, and Communist views of progress, technical and otherwise, while evoking the need for a "messianic" intervention to stop the catastrophic flow of evolutionary time.[78] It would appear that he had departed drastically in these last two major essays from the revolutionary optimism which preceded 1938. On closer inspection, however, when judged in relation to his whole production in the 1930s, we may see these last works of 1939–40 as an accentuation, encouraged by the drift of historical events, of the melancholy and pessimistic strain which had always been present. For at the same time as he was writing the "Work of Art" and the earlier *Arcades* essays of 1935–37, he developed widely contrasting perspectives on the loss of aura, tradition, and experience in a brilliant analysis of the decline of narrative art, "The Storyteller," in which many of the themes of "Some Motifs in Baudelaire" were quite clearly evoked.[79] Earlier in the decade, long after he had been influenced by Brecht, Benjamin wrote pieces on Karl Kraus, Proust, and

76. Ibid., p. 188.
77. Adorno to Benjamin, February 29, 1940, *Über Walter Benjamin*, p. 160; *GS*, I:3, pp. 1131–1132.
78. Benjamin, *Illuminations*, pp. 253–264.
79. Ibid., pp. 83–110. The connection of this essay with "Some Motifs" is made by Pfotenhauer, *Aesthetische Erfahrung*, p. 72. The full notion of the decline of integrated experience appeared already in 1933 in Benjamin's "Erfahrung und Armut," reprinted in *Illuminationen* (Frankfurt a.M., 1961), pp. 313–317.

Kafka in which the laments of each concerning modern life were appreciatively presented and their art seen as an attempt, as Benjamin wrote of Kafka's work, "to postpone the future," the dreaded "last judgment." [80] Such essays may have contained elements of Marxist criticism, but this did not lead Benjamin to explain away his protagonists' despair as simply reducible to their experience of specifically capitalist modernity. Simultaneously with these writings, however, he was composing his most Brechtian of pieces, "The Author as Producer" (1934), in which revolutionary optimism concerning the proletariat and technology is most intensely embodied, albeit with a far more nuanced concept of literary "commitment" than has usually been seen in the essay. [81]

The paradoxical entertaining of seemingly opposed perspectives served Benjamin as the ambiguous organizing principle of his thoughts on the twentieth century. [82] Although there were interlaced elements of hope and dread, lament and utopia in Lukács, and more so in Brecht and Adorno in their different ways, Benjamin alone radically cultivated an ambivalence which makes of his work so explosive a mixture, eluding even the most sophisticated attempts at synthesis. Many of his devotees avoid this fact and, selecting out those elements of his thought which are congenial to them, give very partial and mutually exclusive assessments of his writings. [83] This montage of opposites was not merely a "Janus-face," in which materialist and theological methods are simultaneously developed [84]—as they are so graphically in the Kafka piece and the "Theses on the Philosophy of History." Nor was this simply a matter of juxtaposing aesthetic and social "texts" of seemingly distant meanings. It also pertains to his ambivalent responses to the historical

80. See *Illuminations*, pp. 201–216 and 111–140, and *Reflections*, ed. Peter Demetz (New York, 1978), pp. 239–273. The comment on Kafka appears on p. 129 of *Illuminations*. In arguing this case for Benjamin's ongoing studied ambivalence, I am disagreeing with the argument of Buck-Morss, *Origin of Negative Dialectics*, that a "Brechtian" stage from about 1932–37 was followed, in effect, by a more "Adornoesque" one in 1939–40.

81. Benjamin, *Understanding Brecht*, pp. 85–104.

82. Jürgen Habermas, "Consciousness Raising or Redemptive Criticism," p. 44, notes the ambivalence in Benjamin's treatment of the decay of aura, while Burckhardt Lindner has suggested the wider range of intentional ambiguity in Benjamin. See the latter's essays "Herrschaft als Trauma," *Text und Kritik*, 56 (1977), and "'Links hatte noch alles sich zu enträtseln'," in *Walter Benjamin im Kontext* (Frankfurt a.M., 1978).

83. For example there are the mutually exclusive and mutually hostile accounts of Gershom Scholem, the analyst of Jewish mysticism, as in his recent *Walter Benjamin— Geschichte einer Freundschaft* (Frankfurt a.M., 1975), which belittles the importance of Benjamin's Marxism; and the equally one-sided treatments of German New Leftists (e.g., Hildegaard Brenner, "Die Lesbarkeit der Bilder,") who study only the most Marxist writings.

84. Buck-Morss, *Origin of Negative Dialectics*, pp. 141–143.

decay of tradition and aura, the crisis of a more contemplative literary culture and intelligentsia, and the advent of collective society and mechanical reproduction.

Ambiguity concerning "progress," cultural tradition, technology, mass society, the city—a central motif in much modernist culture[85]—had been in some ways anticipated in Marx's work, as we have seen, in which contradictory responses to the capitalist industrial world are dialectically interwoven. But Marx had unraveled the threads in a hopeful manner, instead of leaving them poised as alternative horns of a dilemma. His thought had refashioned, while socially radicalizing, the rationalist optimism of the Enlightenment: the expectation of victory is only the most obvious sign of a dialectic whose cutting edge is the inexorable transformation of temporal loss (e.g., the decline of craftsmanship and community) into historical gain. Marx was, after all, a product of the mid-nineteenth century. Benjamin's dialectic, however, is at a "standstill," as he once put it; this, he wrote, is the nature of ambiguity.[86] While Adorno's procedure was most often to "expose" the regressive realities of apparently liberating developments, and while Benjamin (such as in the "Work of Art" essay) might occasionally argue the reverse, his work of the 1930s as a whole paradoxically and simultaneously entertains the twin antinomies of an ambivalent stance. It is one of the major limitations of their so-called "debate"—that is, Adorno's critique of Benjamin's work—that this wider perspective was not really present, since Benjamin did not choose to make it explicit. On the other hand, Adorno's critical focus on the moments of revolutionary affirmation and hope in Benjamin's writings caused Adorno to slight those (admittedly receding) utopian components in his own work. In the following chapters, we shall be analyzing the historical, aesthetic, and philosophical roots of their contrasting modernism and Marxism. In doing so, however, we will need to include, but also go beyond, the terms of dispute set forth in Adorno's critical responses to Benjamin's work.

85. This has been stated very persuasively in Wolfgang Sauer, "Weimar Culture: Experiments in Modernism," *Social Research*, 39:2 (Summer 1972), 278–280, and is analyzed, in specific cases (including Benjamin's) in Ivo Frenzel, "Utopia and Apocalypse in German Literature," in the same issue.

86. Benjamin, *Charles Baudelaire*, p. 171.

CHAPTER SEVEN

Benjamin and Adorno

The Development of Their Thought

Instead of a theoretical synthesis, Benjamin's writings reveal an explosive cross-fertilizing of intellectual currents and historical experiences which were registered as though on a seismograph. In many ways, his alienation as a child and adolescent from his environment could not have been greater.[1] Born in 1892 in upper-middle-class Berlin and subjected to the pompous, hypocritical, and stuffy atmosphere of Wilhelmine culture, he always felt estranged from the new German metropolis, refusing many of its tastes and mannerisms.[2] His parents' economic position rested upon his father's successful oriental carpet and antique auction business,[3] which provided Benjamin with an early exposure to the fetishism of artistic commodities: writing years later of his youthful home as a "mausoleum," and of his parents as smugly self-confident assimilated Jews, he was often repelled, for example, by the way his mother and father showed off their rich treasures for their guests.[4] The authoritarian gymnasium "prison" was equally insufferable, and Benjamin soon gravitated in late adolescence toward the *Wandervogel* or youth movement, the widespread revolt of middle-class youth of the era against the patriarchal repressiveness of family and school.[5] First at his

1. The point is made very well by Burckhardt Lindner in "'Links hatte noch alles zu enträtseln'," *Walter Benjamin im Kontext*, p. 7.
2. Werner Fuld, *Walter Benjamin: Zwischen den Stühlen* (München, 1979), pp. 61–64. This book is now the most important study of Benjamin's life.
3. Ibid., pp. 19–20.
4. Hannah Arendt, "Introduction," in Benjamin, *Illuminations*, pp. 28–29; Benjamin, *Reflections*, p. 10.
5. Benjamin wrote bitterly in the 1930s about the oppressive school discipline and his resultant youth movement activities. (*Reflections*, pp. 18–20, 49.) On this involvement

Berlin gymnasium and then at the Universities of Freiburg and Berlin in
the years 1912–14, he came under the influence of Gustav Wyneken's
idealist and metaphysical views of educational reform and a free youth,[6]
although he distanced himself from the youth movement as it moved
rightward.

At the same time, Benjamin was influenced to some degree by a more
technically philosophical idealism in Heinrich Rickert's neo-Kantian
lectures at Freiburg[7] (although he never liked any of his professors[8])
and studied Kant's critiques of Anglo-French empiricism.[9] Although he
was later to criticize the neo-Kantians' unhistorical metaphysics, there
are some neo-Kantian elements in his work. There is, for example, an
affinity between Benjamin's view of language (one of the central concerns of his early development) and that of the neo-Kantian Ernst Cassirer, who was influenced by French symbolist aesthetics. Cassirer argued extensively that linguistic "descriptions" of reality (whether those
of myth, science, or art), far from being arbitrary signs or attempts at
representation, are symbolic forms given to sense perceptions.[10] While
absorbing a similar kind of Kantian "formalism," Benjamin found Hegel distasteful as early as 1918.[11] This was to be a later source of friction
with Adorno, whose Marxism drew heavily on the Hegelian dialectic of
subject and object mediations.

Far more decisive for Benjamin's entire intellectual development,
however, were two other currents which he first absorbed and reworked
during the years of the First World War and the early Weimar period.
The first of these was the heritage of French symbolist poetics; the second, of Jewish mysticism. In May 1913, Benjamin visited Paris for the
first time. For most of the rest of his life, it was to remain a central mag-
net of his critical output,[12] both as city (the experience of urban modernity, for which Paris was the great model, was later to become a major

---

see Fuld, *Walter Benjamin*, pp. 35–61, and Bernd Witte, *Walter Benjamin—Der Intellektuelle als Kritiker: Untersuchungen zu seinem Frühwerk* (Stuttgart, 1976), pp. 15–22.

6. Witte, *Walter Benjamin*, pp. 15–16.

7. Benjamin, *Briefe*, Vol. 1, p. 41; Vol. 2, p. 857. Lieselotte Wiesenthal, *Zur Wissenschaftstheorie Walter Benjamins* (Frankfurt a.M., 1973), pp. 9–24, discusses Benjamin's relation to the whole "Marburg School" of neo-Kantianism.

8. Gershom Scholem, *Walter Benjamin*, pp. 24, 32.

9. Benjamin, *Briefe*, Vol. 1, pp. 47, 50, 61, 81.

10. Pfotenhauer, *Aesthetische Erfahrung*, p. 137; David Biale, *Gershom Scholem:
Kabbalah and Counter-History* (Cambridge, Mass., 1979), p. 253, n. 111. In "Probleme
der Sprachsoziologie: Ein Sammelreferat," *Zeitschrift für Sozialforschung*, 4 (1935),
246–268, Benjamin cited Cassirer's work on language quite approvingly.

11. Benjamin, *Briefe*, Vol. 1, pp. 166, 171. Fuld, *Walter Benjamin*, p. 182.

12. Fuld, *Walter Benjamin*, p. 42.

preoccupation[13]) and as home of French modernist art. In the years 1914 through 1916, he read Baudelaire and Mallarmé avidly.[14] Proust came after 1919. As early as 1915, Benjamin was doing translations of Baudelaire's poetry into German, which were to be published in the early 1920s. Translations of Proust and Verlaine followed in 1926–27, as did a new fascination with the contemporary surrealists.[15] Before the war, Benjamin had read very little modern literature. In 1915 and 1916, however, at the age of twenty-three, as he wrote later, he was "captivated by the theory of language in the works of Stéphane Mallarmé."[16] But it was not only the French symbolists who captured his imagination. Benjamin was attracted very early to the poetry of Stefan George and Hugo von Hofmannsthal, two of the most significant symbolists in the German language, although he was critical of the conservative uses to which they annexed their art. In the early 1920s, Benjamin corresponded frequently with Hofmannsthal, who was very enthusiastic about Benjamin's work, shared his focus on language as a counter to subjectivism, and published his long essay on Goethe's "Elective Affinities" in his own journal.[17]

In his first important article, "On Language as Such and the Language of Men" (1916), Benjamin developed the symbolist insistence that language communicates itself and not subjective or intersubjective meanings or mental pictures of objects. The view that the material density of language was constitutive of the world to be apprehended was already a basic premise for Benjamin: "The language of this lamp," he wrote, "does not communicate the lamp . . . but: the language-lamp, the lamp in communication."[18] In another early article, "On the Mimetic Faculty" (1920), Benjamin speaks of the crucial human capacity to "produce evanescent similarities" in a "flash." Such abilities are aided by the presence everywhere of "natural correspondence," but an-

---

13. The fullest treatment of Benjamin's fascination with the city is in Henning Günther's *Walter Benjamin: Zwischen Marxismus und Theologie* (Olten, Switzerland, 1974), pp. 165–188.

14. Benjamin, *Briefe*, Vol. 1, pp. 120, 133, 171, 198, 213; Fuld, *Walter Benjamin*, p. 69; "Curriculum Vitae Dr. Walter Benjamin," in Siegfried Unseld, ed., *Zur Aktualität Walter Benjamins* (Frankfurt a.M., 1972), p. 53.

15. Fuld, p. 79, 121; and *Zur Aktualität Walter Benjamins*, p. 232. Benjamin's major study of surrealism, published in 1929, is translated in *Reflections*.

16. Fuld, *Walter Benjamin*, pp. 64–69. Witte, *Walter Benjamin*, pp. 32, 99–106, 164–165.

17. Witte, *Walter Benjamin*, pp. 32, 99–106, 164–165, 194. Fuld, *Walter Benjamin*, p. 140. Adorno commented critically (see Adorno, *Über Walter Benjamin*, pp. 38, 52) on Benjamin's attraction to George's aestheticism.

18. Benjamin, *Reflections*, pp. 314–316, 324.

cient peoples and young children (whose logic is associative and analogical) are far more familiar with this than modern adults.[19] For the
next two decades, Benjamin's poetically conceived philology took its
cue from such sources. Charles Rosen has defined Benjamin's symbolist
inspiration in the following manner:

ANOTHER
WAY OF
TELLING

> The idea must appear to arise solely from the juxtaposition of words as they
> reflect each other—this implies that more than one facet of the meaning of each
> word is used to create these reflections. . . . The independent initiative of the
> words is ensured by systematically weakening the linear movement, the flow of
> the sentence traditionally cultivated in literary style. It is in language emanci-
> pated from communication that Benjamin placed the representation of the
> Ideas. . . . As Mallarmé treats words Benjamin treats ideas: he names them, jux-
> taposes them and lets them reflect off the other. Renouncing direct argument, he
> relies upon the ideas through language to produce their own cross-meanings:
> his arrangements are material for contemplation, they force the reader himself
> to draw the meaning from the resonances of the ideas. . . . Like Mallarmé's po-
> etry, Benjamin's criticism is allusive, not coercive. Where it goes beyond Sym-
> bolism is in the more modern Surrealist use of shock, . . . the yoking-together of
> incongruities. . . . The extremes are juxtaposed with little or no mediating com-
> ment, and the Idea arises in the silence between them.[20]

At the same time that Benjamin was first deeply engaged with symbolism, 1915–16, he came into close contact with Gershom Scholem,
who was later to become well known as the most profound modern in-
terpreter of the traditions of mysticism within Jewish history.[21] Although Benjamin never fully embraced Scholem's Zionism (while the
latter, in turn, was very hostile toward Benjamin's later interest in
Marxism[22]), the two men reciprocally influenced each other's perspectives on Judaism, language, and history for over two decades.[23]
Scholem, who emigrated to Palestine in 1923, encouraged Benjamin to
follow him there; although he never did, Benjamin entertained the possibility for many years.[24] In 1917, Benjamin married Dora Kellner,
whose father was a major Zionist pioneer and a close friend of Theodor
Herzl.[25] Through such relationships, as well as his reading of the mysti-

19. Ibid., pp. 332–336.

20. Charles Rosen, "The Origins of Walter Benjamin," *New York Review of Books*,
November 10, 1977.

21. See the excellent study by David Biale, *Gershom Scholem*.

22. Benjamin, *Briefe*, Vol. 2, pp. 525–533 (an exchange on Marxism between them).

23. Biale, *Gershom Scholem*, pp. 103–104. See also Benjamin to Scholem, April 25,
1930, in Benjamin, *Briefe*, Vol. 2, p. 513.

24. Scholem, *Walter Benjamin*, pp. 173–195; Benjamin, *Briefe*, Vol. 2, esp. pp. 455,
461 and 478.

25. Scholem, *Walter Benjamin*, pp. 30–31.

cal philosophies of Ernst Bloch and Franz Rosenzweig in 1919–20,[26] there developed an important strain of Jewish theology in Benjamin's intellectual life.

This Jewish component in his thought—which was to interact first with his symbolist aesthetics and then with his Marxist social theory—requires some wider, although brief, historical considerations. With the Jewish background of Lukács, Adorno (who was half-Jewish), and Benjamin in mind, not to mention Marx himself, we might speculate about the indirect sources in Jewish tradition of their intellectual creativity: Jewish existence as a "people of the book," deriving in part from a need to focus on the interpretation of shared sacred texts as an essential vehicle of ethnic continuity in the diaspora[27]; the historically conditioned verbal ability of Jews as a source of economic survival and psychic defense against feelings of inferiority and insecurity in anti-Semitic environments; the stimulation to conceptual thought and textual analysis which the ancient prohibition on graven images of the deity encouraged[28]; or the particular social sources of the outburst of innovative work among Central European Jewish intellectuals in the half-century before the Holocaust. The last of these has often been related to new cultural opportunities coupled with only partial emanicipation, a continuing marginal social position which allowed Jews a greater freedom from theoretical orthodoxies within their various fields.[29] Speaking more specifically, we know that Benjamin, along with Scholem and many other young Jewish intellectuals of the early twentieth century, reacted virulently against the liberal assimilationist milieu of his successful bourgeois parents. In this light, it has often been suggested that Marxism, as well as Zionism, was a common form of political revolt among such young Jewish intellectuals against their "outsider" status or

26. Scholem, "Walter Benjamin," in *Leo Baeck Yearbook*, 10 (1965), p. 132; Benjamin, *Briefe*, Vol. 1, pp. 217–221, 234, 249.
27. Cecil Roth, *A History of the Jews* (New York, 1970), pp. 124–132.
28. William Johnston speculates in such ways in his *The Austrian Mind*, pp. 23–29.
29. Howard Sachar, *The Course of Modern Jewish History* (New York, 1958), pp. 394–398; Oscar Handlin, "The Jews in the Culture of Middle Europe," in Max Kreutzberger, ed., *Studies of the Leo Baeck Institute* (New York, 1967), pp. 159–175; Stanley Rothman and Philip Isenberg, "Sigmund Freud and the Politics of Marginality," *Central European History*, 7 : 1 (March 1974), 65–69. For a recent overview of Jewish intellectual creativity in the years 1890–1933, focusing on sixteen examples (including Benjamin), see the interesting popularized account in Frederic Grunfeld, *Prophets Without Honour* (New York, 1980). In *The Ordeal of Civility: Marx, Freud, Lévi-Strauss and the Jewish Struggle with Modernity* (New York, 1974), John Murray Cuddihy views that creativity in the light of the Jewish intellectuals' discomfort in modern societies, and resultant desire to "expose" their undersides.

the myopically self-confident business strivings, or German nationalism, of their parents.[30]

As far as the Jewish contribution to aesthetic modernism is concerned, we have been warned recently against assuming that most modernists or their supporters were Jewish, or that most Jewish intellectuals were modernists in the decades 1890–1930.[31] With this important qualification in mind, it seems hard to deny the disproportionately high number of Jews (relative to their part in the population) in the expressionist movement, in the flowering of fin-de-siècle Viennese and 1920s Weimar culture, or among the intellectual defenders of modernism.[32] Benjamin and Adorno were not only Marxists after 1928, but had been in *aesthetic* revolt against bourgeois society and traditional cultural life before that. Their parents' commercial existence, the "taint" of that life of trade which has been assumed to be "natural" to Jews, was resisted by them through the most extreme forms of modern cultural rebellion against liberal bourgeois life. In both Benjamin and Adorno in different ways, an aesthetically aristocratic element formed part of their disdain for capitalist society (as it had with Lukács). There was some continuity here in the midst of generational shift. Both Benjamin's and Adorno's parents catered to the aesthetic life of their bourgeois patrons: Benjamin's father dealt in oriental rugs and Adorno's father sold fine wines, while Adorno's mother was a concert singer (and his aunt, a strong influence upon him, a pianist).[33]

Yet, Benjamin alone, and not Adorno or Lukács, was *directly* influenced by aspects of the Jewish intellectual heritage itself, although Adorno was to give considerable attention in the 1940s (along with the

30. For example, see Arendt, "Introduction," pp. 28–38.

31. Peter Gay, "Encounter with Modernism: German Jews in German Culture, 1890–1914," in *Freud, Jews and Other Germans* (London, 1978). A particularly strong example of the tendency criticized by Gay is present in Walter Laqueur, *Weimar: A Cultural History* (New York, 1973), pp. 72–77.

32. See Laqueur, *Weimar*, pp. 72–77, although he exaggerates; the importance of Jewish figures studied in Carl E. Schorske, *Fin de Siècle Vienna*, and Helmut Gruber, "The Politics of German Literature: A Study of the Expressionist and Objectivist Movements," Doctoral dissertation, Columbia University, 1962. Gruber chooses forty-one expressionists and finds that half of them are Jewish. (See pp. 15–17.)

33. Buck-Morss, *Origin of Negative Dialectics*, p. 1. This pattern was probably more common in Vienna where the aestheticism of the late nineteenth-century intelligentsia was shared with the bourgeois class as a whole. This is a major interpretive thread in Schorske, *Fin de Siècle Vienna*.

34. See Martin Jay, *Dialectical Imagination*, pp. 31–35 and 219–252 on the Jewish background of many of the Frankfurt school members, and the 1940s analysis of anti-Semitism in which Adorno played an important role. See also Jay's study "The Jews and the Frankfurt School: Critical Theory's Analysis of Anti-Semitism," *New German Critique*, 19 (Winter, 1980), 137–150.

whole, largely Jewish, Frankfurt school) to anti-Semitism and racial prejudice in modern society.[34] Benjamin, in fact, was part of a renaissance not merely of Jewish intellectual creativity but of Jewish religiosity in the decades after 1900. As part of the wider revolt against positivism and scientism, writers like Scholem, Benjamin, Buber, Bloch, Rosenzweig, and Kafka rebelled against the deracinated middle-class "practicality" and stolid respectability of the previous generations of liberal assimilationist Jews. Such figures began to cultivate apocalyptic and mystical countercurrents within the Jewish tradition (e.g., the Kabbalah) which had been frowned upon in the rationalistic "Enlightenment" perspective of "emancipated" nineteenth-century Jewry.[35] Such currents were to form a permanent part of Benjamin's intellectual baggage and were by no means dislodged when he embraced the materialist perspectives of Marxian theory.[36]

The Kabbalah was a body of medieval mystical teachings which gained influence among many Jewish groups after the expulsions from Spain around 1500. In these teachings, Benjamin found the means to reinforce and to metaphysically extend the view of language which he was learning from the symbolist poets. In *Major Trends in Jewish Mysticism* (1940), Scholem explained that the Kabbalistic mode of interpretation of Jewish sacred texts served to revive primitive and mythical modes of thought by restating rabbinical tenets in paradoxical form, thus giving them a suggestive ambiguity which heightened the sense of mystery.[37] For the Kabbalist, the entire cosmos is an endless network of correspondences and correlated symbols; everything mirrors everything else. The dimension of time proper to the comprehension of these symbolic connections, and thus the unlocking of their religious power, was in the "momentary totality" of a mystical "now," the fleeting instants of true understanding.[38] What distinguished such Jewish mystical doctrines from non-Jewish varieties was the degree of (1) impersonal, objective description, rather than self-expressive autobiographical confession; and (2) "their metaphysically positive attitude towards language as God's own instrument."[39]

All of these concepts provided new substance and direction for Ben-

35. Leon Wieseltier, "The Revolt of Gershom Scholem," *New York Review of Books*, March 31, 1977.

36. The most extensive treatment of the relation between the theological component and Marxism in Benjamin's work is Henning Günther, *Walter Benjamin*, pp. 21–90.

37. Gershom Scholem, *Major Trends in Jewish Mysticism* (New York, 1946), pp. 22–25, 29, 35.

38. Ibid., pp. 26–27.   39. Ibid., p. 15.

jamin's symbolism. The Kabbalistic notions of cosmic and natural correspondences, the freezing of time in an epiphany of "now," and the necessity of an impersonalized language all dovetailed nicely with French
symbolist poetics. Benjamin incorporated the Kabbalists' sense of primitive paradox into his view of the power of archaic remembrance. This
was to be accomplished in part through the qualities of language, which
to Benjamin was an ultimate reality coextensive with God's creation. In
paradise, Benjamin wrote in 1916, "the life of man in pure language-
mind was blissful," since God's creation was being completed through
the linguistic power of giving names to things, just as God had done in
Genesis. Such "naming," when done today, reestablishes the primordial
"magic spark" between language and objects. In symbolist fashion,
Benjamin held that "spark" to be a receptivity to the language of things,
"from which, in turn, soundlessly, in the mute magic of nature, the
word of God shines forth." After the Fall, however, and the curse of
Babel, language was transformed into mere speech, an instrumentalized
system of signs used for the purpose of communicating "something
(other than itself)," thereby dissolving its Edenic creativity and symbolic mystery.[40]

To Benjamin, literary interpretation, in treating texts as containers of
an untapped sacredness, might unleash such revelatory power: if the
smallest details, for example, were placed, against their intention or
everyday meaning, into a constellation with the present, then the critic
would have "redeemed" the "object" through the symbolic networks
contained in metaphorical language. This "constellation with the present" suggests that the archaic religious past was to be not so much "re-
captured" as given new meaning through the eyes of the present.[41] In
another direction, the translator, in mediating between languages,
could serve to approach the central reality of God's word by freeing the
meanings from only one form of them. In such ways, the truth will have
been illuminated not as "an unveiling which destroys the secret" (of language), but as the "revelation which does it justice."[42] Through his symbolist and Jewish mystical sources, Benjamin thus harnessed theological
teaching to hermeneutic practice. Even after absorbing elements of

40. Benjamin, Reflections, pp. 314–33; Biale, Gershom Scholem, pp. 105–106.
41. Pfotenhauer, Aesthetische Erfahrung, p. 53; Buck-Morss, Origin of Negative Dialectics, p. 210 n.; Adorno, "On Walter Benjamin," Prisms, pp. 233–255.
42. Quoted in Arendt, "Introduction," p. 41. See also Benjamin, Illuminations, pp.
69–82, an essay entitled "The Task of the Translator," written in 1923.
43. Benjamin, Briefe, Vol. 2, p. 524.

Marxism, Benjamin wrote, in 1931: "I have never been able to do research and think in any way other than, if I may so put it, in a theological sense—namely, in accordance with the Talmudic teaching of the forty-nine levels of meaning in the Torah."[43] What he failed to mention was that, through the logic of metaphor, individual meanings simultaneously suggested other ones.

Aside from the revelatory power of critical exegesis, Benjamin was indebted to Judaism, primarily through Scholem's influence, for his messianic notion of history. For millennia, the exilic powerlessness of the Jewish communities had been compensated through utopian hope in the coming of a Messiah who would redeem the past while inaugurating a secular kingdom of happiness. What was significant for the form of utopianism which Benjamin embraced, however, was that such hope was not in immanent historical development and continuity, but, according to Scholem's interpretation, in an apocalyptic and transcendent intervention.[44] While Scholem emphasized the Zionist redirecting of transcendent longing into secular action, Benjamin largely remained within the perspective of the Jewish exile: his life was to be lived in an endlessly deferred hope.[45] In reviving the older Jewish notions described by Scholem, Benjamin wrote in 1940, in the last two sentences of his last essay: "The future did not become a homogeneous and void space of time to the Jews. For each single second in it was the small door through which the Messiah might enter."[46] Reinforcing the spatial focus of symbolist and Kabbalistic "correspondences," such perspectives were to give a strong anti-evolutionary cast to Benjamin's very unusual Marxism.

It may be that Benjamin's historical pessimism and acute sense of the end of tradition, unleashing joint catastrophic and messianic expectations, was conditioned by an awareness of the dangers to the Jews which he shared with Kafka.[47] More commonly, however, he suggested that it was the World War and its social aftermath which had shattered

44. Scholem, "On the Messianic Idea in Judaism," in *The Messianic Idea in Judaism and Other Essays on Jewish Spirituality* (New York, 1971), pp. 9–36.
45. Leon Wieseltier, "Gershom Scholem and the Fate of the Jews," *New York Review of Books*, April 14, 1977; in his essay "On the Messianic Idea," Scholem emphasized the Zionist rejection of the powerless position of those who live in deferred hope (*The Messianic Idea*, pp. 35–36).
46. Benjamin, *Illuminations*, p. 264.
47. Arendt, "Introduction," p. 37. In his letter of 1938 to Adorno, Benjamin spoke with great anguish about the fate of German Jewry under Hitler. See *Aesthetics and Politics*, p. 139.

any sense of an organically unified, continuously transmitted culture or body of "experience"; and the shadow of that war lay across the Weimar and early Nazi years. In "The Storyteller" (1936), he wrote:

Our picture, not only of the external world but of the moral world as well, overnight has undergone changes which were never thought possible. With the World War a process began to become apparent which has not halted since then. . . . For never has experience been contradicted more thoroughly than strategic experience by tactical warfare, economic experience by inflation, bodily experience by mechanical warfare, moral experience by those in power. A generation that had gone to school on a horse-drawn streetcar now stood under the open sky in a countryside in which nothing remained unchanged but the clouds, and beneath these clouds, in a field of force of destructive torrents and explosions, was the tiny, fragile human body.[48]

Benjamin's movement toward the political left (as was common among Weimar's left intelligentsia), first towards anarchism and then Marxism, was strongly affected by his reactions to the World War. He had been excused from military duty because of his own "fragility"; he was declared unfit as a *Zitterer*, one who "trembles."[49] Nevertheless, the depraved technology of gas warfare, caterpillar tanks, and other instruments of annihilation formed part of his view of the "aestheticized violence" of late bourgeois society.[50]

Yet, Benjamin was not a pacifist. At least in the years following the World War and in revulsion from it, Benjamin showed nihilistic and anarchist attitudes toward bourgeois society (though in a rather distanced and literary manner). The ferocious and violent assault of the dadaists upon meaning and discursive logic attracted him, as did their magical word experiments.[51] After 1918, he began to show, according to Scholem, a marked nihilistic and amoral attitude toward his parents (upon whom he was still financially dependent) and their social class.[52] In 1920, in an essay entitled "Critique of Violence," he seemed obliquely to favor "divine" revolutionary, in contrast to "lawmaking," violence; in addition, he approvingly quoted Georges Sorel at some length.[53]

48. Benjamin, *Illuminations*, p. 84. Similar notions are voiced in "Erfahrung und Armut," in *Illuminationen* (Frankfurt a.M., 1961), p. 317.

49. Scholem, *Walter Benjamin*, pp. 20–21.

50. Benjamin, "Theories of German Fascism" (1930), *New German Critique*, 17 (Spring 1979), 120–128; Benjamin, "The Work of Art."

51. See Scholem, *Walter Benjamin*, pp. 101–104, in which he discusses Benjamin's relation to Hugo Ball, the German dadaist centered in Zurich; see also Benjamin's comments on futurism and dadaism in *Reflections*, p. 184, and "Work of Art," pp. 237–238, 250–251.

52. Scholem, *Walter Benjamin*, pp. 71–72.

53. Benjamin, *Reflections*, pp. 277–300.

What particularly distinguished this anarchistic and "divine" form, and lent it its "purity," was a freedom from the instrumental and purposive rationality of Marxian action, which was interwoven with evolutionary (albeit dialectical) development.[54] Even when he moved toward a more Marxian politics, Benjamin was to retain a strong apocalyptic strain from these earlier years.

Throughout much of his life, Benjamin's "destructiveness" was aimed less at that outer "bourgeois" world that he had come to despise, however, than within, against his own self or personality. His fascination with old books, juxtaposed quotations, architectural fragments and ruins, the technologies of photography and film—and the "reading" of the self as a text or an imagistic montage: all these were part of Benjamin's obsession to unlock the poetic power of objects while extinguishing the subjectivity of the one who unlocks them. The writer who early rejected an aesthetic of self-expression,[55] and would later describe the Baudelairean obliteration of the individual's traces in the big city crowd,[56] was throughout his life afflicted with a sense of his own practical helplessness, pathological hesitation, and liability to sickness. These were the same subjectively paralyzing qualities he found in Proust, the archaesthete, one of his favorite authors.[57] While his voice was "beautiful, melodic and impressive," according to Scholem, Benjamin seemed to some people (including his wife Dora) to be distant from his own body, an incorporeal, elusive, intellectually "distracted" man, who placed a secretive wall around his person.[58] Benjamin wrote bitterly that a dreamy recalcitrance and a tendency to appear thoroughly maladroit had been built up in him by the way in which his mother would use small everyday items of conduct to test his aptitude for practical life,[59] the same kind of "education" which had alienated Kafka from his father and the world.[60]

One escape from the burden of personality lay in a fascination with objects. Another was found through depreciating the significance of temporal continuity, the realm of "mere fulfillment" (of which he had very little, personally, professionally, or politically); and, instead, favor-

---

54. Habermas, "Consciousness Raising," p. 55.
55. Benjamin, *Angelus Novus: Ausgewählte Schriften 2* (Frankfurt a.M., 1966), p. 372.
56. Benjamin, *Charles Baudelaire*, pp. 42–48.
57. Fuld, *Walter Benjamin*, p. 21.
58. Scholem, *Walter Benjamin*, pp. 10–11, 34–35, 121–122.
59. Benjamin, *Reflections*, p. 4.
60. See the well-known *Letter to His Father* (New York, 1966).

ing the spatial sensibility which he absorbed from the French modernists. "In space," Susan Sontag has written of Benjamin, "one can be another person. Time does not give one much leeway: it thrusts us forward
from behind, blows us through the narrow funnel of the present into the
future. But space is broad, teeming with possibilities, positions, inter-
sections, passages, detours. . . ."[61] Beyond the spatial dissolution of self
lay the possibility of its literal liquidation. Death, the symbolist obsession, always haunted Benjamin and was a central theme of his medita-
tions on art and politics, whether baroque, Baudelairean, or fascist. In
1922–23, while writing *The Origins of German Tragic Drama*, which
is saturated with the landscape of death in the catastrophic seventeenth
century, he was described by a friend, Charlotte Wolff, as having a
death longing himself,[62] evidence for which may also be found in various of his letters during this period.[63] In the mid-1920s, he wrote: "In a
dream I took my own life with a rifle. When the gun went off I did not
awake, but saw myself lying there for a time, as a corpse. Only then did
I wake up."[64] In 1940, he was to perform the act with morphine, though
within a situation of immense objective danger: he was fleeing from the
Nazis. Yet before, in 1932, he had also come very close to suicide.[65] This
act, the "only heroic deed available for the *multitudes maladives* of the
cities in reactionary times,"[66] as he wrote in one of the Baudelaire essays, was perhaps his ultimate "empathy with inorganic matter."

To return to his early intellectual development, we may view the major works of Benjamin's pre-Marxist period as an interweaving of symbolist and Judaic themes with the catastrophic historical experiences of
the decade 1914–23. In his doctoral dissertation on the art criticism of
the German romantics (1920), Benjamin de-emphasized romantic subjectivism and nature worship, and concentrated on those aspects of the
work of Schlegel and Novalis which anticipated the French symbolists:
criticism seen not as judgment but as the method of completion of the
work of art, and therefore, by necessity, as poetic itself; the departure
from discursive style and logic in favor of illuminating details as monads
which contained the whole; the notion of poetic construction as the
major subject of poetry itself; the purpose of art as a means to keep

61. Susan Sontag, "The Last Intellectual," *New York Review of Books*, October 12,
1978.
62. Asja Lacis, *Revolutionär im Beruf*, p. 44.
63. Benjamin, *Briefe*, Vol. 1, pp. 281, 325 and 422 (from the years 1921–26).
64. Benjamin, "Einbahnstrasse," *GS*, IV/1, p. 133.
65. Scholem, *Walter Benjamin*, pp. 207–208, 222–223, 232–233.
66. Benjamin, *Charles Baudelaire*, p. 76.

mystical experience alive in secular form; and, possibly most important of all, the view of the mind and the world, distanced from subjectivism, as a hall of mirrors which infinitely reflect one another. In addition, de-emphasizing the romantics' idea of organic natural evolution, Benjamin interpreted the romantic view of history as a messianic longing for uto-pia which distilled a sense of spiritual rupture, crisis, and hope.[67]

A brilliant essay on Goethe's *Wahlverwandtschaften* [Elective Af-finities] followed in 1923. Benjamin interpreted the novel with symbol-ist notions of myth which drew particularly upon Nietzsche.[68] Through the languages of art, he argued, humans are temporarily able to hold the pre-individualistic mythical forces of instinctual chaos and primi-tive barbarism at bay. In doing so, however, in helping to overcome the aimless trail of disasters which is historical time, art must be able to harness these mythical forces and give them some formal order. Yet, in the face of the return of instinctual chaos, human frailty always pre-vails, a symbolic suggestion of Benjamin's own reactions to the violent turbulence of these years.[69]

In his major pre-Marxist writing, *The Origin of German Tragic Drama* (completed in 1925), Benjamin drew together all the strands of his early intellectual and personal development in a most esoteric and erudite reading of the melancholy plays of the seventeenth-century ba-roque. Significantly, he began work on the study in 1916, during the World War, and the text suggests such connections.[70] Benjamin saw German baroque drama, in contrast with the classical literature of the eighteenth century, as expressive of an era of catastrophe, fragmenta-tion, and discontinuity similar to the twentieth century.

In the long methodological introduction, Benjamin set out his own critical strategies. The "things," the concrete phenomena of history, are intentionless "stars" through which the critic constructs an historical "constellation" by juxtaposing what had previously been isolated; in

---

67. Rudbeck, "The Literary Criticism of Walter Benjamin," pp. 31–35; Witte, *Walter Benjamin*, pp. 12–13, 93–95. The elements of continuity between German romanticism and French symbolism are familiar today to comparative literature scholars. See René Welleck, "Symbolism in Literary History," *Discriminations* (New Haven, 1970), pp. 116–119. Mallarmé was apparently deeply interested in Novalis.
68. Scholem, *Walter Benjamin*, p. 79, discusses Benjamin's interest in Nietzsche's view of myth in the years after World War One. See also Gillian Rose, *The Melancholy Science: An Introduction to the Thought of Theodor W. Adorno* (New York, 1978), p. 37.
69. Rudbeck, "The Literary Criticism of Walter Benjamin," pp. 59–62.
70. Witte, *Walter Benjamin*, p. 117; Benjamin, *The Origin of German Tragic Drama* (London, 1977), p. 66. Besides the discussion of the *Trauerspielbuch* in Witte, see also Richard Wolin, "An Aesthetic of Redemption: Benjamin's Path to *Trauerspiel*," *Telos*, 43 (Spring 1980), 61–90.

the process, such past objects are "redeemed" through the truth-creating interventions of the present.[71] In constructing the "Ideas" which give meaning to the fragments, minute details, and quotations which one has found, the critic renews through memory the primordial mode of apprehending words as symbolic and not communicative. "Ultimately this is not the attitude of Plato," Benjamin commented, "but the attitude of Adam,"[72] the Edenic name-giver. In willful self-effacement, Benjamin conceived of the critical process as the production of a mosaic of quotations whose mutual meanings would emerge from their relative placements[73] (a kind of cubistic collage of "found objects"), even if his actual text contained much philosophical-historical commentary.

In interpreting the German baroque, Benjamin focused upon the historical sources of allegory as against the Goethean classical "symbol," and on the seventeenth-century perception of history as a landscape of decay and death. Given the political, military, and social catastrophes of the era—the Thirty Years' War and its aftermath—German baroque dramatists, unable to grant meaning to fragments and ruins in their usual natural setting, used allegorical constructions to rescue the ephemeral world for eternity.[74] While the Goethean symbol is alive and fully palpable, important in itself and in its relation to other things before it signifies any ideas or concepts (the classical "realism" which Lukács applauded), the object is granted its sole meanings by the conceptualizing allegorist. In this way, allegory is the favored mode for a world in ruins, its objects devoid of significance in themselves. Haunted by the idea of catastrophe, the baroque dramatist perceives historical time as an ever-growing pile of debris: "Allegories are, in the realm of thoughts," Benjamin wrote, "what ruins are in the realm of things."[75] Instead of viewing the classical harmonies of nature and antiquity as organically whole living models, the baroque allegorists conceived of both as fractured and decayed.[76] The culminating allegory of this mournful vision lay in the multiform emblematic renderings of death: "Melancholy betrays the world for the sake of knowledge. But in its tenacious self-absorption it embraces dead objects in its contemplation in order to redeem them."[77] Thus, the historical ruin has its bodily equivalent in the depiction of the

71. Benjamin, *Origin*, pp. 34–36.
72. Ibid., pp. 36–37; on the notion of "ideas" here, see Hans Heinz Holz, "Prismatisches Denken," *Über Walter Benjamin* (Frankfurt a.M., 1968), pp. 89–92.
73. Benjamin wrote at the time of his "over 600 quotations, very systematically and clearly arranged" (Benjamin, *Briefe*, Vol. 1, p. 339).
74. Benjamin, *Origin*, pp. 139–140, 224–225.
75. Ibid., p. 178.   76. Ibid., pp. 177–179.   77. Ibid., p. 157.

human *physis* as a corpse,[78] the preeminent allegory of an idea, the *memento mori*. But then such chosen objects self-reflexively reveal the nature of the allegorical literary process itself, in which "life flows out of" the things of this world[79] and they "signify" in inorganic ways such as montage.[80]

Intended as his *Habilitationschrift*, Benjamin's study of the German baroque was turned down by the University of Frankfurt because it was found incomprehensible.[81] Yet, it is likely that Benjamin was dubious about pursuing an academic career in the conservative German universities (even Frankfurt, the most liberal) in the first place, and had wanted the public recognition of a successful habilitation to convince his father to grant him an adequate income to pursue an independent scholarly life.[82] The inflation of 1923 ruined his father's business, however; and even if a larger stipend had earlier been a possibility, it was no longer so. In addition, the chance to edit a journal and act as a consultant collapsed when Benjamin's publisher contact, a certain Littauer, went bankrupt.[83] Although, after 1925, Benjamin adjusted to the new financial situation by barely managing to earn a living in literary journalism, the whole course of events after 1923 made him more conscious than he had ever been before of the economic bases of his own existence as an allegedly "free" intellectual.[84] While the inflation was driving sectors of the *Mittelstand* into the hands of the Nazis, and helping to form a large academic proletariat among university graduates,[85] Benjamin penned a scathing "Tour of the German Inflation" in his collection of contemporary notes, *Einbahnstrasse*, which was written in the years 1924–28. What angered him most was the refusal of the middle classes to accept the controlling influence of money and material interests in their own lives as well as in those of all other members of society, their anachronistic recourse to status concepts emptied of meaning, and their nostalgic yearning for the return of a prewar stability which was a "stabilized wretchedness" for those below them.[86]

78. Ibid., pp. 216–218.   79. Ibid., p. 183.
80. Peter Bürger, *Theorie der Avant-Garde* (Frankfurt a.M., 1972), p. 95.
81. Witte, *Walter Benjamin*, pp. 140–141; Arendt, "Introduction," pp. 24–25.
82. Benjamin, *Briefe*, Vol. 1, p. 293.
83. "Werkbiographie," *Text und Kritik*, 31/32 (1971), p. 82.
84. Witte, *Walter Benjamin*, p. 137.
85. Ringer, *The Decline of the German Mandarins*, pp. 61–67.
86. Benjamin, *Reflections*, pp. 70–76. See Lebovics, *Social Conservatism in Germany and the Crisis of the Middle Classes*, chs. 1–2, on the avoidance of issues of economic class and material interest among the *Mittelstand* in favor of anachronistic notions

In November 1923, Benjamin wrote: "Whoever works seriously as
an intellectual in Germany is threatened by hunger in the most serious
way."[87] The threat of his own impoverishment and proletarianization as
an intellectual, his resentment against the idealist culture of the academic mandarinate, and his reflections on the quite visible class struggles of the Weimar era were slowly moving Benjamin in a materialist
direction. In this process he participated, quite consciously, in the "class
war" between the entrenched German professoriat, tied largely to the
hierarchical traditions of the "feudal" and aristocratic past, and the
now quite large democratic and socialist "free intelligentsia" of urban
Weimar culture (much of it Jewish).[88] But Benjamin, even more than
Tucholsky and Ossietsky (the leading figures of the *Weltbühne* journal),
was a "homeless" man of the left; they, at least, had a secure professional position for the time being. More than most of them, and definitely more than Adorno, he was to continue to experience the direct
threat of hunger and material need, which may in part have made him
emphasize such "infrastructural" necessities more than his younger
friend, who stressed their "mediated" influence. The economic dis-
possession of his parents and his own need to sell essays as a literary
commodity in order to barely survive were "im-mediate," though not
the only, sources of his growing Marxism in the mid-1920s.[89]

In 1924, at the beginning of his economic difficulties, Benjamin first
engaged seriously with a major Marxist study, Lukács's *History and
Class Consciousness*. Though deeply affected by the work,[90] Benjamin
was not optimistic concerning the crisis of bourgeois society. While
Lukács in this book had suggested historical alternatives of socialism or
barbarism (later he was to drop the grain of skepticism within his more
orthodox commitment), Benjamin went further, seeing the victory of
the proletariat as decidedly a matter of doubt. Although the bourgeoisie

---

of social status and moral individualism. Benjamin expanded his attack on the "false consciousness" of both the *Mittelstand* and many literary intellectuals in his 1930 essay, "Die
Politisierung der Intelligenz," reprinted in *Angelus Novus*, pp. 422–428.

87. Benjamin, *Briefe*, Vol. 1, p. 311.

88. On the conflict between professors and free-lance intellectuals, see Ringer, *The
Decline of the German Mandarins*, p. 161. Sauer, in "Weimar Culture," gives a fine short
description of the rise of a "free intelligentsia" in Germany after 1890. For a careful study
of one pivotal group of left "free-lancers" in the 1920s, see Istvan Deak, *Weimar Germany's Left Intellectuals: A Political History of the Weltbühne and Its Circle* (Berkeley,
Calif., 1968). On Benjamin's own rejection of the culture and social attitudes of the University Professors, see Fuld, *Walter Benjamin*, p. 234.

89. Bernd Witte, "Benjamin and Lukács," *New German Critique*, 5 (Spring 1975),
25–26.

90. Benjamin, *Briefe*, Vol. 1, pp. 350, 355, 381.

was in eclipse, historical development was tending toward an immense conflagration and fatal catastrophe through its own self-destruction, which might well mean the advent of fascism. The only hope was an intervention by the proletariat (eschatological, in effect), to halt the temporal drift. From the outset, Benjamin's Marxism was squarely aimed against any trust whatsoever in historical evolution, which, in 1928, he saw, metaphorically, as a burning fuse moving toward the dynamite: "If the abolition of the bourgeoisie hasn't been achieved by a certain almost calculable point in the economic and technical development (inflation and gas warfare are signals of its approach), then everything is lost. Before the spark reaches the dynamite, the burning fuse must be severed. The moment of intervention, the danger and tempo are technical, not chivalrous, questions."[91]

Benjamin never joined the Communist Party, though he considered doing so for a time, as an "experiment" in political commitment.[92] His brother was a Communist who worked, as a doctor, in the poorest sections of East Berlin and had some influence upon him in these years.[93] More importantly, in 1924, Benjamin met and fell in love with a Latvian Communist and pioneer of proletarian children's theatre named Asja Lacis, who later introduced Benjamin to Brecht, fought hard against his Jewish mystical interests, and was the direct cause of Benjamin's one visit to Moscow, in the winter of 1926–27.[94] (For a few years now, Benjamin's marriage to Dora had been in collapse; both went their separate ways, Benjamin taking many trips abroad.)[95] In Moscow, Benjamin was impressed by the constructivist theatrical, literary, and cinematic avant-garde and such ties to the working class as it had through the "worker-correspondent" movement to literarize social and technical experience.[96] Soon after returning to Berlin, he wrote rhapsodically of the liberating effects of the new cinema of Eisenstein in a way which partly anticipated, two years before any close relation to Brecht, his later theses in the "Work of Art in the Age of Mechanical Reproduction."[97] Yet, although he was enthusiastic about the potentials of the new technology

91. Benjamin, "Einbahnstrasse," *GS*, 4:1, p. 122, quoted and analyzed in Witte, "Benjamin and Lukács." I have altered the translation somewhat.
92. Benjamin, *Briefe*, Vol. 1, pp. 368, 425–426.
93. Lacis, *Revolutionär im Beruf*, p. 43.
94. Ibid., pp. 42–51; Benjamin, *Briefe*, Vol. 1, pp. 344–359.
95. Scholem, *Walter Benjamin*, pp. 98–99, 117–122.
96. Lacis, *Revolutionär im Beruf*, p. 51; Witte, "Benjamin and Lukács," pp. 15–18, 21–22.
97. Benjamin, "Diskussion über russische Filmkunst und kollektivische kunst überhaupt," (1927), *Alternative*, 56/7 (October–December 1967), 219–220.

and collective life which he found, as well as the severing of power from money, there was also a notable coolness, detachment, and irony in his private reflections on Moscow, especially in his comments on the growing evidence of bureaucratic and party dictation.[98]

What attracted Benjamin to communism was that it was the opponent of the Western bourgeoisie, a negating force, and less that it presented positive solutions which Benjamin could ever simply embrace[99] (although "The Author as Producer" and "The Work of Art" seemed to suggest that he had). Marxism, like the nihilism and anarchism which were never to be displaced entirely by it,[100] served Benjamin, in part, to make his work indigestible to the right. Scholem commented to Benjamin in 1931 that the Russians would have no use for his "dynamite" except in the bourgeois camp, since it was so distant from a party point of view. In answer, Benjamin, instead of contradicting the suggestion, wrote that he sought to "methylate" his work, "like spirits, to guarantee its unpalatability to the other side—at the risk of making it unpalatable to everyone."[101] While Benjamin took the Marxist theoretical component in his work quite seriously, and at least after 1933 read *Capital*, the 1844 Manuscripts, and Marx's political writings very carefully, there was something in him of Karl Kraus's view of the Communists, which he quoted approvingly in his essay on the great satirist: "Communism . . . the devil take its practice but God preserve it as a constant threat over the heads of those who have property and would like to compel all others to preserve it, driving them, with the consolation that worldly goods are not the highest, to the fronts of hunger and patriotic honor."[102] Similarly, almost one hundred years before, Heine had written: "From hate for the partisans of nationalism I could almost love the Communists."[103] Indeed, "almost." Although the idea of collective proletarian solidarity was attractive as a counter to the "bourgeois" obsession with self, Benjamin knew quite well that he would not be able, "under any circumstances," as he once wrote, "to form a united front, be it even with my own mother."[104]

It is a mark of the heuristic and ambiguous quality of Benjamin's

98. Benjamin, *Reflections*, pp. 102–110.
99. Benjamin, *Briefe*, Vol. 1, p. 52.
100. Rolf Tiedemann, "Nachwort" to Benjamin, *Charles Baudelaire: Ein Lyriker im Zeitalter des Hochkapitalismus* (Frankfurt a.M., 1967), pp. 185–190.
101. Benjamin, *Briefe*, Vol. 2, p. 531.
102. Benjamin, *Reflections*, p. 272.
103. Quoted in Fuld, *Walter Benjamin*, p. 217.
104. Benjamin, *Reflections*, p. 11.

Marxism that at the same time, 1929, that he became fascinated with Brecht and Brecht's theatrical practice, he came closer to Adorno (the two had met in Frankfurt in 1923[105]), who disapproved so strongly of Brecht's influence upon him. Benjamin found in Brecht a quality of "crude thinking" which Adorno despised but which, according to Benjamin, forced theoretical flights to be related to basic material realities experienced by the masses.[106] To him Brecht was a kind of reality principle, in touch with the proverbial idioms of everyday plebeian language, which would help Benjamin to break away from the esotericism of his own style and thought.[107] Yet, he remained sufficiently independent of Brecht throughout the next decade to maintain intellectual connections not only with Adorno but, more importantly, with the Jewish mysticism he learned with Scholem's aid, and with the symbolist and surrealist modernisms which always played into his work. Clearly, no brand of Marxism, whether Brecht's or Adorno's, could alone contain his protean forms.

Benjamin's drift toward Marxism in the years 1925–29 coincided with and was influenced by a shift in his conception of his social role. Whereas up to 1924 (when his *Habilitationschrift* was rejected) he remained within a hermetic, mystical, and aestheticized world, and his writings were, to a large extent, the narcissistic self-reflections of a melancholy intellectual, for the next eight years Benjamin sought through his journalistic activity (as literary reviewer) to reach a broader public of educated readers. Attempting to make this largely bourgeois intellectual audience sensitive to the bankruptcy of traditional bourgeois society and culture as he saw it, Benjamin also endeavored to scrutinize the social bases of his own literary activity within the capitalist marketplace. While strongly sympathizing with the struggles of the proletariat, he knew full well that his function was to be a critical force within, though hostile to, bourgeois cultural life.[108] Unlike Brecht, Benjamin never played at being a proletarian or aimed his work directly toward the working class.

In 1926, Benjamin moved to Paris. Apart from his travels and the necessity to return to Berlin for short trips in the next six years to find work, he was to remain there until his death in 1940.[109] In the years

105. Benjamin, *Briefe*, Vol. 2, p. 494; Scholem, *Walter Benjamin*, pp. 197–199.
106. Benjamin, *Understanding Brecht*, p. 81.
107. Habermas, "Consciousness Raising," p. 31; Arendt, "Introduction," pp. 14–16.
108. Witte, *Walter Benjamin*, pp. ix–xi, 136, 162–163.
109. Scholem, *Walter Benjamin*, p. 160.

1918–24, he had studied German literature from the baroque to the romantics with symbolist perspectives drawn from Baudelaire and Mallarmé. Immediately upon his arrival in the French capital, he threw himself into the further study of modern French literature, including Proust[110] and Valéry[111] (the latter-day symbolists), but also, for the first time, the contemporary surrealists. To Hofmannsthal he wrote in 1927 that he was far more interested in current French, in contrast to German, literary currents and was seeking to come close to their spirit.[112] Although the path of Breton, Aragon, and other surrealists toward communism in these years interested him, it was their guerilla war against bourgeois culture which most drew his attention. In his major piece on the movement, "Surrealism: The Last Snapshot of the European Intelligentsia" (1929), Benjamin hailed the surrealists' disclosure of public space within the interior of the allegedly subjective private self. At the same time, he described the surrealists as having broken from the commodified world in their materialist or "profane illumination" of the "enslaved" face of objects. Benjamin then enthusiastically examined the surrealist experience of Paris in which the visual images of the metropolis were recorded in a startling montage fashion.[113] The distillation of urban "shocks" in Aragon's *Le Paysan de Paris* particularly enthralled him and became an inspiration for the entire *Arcades* study.[114]

While Benjamin's Marxist and surrealist interests developed after 1928, his symbolist and Jewish mystical tendencies had by no means faded. He still seriously considered emigrating to Palestine in the late 1920s,[115] and to Russia in the mid-1930s.[116] Throughout the years after 1929, his relations with Brecht, Scholem (by letter), and Adorno placed him in a field of tension between what would appear to have been mutually exclusive forces. While Adorno entreated him to come to New York (where the Institute of Social Research had been relocated) and Scholem urged Jerusalem upon him, Brecht advised that he come to live close to him in Denmark. Benjamin declined them all, preferring to remain in Paris.[117] He feared that any such moves would make him too dependent

110. Benjamin, *Briefe*, Vol. 1, pp. 395, 403–406, 409–412.
111. Scholem, *Walter Benjamin*, p. 119.
112. Benjamin, *Briefe*, Vol. 1, pp. 446–447.
113. Benjamin, *Reflections*, pp. 177–192.
114. Scholem, *Walter Benjamin*, p. 170.
115. Ibid., pp. 173–195; Benjamin, *Briefe*, Vol. 1, pp. 261–262, 278–281, 454–458.
116. Rosemarie Heise, "Der Benjamin Nachlass," *Alternative*, 56/7 (October–December 1967), 188–189.
117. Jay, *Dialectical Imagination*, p. 197.

on any one of his friends, both financially and intellectually.[118] Instead, he confronted each (most often implicitly) with the perspectives of the others: urging Marxism against Scholem and politics against Adorno, he countered Brecht with his metaphysics and his work on Baudelaire and Kafka. Hence, he described himself in 1938 "as a man at home between the jaws of a crocodile which he holds apart with iron struts."[119]

Benjamin's writings of the 1930s, in which utopia and catastrophe were set in counterpoint, were composed against a personal background of continual economic insecurity and growing despair about the state of the world. The divorce from Dora did not come until 1930, and only after a long and anguished battle (which he lost) over his financial responsibility toward her in the future.[120] "War weary on the economic front," and in anguish over the growth of Nazi strength, in 1931 and 1932 he came close to suicide.[121] Clearly, as in the case of many modern writers, literary expression was for him an at least temporary "counter-toxin" against his own "decomposition," as he put it in a letter to Scholem at the time.[122] Another "counter-toxin" may have been a desperate hope in the Soviet Union, which Benjamin critically supported (albeit with misgivings about the bureaucracy and the purge trials) up to the Hitler-Stalin pact of 1939.[123] (This, of course, was to play a role in his conflict with Adorno.) Intellectually isolated and living very poorly in Paris, Benjamin was helped somewhat by the granting of a small stipend from the Institute of Social Research beginning in early 1934, but he resisted Horkheimer's and Adorno's pleas for him to join the Institute in exile in the United States.[124] Even with the most acute awareness of his exposed position as a left-wing Jewish refugee from Germany, should the Nazis invade France, he nonetheless insisted to Adorno in January 1938 that "there are still positions in Europe to defend."[125] Later the same year, Adorno's decision to deny publication of the "Paris

118. Benjamin, *Briefe*, Vol. 2, p. 599; Arendt, "Introduction," p. 52.
119. I have expanded the range here of a point made by Irving Wohlfahrt in "No-Man's Land: On Walter Benjamin's 'Destructive Character,'" *Diacritics*, 8 : 2 (September 1978), 49, and "On the Messianic Structure of Walter Benjamin's Last Reflections," p. 196. The quote is from Buck-Morss, *Origin of Negative Dialectics*, p. 155.
120. Scholem, *Walter Benjamin*, pp. 196–205.
121. Ibid., pp. 207–208, 222–223, 232–233.
122. Benjamin, *Briefe*, Vol. 2, pp. 555–556.
123. Buck-Morss, *Origin of Negative Dialectics*, p. 150; Scholem, *Walter Benjamin*, pp. 274–275; and Rolf Tiedemann, "Historischer Materialismus oder politischer Messianismus?," in Peter Bulthaup, ed., *Materialien zur Benjamins Thesen über den Begriff der Geschichte* (Frankfurt a.M., 1978), pp. 101–102.
124. Fuld, *Walter Benjamin*, pp. 240–241; Jay, *Dialectical Imagination*, p. 197.
125. Jay, *Dialectical Imagination*, p. 197.

of the Second Empire" essay threw him into the deepest depression, since it further threatened his economic livelihood and strengthened his sense of isolation; revision of the essay, however, under the circumstances of gathering war clouds, presented great difficulties.[126] Yet, beyond this latest blow and throughout the late 1930s, financial difficulties, pain over the growing plight of the Jews of Germany,[127] and a sense of imminent world catastrophe plagued Benjamin.[128]

After the Nazi-Soviet pact and the Nazi invasion of Poland, Benjamin penned his last reflections on history, which pilloried all notions of evolutionary progress and stressed a "hope in the past" through "seizing hold of a memory as it flashes up at a moment of danger." Three months after the fall of France, however, on September 26, 1940, Benjamin took his own life on the Spanish border. Although he had an American visa, nothing drew him to the United States. As Hannah Arendt (who knew him in Paris) says of his expectations there: "People would probably find no other use for him than to cart him up and down the country to exhibit him as the 'last European.'" Not having a French exit visa, since these were invariably denied to German refugees by the Vichy regime, which was eager to please the Nazis, Benjamin had reluctantly planned to escape across the Franco-Spanish border with a party of refugees via a usually unguarded road, and from there to go to Lisbon and a ship to the United States. Just that day, however, the Spanish had closed the border. Exhausted from the journey and with a cardiac condition, unhappy about an American exile, and in fear of being returned to the Gestapo (which had already seized his Paris apartment), Benjamin swallowed fifteen tablets of a morphia compound and died in agony.[129]

❖ ❖ ❖

Unlike Benjamin, whose contempt for bourgeois existence was influenced by a sharp and long conflict with his parents, Adorno regarded his own childhood as a lost paradise, sheltered from harsh realities, and this was to serve him as an image of a liberated utopian future.[130] His

---

126. Fuld, *Walter Benjamin*, p. 276; Buck-Morss, *Origin of Negative Dialetics,* p. 158.

127. Benjamin to Adorno, December 9, 1938, *Aesthetics and Politics*, p. 139.

128. See, for example, his letter of 1935 in Benjamin, *Briefe*, Vol. 2, p. 698.

129. Arendt, "Introduction," pp. 17–18; Jay, *Dialectical Imagination*, pp. 197–198.

130. Carlo Petazzi, "Studien zu Leben und Werk Adorno," *Text und Kritik* 56 (1977), 24; Jürgen Habermas, *Philosophisch-Politische Profile* (Frankfurt, 1971), pp. 188–189; George Lichtheim, "Adorno," in *From Marx to Hegel*, p. 128.

father, a successful wine merchant, provided economic security without interfering with his son's absorbing interests in music and philosophy. He was brought up by his mother, a professional singer, and his aunt, a pianistic accompanist who taught him the piano at an early age and thus provided him with a model of active musical engagement. At home in this aesthetically cultivated German bourgeois environment, Adorno was further protected from German political realities by the liberal tone of his native city, Frankfurt, and by the fact that he was too young to fight in the First World War or to be affected profoundly by its shattering impact upon German society.[131] He was only eleven years old in 1914.

The crisis of bourgeois society in the early 1920s was felt by Adorno in terms of the philosophical issues he grappled with at the University of Frankfurt, where he was to receive his doctorate in 1924. He studied there with the unorthodox neo-Kantian Hans Cornelius, in whose seminars he came to know a lifelong friend and later co-worker, Max Horkheimer. Adorno and Horkheimer shared a common interest in the phenomenological perspectives of Edmund Husserl, in which, they felt, the crisis and dissolution of bourgeois idealism was most acutely registered. Adorno's doctoral thesis explored Husserl's attempt to find secure knowledge in the world's objects, the "things in themselves," while he emphasized Husserl's fear that such transient phenomena provided little ground for truth.[132] Yet, there were nonacademic sources of his later outlook. He was deeply impressed by Ernst Bloch's *Geist der Utopie* (1918), which utilized utopian expressionist motifs in linking messianic hope and an eschatological Marxism. While Lukács's and Benjamin's work around this time shared strong elements of this apocalyptic vision, Adorno, unlike the others, was attracted to the expressionist form within which it was framed.[133] In 1942, he wrote of Bloch as "the philosopher of Expressionism in which the word knowledge and expression are one and the same. Already that was not gladly seen in Germany."[134] While he was later to emphasize how Schoenberg and Kafka objectified the often rhetorical expressionist procedures, Adorno's first decisive experience of the possibilities let loose by cultural disintegration was through the expressionist movement.[135] From the very

131. Buck-Morss, *Origin of Negative Dialectics*, pp. 1–2.
132. Ibid., pp. 3–10.
133. Petazzi, "Studien," pp. 27–28.
134. Quoted in Buck-Morss, *Origin of Negative Dialectics*, p. 4.
135. His first published article, written at age eighteen, showed the shattering of tra-

beginning, then, Adorno's concern for an embattled subjectivity contrasted with Benjamin's delight in the symbolists' linguistic suspensions of personal utterance.

In the spring of 1924, Alban Berg, the devotee of Schoenberg, came to Frankfurt for a performance of his expressionist masterpiece *Wozzeck*. Adorno, deeply moved by the music, met the composer, and the two immediately agreed that Adorno was to come to Vienna as Berg's student in composition. The two years in which he stayed in the Austrian capital (1925–26) were pivotal ones for Adorno's education as an aesthetic and social thinker. In the decade before World War I, and especially after the fall of the Habsburg monarchy in 1918, Vienna lived on as an empty shell of its baroque Catholic and Imperial past, a city filled with reminders of desolation and slow death heightened by continued bureaucratic suffocation and, in the 1920s, new economic malaise.[136] Aristocratic and bourgeois traditions were not simply abandoned or attacked by its artists, as they were among the dadaists and constructivists of contemporary Berlin, but were seen in a visible state of advanced rigor mortis: many of Vienna's most gifted modernist writers and musicians—Musil, Broch, Hofmannsthal, Kraus, Schoenberg, Berg, and Webern (as well as Kafka, from Prague)—felt less that they had been liberated from traditional social and cultural forms than that they must demonstrate the historical self-destruction and exhaustion of those forms *from within*. This immanent perspective, wherein tradition lived on only through its historically necessary overcoming (a perfect paradigm for an Hegelian *Aufhebung*, or "negation," which simultaneously "elevated" and "preserved"), was to form one of the abiding features of Adorno's historical method of social and aesthetic analysis.

To Schoenberg, whose work particularly affected Adorno, the justification for the emergence of polytonality lay in the inner evolution of musical logic in the nineteenth century; he was merely developing its objective unfolding toward the final dissolution of the classical tonal center.[137] Adorno argued in 1925 that Schoenberg's cultural radicalism was necessitated by the very concern for historical tradition which conservatives used to justify their attacks upon the modern. By 1929, Adorno saw such resistance to change in Marxist terms, i.e., as serving

---

ditional forms in expressionist writing: T. Wiesengrund, "Expressionismus und künstlerische Wahrhaftigkeit: Zur kritik neuer Dichtung," *Die Neue Schaubühne*, 2:9 (1920), 233–236. This has been reprinted in *GS*, Vol. 2, pp. 609–611.

136. Johnston, *The Austrian Mind*, pp. 73–75, 391–392.

137. Buck-Morss, *Origin of Negative Dialectics*, pp. 13–14, where Schoenberg's *Harmonielehre* (1911) is examined.

the ideological purposes of class privilege: "Disputing the decay of works in history serves a reactionary purpose; the ideology of culture as class privilege will not tolerate the fact that its lofty goods ever decay, those goods whose eternity is supposed to guarantee the eternity of the class's own existence."[138]

By the late 1920s, Adorno stressed the necessity of a dialectical superseding of tradition, not its cavalier overthrow. The expressionism of Schoenberg's student, Webern, had to be situated historically as the completion and simultaneous reversal of romantic individualism, he wrote; a similar reversal of tradition was accomplished in Berg's *Wozzeck*.[139] In 1932, Adorno argued that Schoenberg's Freudian-like revelation of the disintegrating ego and the pressures of the unconscious had required radical new objective musical means: the end of false harmonies and the emancipation of dissonance. These would provide formal communication of the urgent expressive material.[140]

Schoenberg's roots were clearly in the expressionist revolt against fin-de-siècle Viennese aestheticism. Like his fellow Viennese Karl Kraus, whom he deeply admired, and Adolf Loos, the architect, Schoenberg championed modern "truth" against the poetic language and "illusionary" facades of impressionist, *art nouveau*, and symbolist "beauty."[141] In Schoenberg's work, art becomes a vital medium for the radical expression of the emotional "truths" of personal anguish (sexual and otherwise). While his theoretical writings make clear how "expression" was to be developed via the objective musical material (and thus he clearly distinguished himself from the more purely subjective expressionists, such as Werfel and Toller), there is no mistaking the explosive dynamics and intense emotional overload of the music itself, especially before 1914.[142]

But emotional rebellion need not mean political engagement. Schoenberg, like so many of the other major Viennese artists, remained a cultural revolutionary, even if not an "aesthete." While modernist cultural rebels in Paris, Berlin, and Moscow were attempting to wed their art to

138. Ibid., pp. 44–45.
139. Buck-Morss, *Origin of Negative Dialectics*, pp. 15, 201n.
140. Adorno, "On the Social Situation of Music," *Telos*, 35 (Spring 1978), 133–137. This was originally published in the first edition of the Frankfurt Institute's journal *Zeitschrift für Sozialforschung*.
141. Allan Janik and Stephen Toulmin, *Wittgenstein's Vienna* (New York, 1973), pp. 67–112.
142. This is shown very well in the analyses of Schoenberg in Schorske, *Fin de Siècle Vienna*, pp. 344–364, and Charles Rosen, *Arnold Schoenberg*, 1–22. As in chapter two, I have drawn upon Walter Sokel's distinction between objectified and subjective expressionism in his *The Writer in Extremis*, pp. 50–51, 106–113, 161.

revolutionary action after 1918, Schoenberg's battle with bourgeois society took organized form in the sanctuary of his "Society for the Private Performance of Music," a circle of his devotees who met from 1918
to 1921, seeking means to avoid commercial pressures in the production
and reception of their music.[143] Something of this same exclusive modernist coterie, holding the masses and the commodified world at bay as
much as possible, remained around Schoenberg in the late 1920s and
deeply attracted Adorno[144] (although he found Berg personally far more
accessible).[145] Adorno's experience of this avant-garde enclave was important in forming his notion of available forms of critical "negation"
in late bourgeois society: although given philosophical form with the
aid of Marxian categories, Adorno's concept of "negation" was to be
largely denuded of political weight and class analysis. With no collective revolutionary "subject," all that could be hoped for was the protest
of the avant-garde against the repressive social whole and the dialectical "moments" of utopian transcendence expressed in avant-garde
work.

In the late 1920s, Adorno spent time in Frankfurt with Horkheimer,
while completing his postdoctoral work. He then moved to Berlin in
1930, where he participated in intellectual circles which included Ernst
Bloch, Siegfried Kracauer, Walter Benjamin, and Bertolt Brecht.[146] These
figures, all of whom were indebted to modernist social thought and art,
were attempting to develop a critical Marxian aesthetics at variance
with official Communist versions. These years saw Adorno's first reception of Marxian methods of analysis. Along with many of his friends,
Adorno was deeply influenced by Lukács's *History and Class Consciousness*, and by 1928 he was incorporating Lukács's critiques of
bourgeois ideology into his own writings.[147] (*Ideologiekritik* he shared
more with Horkheimer than with Benjamin; the writings of the latter
were relatively free of this mode of social analysis.[148]) Yet, Adorno and
Horkheimer did not, of course, fully embrace Lukács's perspective even
in the relatively critical form of *History and Class Consciousness*. Both
completely rejected Lukács's "identity theory," the claim that the objective understanding of history and the self-understanding, the class consciousness, of the proletariat, when properly directed by the Commu-

143. Rosen, *Schoenberg*, pp. 65–69.
144. Jay, *Dialectical Imagination*, p. 22.
145. Buck-Morss, *Origin of Negative Dialectics*, pp. 15–16.
146. Ibid., pp. 17–20.
147. Ibid., pp. 20–21, 25–28.
148. Lindner, "Herrschaft als Trauma," p. 82.

nist Party, were in unity. For them the relation between theory and
practice had to be highly mediated; the validity of theory was to be
strictly independent of instrumental needs of party or working class.[149]
While Adorno occasionally cited the injustices of class that were in-
flicted upon the proletariat, his philosophical position was rooted in the
individual rational subject, even if he viewed the individual historically
and within a mediating social whole. In his cultural criticism, Adorno
repeatedly emphasized, beginning in the late 1920s, that the individual
writer or musician best serves social purposes by working out the inner
problems of his aesthetic material, instead of construing his work as a
contribution to presently existing social collectives[150] (an argument
which we have seen him use against Brecht and Benjamin in the 1930s).

It was from such considerations that Adorno would find Benjamin's
political position of the mid-1930s dangerously close to that of Brecht
and Lukács. Though critical of Benjamin's work by the mid-1930s,
Adorno had been strongly influenced by some of his writings in the
years 1928–31, especially the methodological introduction to the pre-
Marxist *Origin of German Tragic Drama*. In her book *The Origin of
Negative Dialectics*, Susan Buck-Morss has convincingly demonstrated
the impact of this statement of Benjamin's method upon Adorno's own
form of Marxian analysis (the two had talked at length about this in
1929); in doing so, she attempts to distinguish Adorno from other members of the Frankfurt Institute for Social Research, which was to be led
by Horkheimer after 1931 (but which Adorno did not join until seven
years later). Using in particular Adorno's "The Actuality of Philosophy," an inaugural address as a new member of the philosophical faculty of the University of Frankfurt, and another talk of 1932, "The Idea
of Natural History," Buck-Morss has shown how Adorno saw history
appearing as "concrete configurations within the phenomena," and
often its most apparently insignificant details. Unlike Horkheimer, who
concentrated upon the ideological decoding of bourgeois social thought
with philosophical categories drawn from Hegel, Marx, and Freud,
Adorno fastened upon the most minute microscopic analysis of the empirical, conceptless particulars of cultural artifacts. The significance of
these details lay in their very contingency as a unique and concrete material "picture" of the social whole. The philosopher's purpose was not
to attempt to find any universal, transhistorical truths, which were illusory (Horkheimer would agree with this), but to construct "constella-

149. Buck-Morss, *Origin of Negative Dialectics*, pp. 27–32.
150. Ibid., pp. 82–87.

tions" of discontinuous, transitory particulars so that they yielded some measure of fleeting historical truth unintended by the makers of the phenomena (such as the jazz performer or Schoenberg).[151] Using language strikingly similar to Benjamin's, Adorno said in his inaugural address:

> The text which philosophy has to read is incomplete, contradictory and fragmentary. . . . Authentic philosophic interpretation does not meet up with a fixed meaning which already lies behind the question, but lights it up suddenly and momentarily, and consumes it at the same time. . . . Interpretation of the unintentional through the juxtaposition of the analytically isolated elements and illumination of the real by the power of such interpretation is the program of every authentically materialist knowledge. . . . For the mind is indeed not capable of producing or grasping the totality of the real, but it may be possible to penetrate the detail, to explode in miniature the mass of merely existing reality.[152]

History received its significance only through the unavoidable reference of our position in the present, and needed the philosophically knowing subject to decipher its meanings as they are sedimented in the concrete minute details of cultural material.[153] All of this had been suggested in Benjamin's introduction to the *Trauerspielbuch*. But Adorno was very selective in his reception of the pre-Marxist Benjamin. It was not merely that he avoided the forms of theological and mystical affirmation within which Benjamin had conceived his method of immanent criticism and microscopic analysis.[154] He never shared Benjamin's notion of critical linguistic intervention as the constructing of a radically spatial constellation wrenched from historically evolutionary time; he insisted as early as 1925 on the temporal, dialectical *Aufhebung* of cultural tradition. Similarly, while Benjamin's early and later writings pressed toward the elimination of authorial subjectivity (that of his interpreted texts or his own), Adorno always insisted on a mediation of subject and object. Benjamin's method of historical criticism proceeded throughout his career along metaphorically poetic and impersonal lines, the linking of imagistic correspondences inspired by the symbolists (even if such "images" were produced by one influenced by Marxian or other concepts). Adorno, on the other hand, explicitly and systemat-

---

151. Ibid., esp. pp. 44–46, 88–114. See also Lindner, "Herrschaft als Trauma," pp. 78–91.

152. Adorno, "The Actuality of Philosophy," *Telos*, 31 (Spring 1977), 126–127, 133.

153. Buck-Morss, *Origin of Negative Dialectics*, pp. 50–53.

154. This is the major distinction which Buck-Morss cites between the *Trauerspielbuch* introduction and Adorno's method. See pp. 90–95 of *Origin of Negative Dialectics*.

ically interpreted his microscopic details with the aid of sociological and philosophic categories. While expressionist disclosures of threatened individual personality were his favored raw material (which Benjamin had long rejected as the product of a bourgeois preoccupation with the private "soul"), Adorno theoretically mediated his data in a way which Benjamin's "correspondences" disallowed.

In his first piece of Marxian criticism which showed the influence of some of Benjamin's methods, "Die Oper Wozzeck" (1929), Adorno already showed his distance from his older friend. In spite of Berg's intent, there was a structural convergence between the inner logic of the expressionist music and a Marxist critical understanding of contemporary society, Adorno alleged: "The suffering of every individual has entered into the class struggle and turned itself against the continuance of the bourgeois order." [155] Although the reference to "class struggle" was unusual for Adorno, the appreciative examination of expressionist subjectivity with dialectical theory was not. The contrasts between Benjamin and Adorno by the late 1930s were due far less to any shift in Benjamin after 1928, or to any sharp move away from the baroque book—the method of analysis to which Adorno urged him to return—than to the more graphic unfolding of differences which were present in the two thinkers from the earlier stages of their "careers." [156] One final contrast of their formative years before 1928 may be worth suggesting here: as we have seen, Benjamin's post—World War I outlook contained revolutionary political undertones of an anarchistic nature, and the impact of the German inflation made him view his situation as analogous with, though not identical to, that of the proletariat by the mid-1920s. Both of these ingredients were foreign to Adorno's posture, in which Marxist analytical methods were used in depoliticized forms and with little reference to the working class.

Apart from the highly selective absorption of critical methods from

155. Buck-Morss, *Origin of Negative Dialectics*, pp. 23 and 211n.
156. I have emphasized this point because Buck-Morss in her important book on Adorno sees his critiques of Benjamin entirely within Adorno's perspective, that is, as resulting from Benjamin's break from a "common program" which they allegedly shared in 1928–29. Adorno, however, was highly selective in his reception of Benjamin in these years, as I have attempted to show. Buck-Morss interprets Benjamin's early work (before surrealism and Brecht in the late 1920s) as leading, in effect, more toward Adorno's appropriation of it than toward Benjamin's own later thought. This is made clear in a fine review of *The Origin of Negative Dialectics* by Peter Hohendahl in *Telos*, 34 (Winter 1977–8), 134–137. In the 1950s Adorno came to see the continuities in Benjamin's work, suggesting now the roots of his *Arcades* study and "Work of Art" essay in the pre-Marxist writings. See, for example, "A Portrait of Walter Benjamin," *Prisms*, pp. 227–242.

Lukács and Benjamin, and the first suggestions of Freudian categories, Adorno's early Marxist studies show the imprint of a major social development of the Weimar Republic: the rationalization and monopolization process within German industry, which proceeded very swiftly in the aftermath of the inflation of 1923. The growing concentration of capital and the buying out of smaller businesses; the increasing tendency to bypass market mechanisms and the dynamics of competition and to fix prices and directly create expanded consumer demand; the use of American business techniques of mass production and the rationalization of the labor process to raise work productivity and decrease spontaneous operations; the cult of advanced technology, administrative efficiency, and "matter-of-factness" [157]—all of these features of the postcompetitive, postliberal capitalism of the Weimar Republic were to be given theoretical treatment in the work of the Frankfurt School. In the first issue of its journal, *Zeitschrift der Sozialforschung*, Adorno published his major early statement on the social analysis of music, which suggested such processes of administered capitalism [158] a few years before Friedrich Pollock was to conceptualize these developments for the Institute through the theory of "state monopoly capitalism." [159] In this view, the state was now operating to aid corporate technical and administrative control and coordination of the economy in a postcompetitive way.[160] This was to be a significant feature of the Frankfurt School's brand of Marxian analysis and found its way into the major collaborative work of Adorno and Horkheimer in the 1940s, *The Dialectic of Enlightenment*, in which the "Culture Industry" chapter appeared.

In his two essays on "The Social Situation of Music" (1932), Adorno

157. See, especially, Robert Brady, *The Rationalization Movement in German Industry: A Study in the Evolution of Economic Planning* (New York, 1970). On the relation of this aspect of Weimar history to the Frankfurt School, see Slater, *Origin and Significance of the Frankfurt School*, pp. 16–21.

158. Adorno, "On the Social Situation of Music," pp. 128–164.

159. See Jay, *Dialectical Imagination*, pp. 152–155, on Pollock's work. Siegfried Kracauer, a friend of Adorno's family whom he had studied with as early as 1917 (Buck-Morss, *Origin of Negative Dialectics*, p. 2) and remained close with for decades, had examined the rationalization of labor and the penetration of the machine and conveyor belt methods in clerical offices in the 1920s, in his pioneering analysis of the lower middle classes, *Die Angestellten* (Frankfurt, 1930). "Das Ornament der Masse," a Kracauer essay of 1927 (reprinted and translated as "The Mass Ornament" in *New German Critique*, 5 [Spring 1975], 67–76) had elucidated the impact of technification in forms of popular culture as well. On Kracauer and his relation to Adorno, see Martin Jay, "The Extraterritorial Life of Siegfried Kracauer," *Salmagundi*, 31/32 (Fall 1975–Winter 1976), 49–106.

160. Slater, *Origin and Significance of the Frankfurt School*, pp. 20–21.

saw the historical changes of the rationalization process appear, in a highly mediated way, within the "Neue Sachlichkeit" or objectivist music of Weimar culture in the 1920s. The connection was not completely farfetched: many writers, artists, and composers related to this current were positively responding to the American (or Soviet) cult of technology in their various attempts to destroy the remnants of romantic and expressionist subjectivity in their work.[161] Whereas Schoenberg's music evolved an objective principle of order dialectically, from out of the subjective psychic sources of his material, the "matter-of-fact" objectivists, Stravinsky and Hindemith, Adorno now argued, artificially revoked all individual expression in their anachronistic reversions to prebourgeois musical forms. Adorno wove into his defense of Schoenberg and Berg parallel motifs from their Viennese contemporaries Karl Kraus, Adolph Loos, Sigmund Freud, and Oskar Kokoschka.[162] Whereas this Viennese culture mounted a powerful protest against the increasingly technified and rationalized social whole precisely by demonstrating the shortcircuiting of individual expression in the contemporary world, Stravinsky, Hindemith, and the new "objectivists" were embracing the alienation of the self in the most advanced industrial economies: "The estate-corporate organization of a highly industrial economic context is manifested, which in objectivist music appears as a conforming image." Both in the manner of its composition and of its reproduction, objectivist music shows the same "limitation of . . . freedom and the same tendencies towards technification and rationalization experienced outside of music in social and economic developments. The perfection of the machine and the replacement of the human forces of labor through mechanical forces has become a matter of reality in music as well."[163] But the "transition from competitive to monopoly capitalism" (to which Adorno specifically referred), which is concealed in the very processes which appear to make society more "rationalized," must be understood as creating a still more irrational order than the older liberal bourgeois one.[164] ("Irrational" was meant here in the Marxian sense of misdirecting social resources against the real fulfillment of human needs.)

161. On the widely dispersed *Neue Sachlichkeit* phenomenon in the Weimar arts and social thought, see the illuminatingly broad studies: Willett, *Art and Politics in the Weimar Period, 1917–1933*, and Lethen, *Neue Sachlichkeit*.
162. Adorno, "On the Social Situation of Music," pp. 133–138.
163. Ibid., p. 148.
164. Ibid., p. 149.

In this way, Adorno first suggested, under the impact of the American-influenced economy of the Weimar Republic, the view of contemporary capitalist society which was to receive full expression in *Dialectic of Enlightenment*, written in the United States in 1944–45. The next step, to perceive the advent of fascism as a continuation of the iron system of administered capitalism, and thus to view American realities with Nazi society frequently in mind (the distorting perspectives of Adorno's later American exile), was also hinted at in his 1932 essays on music. Thus, Adorno's developing social thought reflected, in part, American-German interactions since the stabilized capitalism of the mid-1920s, but also some of his own heavily "dialectical imagination." [165] It has been suggested that the polarities of Adorno's thought—utopian hope and darkly pessimistic assessment—were partly formed in the double impact upon him of utopian expressionist culture of 1918–22 and the destruction of its messianic outlook in the sobering era of economic, political, and cultural restoration after 1924 in Germany. [166] What this forgets is that Adorno's expressionism was largely formed in the Viennese crucible (which never had a millenarian phase), and that his utopian dimension was a highly subordinated affair from 1925 on. Armed with the bleak vista of the disintegration of the bourgeois "autonomous" individual, Adorno used the postliberal technical rationalization of the Weimar economy to transfer that lament (so strong in Vienna) to the analysis of advanced industrial societies such as Nazi Germany and the United States.

Although he continued to turn out dialectical essays on music, Adorno's major works of the decade 1928–37 were neither examinations of modern capitalism nor of its art, but rather critiques of the latest phases of bourgeois philosophy. Unlike his friend Horkheimer, Adorno was far less a sociologist than a philosopher, even if he relied on ultimately social categories, and Horkheimer's was a highly philosophical social science. [167] While Horkheimer's essays revealed a profound moral indignation at social injustice, with a growing trace of Schopenhauerian futility at fighting it, Adorno was preoccupied with the problem of truth (albeit always a social, historical truth, not an eternal one). [168] These differences did not prevent them from working very

165. The term "dialectical imagination" is the title of Martin Jay's study of the Frankfurt School.
166. Petazzi, "Studien zu Leben und Werk Adorno," p. 28.
167. Buck-Morss, *Origin of Negative Dialectics*, pp. 66–68, 234n.
168. Ibid., pp. 9, 67.

closely together after 1936, however, or Adorno's being influenced by the Institute's work before 1938 (by which time he formally joined the group in New York). All the same, Adorno's philosophical studies of Kierkegaard (written in 1928–33) and Husserl (1934–37) were largely independent of the Institute, although compatible with some of its major directions under Horkheimer.

As in his musical analyses, Adorno attempted to demonstrate the dialectical self-destruction of tradition in the late "bourgeois" philosophies of the existential and phenomenological thinkers. As Schoenberg, Berg, and Webern had completed the "sublation" (*Aufhebung*) of romantic individualism, so Kierkegaard and Husserl had revealed, in spite of themselves, the self-liquidation of all bourgeois idealism which attempts to construct the world out of a pure subjectivity. Adorno's analysis was not intended merely to "expose" the ideological biases of idealism, but to reveal its (quite unintentional) social truth: both the philosophical fallacy of viewing the world as entirely self-constituted, and also the historical one of assuming the possibility of real integrated experience (*Erfahrung*) under late bourgeois administered conditions.[169] Later, in the 1950s, in a study of Martin Heidegger, Adorno was to continue these lines of argument in a devastating polemic against the fashionable language of existential "authenticity."[170] Although Husserl had in some ways gone beyond psychologism, and Adorno had learned much from his microscopic analysis of the perception of objects, Adorno sensed that even here there was a yearning, as among the existentialists, for unhistorical "essences" beyond appearance.[171]

These bourgeois philosophers reduced the object to the subject, Adorno charged, instead of dialectically mediating one with the other. Reversing the problem, orthodox Marxists and bourgeois positivists eliminated the role of the active subject in cognition and in history. Adorno was opposed in this way to all theories of "identity" in which the contradictions between particular and whole, individual and collective, history and nature, and object and subject were falsely harmonized, or even eliminated, as they were increasingly in practice in monolithic advanced industrial societies. He had learned a great deal, as had Horkheimer, from Hegel's dialectical reversals of oppositional categories wherein each antinomy, when developed to its logical conclusion,

169. Ibid., pp. 114–121; Jay, *Dialectical Imagination*, pp. 68–70.
170. See Adorno, *The Jargon of Authenticity* (London, 1973).
171. Jay, *Dialectical Imagination*, pp. 68–69.

disclosed the other without becoming identical with it.[172] Yet, the premises of Hegel's work, the positing of an ultimate identity of logic and Being, of mind and reality, and the ontological claims of absolute truth, were foreign to Adorno's more modern and limited ambitions, which he shared with the members of the Frankfurt School around Horkheimer, including Herbert Marcuse. (Dialectic was not reducible, moreover, to logical categories, as Marx had shown.) There was no ultimate ground of knowledge or reality, only contingent, fragmentary glimpses of historical truth which lay in an irresolvable and continually shifting "force-field" between subject and object.[173] Hence, while Adorno's philosophical work of the 1930s, as well as his musical analyses, showed some of the influence of Benjamin's methods—the Kierkegaard study, for example, decoded the thinker's concrete historical "constellation" and "image" of the "bourgeois interior"[174]—it was also allied to the kind of dialectical studies being carried out by Horkheimer, Marcuse, and other members of the inner circle of the Frankfurt School in this decade.

In the next chapter, the work of the Frankfurt School will be discussed at greater length; at this point, we need only briefly cite other common features of their work which Adorno shared from the mid-1930s on. Besides the historical theory of postliberal administered capitalism, and the philosophical stress upon dialectical mediation, the Frankfurt School began in the early 1930s to utilize psychoanalytic concepts in social analysis, in large part as a result of an increasing pessimism about the revolutionary potential of the working class. Freudian theory, they hoped, would help explain the psychic sources of mass instinctual conservatism—"the misplaced love for the wrong which is done them," as Adorno and Horkheimer wrote in Dialectic of Enlightenment—if properly filtered through a revised Marxian perspective on industrial society.[175] Earlier, in his Habilitationschrift of 1926, Adorno had drawn upon Freud in his attempts to find rational knowledge in the workings of the unconscious, and had set Freud's investigations against the variety of irrationalist philosophies pervasive in Germany in the 1920s.[176] By the late 1930s, with the aid especially of Erich Fromm's article for the Institute's collective work Studien über Autorität und Familie, as well as of Horkheimer's essays, Adorno stressed the Freudian analysis of masochistic dependence on authority in his articles on jazz

172. Ibid., pp. 46–49.   173. Ibid., pp. 46–47.
174. Buck-Morss, Origin of Negative Dialectics, pp. 114–121.
175. Jay, Dialectical Imagination, pp. 36–37, 105, 116.
176. Buck-Morss, Origin of Negative Dialectics, pp. 17–19.

and mass culture.[177] Thus, psychoanalytic theory provided access to problems of mass conformity and authoritarianism in advanced societies, and, concomitantly, psychosocial perspectives on the liquidation of the individual in a world of technical domination.

Whereas the Institute focused in the 1930s upon the disregard for objective material existence of various forms of bourgeois individualist and irrationalist thought, by the late 1930s, in true dialectical fashion, a deepening concern for the eclipse of individual subjectivity came into play.[178] It was this alarm which Adorno voiced to Benjamin in his letters of 1935–38, which criticized the latter's apparent "identification with the aggressors," technological and collective, and charged Benjamin with denying a role to the rational "subject" in the process of cognition. Whereas Benjamin's "discovery" of the unconscious bypassed Freud and took the impersonal form of the surrealists' public image-space within the "private" mind,[179] by the end of the 1930s Adorno had come to cite a destruction of individual subjectivity as the most disastrous threat to any hopes for a different, more hopeful, future. Now, he insisted over and again, with any remaining flickers of real negation gone from the collective subject (i.e., the workers), the vulnerable individual alone, in his/her immensely crippled existence, retained the last vestiges of resistance to the increasingly homogenized social whole; these vestiges, he emphasized, must be carefully nurtured. In his most plaintive and personal expression, in some ways his most lucid work, *Minima Moralia: Reflections of a Damaged Life*, written in the United States in the early 1940s, Adorno wrote:

In face of the totalitarian unison with which the eradication of differences is proclaimed as a purpose in itself, even part of the social force of liberation may have temporarily withdrawn to the individual sphere. If critical theory lingers there, it is not only with a bad conscience. . . . While the individual, like all individualistic processes of production, has fallen behind the state of technology and become historically obsolete, he becomes the custodian of truth, as the condemned against the victor.[180]

Adorno arrived in the United States in 1938 to join the Frankfurt School in New York. Preoccupied with his own intellectual career and culturally rooted in Central Europe, he had stayed in Germany as long as possible. When, in 1934, he saw that emigration was necessary, his

177. Jay, *Dialectical Imagination*, p. 194.
178. Ibid., pp. 52, 276–277.
179. Benjamin, *Reflections*, pp. 177–192.
180. Adorno, *Minima Moralia* (London, 1974), pp. 17–18, 129.

first choice was Vienna, but his application to continue his studies was rejected by the philosophy faculty at the University. Instead, he went to England, where he studied at Merton College, Oxford, whose refined academic atmosphere appealed to him. For the next three and a half years, however, he made frequent trips back to Germany, visiting his family in Frankfurt and his future wife Grete Karplus in Berlin.[181]

Even more than other members of the Frankfurt Institute, Adorno was to feel intensely alienated from American society and intellectual life. Because of his superficial connections to Judaism and his distance from all politics, Adorno had felt far more at home in pre-Nazi Germany than had Benjamin. Now, in the United States, Adorno's cultural pessimism and left-wing brand of elitism deepened. Working on a Princeton University Radio Research Project under the direction of sociologist Paul Lazarsfeld, Adorno reacted strongly against its purely empirical and quantitative study of audience reception of radio programs. These techniques, he alleged, merely validated the commercial claims that the public's views were spontaneous and that the consumers were the arbiters of what was produced. Instead, only critical social theory could demonstrate the administered forms of "taste" and "choice," the production of a "reified, largely manipulable consciousness scarcely capable any longer of spontaneous experience." The audiences' reactions were preformed, the internalization of the smooth "commands" of the apparatus. (Adorno arrogantly brushed aside with philosophical objections any need to empirically verify such claims.) In first coming to the United States in 1938, Adorno wrote almost thirty years later, "I had not realized how far 'rationalization' and standardization had permeated the so-called mass media."[182]

While his cultural defensiveness vis-à-vis the collective and technified forms of advanced capitalism increased in the United States, as well as his political pessimism regarding qualitative structural change, in certain ways Adorno now moved closer toward a Marxian analytical framework. American culture and society cured him, he felt, of any lingering idealist assumptions of the primacy or autonomy of *Geist* or aesthetic cultivation.[183] The near total commodifiction of cultural life in the United States, the dominance of exchange values in a society which was

181. Rose, *The Melancholy Science*, p. 9; Buck-Morss, *Origin of Negative Dialectics*, pp. 136–138; Jay, *Dialectical Imagination*, p. 68.

182. Adorno, "Scientific Experiences of a European Scholar in America," *The Intellectual Migration*, ed. Donald Fleming and Bernard Bailyn (Cambridge, Mass., 1969), pp. 340–349.

183. Ibid., p. 367.

having increasing influence in Europe and was the wave of the future, made him stress more than ever before the corporate bureaucratic structures of ultimate decision-making.[184] The very homogenizing effects of "mass culture," and the espousal of a bogus ideology of equality, might have the effect, he hoped in 1942, of actually illuminating the still entrenched socioeconomic class disparities.[185] One of the central arguments of the *Dialectic of Enlightenment* (written in the early 1940s) was that "progress" in technological rationality, without revolutionary changes in social and economic structure, was causing the return of mythic barbarism as a primary feature of advanced capitalist society. Yet, an increasing disillusionment with *any* political praxis to bring about the changes he felt were needed, and a growing sense of the interlocking monolithic quality of the social whole, make it easy to overlook these Marxist aspects of his work.

Dialectic of Enlightenment, Minima Moralia, and the *Philosophy of Modern Music,* the three major works of Adorno's American exile, contained many passages which assimilated American society to that of Nazi Germany. Only the suggestion that direct terror and coercion differed from gentler, but no less effective forms of enforced conformism was advanced to distinguish between the widely contrasting realities.[186] But even more significant as an indication of Adorno's historical outlook were a number of passages in which contemporary American capitalist society was distinguished from the *relatively* precapitalist structures of Central Europe before World War I. Although the old society could never return, Adorno emphasized that, because of its "feudal" remnants, it had allowed a freedom from exchange value, the false "identification" of things because of their translation into purely quantitative, monetary equivalencies. These pockets of freedom from what in the United States was an all-pervasive capitalism allowed a final flowering of European thought and culture, including that of the modernists. Using this historical contrast to highlight the present state of affairs, without arguing (as Lukács had) that nineteenth-century European high culture could be simply adapted for the twentieth century, Adorno and Horkheimer wrote in *Dialectic of Enlightenment*:

It was pre-Fascist Europe which did not keep up with the trend toward the culture monopoly. But it was this very lag which left intellect and creativity some

---

184. This is evident in the "culture industry" chapter of *Dialectic of Enlightenment,* pp. 120–168.

185. Buck-Morss, *Origin of Negative Dialectics,* p. 187.

186. Jay, *Dialectical Imagination,* p. 172.

degree of independence and enabled its last representatives to exist—however dismally. In Germany the failure of democratic control to permeate life had led to a paradoxical situation. Many things were exempt from the market mechanism which had invaded the Western countries. The German educational system, university, theaters, with artistic standards, great orchestras and museums, enjoyed protection. The political powers, state and municipalities, which had inherited such institutions from absolutism, had left them with a measure of freedom from the forces which dominate the market, just as princes and feudal lords had done up to the nineteenth century. This strengthened art in this last phase against the verdict of supply and demand.[187]

To Adorno, this same older culture, in decline, spawned the avant-garde protests against capitalist alienation, such as those he deciphered in the works of the Schoenberg circle. (Here was the historical context for Adorno's insistence upon the dialectical reversal of tradition, and not its cavalier abandonment.) But in the United States, such resistance to market criteria, the very possibility of a critical culture, was thwarted by the ubiquity (and internalization) of exchange values so manifest in the products of the "culture industry." "The United States . . . displays capitalism in a state of almost complete purity, without any pre-capitalist remnants," Adorno wrote in 1967, by which time he could fully assess the increasing West European resemblance to this state of affairs. (This was precisely what had drawn Brecht, the advocate of a "refunctioned" capitalist technology, *toward* America in the 1920s.) Adorno's parents, like many Austrian and German business people (especially the Jews among them), had sought to justify their wealth by fostering the intellectual and aesthetic education of their children. But the United States, in comparison, was an unapologetic, frankly acquisitive society whose cult of practical business success, as Richard Hofstadter has shown, was marked by a decided disrespect for aesthetic values and speculative critical thought[188]—the precise strengths of Adorno's cultivated European makeup. In *Minima Moralia*, Adorno valorized the "feudal" remnants which distinguished Europe from the United States. It is worth quoting at length.

In Europe the pre-bourgeois past survives in the shame felt at being paid for personal services or favours. The new continent knows nothing of this. . . . What was thought disreputable about artists and scholars was what they themselves most rebelled against, remuneration, and Hölderlin, the private tutor, as much as Liszt, the pianist, underwent precisely in employment those experi-

---

187. Adorno and Horkheimer, *Dialectic of Enlightenment*, pp. 132–133.
188. Hofstadter, *Anti-Intellectualism in American Life*, p. 251. The long discussion of the business component in American anti-intellectualism is on pp. 233–298.

ences which led them into their opposition to the dominant consciousness. . . .
Even if the greater force of bourgeois utility overcame and overcompensated
such reactions, the doubt nevertheless remained whether man was made merely
to exchange. The remnants of the old were, in the European consciousness, ferments of the new. In America, on the other hand, . . . the self-evidence of the
maxim that work is no disgrace, the guileless absence of all snobbery concerning the ignominy, in the feudal sense, of market relationships, the democracy of
the earnings principle, contribute to the persistence of what is utterly anti-
democratic, economic injustice, human degradation. It occurs to nobody that
there might be services that are not expressible in terms of exchange value. This
is the real pre-condition for the triumph of that subjective reason which is incapable of thinking truth intrinsically binding, and perceives it solely as existing
for others, as exchangeable. If across the Atlantic the ideology was pride, here it
is delivering the goods.[189]

Such remarks neglected important historical contrasts between the
United States and Central Europe in the 1930s and early 1940s. That
German and Italian fascism flourished among precapitalist elites who
disdained commerce, even if fascism functioned to strengthen the economic power of big business, did not engage Adorno's attention. The
very pervasiveness of capitalist ideology and practice in American
society, moreover, with no revolutionary or even moderate socialist
threats to endanger it (as on the European continent), had also allowed
the social system to prevail without recourse to truly authoritarian
measures. Obviously, the tradition and reality of constitutional legal
safeguards, and the long experience of political life, played an important role here also. Be that as it may, Adorno's comments on American
society suggest how strong the opposition to the instrumentalizing of
art and thought and to commercially induced "identities" was in Adorno's own anti-capitalism, formed in the rich aesthetic culture of Central
Europe's "feudal" remnants.

Adorno was not suggesting a return to aristocratic or academic privileges on the nineteenth-century German model. He was not a "mandarin" seeking to use idealist philosophy and traditional culture as a defense of vested social interests for the educational elite, as were the
professors described in Fritz Ringer's study of the German academic
community and its long rearguard battle against modern capitalist society in the decades 1890–1933.[190] While Adorno shared the common
German academicians' cultural elitism, their distrust of instrumental
reason and utilitarian, positivist values, and their defensiveness toward

189. Adorno, *Minima Moralia*, pp. 195–196.
190. Ringer, *Decline of the German Mandarins*.

a modern technological mass society (in short, the "West"), he did not counter "modern" vulgar materialism with an equally vulgar idealism which hid material injustices and sensate unhappiness behind a fog of lofty rhetoric. He also did not reify traditional idealist culture and thought as a body of truth protected from the shifting movements of history. In addition, Adorno rejected the nationalist ideologies and *Gemeinschaft* appeals through which many professors politically channeled their cultural laments.[191]

Yet, there was a group of "modernist mandarins" who resisted the reactionary nostalgic views of their colleagues, realistically understood the historical inevitability of industrial society, and studied its features with social-science methods influenced, in part, by historical materialism (Weber, Tönnies, Simmel, Brentano, and Troeltsch were its leading lights), even while they shared the nationalist politics and pessimistic social outlook.[192] If they may be described as mandarins of the "center" (which reflects something of their moderately "conservative" or "liberal" politics), then Adorno may perhaps be seen as a kind of "mandarin" of the left, as long as we do not take this so literally that we reduce his thought simply to a defense of vested institutional or social privileges; the term should be understood metaphorically as suggesting a general social outlook. Another vital qualification would also be necessary: Adorno repeatedly stressed the historically necessary dialectical reversal of nineteenth-century high culture in the best advanced work of the modernists. Although historical traces of the social outlook of the older intellectual elite remained within Adorno's thought, they were refracted through the prisms of the aesthetically modern (a common conjuncture in the Viennese avant-garde) and the socially Marxist. All the same, whereas Lukács attempted to compensate for his patrician beginnings with his espousal of a popularly received realist art, Adorno did not apologize for the aristocratic sources of his culturally avant-garde posture, which had been filtered through the aesthetically cultivated *haute bourgeoisie* of Frankfurt and Vienna. Although there were genuine socialist and democratic strains in his critiques, the note of traditional upper-class aesthetic disdain for a commodified mass culture is unmistakable. He himself had written of this aristocratic-socialist anti-capitalism in true dialectical fashion: "The remnants of the old ['snobbery concerning the ignominy, in the feudal sense, of market rela-

---

191. Jay, *Dialectical Imagination*, pp. 294–295.
192. Ringer, *Decline of the German Mandarins*, pp. 128–143, 202–212, 269–281.

tionships, the democracy of the old earnings principle'] were, in the European consciousness, ferments of the new." [193]

Adorno's "aristocratic" left-wing assaults upon American mass culture historically coincided with a conservative form of "populist" surge in American intellectual life beginning in the middle 1930s. In the face of Hitlerism and Stalinism, and with the apparent success of New Deal policies to avert the worst ravages of the depression, many American liberal and previously radical writers began in the late 1930s to celebrate "native" national values, rural life, and the American political consensus. In this context, American culture was now hailed as a truly democratic expression of the popular will, its relationship to capitalist economics sidestepped within the perimeters of conflict now seen in the world: the battle between popular "democracy" and "totalitarianism." [194] While Adorno and his Frankfurt School colleagues rarely referred to any of this nativist ideology specifically, many of their arguments regarding American mass culture may be seen as a critical response to this kind of "populist" defense of American capitalism. The very term "culture industry" had been intended, as we have seen, to undercut the assumption of spontaneity and free choice implied in the concept of "popularity." (Unfortunately, Adorno and his colleagues went to the other extreme and assumed voluntary servitude on the part of the "manipulated.")

Almost alone among German-Jewish exile intellectuals (including his Frankfurt School associates), Adorno was anxious to return to Germany after the end of the war. Besides homesickness, he acknowledged later that the German language also drew him back because of the "special elective affinity" of that language to philosophy, and especially to the speculative aspects of philosophy. [195] Here, of course, was an indirect reference to Adorno's intense discomfort in the American cultural en-

193. This does not mean that an aristocratic "strain" makes one a conservative elitist. There were strong anti-authoritarian, anti-ascetic and democratic aspects of Adorno's critiques of "popular culture." My own analysis of Adorno's posture should be distinguished from writers such as Edward Shils who disregard the differences between Adorno's left polemics and those of high culture conservatives. To Shils they are all simply elitist European exiles who loathe the "democratic" mass culture of the people. (See "Daydreams and Nightmares: Reflections on the Critique of Mass Culture," *Sewanee Review*, 65 [1957], 600.) At the same time I have associated Adorno more closely with the "mandarins" of Ringer's study than does Martin Jay (*Dialectical Imagination*, pp. 294–295) who does not consider the "modernist mandarins."

194. Richard Pells, *Radical Visions and American Dreams: Culture and Social Thought in the Depression Years* (New York, 1973), pp. 292–329.

195. Adorno, "Auf die Frage: was ist deutsch?," *Stichworte: Kritische Modelle 2* (Frankfurt, 1969), p. 110.

vironment. In addition, however, it pointed to a central observation which continued to govern and justify his work in the decades of the 1950s and 1960s in West Germany: "Philosophy, which once seemed obsolete," he wrote in 1966, "lives on because the moment to realize it was missed." [196] With a wide audience for his writings, and at the center of the now celebrated Frankfurt School, resettled in its native land, Adorno continued to pour out works of sociology, music criticism, and philosophy at a furious pace. Nevertheless, although he felt less alien from his environment than in the United States, Adorno continued to cast his writings in a melancholy pessimistic mold. [197]

In the last decade before his death in 1969 at the age of 66, Adorno wrote his final major statements, *Negative Dialectics* (published in 1966) and *Aesthetische Theorie* (unfinished at his death and posthumously published in 1970). [198] Before that time, through the publication of the first editions of Benjamin's writings, [199] Adorno did immense service by rescuing the completely unknown *oeuvre* of his unfortunate friend from oblivion and contributing so much to its belated influence. Benjamin's work continued in the postwar decades to stimulate his own, both in agreement and disagreement. In the remaining two chapters of this book, I shall compare their modernist versions of Marxism and their Marxist "interventions" into twentieth-century culture. In the case of each thinker, however, the weight of personal biography and historical experience which we have noted in this chapter will be apparent: the contrasting structures, for example, of Parisian symbolism and surrealism or Viennese expressionism and psychoanalysis; of Jewish messianic time ruptures or German dialectical evolutions; of suspended or mediated subjectivities; of political anger and historical ambiguity or near total political pessimism; and, finally, of direct experience of the market in literary goods or more distanced observation of its erosion by the administered social whole.

196. Adorno, *Negative Dialectics*, p. 3.
197. Jay, *Dialectical Imagination*, p. 256.
198. Both were published with Suhrkamp Verlag, the disseminator of most of the writings of Adorno, Benjamin, Marcuse, Horkheimer, Bloch, Brecht, etc.
199. Benjamin, *Schriften*, 2 vols. (Frankfurt a.M., 1955), *Illuminationen* (Frankfurt a.M., 1961), and *Angelus Novus* (Frankfurt a.M., 1966), were the first collected editions before the *Gesammelte Schriften* began to appear in 1972. For a complete list of the publications of Benjamin edited by Adorno from 1950 to 1966, see *Zur Aktualität Walter Benjamins*, pp. 273–277.

CHAPTER EIGHT

Marxism Much Revised

In contrast to Brecht and Lukács, Benjamin and Adorno were not "Marxists" in any simple sense of the term. As we have seen, many other currents of thought played equally important roles in the work of the latter two (Benjamin especially); their "Marxism" was a highly selective, even truncated, affair. Adorno largely avoided class struggle categories and totally dismissed the classical notion of the proletariat's central function in historical change. Benjamin, on the other hand, while adopting a few major Marxian arguments, often used these in a largely metaphorical fashion, one of the strategies of his "crossroads" position between Marx, Mallarmé, and Gershom Scholem. Brecht may have been "modern," experimental, and open-ended in comparison with the Communists, but he appears to be orthodoxy itself when compared to Adorno or Benjamin. Though the latter two shared many of Brecht's critical attitudes toward Lukács's literary classicism,[1] neither Benjamin nor Adorno could abide, for example, the productivist, left-utilitarian, and French Enlightenment mold of Brecht's Marxism. (The playwright had hailed the sciences, for example, "for all their success in exploiting and dominating nature."[2]) Neither Benjamin nor Adorno would have ever rationalized the Stalinist dictatorship in terms of the

---

1. See Benjamin's conversations with Brecht in 1934–38 (*Understanding Brecht*, pp. 105–121) and Adorno's powerful critique of Lukács, "Reconciliation Under Duress" (1958), translated in *Aesthetics and Politics*, pp. 151–176. In this article Adorno makes strictures upon Lukács similar to those made by Brecht, but also observations which, in other places, he aimed against the dramatist (as in "On Commitment," also translated in the book, pp. 177–195).

2. *Brecht on Theatre*, ed. John Willett, p. 184.

alleged progressive value of increased socialist industrial production, an
ascetic technocratic perspective which Benjamin acidly attacked in his
last reflections upon history,[3] and Adorno savaged in his sustained assaults upon the technical domination of nature.

Benjamin and Adorno were far more distant from Soviet Communism and Leninism than were Gramsci, Bloch, Lukács, Brecht, or later
"Western Marxists" (such as Althusser, Lefebvre, or Coletti). This
partly resulted from, and contributed to, a refreshing freedom in their
transformations of the Marxian canon, and a wider awareness and less
crudely utilitarian understanding of modernist culture in the West. But
there is another side to this. Benjamin and Adorno were free not merely
from the Communist Party, but also from all experience of politics and
actual working-class movements (even though Benjamin sought to overcome this partly by building literary bridges, on occasion, between intellectual and working-class "production"). Although the Marxist aesthetics of Benjamin and Adorno benefited immensely from poetic or
musical talents and intimate acquaintance with a vast terrain of modern
cultural experience—so that their treatments of art reveal a concrete attention to aesthetic detail and a mastery of advanced formal languages
usually missing in Marxist criticism—their writings often suffer from a
lack of historical specificity and communicative directness. Such qualities revealed, in part, the total lack of any meaningful relation to social
action. This may have been largely a matter of choice and predisposi-
tion: it is hard to imagine either of them, but especially Adorno, active
in any trade union or political movement, no matter how attractive the
institutional frameworks. Part of the problem of course was caused by
historical realities of the Hitler-Stalin era: the great difficulty of inter-
relating an open critical Marxist theory and practical action after the
Stalinization of the KPD in the mid-1920s; the increasingly sclerotic and
conservative behavior of the SPD and many of the German trade unions
in the 1920s; and, finally, the utter debacle and destruction of the left in
the wake of the Nazi seizure of power.[4] (Benjamin did at least address
himself directly to the political education of the broad intellectual middle classes in his journalistic activity from 1926 to 1932.) Whichever
side one chooses to emphasize (their personal predispositions or the historical situation), the fact remains that Benjamin's and Adorno's sophisticated body of thought was eroded from within by an excessive dis-

3. Benjamin, *Illuminations*, pp. 258–289.
4. See *Dialectical Imagination*, pp. 36–37, and Russell Jacoby, "The Critique of Automatic Marxism," *Telos*, 10 (Winter 1972), 119–146.

tance in its esotericism from the vital and mundane problems of the nonintellectual population. This is not to suggest, of course, that all intellectual activity should be subordinated to immediate historical exigencies or the ordinary problems of working people, but that critical social theory (including that focused upon cultural life) suffers substantially from too great a remoteness from these realities. Benjamin and Adorno were each well aware of this and sought to mediate their work with such considerations. Yet, both retained stylistic elements of a private language in their writings, a language fully open only to initiates, even if Benjamin made important efforts to overcome his own esoteric tendencies. In Adorno's writings, in particular, the disillusionment with the "masses" and with political action is so total and abstract as to serve, in part, as a rationalization of his own hermetic theorizing.

The highly esoteric quality of the writings of Benjamin and Adorno weakened the real advances they made over Brecht's or Lukács's "cruder" Marxism. For all its faults, Brecht's work has richly fertilized critical-minded filmic and theatrical productions in many places in the world, and there is at least a latent potential in his methods for the social activation, based on firmer historical understanding, of his audiences. Lukács's writings, in addition, have been a source of great inspiration to many intellectuals attempting to democratize communism in Eastern and Western Europe, although (especially in the 1930s and 1940s) his work in certain ways justified the communist status quo (as did Brecht's). The greater penetration of Benjamin's and Adorno's analytical work was purchased, on the other hand, at the expense of its social insularity as an interesting source for largely academic research (of which the present study is, of course, an example). Perhaps all this merely reflects the different talents that each of the four men possessed— or the dilemmas always facing critical intellectuals, especially those of the left. In any case, it seemed necessary to make this observation before embarking upon the study of our last, and here much revised, versions of "Marxism."

Benjamin did not "apply" Marxism to art after 1925. He introduced into his writings a new source of poetic metaphor, one which pointed toward the social world interpreted in Marxian theory and which thereby intensified the complex reverberations between the antinomies within his thought-world. In this way, Jewish mystical theology (in particular its revelatory and messianic strains) was now simultaneously juxtaposed and poetically interrelated with selected aspects of Marx's materialism. Political and religious directions, Benjamin wrote in 1926, were now to be paradoxically transformed "from one into the other (in either direction)."[5] Benjamin's pivotal absorption of symbolist modernism provided the connective method—in particular, the evocative, enigmatic, and resonating power of metaphorical statement. The theological substance was presented in the most profane manner possible, while the mundane and secular world was approached as a numinous and sacred text.[6] The classic formulation of this appeared in Benjamin's essay on surrealism (1929):

> The true, creative overcoming of religious illumination does not lie in narcotics. It resides in a *profane illumination*, a materialistic, anthropological inspiration, to which hashish, opium, or whatever else can give an introductory lesson. (But a dangerous one; and the religious lesson is stricter.)[7]

Adorno had chided Benjamin for combining mystical enumeration, the theological motif of "naming," with economistic facticity in his first Baudelaire essay. What might be said more broadly is that Benjamin's "profane illumination" contained the most ambiguous mixture of auratic and politically de-aestheticized qualities, the confrontation of his essentially poetic and mystical approach to language with a selective Marxist substance which threatened to liquidate that approach (as did his counter-toxin of Brechtian *Entzauberung*). In the surrealist essay, for example, Benjamin hailed in surrealist work the materialist revelations of palpable physical objects which lay within the visual interiors of the self. Breton is closer to the "things" that Nadja is close to than he is to her, Benjamin emphasized. Surrealist writings evoked the "revolutionary virtue" of living in a "glass house" where "discretion concerning one's own existence" was abandoned in favor of public collective life.[8]

Marxism provided Benjamin with social categories for his war on the private and subjective, and, at the same time, gave new meaning to his modernist aesthetics. In his "Tour of the German Inflation," he had attacked the bourgeois family for its "regime of private affairs," claiming that "the shift of erotic emphasis to the public sphere is both feudal and proletarian."[9] That Marx had viewed collective action and social control of production as a means to *free* the subjective personality in a

---

5. Benjamin, *Briefe*, Vol. 1, pp. 425–426, May 29, 1926, to Gershom Scholem.
6. Witte, *Walter Benjamin*, pp. 178–181.
7. Benjamin, *Reflections*, p. 179.   8. Ibid., pp. 179–180.   9. Ibid., p. 91.

new associated life, and thus to make good the claims of the bourgeois revolution on a new basis, did not concern Benjamin. For him, Marxism continued the approach of his own theories of language: it added a political significance to the impersonal poetics of the symbolist or surrealist object.

In suggesting Marxian motifs, Benjamin often utilized the most concrete visual imagery in presenting his thoughts, a procedure which unlocked many meanings which the Marxian ones did not exhaust. Describing his central focus as a critic (the "redemption of the past" through the construction of new hidden "constellations" with the present), he reassembled the method in Marxist terms: "The historical material, turned by the plough of Marxist dialectics, would have become a soil capable of giving life to the seed which the present had planted in it." [10] Such poetic language was no mere ornamental medium for "expressing" Benjamin's thoughts. The material density of his words attaches the reader of such sentences to the very images which they evoke; those palpable objects then release *their* significance through the aid of the sentence. In his last reflections on history, Benjamin, now explicitly asserting the religious components of his thought, presented historical materialism as a puppet in Turkish attire playing chess guided by the "hunchback dwarf" of theology who sits inside him and guides his hands. The allegorical image concludes: "The puppet called 'historical materialism' is to win all the time. It can easily be a match for anyone if it enlists the services of theology, which today, as we know, is wizened and has to keep out of sight." [11] Here Benjamin explicated his fable, but its mysterious resonance remained intact. The poetic form was not a "covering" but part of the very nature of his Marxist "content." It lent to his essays a quality of extreme indirectness and enigmatic suggestion which heightened the experimental qualities of his "commitment."

Far from encouraging the theological analogies within which Benjamin viewed the social and historical theories of Marxism (as has been claimed), [12] Adorno sought to direct Benjamin toward a more purely secular form of discourse. [13] More fundamentally, Adorno hinted at the metaphorical manner in which Benjamin presented the relationship between the "superstructure" and "corresponding features" of the "in-

---

10. Benjamin, "Eduard Fuchs: Collector and Historian" (1937), *New German Critique*, 5 (Spring 1975), 32.
11. Benjamin, *Illuminations*, p. 253.
12. Brenner, "Die Lesbarkeit der Bilder," pp. 55–56.
13. Jay, *Dialectical Imagination*, p. 201.

frastructure," instead of "mediating cultural traits . . . through the total social process."[14] For this reason, Adorno was disappointed with the way in which powerful ideas were being presented "as a mere as-if" construction. But Adorno missed the full extent of Benjamin's metaphorical imagination: Benjamin was not merely eschewing explicit mediating analyses and philosophical discursive logic; he was poeticizing causal analysis away in many cases by replacing it with the relational language of symbolist "correspondences." While introducing Marxian-influenced analogies such as those between Baudelaire's poetry and the fetishized commodity structure (thereby attempting to undercut Baudelaire's aestheticism), Benjamin was simultaneously developing a Marxism in symbolist form, weakening its claims to "scientific" explanation. Thus, the strongest antidote to his own youthful aestheticism, Marxian materialism, was to this extent itself aestheticized. Seeing the danger, Benjamin paradoxically embraced the "decay of aura" and the "politicization" of art. Adorno, drawing on Freudian theory, interpreted such maneuvers on Benjamin's part as masochistic "identification" with technological and collectivist "aggressors,"[15] instead of considering the genuine ambivalence in Benjamin's view of the crisis of cultural tradition—a refusal to choose between alternative perspectives which he posed in the most extreme manner possible.

Benjamin had always been fascinated by the "redemptive" and "illuminating" power which he found enclosed in the physical objects of the world. In Benjamin's use of the most concrete visual imagery, he viewed himself, in effect, as a linguistic medium in service to the power of these objects. Yet, like the early French symbolists, who were obsessed with the ephemerality of life's passing moments, this perspective took a most melancholy cast as a meditation on death, which was a central theme of much of Benjamin's work, from the baroque book to the Paris studies. In a most unique manner, Benjamin's Marxism continued his lifelong inquiry into the aesthetics of death; but now, via the theory of reification and commodity fetishism, he sought to cure the traces of decadent necrophilia in himself by construing it in relation to the market economy and fascist violence, both of which he equally despised.[16]

14. Adorno to Benjamin, November 10, 1938, *Aesthetics and Politics*, p. 128.
15. Adorno, *Über Walter Benjamin* (Frankfurt a.M., 1970), pp. 58, 64. These are in two short pieces written in the 1950s and 1960s. The point was already implied, however, in the letter of March 18, 1936, to Benjamin, where Adorno criticizes his "Work of Art" essay: ". . . it is as though you feared a consequent onrush of barbarism . . . and protected yourself by raising what you fear into a kind of inverse taboo." *Aesthetics and Politics*, p. 123.
16. In the now vast literature on Benjamin it is quite surprising that this theme of

The aesthetic glorification of dead commodity objects, reified from their living connection to the labor process in which they were created, formed a central focus of Benjamin's major Marxist inquiry, the study of nineteenth-century Paris and the origins of capitalist modernity. As we have seen, he wrote in the draft outline of the whole project: "Fashion prescribed the ritual by which the fetish commodity wished to be worshipped. . . . In relation to the living it represents the right of the corpse. Fetishism, which succumbs to the sex-appeal of the inorganic, is its vital nerve; and the cult of the commodity recruits this to its service." [17] In the two completed essays on Baudelaire, Benjamin explored the dissolution of personality through the poet's empathy with inorganic matter and decayed goods (a symptom of his own existence as a salable commodity in search of customers),[18] and through the poet's "intoxicated" surrender to the unassimilable "shocks" of urban *Erlebnis*, the ephemeral, new, and unexpected found in the shifting metropolitan crowds. In both the baroque book and the studies of Paris, the corpse functioned as a central allegorical figure; in the second case, however, as Benjamin once explained, it is seen "from within" [19] by the poet, who is subject to the prostituted fetishism of his own commodity "soul." There was clearly a biographical influence upon this analysis: Benjamin's own sense of himself as a "commodity" in the literary market, and as a connoisseur of the deathly loss of selfhood in the modern anonymous city.[20]

In struggling against such reification (as he had come to view this process with the aid of Lukács's *History and Class Consciousness*), Ben-

---

death has been largely neglected. Witte, *Walter Benjamin*, p. 132, suggests the general significance of death in his aesthetic theories but does not clarify this very much. There is a good short discussion of Benjamin's view of the modern city in relation to death in Günther, *Walter Benjamin*, pp. 174–176. Many commentators on *The Origin of German Tragic Drama* have not missed its central importance in that work, but do not show his later and very different handling of the theme in the *Arcades* study or the essays which deal with fascism. For a good discussion of various treatments of death in selected works of modern literature, see Theodore Ziolkowski, *Dimensions of the Modern Novel* (Princeton, N.J., 1969), chaps. 6 and 7. Ziolkowski stresses the connection of the death obsession with the experience of ephemerality discussed in the *Lebensphilosophie* of Dilthey, Simmel and Nietzsche, and views modernist simultaneity as a defense against irreversible time. Illuminating comments on the specifically symbolist preoccupation with death may be found in Anna Balakian, *The Symbolist Movement*.

17. Benjamin, *Charles Baudelaire*, p. 166. There is a good discussion of the concept of commodity fetishism in Benjamin's whole *Arcades* study in Pfotenhauer, *Aesthetische Erfahrung*, pp. 59–63.

18. Benjamin, *Charles Baudelaire*, pp. 55–61.

19. Benjamin, "Zentralpark," *GS*, I/2, pp. 681, 684.

20. Besides his treatments of Baudelaire's Paris, see Benjamin's comments on the death-like nature of capitalist Berlin in the mid-1920s, in *Reflections*, pp. 97–98.

jamin paradoxically sought to enlist the services of his attraction to dead objects in the effort to impart new life to them. His method of "profane illumination" of the "things" of the physical world was to "explode" them from their ordinary and habitual existence as commodified "enslaved and enslaving objects," and thus liberate them, in effect, for a changed social usage. A central feature of this technique was defamiliarizing estrangement through viewing objects up close but from many angles, a montage distancing technique which Benjamin had been using all along but for which Brecht was to provide a conceptual handle. In an essay of 1950, Adorno perceptively commented on his friend's work: "By permitting thought to get, as it were, too close to its object, the object becomes as foreign as an everyday, familiar thing under a microscope. The technique of enlargement brings the rigid in motion and the dynamic to rest. The core of Benjamin's philosophy is the idea of the salvation of the dead as the restitution of distorted life through the consummation of its own reification down to the inorganic level." [21]

In his Marxist phase, the notion of so redeeming dead objects for a better society gave a constructive turn to Benjamin's otherwise paralyzing morbidity. His scathing indictment of fascist politics provided still another means of undermining the strain of symbolist decadence in his outlook. After 1930, Benjamin developed his notion of the cult of death in modern capitalist culture by citing the aestheticized intoxication with technological warfare in fascist ideology, fascist nostalgia for World War I (in Marinetti and Ernst Jünger), and fascist preparations for the next war. Rather than "identifying with the aggressor" in his hopeful assessment of modern technology, as Adorno claimed, [22] Benjamin sought instead to suggest utopian possibilities which must be rescued from the current annihilative and aggressive violations of its potential. Suggesting that fascist aestheticizing of warfare and pseudorevolutionary politics was a culmination of late nineteenth-century decadence, rendered possible by the social misdirection of technical capacities, Benjamin saw the climax of voluntary reification in the fascist lust for universal self-destruction "as an aesthetic pleasure of the first order." [23]

Besides his own unique deployment of the concepts of reification and commodity fetishism, Benjamin made much of the central Marxian analysis of capitalist contradictions between forces and relations of production. In the essays "The Work of Art in the Age of Mechanical Re-

21. Adorno, "A Portrait of Walter Benjamin," pp. 240–241.
22. Adorno, Über Walter Benjamin, pp. 58, 64.
23. Benjamin, Illuminations, p. 242.

production" and "The Author as Producer," Benjamin applied these categories to the new media in capitalist society. He was to draw frequently upon this conceptual apparatus, as Brecht had done with regard to the emancipation of avant-garde literary productions from the ideological constraints within which they were held. But for Benjamin, technology was no mere scientific "fact," and its "progress" was no necessary boon to humanity. Whereas Marx could not have been fully aware of the destructive possibilities which might be unleashed through modern machinery, though he had emphasized the social regression and alienated labor in its manufacture, Benjamin stressed how, in the First World War, technology fully "betrayed man and turned the bridal bed into a bloodbath." [24] In examining fascism, Benjamin argued that the aesthetic manipulation of destructive violence served to mask the property system in whose defense such "technological holocausts" occurred (an oversimplified causality); and he wrote in 1930 that only proletarian revolution may lead to a use of technology as a "key to happiness and not a fetish of decay." [25] Clearly, unlike Adorno, Benjamin was suggesting a misuse of the otherwise liberating potential of modern technical capacities. On the other hand, while appearing to follow Brecht's more optimistic view of technology, proletarian struggle, and "production aesthetics," Benjamin increasingly criticized (in the course of the 1930s) the notion of linear "technological progress" and Enlightenment "domination of nature." In one of the *Theses on the Philosophy of History*, he attacked the idolatry of technology and labor in the SPD's "vulgar Marxism," a secularized version of Protestant asceticism, and its implicitly exploitative attitude toward the natural environment (an attitude which Brecht shared in certain ways, as we have seen). All this presaged the "technocratic features later found in Fascism," he commented. [26] Here he was on common ground with Adorno and Horkheimer, whose *Dialectic of Enlightenment* similarly argued that fascism was the culmination of the Enlightenment tendency to repress nature without and within in the pursuit of a reified technological "rationality." Reversions to barbarism in the modern world were the revenge, in effect, of a brutalized nature. But Benjamin had not implicated Marx in all this, choosing instead to compare "vulgarized" Marxism with the technocratic tendencies of bourgeois society. Adorno, on the other hand, less ambivalent than Benjamin and thoroughly out of sym-

24. Benjamin, *Reflections*, p. 93.
25. Benjamin, "Theories of German Fascism," p. 128.
26. Benjamin, *Illuminations*, pp. 258–259.

pathy with the productivist aspects of Marx's synthesis, was to state in 1969 that Marx wanted to turn the whole world into a giant workhouse.[27]

Benjamin did not see fascism simply in terms of aestheticized violence or the annihilating uses of a misdirected technology. He also expanded on the incipient "mass" analyses in Marx's work. In his study of Baudelaire, Benjamin drew heavily upon the *Eighteenth Brumaire*, wherein Marx had suggested a connection between atomized masses and modern Caesarist dictatorship (particularly in his treatment of peasants and urban *lumpenproletariat*). But whereas Marx viewed such manipulable "masses" as an anachronistic holdover soon to be replaced by the steady march of proletarian class formation, Benjamin seemed less sure. In "Paris, Capital of the Nineteenth Century," he referred to the "ambiguity" which is peculiar to the social relations and events of the modern epoch.[28] In the two long essays on Baudelaire, he seemed to suggest that in the maturing era of bourgeois rule there were combined elements of mass and class society. A consumer capitalism tends to isolate its customers as an atomized and amorphous mass, thus helping to dissolve the structured class differences which were otherwise more apparent. This very same amorphous "mass," the "crowd," was the social element within which Baudelaire's poetry was conceived, with its attempts to parry the shocks of unassimilated occurrences (*Erlebnisse*). The erosion of integrated experience and self-possession in the atomized consumer flow became a source of the symbolist cultivation of the ephemeral moment wrenched from temporal continuity. But on a political level, Benjamin argued that in fascist states such massification, "the accident of the market economy which brings [people] together" as buyers, was being made "permanent and obligatory" as a "fate in which the 'race' gets together again."[29]

In the essay "Some Motifs in Baudelaire," Benjamin viewed the assembly-line workers' passive adaptation to the machine, their endless repetitions of physical movements, as analogous to the conduct of passersby in a crowd: both of these groups are conditioned to act in a behavioristic manner, automatically, as an unreflective reaction to unassimilable shocks. Instead of leading to conscious class solidarity as a result of shared experiences of alienated labor on the job (Marx's view), such daily bombardment, Benjamin implied, might just as well create a

27. Jay, *Dialectical Imagination*, p. 57.
28. Benjamin, *Charles Baudelaire*, p. 171.
29. Ibid., pp. 62–63.

manipulable and amorphous collection of traumatized automatons.[30] Although this was the only place in which he voiced such fears, it is clear that by 1939, when this essay was written, Benjamin was more skeptical than he had ever been before of the Marxian prognosis of proletarian action. It is illuminating in this connection that his object of inquiry, the France of Louis Napoleon, and his contemporary point of reference, Hitler's Germany, have been the most common historical sources for sociological theorists of mass society who have been anxious to refute Marx's expectations concerning class struggle.[31]

Whatever doubts about Marxian class analysis the fascist era had stimulated in Benjamin, the advent of Hitler intensified, on the other hand, his materialist views of culture. Like Brecht and Adorno in their different ways, he stressed that the "cultural treasures" which Communists simply wanted to take over and reuse had been transformed by new technologies of reproduction, or had deteriorated in the process of being converted into commodities or the booty of the military victor. Sensitized by the fascists' appropriations of classical and romantic culture, and by their dashing of the hopes of earlier generations for a freer and more just future, Benjamin indicted historicist notions of culture which dignified its alleged "transmission":

Whoever has emerged victorious participates to this day in the triumphal procession in which the present rulers step over those who are lying prostrate. According to traditional practice, the spoils are carried along in the procession. They are called cultural treasures, and a historical materialist views them with cautious detachment. For without exception the cultural treasures he surveys have an origin which he cannot contemplate without horror. They owe their existence not only to the efforts of the great minds and talents who have created them, but also to the anonymous toil of their contemporaries. There is no document of civilization which is not at the same time a document of barbarism. And just as such a document is not free of barbarism, barbarism also taints the manner in which it was transmitted from one owner to another. A historical materialist therefore dissociates himself from it as far as possible. He regards it as his task to brush history against the grain.[32]

The last sentence of this passage suggests the extreme anti-evolutionary notion of "history" which marked Benjamin's unusual (and selective) reading of Marxism. We have seen on many occasions how Benjamin viewed with horror the linear continuum of historical sequence as

30. Benjamin, *Illuminations*, pp. 175–177.
31. Edward Shils, "The Theory of Mass Society," in *Center and Periphery: Essays in Macrosociology* (Chicago, Ill., 1975), pp. 91–107.
32. Benjamin, *Illuminations*, pp. 256–257. See also the 1937 article, "Eduard Fuchs," pp. 36–38.

a catastrophic "pile of debris," and how he viewed revolutions and "profane illumination" as a rupture in time on the model of the messianic "interventions" of Jewish hope. Many ingredients went into the formulation of this basic structure of his thought, which was implicit as early as 1915.[33] Besides Jewish apocalypticism,[34] Benjamin found in symbolist poetics the fundamental contrast between additive time and the mysterious and liberating "epiphanies," the "space-bound" "correspondences" between synchronized ancient and modern experiences.[35] In addition, as Lukács had done in *History and Class Consciousness*,[36] Benjamin described linear time as an empty ritual of meaningless repetitions, and, as such, a central ingredient of alienated labor.[37] We might also mention the "freezing" of historical time which Benjamin cited in Brecht's epic theatre.[38] Beyond these sources, and strengthening Benjamin's sensitivity to them, was his own reaction to the catastrophic "sequence of events" of his own lifetime: the First World War; the fascist "evolution" out of the crisis of middle-class society; the dogmatic trust in progress and in the historical inevitability of victory which had crippled the political effectiveness of organized Marxism in the fascist era; the beginnings of the full-scale persecution of the Jews (strengthening the need for apocalyptic redemption); and the final bankruptcy, for Benjamin, of Communist politics in the Nazi-Soviet pact of 1939. All of these historical ingredients helped to mold Benjamin's full blast against the theory of progress in *Theses on the Philosophy of History* (1940).

In this extraordinarily cryptic essay, Benjamin spelled out most fully his distinction between the linear continuum of historical evolution— what he called here "empty, homogeneous time"—and the explosion of additive sequence and immanent development in "messianic time," which draws upon the power of revolutionary memory as an "historical time-lapse camera" to produce a "time filled by the presence of the now" (*Jetztzeit*), the mystical "*nunc stans.*"[39] "[Every] second of time

33. Habermas, "Consciousness Raising," pp. 38–39.

34. On the personal and theological sources of Benjamin's assault on the idea of progress and view of time ruptures, see Gershom Scholem, "Walter Benjamin and His Angel," in *On Jews and Judaism in Crisis* (New York, 1976), pp. 198–236. On the pessimistic bases of Jewish apocalyptic messianism, see Scholem, *The Messianic Idea in Judaism*, pp. 10–11.

35. See Benjamin, *Charles Baudelaire*, pp. 81–90.

36. Lukács, *History and Class Consciousness*, pp. 88–90. A recent more empirical study of such alienation is contained in E. P. Thompson, "Time, Work Discipline and Industrial Capitalism," *Past and Present*, 51 (1967).

37. Benjamin, *Illuminations*, pp. 176–180.

38. Benjamin, *Understanding Brecht*, pp. 18–21.

39. Benjamin, *Illuminations*, p. 261. See also, on this distinction, "Eduard Fuchs," pp. 28–29.

was the strait gate through which the Messiah might enter," he wrote of the ancient forms of Jewish hope. While the "angel of history" gazes upon the incremental growth of destruction which is the movement of the present into the past, a storm from paradise propels it into the future, a storm called "progress." In hopes of arresting this "pile of debris" which "grows skyward," true revolutionary classes seek to perpetuate the moment in which the ordinary sequence of ticking seconds is ruptured.

The awareness that they are about to make the continuum of history explode is characteristic of the revolutionary classes at the moment of their action. The great revolution introduced a new calendar. The initial day of a calendar serves as a historical time-lapse camera. And, basically, it is the same date that keeps recurring in the guise of holidays, which are days of remembrance. Thus the calendars do not measure time as clocks do; they are monuments of a historical consciousness of which not the slightest trace has been apparent in Europe in the past hundred years. In the July revolution an incident occurred which showed this consciousness still alive. On the first evening of fighting it turned out that clocks in towers were being fired on simultaneously and independently from several places in Paris.[40]

The essay suggests how Benjamin wanted to go much further than Marx in revising the liberal notion of linear progress. He was not merely viewing history as a dialectical development with combined technical progress and social regression; he now fully spelled out a need to arrest, in effect, the very flow of clock-time. Sensing the discrepancy between his own view and that of Marx, he sought to use Marx selectively in developing his "historical time-lapse camera": the *Theses* referred, significantly, to Marx's *Eighteenth Brumaire*, wherein Robespierre is described as having invoked ancient Rome as a "past filled with the time of the now," as Benjamin put it, "which he blasted out of the continuum of history."[41] But Benjamin failed to acknowledge that, according to Marx, the bourgeoisie had used this revolutionary imagery in order to disguise the fact that it was serving its own class-bound interests; the proletarian revolution would not need to invoke the past, but would be able to draw its poetics from the future.[42] In preparatory notes to the *Theses*, Benjamin claimed that, for Marx, a "classless society is not to be conceived as the endpoint of an historical development," "but bears much more messianic features."[43] Yet, in so arguing,

---

40. Benjamin, *Illuminations*, pp. 261–262.
41. Ibid., p. 261.
42. *The Marx-Engels Reader*, 2d ed., pp. 596–597.
43. Benjamin, *GS*, I/3, p. 1232.

he was avoiding the obvious grounding of Marxian eschatology in the immanent self-contradictory development of capitalism over time. Elsewhere he was on firmer ground, contrasting the pessimistic bases of his apocalyptic hopes with the strong remnants of "progressivist" thought in Marx. In the mid-1930s, he wrote: "Marx says that revolutions are the locomotives of world history. But perhaps they should be seen in a wholly different manner. Perhaps revolutions are a grasp for the emergency brake which humanity makes in its trainride." [44] Such a degree of despair over the evolutionary course of things, and such a focus on the rupturing of time, link Benjamin's philosophy of history with the more "anarchistic" Blanqui and Nietzsche (both of whom he cited in the *Theses*) more than with Marx, even if Benjamin introjected some Marxian social contents into these radical discontinuities.

Benjamin's hermeneutic method and his concept of revolutionary action focused his "Marxism" on what the German literary critic Peter Szondi has aptly described as a "hope in the past," choosing the phrase from a passage in the *Theses*. This was not a desire to regress in time, but a rescuing of the hopes of earlier generations for the present juncture, a redemptive action aimed against the course of evolution in which those hopes had been dashed (as the murderous abuse of modern technology in the twentieth century had violated the initial possibilities it had contained in the "childhood" of the modern, the early nineteenth century). [45] This is what Benjamin meant when he cited the invocation of the Roman republic in the French revolution, quoted Karl Kraus's dictum, "the origin is the goal," or examined the release from temporal sequence and the drift toward death in Baudelarian "correspondences," Proustian "remembrances of things past," or his own recollections of childhood. In the fascination of old photographs, for example, he searched for "that imperceptible point at which, in the immediacy of that long past moment, the future so persuasively inserts itself that, looking back, we may discover it." [46]

The word "immediacy" points toward Benjamin's difference from Adorno on this critical matter. Whereas the dialectician sought the mediation of past and present, and criticized Benjamin's "unhistorical" coupling of the "archaic" and the "new," [47] Benjamin's constellations seemed to synchronize moments of the "enslaved" past with the needs

44. Ibid.
45. Peter Szondi, "Hope in the Past," *Critical Inquiry*, 4:3 (Spring 1978), 491–506.
46. Benjamin, "A Short History of Photography," *Screen*, 13 (Spring 1972), 7.
47. Adorno to Benjamin, August 2, 1935, *Aesthetics and Politics*, p. 112.

of the present. As against an additive notion of tradition, the linear transmission of "treasures," Benjamin sought "explosions" of the continuum so that he might, selectively, pick up the promising, untransmitted, and out-of-the-way "debris," the refuse of civilization, as does the "hero" of the modern city in Baudelaire, the ragpicker.[48] Collecting and rearranging neglected details, quotations, images of old engravings, objects, or texts had long been an obsession with Benjamin. By 1940, however, the question of rescuing the utopian hope of the hidden past from its later misappropriations (e.g., by the Nazis) was an urgent matter, one which would strengthen the weakened powers of socialist resistance. Although the sufferings of past generations would never be fully "redeemed," to Benjamin (unlike Marx) the memory of enslaved ancestors, more than liberated grandchildren, must guide the "avenging" work of the "last enslaved class."[49]

To articulate the past historically does not mean to recognize it "the way it really was" (Ranke). It means to seize hold of a memory as it flashes up at a moment of danger . . . which affects both the content of the tradition and its receivers. The same threat hangs over both: that of becoming a tool of the ruling classes. In every era the attempt must be made anew to wrest tradition away from a conformism that is about to overpower it. . . . Only that historian will have the gift of fanning the spark of hope in the past who is firmly convinced that *even the dead* will not be safe from the enemy if he wins. And this enemy has not ceased to be victorious.[50]

❖   ❖   ❖

Benjamin's metaphorical constructions, theological allusions, and anti-linear "time-lapse camera" of history did much to reposition Marxism in a triangular field with Jewish mysticism and French aesthetic modernism, although certain Marxian concepts were used in relative "purity": class struggle (qualified by much less hope in the victory of the proletariat); contradictions between forces and relations of production (with a more twentieth-century perspective on the dangers of technocracy and technical warfare); and commodity fetishism (although with Benjamin's own understanding of the worship of "dead objects").

48. Benjamin, *Charles Baudelaire*, pp. 79–80.
49. Benjamin, *Illuminations*, p. 260.
50. Ibid., p. 255. Benjamin's *Theses* have provoked wide discussion, as they should. Other treatments, more detailed than my own, may be found in Scholem, "Walter Benjamin and His Angel"; Gerhard Kaiser, *Benjamin Adorno: Zwei Studien*, pp. 1–74; Irving Wohlfahrt, "On the Messianic Structure of Benjamin's Last Reflections"; and the collection edited by Peter Bulthaup, *Materialien zur Benjamins Thesen über den Begriff der Geschichte*.

Adorno's "Marxism" was no less idiosyncratic, even if both he and Benjamin shared some common ground with other "Western Marxists," such as an abandonment of the belief in automatic progress and a stress on consciousness and culture within the social totality. But if Adorno, too, developed a unique deployment of Marxian categories, his sources were neither Jewish nor French, but within the "immanent" development of critical-minded Austro-German thought and culture as he interpreted it.

Given Adorno's focus on dialectical methods, it is best to begin with his own, while comparing them with Marx's dialectic. Adorno shared Benjamin's micrological methods in which particular contingent phenomena were socially deciphered as they appeared in cultural life. Yet, although there was overlap here, the contrasts were always at least as sharp. The watchwords of Adorno's dialectical approach were "non-identity" and "mediation." He steadfastly refused to derive reality from some ultimate ground. Neither the subject nor the object, "totality" nor concrete particulars, nature nor history, etc., should ever be reduced to one or the other; they were each in a "force-field" of tension and retained elements which distinguished one from the other. "Dialectics," he wrote, "is the consistent sense of non-identity. It does not begin by taking a standpoint. My thought is driven to it by its own insufficiency." [51] At the same time, all parts of the totality are in perpetual mediation, but this relation is not extrinsic to them, but inheres in their very structure: "Mediation is in the object itself, not something between the object and that to which it is brought." [52] More consistently than Marx, whose later work sometimes appeared to dismiss the active role of the subject in history, Adorno always stressed the mediated relation between object and subject, the tendency of each pole to disclose, in its inner structures, the constituting influences of the other. In this way, he differed from Benjamin, who had a lifelong tendency to view himself as a medium for the ambiguous language of objects while interpreting Marxism as the revelation of public, collective image-space. The careful reader of Adorno's essays will note how often he juxtaposed seeming opposites—e.g., nature and history, psyche and society, affirmation or negation—so as to mediate them by developing each of the apparent antinomies out of the other in mutual critique, a dialectical procedure which he owed to Hegel even more than to Marx. He urged this method upon Benjamin, whose metaphorical connectives tended toward an un-

51. Adorno, *Negative Dialectics*, p. 5.
52. Quoted in Williams, *Marxism and Literature*, p. 98.

mediated simultaneity of disparate perspectives. In the Hegelian Marxist framework, moreover, was Adorno's consistent and imaginative treatment of the *Aufhebung* of tradition, reversals in which continuity and negation each played a role (as in the analyses of Husserl and Schoenberg). This method distinguished Adorno's historical outlook from Benjamin's more total rejection of linear development. (It should be added here, however, that Adorno found Hegel wanting in dialectical consistency, for the latter had predicated his philosophy on a reduction of being to mind that was as erroneous as the orthodox Marxists' opposite reduction of consciousness to matter.[53] Furthermore, Adorno would not follow Hegel's belief in necessary historical progress, or related metaphysical claims to absolute truth, for, as a modernist, he stressed the relativity and provisional contingency of all searches for knowledge. Assertions of absolute certainty were chimerical, an attempt to arrest the continually dissolving workings of time.[54])

Adorno had learned much from Marx's materialist dialectic and his critiques of Hegelian idealism, although he had always rejected the pivotal Marxian affirmation of the proletariat as the collective agency of revolutionary change. Even before the Nazi victory in 1933, he saw the industrial working class as an integrated and passive reflection of capitalist society.[55] With this perspective, Adorno soon began to view theory as the only "practice" left. Yet, this was not the only major departure from Marx. Adorno also differed in strongly favoring the "totality" model for the understanding of society, in which there are endless interactions within the whole social process, over the so-called "base-superstructure" model, in which a causal focus is placed on productive forces and class relations. Marx had used both of these forms of argument[56]; Adorno usually relied on the former. For Adorno, as for Horkheimer and Marcuse of the Frankfurt School, dialectics was not causally dependent upon fissures in the so-called "base," just as it was not simply an objective process outside human consciousness (as orthodox Marxists claimed).[57] In studying cultural developments, Adorno

53. Jay, *Dialectical Imagination*, pp. 46–47; M. T. Jones, "Constellations of Modernity," pp. 173–177.

54. Buck-Morss, *Origin of Negative Dialectics*, pp. 46–53; Jay, *Dialectical Imagination*, pp. 68–69. Analogously, Adorno criticized conservatives who seek to freeze traditional culture as a value above history (*Prisms*, p. 22).

55. Adorno and Horkheimer, *Dialectic of Enlightenment*, p. 37; Adorno, *Minima Moralia*, pp. 113–114. For expressions of this in the early 1930s, see "On the Social Situation of Music."

56. Melvin Rader, *Marx's Interpretation of History* (Oxford, 1979), chaps. 1 and 2.

57. Jay, *Dialectical Imagination*, pp. 52–56.

viewed the forces of production as intrinsic, i.e., as contained *within* aesthetic activity: whereas the exacting Schoenberg had further evolved the "forces of [musical] production" that were available to him (the immanent logic of formal, compositional development), the alienated "relations of production" had extrinsically dictated the "techniques" of the culture industry for commodified consumption.[58] Although Adorno might refer, on occasion, to the more common Marxian notion of "forces of production,"[59] his own intense suspicion of a reified and repressive technological apparatus, and his insistence upon an "immanent" analysis of advanced art, made him largely replace the classical Marxian formula with his own.

In adopting the notion of an administered post-market capitalism as a key to contemporary history, Adorno tended, especially by the early 1940s, to view contemporary society as an increasingly unmediated, seamless web of "identities"—between a voluntarily compliant individual and a repressive social whole, the working class and "management," and economic and political "domination." (This was the case even though Adorno now and then might refer to the crucial influence of corporate business within the whole, and viewed the exchange economy as intact.)[60] This meant that the Marxian notion of a causal derivation of power from the class control of production, the lever in terms of which to mount specifically focused collective actions, was eroded, increasingly replaced by the specter of an interlocking and monolithic "system"[61] (as the "New Left" was to call it in the 1960s).

Adorno tended to reverse the usual direction of Marx's historical argument. In Marx's dialectic, transcending forces evolved out of the very structures of seemingly stable domination (that is, most importantly, the proletariat evolved out of the collectivizing and dehumanizing experience of capitalist labor). Adorno, however, saw affirmative and conforming realities hidden beneath apparent "liberation" (as in his studies of mass culture); only the isolated avant-garde retained an element of "negative" resistance and genuine utopian hope, without, at the same time, being able to totally escape a "reflection" of the administered "whole." The very terms "affirmation" and "negation" show the sharp alteration of Marx's historical class analysis (of contradictory tenden-

58. Rose, *The Melancholy Science*, pp. 118–121.
59. Adorno, *Minima Moralia*, p. 194; "A Social Critique of Radio Music," *Kenyon Review*, 7:2 (Spring, 1945), 208–217.
60. Adorno and Horkheimer, *Dialectic of Enlightenment*, pp. 120–121.
61. See for example, Adorno, *Prisms*, p. 34.

cies *within* capitalist production) to a dialectic between the vast majority inside and the very few relatively outside the all but total "system."

Without historically examining how an "administered capitalism" had developed out of the nineteenth-century "market economy," or how it might evolve into something else (other than fascism), Adorno and Horkheimer, by the late 1930s, stressed one feature above all of the contemporary world: the near total elimination of an integrated and autonomous bourgeois subjectivity which had previously been sustained by the more "anarchic" play of economic and social forces. Although Adorno showed traces in his social outlook of a *pre*capitalist disdain for all commercial values, the bourgeois "individualist" era of the nineteenth century appeared to him to be preferable to an advanced coordinated capitalism, if only as a stick with which to beat the present.

Adorno's handling of the notion of reification was related directly to his analysis of the plight of the individual. Benjamin had construed reification in terms of the worship of "dead" objects; Adorno saw it in the deathlike exchangeability of atomized persons in the contemporary "masses." [62] Whereas Benjamin suggested elements of a "mass" analysis within a perspective that was still guided by the conflict of classes at the point of production, Adorno retained traces of a class-conflict perspective within a predominant view of contemporary "concentrated power and dispersed impotence." [63] What lay behind the increasing identity of persons, according to Adorno, was the growing dominance of an abstract, formal equality and exchangeability in the interwoven structures of bureaucratic administration and economic trade. This, in fact, was vital to the smooth functioning of the harmonized, anonymous, and impersonal economic system of contemporary capitalism. [64] In Adorno's theory, the focus of the Marxian concept of commodity fetishism was shifted from the capitalist labor process to commercial exchange values in a twentieth-century bureaucratic and consumer society. [65]

In the era of fuller economic competition, society of course mediated

62. Adorno, *Minima Moralia*, pp. 231–232.
63. Ibid., p. 204.
64. Rose, *Melancholy Science*, pp. 43–47, 64–65, 86–91. In 1966, in *Negative Dialectics* (pp. 189–92), Adorno drew back from the concepts of alienation and reification, judging them to be a form of subjectivist or idealist criticism of how people "feel" or "think" about conditions. What was needed, he emphasized, was an examination of the objective "cause" of reification in the conditions themselves. This was part of a wider focus in the book on the constituting activity of the object (see, for example, pp. 183–184), since by that time, so Adorno felt, the "subjective" was being increasingly isolated and lionized.
65. See, for example, Adorno, "The Fetish Character of Music," pp. 278–279.

the lives of individuals (who were therefore not "autonomous" in the classical liberal sense), and such freedom as existed for bourgeois "subjects" was sustained by the maintenance of class privileges. It was neither desirable nor possible to return to that world, Adorno made clear. All the same, he used the relatively "individualistic" era of the nineteenth century, with its clear contradictions, conflicts, and mediations, as a means of attacking the administered "identities" of the present. The historical bases of this argument were most clearly articulated in an important passage from *Dialectic of Enlightenment*:

The individual . . . arose as a dynamic cell of economic activity. Emancipated from tutelage at earlier stages of economic development, he was interested only in himself: as a proletarian, by hiring his services through the labor market, and through continual adaptation to new technical conditions; and, as an entrepreneur, through tireless attempts to approximate the ideal type *homo economicus*. Psychoanalysis represented the internal "small business" which grew up in this way as a complex dynamic system of the conscious and unconscious, the id, ego and super-ego. . . . The complex mental apparatus made possible to some extent that free interplay of subjects on which the market economy was based. But in the era of great business enterprises and world wars the mediation of the social process through innumerable monads proves retrograde. The subjects of the economy are psychologically expropriated, and the economy is more rationally operated by society itself. The individual no longer has to decide what he himself is to do in a painful inner dialectic of conscience, self-preservation and drives. Decisions for men as active workers are taken by the hierarchy ranging from the trade associations to the national administration, and in the private sphere by the system of mass culture which takes over the last inward impulses of individuals, who are forced to consume what is offered to them. . . . In the system of liberalism, individuation of a sector of the population belonged to the process of adaptation of society as a whole to technological development, but today the operation of the economic apparatus demands that the masses be directed without any intervention from individuation.[66]

Adorno (and Horkheimer) turned to Freud and Nietzsche for help in understanding the psychic sources of individual self-surrender to the apparatus of "repression." Seeking to derive a democratic critique of "mass society" from Freud's most conservative study, *Group Psychology and the Analysis of the Ego* (1921), Adorno linked Freud's treatment of individual identifications with the group and its authority to the theory of administered capitalism. In an article first published in 1951 on psychoanalytic insights into fascism, Adorno wrote: "Accord-

---

66. Adorno and Horkheimer, *Dialectic of Enlightenment*, pp. 202–204. See also Horkheimer's similar, but more extended, description of this process in *Eclipse of Reason* (New York, 1947), pp. 140–143, written soon after.

ing to Freud the problem of mass psychology is closely related to the
new type of psychological affliction so characteristic of the economic
era which for social-economic reasons witnesses the decline of the individual and his subsequent weakness. While Freud did not concern himself with the social changes, it may be said that he developed within the
monadological confines of the individual the traces of its profound crisis and willingness to yield unquestioningly to powerful outside, collective agencies." [67] The masochistic passivity, ego surrender, and dependence on authority which Freud analyzed in the "masses" paved the
way, according to Adorno, to the near total eclipse of the individual
subject; there remains little or no "self" to surrender. In the "totally administered society," and especially in its fascist form, Adorno saw the
virtual end of the mediations of the individual and society still present
in Freudian theory:

The psychology of fascism is largely engendered by manipulation. . . . This
shows a tendency toward abolition of psychological motivation in the old, liber-
alistic sense. . . . Fascism perpetuates dependence through the expropriation
of the unconscious by social control. . . . The psychological impoverishment
of the subject that "surrendered itself to the object" in Freud anticipates the
post-psychological de-individualized social atoms which form the Fascist
collectives. [68]

In describing how the subject prepares for its own elimination,
Adorno drew upon Freud's notion of archaic and infantile regression in
the group's alleged "passion for authority." [69] Whereas Benjamin often
used metaphorical couplings of primitive and modern world as an overcoming of empty time, a redemption of the past, or a foreshadowing of
a "classless society," Adorno viewed these as archetypal and mythical
repetitions, induced by the static features of late capitalism, and culminating, above all, in the advanced barbarism of the Nazis.

Adorno and Horkheimer drew upon Freud in full awareness of (1)
his tendencies toward a reduction of social processes to biology or psychology,[70] and (2) his failure to actively champion full sensual happiness
as a good.[71] They simply reinterpreted these with an eye for the social
sources of such pitfalls, something that Freud himself hinted at. In addi-

67. Adorno, "Freudian Theory and the Patterns of Fascist Propaganda," *The Essential Frankfurt School Reader* (New York, 1977), p. 120.
68. Ibid., pp. 135–136.
69. Ibid., pp. 123–124.
70. Adorno, "Sociology and Psychology," *New Left Review*, 46 (November–December, 1967), 46–47.
71. Adorno, *Minima Moralia*, pp. 60–61.

tion, the classic "Oedipus complex," the dynamic out of which "autonomy" could develop, had been rendered obsolescent, they felt, by the decline of the mediating family in the contemporary process of socialization, a prime aspect of the now more direct anchoring of social controls within the individual subconscious, and by the current immense difficulties in the formation of ego strength.[72]

Although the indebtedness of Adorno to Nietzsche is less obvious, it was no less important. Nietzsche was a major source, along with Hegel, for Adorno's and Horkheimer's critique of French Enlightenment "rationality" as tending toward an instrumentalized domination of nature outside and within human beings.[73] (They drew back, it should be added, from Nietzsche's ahistorical affirmations of "life"—what kind?—and from his irrationalist strains, immensely heightened by his "followers.")[74] The analyses of ascetic and masochistic ingredients in mass culture and economic "rationality" owed a debt to Nietzsche's earlier critiques, especially in *The Genealogy of Morals*,[75] although Nietzsche did not relate these to specifically capitalist tendencies and took a wholehearted aristocratic stance toward the new society. As against a more purely objectivist Marxian focus upon material interest, Nietzsche developed an embryonic depth-psychology of impotent fear when he examined the alleged need of modern "masses" for order, certainty, compulsive work, and familiar routine[76]—the very self-surrender which Adorno deciphered in jazz and film audiences, not to mention fascist collectives. Rejecting this hunger for certainty and an all-embracing system, Adorno followed Nietzsche's anti-systematic philosophizing right down to the syntax of his style; both men wrote essays which cultivated fragmentary and aphoristic incompletion. Both were

72. This had been made clear in Horkheimer's contribution to the Institute's *Studien Über Autorität und Familie* (Paris, 1936) reprinted as "Authority and the Family" in a collection of his essays, *Critical Theory* (New York, 1972), pp. 47–128. On Adorno's and Horkheimer's use and revision of Freud, see Jay, *Dialectical Imagination*, chaps. 3, 4 and 7; Rose, *Melancholy Science*, pp. 91–5; and Jessica Benjamin, "The End of Internalization; Adorno's Social Psychology," *Telos*, 32 (Summer, 1977), 42–64.

73. Nietzsche was cited a number of times in this regard in *Dialectic of Enlightenment*, e.g., pp. 94, 128, 119 and 154, but was also influential in many formulations which did not explicitly invoke his name: for example, the argument relating civilization, instinctual renunciation and self-sacrifice in chapter 2 on Odysseus, is heavily indebted to Nietzsche's *Genealogy of Morals*.

74. Adorno, *Minima Moralia*, pp. 97–98; Rose, *Melancholy Science*, pp. 24–25.

75. Jay, *Dialectical Imagination*, p. 50.

76. James Miller, "Some Implications of Nietzsche's Thought for Marxism," *Telos*, 36 (Summer, 1978), 35–39. Adorno discussed the relation between fear, economic "rationality," and identifications with repressive authority in this way, in "Sociology and Psychology," pp. 71–72.

moralists who sought to avoid the grounding of their negations in the illusory recourse to static first principles, an important attribute of a shared modernism[77] (as against Marx's often fixed and seemingly metaphysical expectations of future progress through proletarian class consciousness, Adorno felt).

Adorno's attack on bourgeois (and vulgar Marxist) views of rational progress in history reached its height in *Dialectic of Enlightenment*, to which we have frequently referred. Drawing upon many of the disparate sources of their complex intellectual endowment, Adorno and Horkheimer collaborated here in indicting not merely capitalist society, but the entire tradition of manipulative, calculating, and narrowly technical rationality which they saw in Western Civilization since the Greeks. There is no doubt that the work, filled with brilliant insights, suffers greatly from an overextended usage of the authors' virulently antipositivist concepts (which often caused them to reduce the eighteenth-century Enlightenment to anticipations of the later positivism). While implying (in the Marxist tradition) that without a truly democratic socialist society "Enlightenment" would mean the endless perpetuation of increasingly rationalized forms of exploitation (although that society seemed most unlikely to develop), they shifted the focus of their social theory, more than ever before, away from historically specific class analysis. Not only was the problem of capitalist "instrumental rationality" read backwards into the ancient past (unhistorically overextending their already too broad notion of bourgeois society), but the central emphasis now fell upon a technological "domination of nature" which seemed to pervade the history of Western science, philosophy, and economic life. Using Hegel's critiques of empiricism and his distinction between formal and substantive logic, they suggested that science embodies a necessarily conformist epistemology, the "obedient subjection of reason to what is directly given," and recreates the mythical superstition of primitive peoples in the face of "brute facts."[78] What was needed instead was the "determinate negation of each immediacy," they wrote.[79] Against all forms of scientism, positivism, and the cult of technology, they stressed the ability of a substantive reason (Hegel's *Vernunft*, in contrast to *Verstand*, "understanding") to "formulate 'global' judgments, prescribing the ends to be followed and not only the means of achieving ends that

---

77. Rose, *Melancholy Science*, p. 19. On pp. 18–26, Rose handles brilliantly the many aspects of Adorno's relation to Nietzsche.
78. Adorno and Horkheimer, *Dialectic of Enlightenment*, p. 93.
79. Ibid., pp. 26–27.

are themselves determined irrationally." [80] Thus, while drawing upon Weber's pessimistic analysis of the instrumental and bureaucratic "rationalization" of the modern world, they felt free to judge this process from a perspective outside Weber's "iron cage." [81] One key to this lay in turning Weber's view into a more critical tool via its Marxist redefinition in the early 1920s: Lukács's theory of reification.

Following Marx, Benjamin had been ambivalent about industrial modernity, as his pointedly contrasting treatments of the "decay of aura" revealed. Adorno and Horkheimer, on the other hand, disregarding the positive achievements of industrial modernity, vilified the machine age and collectivist society in a generalized attack on reified forms of life therein. While industrial labor forced an endless repetition of movements, humans were treated—and treated themselves—as repeatable atoms, exchangeable objects of rule under a repressive regimen of merely formal equality. [82] But behind such arguments lay a critique of the productivist manipulation of nature. To Adorno and Horkheimer, the Enlightenment tradition gave theoretical expression to the growing social practice (heightened by industrial capitalism) of treating both physical and human nature as objects of exploitation. Thus, the Enlightenment hope for emancipation from myth and repressive authority was already betrayed when it viewed nature (including human drives) as separate from—and in adversary relation to the knowing "subject," who must learn to manipulate nature for utilitarian advantage. This, the authors felt, facilitated subordination of "rationality" to technocratic efficiency and brought an alienation from nature and from the objectified nature within oneself. [83] Instead of temporal historical development, for example, Enlightenment natural law (of unchanging physical patterns) gave expression to the mythical repetitions of the growing commodity economy.

In advanced industrial society, however, exploited nature has its revenge, as it were, and the full force of its reified condition becomes apparent. For Adorno and Horkheimer, the structures of an administered capitalist monolith become all but immovable, its coordinated personnel perpetuating a stabilized harmonious network of institutions while manipulating millions of consumers. In the midst of a seeming "domination of nature" (the triumph over mythical thought and human weak-

80. Leszek Kolakowski, *Main Currents of Marxism* (London, 1979), Vol. 3, p. 346.
81. I am alluding here to the title of Arthur Mitzman's *The Iron Cage: An Interpretation of Max Weber* (New York, 1970).
82. Adorno and Horkheimer, *Dialectic of Enlightenment*, pp. 11–13.
83. Ibid., pp. 4–10.

ness), primitive impotence in the face of the ominous powers of the natural world resurfaces at a later historical stage, the creation of a socially constructed, industrialized "second nature": "The impotence of the worker is not merely a stratagem of the rulers, but the logical consequence of the industrial society into which the ancient fate—in the very course of the effort to escape it—has finally changed." [84]

To Adorno and Horkheimer, barbarism resurfaces in the twentieth century through the return of a "nature" which had been thwarted and brutalized by a technocratic civilization. The very instincts repressed in the self and the body politic by a calculating reason periodically burst forth, but in doing so they express a destructive resentment against civilization for the "iron cage" within which they have been held. In a chapter on de Sade (with asides to Nietzsche), Adorno and Horkheimer suggested a theory of "fascism" as the "return of the repressed": "The odious overpowering longing to return to a state of nature is the cruelty produced by an abortive civilization: barbarism, the other face of culture." [85]

Thus, Adorno's dialectical critique of the "modern archaic" in mass culture, which contrasted widely with Benjamin's "redemptive" correspondences between prehistory and the new, was part of a wider assault upon the mythically repetitive features of modern capitalist society as he saw it. Whereas Benjamin called for explosive ruptures in time to arrest the ongoing, endlessly repetitive catastrophic process, Adorno lamented that the process was *not* ongoing but turned back upon itself in continual regression born of its own dynamics of "Enlightenment." In his critique of the *Arcades* study, Adorno had cautioned Benjamin against using the relation between "the oldest and the newest" as a "utopian reference to a classless society instead of as a sign of modern barbarism." [86] But against the ubiquitous social pattern which Adorno saw in contemporary society, he could urge no collective solutions or modes of action, only his own dialectical theory and the nonrepetitive, self-constituting time which still breathed in other avant-garde outsiders, such as Schoenberg's musical "subject."

For Benjamin, the proletariat retained a possible future role as active revolutionary agency. At the same time, he undercut the Marxian analysis of a temporal unfolding of such a role, the interrelation between capitalist evolution and revolutionary change. (Typically, he was ambiguous

84. Ibid., pp. 27–28.
85. Ibid., pp. 111–112.
86. Adorno to Benjamin, August 2, 1935, *Aesthetics and Politics*, p. 112.

here, for in one of his scenarios he was hopeful about the evolutionary development of the technical age of the masses.) In *Dialectic of Enlightenment*, however, the overwhelming focus was upon a seemingly irreversible historical process and its ineluctable betrayal of the dreams of freedom and justice. While utopian hope might be contained in the "damaged lives" of individual isolated cultural outsiders, there was nothing to explain how their work might connect in the future to any larger movement for change. Seemingly incapable of realization, "utopia" existed only as a necessary philosophical "negation" of the existent, the premise of a critical theory which refuses reconciliation to the status quo.[87] But did this not make "transcendence" of the given into something of an ahistorical abstraction, since it did not depend upon an historically derived argument for its social possibility, but on a view of art and philosophy as always containing a utopian "moment"? (The problem was not solved by simply showing that the total impasse was a creation of historical development.)

When judged in terms of Adorno's philosophical expectations of true "revolutionary" transcendence, the working class or any other large collective body would, of course, be totally inadequate, whatever its present state of "consciousness." "It will never be as pure a negation . . . of the system as you want."[88] In this way, a theoretical hyperradicalism justified inactivity and helped to undercut any advocacy or practice of long-term incremental social transformations, whether called "evolutionary" or "revolutionary." One might well agree with Adorno when he criticizes a form of tolerance which justifies loving "people as they are" in such a way as to hate "what they might be."[89] Yet, Adorno's description of the "might be" is usually far less an extrapolation from the historically realizable (for example, the more truly democratic and unburdening use of modern technical capacities) than a "hope" so impossible of realization that its inevitable defeat serves to darken the darkness. That may be the major effect of utopian visions such as this one in *Minima Moralia*:

In the magic of what reveals itself in absolute powerlessness, of beauty, at once perfection and nothingness, the illusion of omnipotence is mirrored negatively as hope. It has escaped every trial of strength. Total purposelessness gives the lie

87. See concluding remarks in Jay, *Dialectical Imagination*, pp. 278–280, and Buck-Morss, *Origin of Negative Dialectics*, pp. 189–190.

88. Terry Eagleton, "German Aesthetic Duels" (a review of *Aesthetics and Politics*), *New Left Review*, 107 (January–February, 1978), 31.

89. Adorno, *Minima Moralia*, pp. 24–25.

to the totality of purposefulness in the world of domination, and only by virtue of this negation, which consummates the established order by drawing the conclusion from its own principle of reason, has existing society up to now become aware of another that is possible.[90]

Adorno's utopia bore the traces of aesthetic fantasy and imagination, as did Benjamin's. Both men did not merely interpret art with selected Marxian categories, such as those we have examined in this chapter (reification, dialectic, class, etc.); the very meaning of these categories, as we have occasionally seen, was informed by the aesthetic and cultural orientations present in each of them from earlier years, or developed by them in later ones. (We saw earlier how a similar pattern obtained in the cases of Brecht and Lukács). In the remaining chapter of this book, the forms of this cultural stance will become more apparent as we view the contrasting modernist analyses which Benjamin and Adorno developed, the focus of their unparalleled contributions to a Marxist aesthetics.

90. Ibid., pp. 224–225.

CHAPTER NINE

Modernist Alternatives

The alternative modernisms of Benjamin and Adorno may be distinguished by focusing on the Paris-Moscow axis of the former and the Viennese pivot of the latter. In this final chapter, this contrast will be studied in detail and developed in relation to the differing views of each thinker on the question of art and politics. It is well to recognize at the outset, however, how much the two aesthetic thinkers shared. Both saw criticism on the model of avant-garde art—open-ended, fragmentary, and uncompromisingly complex—requiring the reader to think it through and actively compose it anew in the process. Unlike almost all others in the tradition of Marxist aesthetics, moreover, they refused to move quickly from the small details of a literary or musical text in a sweeping subordination of particular to general social analysis. (This was especially a failing of Lukács's approach, particularly when he analyzed the moderns.) Adorno spoke for both himself and Benjamin when he wrote: "The concept must submerge itself in the monad until the social essence of its own dynamics becomes evident."[1] More than Brecht, Lukács, or Marx, each man understood (and their artful essays exemplify) that form is "the final articulation of the deeper logic of the content itself," an understanding which enabled them to transcend the empty debate between formalist and sociological theories of art.[2] This understanding was embedded in the construction of Brecht's best plays, but his occasional critical analyses of other literature were often di-

1. Adorno, *Philosophy of Modern Music*, p. 25.
2. Jameson, *Marxism and Form*, pp. 328, 331, 403.

rected toward their uses for his own theatrical practice; the dislodging
and "refunctioning" of certain modernist techniques, which he recom-
mended against Lukács's theories, did not allow the inner dialectic of
form and content to be carefully assessed.

Unlike Brecht and Lukács—who argued over the realist and popular
potentials of the nineteenth-century novel or the modern collectivist
theatre—Benjamin and Adorno were drawn to seemingly hermetic and
less representational art forms, such as highly demanding examples of
modern poetry or music. Given the crucial role that each man ascribed
to the critic as illuminator of unintended social and historical meaning,
Benjamin and Adorno affirmed that "intervention" precisely on this apparently private and "asocial" terrain. At the same time, respecting the
concrete, sensuous materials within a poem or composition, they
sought to keep these alive in the process of their historical examination.
The very distance between the poetic or musical text and the historical
analyst, which allowed considerable space for the critic's imagination,
seemed to highlight the necessity of *not* violating the object under scrutiny. In analyzing and summarizing Benjamin's and Adorno's immensely
dense and highly allusive essays, some of these qualities which I have
been describing may not always be apparent. For this reason, it is worth
emphasizing the obvious: there is no substitute for reading these two
sovereign cultural thinkers, just as there is no substitute for reading
Baudelaire or listening to Schoenberg.

❖   ❖   ❖

Before discussing Benjamin's explicit treatment of modernism, it is useful to begin with his book on German baroque drama. The culmination
of his pre-Marxist studies, the *Trauerspielbuch* contained as its hidden
agenda a modernist assault on German classical aesthetics.

Instead of the German classical culture of organic harmony, a unity
between living and symbolizing particulars and general whole, with
antiquity as a "model" (the Goethean world bequeathed to Marx
and Lukács), Benjamin evoked a seventeenth-century art which self-
consciously rearranged the ephemeral fragments of a broken cosmos, of
which the classical—as a "ruin"—was a part.[3] Allegory played a major
role here. Ripping objects out of their "natural" context, the allegorist
gave them new meanings in a constructed montage of "dead" fragments. Benjamin had seen that, since Baudelaire, the modern use of

3. Benjamin, *Origin of German Tragic Drama*, pp. 166–167, 177–179.

symbols (especially in the French tradition) tended toward a new version of baroque allegory. Words, for example, immediately suggest associations, instead of developing their meanings in the linear succession of the text, while metaphorical mythical references direct attention outside the form and tend toward the dissolution of that form's self-enclosed status.

Lukács was not wrong in seeing Benjamin's baroque study, upon its republication in 1955, as a most lucid defense of the avant-garde. First in *Realism in Our Time* and then in his *Aesthetik* (1963), Lukács criticized Benjamin's *Trauerspielbuch* for its apparent acceptance of a world of deathlike fetishized objects, unmediated by human social interaction. The Goethean premises of Lukács's critique were evident throughout: against modernist fragmentation and discontinuity, he upheld a closed organic totality of the world; against the allegorists' endowment of the world's decayed particulars with meaning, he contrasted the living, unique, and interrelated phenomena which the Goethean "symbol" preserved when creating the beautiful illusion (*schönen Schein*) of an artwork.[4] In doing so, Lukács accentuated the classical strain in Marx's aesthetics, while Benjamin eliminated it. In the late 1930s, Benjamin acknowledged his distance from Marx on this score. Criticizing the traces of classicism which can "still be recognized in Marx," he attacked the notions of "beautiful illusion" and harmonic unity, the use of classical antiquity as a model, and the continued presence of an idealist contemplation of art.[5]

For Benjamin, the rescuable past was not a model of harmony but only redeemable in its hidden scraps and fragmented "debris." Constellations with the present, which the critic or "revolutionary classes" constructed through an historical "time-lapse camera," could not make the world whole again. To arrest the disastrous linear continuum and make a space for a different future, the fleeting moment must be invested with the fullness of which it is capable, the liberating weight of metaphorical relations established between then and now, there and here. This alone would be appropriate to an age whose masses "desire to bring things 'closer' spatially and humanly." In developing this out-

4. Lukács, *Realism in Our Time*, pp. 40–45; "On Walter Benjamin," *New Left Review*, 110 (July–August, 1978), 83–88. Peter Bürger has also discussed Benjamin's theory of allegory as a defense of modernism, but does so in a more sympathetic light. See his *Theorie der Avant-Garde*, pp. 93–97, in which allegory, in Benjamin's view, is carefully analyzed in relation to modernist montage.

5. Benjamin, "Eduard Fuchs," p. 37.

look, Benjamin drew upon (1) modern Parisian poetics, including the work of Baudelaire, Mallarmé, Proust, Valéry, and Breton; (2) the technical challenges of new media such as photography and cinema; and (3) the Moscow constructivism evident in Brechtian theatre. Against a hollowed classicism pervasive in his native country, he constructed an aesthetic counterfoil from Germany's enemies in the First World War, a modernist Franco-Russian alliance.

We have already analyzed from a number of angles Benjamin's indebtedness to the symbolists. We saw how Benjamin undercut Baudelaire's aestheticism and "cult of the new" by relating his poetry to the forms of commodity fetishism in capitalist society, while at the same time attempting to derail the evolutionary focus and "base-superstructure causality" of orthodox Marxism through the symbolists' spatializing metaphor. Against the burden of his commodified role, and the empty flow of exchangeable seconds connected with it, Baudelaire appropriated the prehistoric or ancient past and aesthetically harnessed the passing, transient moment. The "constellations" which Benjamin read in Baudelaire's poems were not presented in a linear, discursive manner but as an evocative montage in the style of Mallarmé or Valéry.

Throughout, Benjamin highlighted both Baudelaire's submersion of self in language and the deathly lure of surrendering to the crowd, or to the commodity object, in the pursuit of new poetic material. Clearly, one function of the whole *Arcades* project for Benjamin was to work through and critically assess his own similar forms of symbolist "decadence." There was no question of simply appropriating Baudelaire's or Mallarmé's sensibility whole, especially not their anti-political cult of art and their reactionary disdain for the masses. But it is clear that Benjamin retained important aspects of the symbolist heritage. It is useful here to draw them together: a self-reflexive and depersonalized theory of language freed of merely representational or "subjective" communicative functions (a theory in which the psyche is seen as a linguistic medium); a cultivation of metaphorical, ambiguous, and enigmatic approaches to the magical poetic "object"; an ambivalence toward and a fascination with death and the void[6]; a focus on the ephemeral moment and liberating spatialized ruptures in time, a sensibility attuned to the urban metropolis; a refusal to mediate his materials with philosophical or historical theory, but instead an attempt to suggest or insinuate their

6. In recollections of his childhood, Benjamin wrote: ". . . the places are countless in the great cities where one stands on the edge of the void" (*Reflections*, p. 11).

social historical meanings through the juxtaposition of objects, thereby retaining their aesthetic sensuous resonances[7]; and, finally, a politically redirected "hope in the past" which drew particularly upon the apolitical "symbolist" novels of Marcel Proust.

Proust's *À la Recherche du Temps Perdu* was for Benjamin "the greatest achievement of recent decades" in literature.[8] The novelist had an immense attraction for him; he felt such an affinity with Proust that he was afraid of excessive dependency as a result of reading him too much.[9] Nowhere was the symbolists' metaphorical use of memory and recollection more intensively revealed than in Proust's multivolume work. Against the sequential passage of seconds, and to parry the shocks of urban stimuli, Proust sought in "involuntary memory" a "space-bound," "convoluted" time, according to Benjamin, which synthetically created experience through the very act of recollection. As against conscious "voluntary memory," Benjamin explained, the involuntary kind—activated by a chance encounter with an object, a taste, or a smell—has a richer past accessible to it. Benjamin quoted Proust: "[The past is] somewhere beyond the reach of the intellect, and unmistakeably present in some material object (or in the sensation which such an object arouses in us), though we have no idea which one it is." [10]

Benjamin viewed Proustian memory as imparting new meanings to fragments of the past through a process of disassociating them from earlier contexts and resituating them with later occurrences: "For the important thing for the remembering author is not what he experienced, but the weaving of his memory, the Penelope work of recollection." [11] Benjamin was guided by Proustian memory (which collapses time and dissolves people into the objects with which they are mentally associated[12]), when he wrote in his own recollections, *Berlin Chronicle*: "The city, where people make the most ruthless demands on one another . . . and the struggle for existence grants the individual not a single moment of contemplation, indemnifies itself in memory, and . . . the veil it has covertly woven out of our lives shows the images of people less than those of the sites of our encounters with others or ourselves." [13]

7. For an excellent analysis of this method, apart from the Charles Rosen essays on Benjamin's symbolism, see Pfotenhauer, *Aesthetische Erfahrung*, pp. 44–59.

8. Benjamin, "The Image of Proust," *Illuminations*, p. 201.

9. See Benjamin, *Briefe*, Vol. 1, p. 395; Vol. 2, p. 559.

10. Benjamin, *Illuminations*, p. 158.   11. Ibid., p. 203.

12. Roger Shattuck, *Proust's Binoculars* (New York, 1967), pp. 31–37; Erich Auerbach, *Mimesis: The Representation of Reality in Western Literature* (New York, 1956), pp. 478–479.

13. Benjamin, *Reflections*, p. 30.

In developing his "hope in the past," Benjamin constructed a star-tling "constellation" of Proust and Marx: in the 1930s, for example, when the promise of technology was being violated through the rela-tions of production, he called upon the fleeting hopes it engendered at the moments in which that promise first appeared. "To articulate the past . . . means to seize hold of a memory as it flashes up at a moment of danger." One of those images was the remembrance of "enslaved ances-tors" whose hopes must be redeemed in the present.[14] Proust also en-riched Benjamin's messianic and utopian understanding, his evocation of an elegiac happiness which is both restorative and "unheard-of, the unprecedented."[15] To endow Proust with such social and political meaning required that his immersion in the passive, languorous demi-monde of aristocratic Paris be countered through critical social analy-sis. Interpreting Proust's handling of this upper-class society as partly ideological and partly critical, Benjamin viewed its aesthetic snobbery as rooted in a condition of consumerism distant from material produc-tion: "The attitude of the snob is nothing but the consistent, organized, steely view of life from the chemically pure standpoint of the consumer. . . . Proust describes a class which is everywhere pledged to camouflage its material basis and for this very reason is attached to a feudalism which has no intrinsic economic significance but is all the more ser-viceable as a mask of the upper middle class."[16] There was thus a con-nection between upper-class consumerism and the cult of art in the late nineteenth century. In the attempt to self-critically undercut his own es-oteric aestheticism, Benjamin analyzed the current of "l'art pour l'art" as a superstition about "creativity" which masked the process by which the writer was separated from his own means of literary "production." While the cult of art flattered the writer's "self-esteem," it was dan-gerous because "it effectively guards the interests of a social order that is hostile to him."[17] "L'art pour l'art" reflected, moreover, the illusory ideology of "taste" in a consumer society, where passive buyers are in-creasingly distanced from an understanding of the production of the goods they consume.[18] For Benjamin, Proust's "hope in the past" had to be given new social meaning, rescued from such instances of paralyzing impotence as Benjamin himself had experienced in his life.

14. Benjamin, *Illuminations*, p. 260.
15. Ibid., p. 204; Rudbeck, "The Literary Criticism of Walter Benjamin," pp. 114–115.
16. Benjamin, *Reflections*, p. 210; See also Benjamin, *Angelus Novus*, p. 280.
17. Benjamin, *Charles Baudelaire*, pp. 71–72.
18. Ibid., pp. 104–106.

Benjamin's attraction to surrealism, beginning in the late 1920s, was an additional aspect of his attempt to "politicize" art, to redirect modernism away from the "decadent" lassitude of the early symbolists. We have seen how, for Benjamin, the surrealists "exploded" the "bourgeois" self by disclosing unrestricted "public image-space" within the "private" individual, a feature of their "dream writing" in particular (which differed from the more "subjective" materials found through psychoanalysis[19]); how he fixed upon their "profane illumination," through which archaic and contemporary objects were rescued from their "enslaved," habitual state as commodities; and how Aragon's *Le Paysan de Paris* had inspired the discontinuous montage of urban imagery (wherein "inconceivable analogies and connections between events are the order of the day"[20]) in Benjamin's studies of nineteenth-century Paris. The acute visual and spatial sensibility of the surrealists was very close to Benjamin's own, as were the paradoxically aggressive and explosive intentions of their "receptivity" to associated imagery. Whereas symbolist metaphors aimed at the creation of a new melancholy beauty, the surrealists' montage heightened the accent upon shock and defamiliarizing as well as destroying more forcefully than did symbolist work all pretensions of art to being an organic or hermetic "self-enclosed world" (something which Benjamin found all too apparent in Mallarmé,[21] for example, and might well have cited in Proust). Just as surrealists, following from dada and cubism, had destroyed the illusion of art's "autonomy" by introducing fragments of reality ("found objects") into their work, so Benjamin purposefully juxtaposed textual quotations with the "brutal heteronomies of economic chaos," undercutting the "asylum of their pre-established harmonies."[22] (We have seen Adorno's strong objections to this critical method, which differed from his own more immanent critique of artistic autonomy.)

Benjamin found in surrealism a materialist "optics" which resisted bourgeois culture more effectively than the official Marxist parties were able to do. Yet, he viewed the surrealists' work as midway between contemplative aestheticism and active communist politics, the latter of which they had begun to toy with in the late 1920s. His 1929 essay on

19. Benjamin, *Angelus Novus*, pp. 158–161. Hermann Schweppenhauser, "Physiognomie eines Physiognomikers," *Zur Aktualität Walter Benjamins*, pp. 153, 162, discusses Benjamin's disinterest in inner life and focus on only its visible "materialisations"; psychology was for him, according to Schweppenhauser, an "objective topography."
20. Benjamin, *Reflections*, p. 183.
21. Benjamin, "Einbahnstrasse," p. 102.
22. Witte, *Walter Benjamin*, pp. 152–153.

the movement was both a study of its tentative moves in this "disciplined" political direction and a self-analysis of his own position between the pressures of art and politics. While criticizing the remnants of occult and romantic mystification in their work (he was always far more attentive to the semantic meanings of language, for example, while the surrealists might indulge in pure word intoxication[23]), Benjamin sympathetically discussed the surrealists' fitful attempt to "win the energies of intoxication for the revolution." Contrasting the surrealists' political "image-space" with the moralistic and optimistic "metaphors" of social democratic politics, Benjamin viewed the surrealists as coming "ever closer to the Communist 'answer,'" the "organization of pessimism . . . all along the line": "mistrust in the fate of literature, mistrust in the fate of freedom, mistrust in the fate of European humanity, but three times mistrust in all reconciliation: between classes, between nations, between individuals. And unlimited trust only in I. G. Farben and the peaceful perfection of the air force."[24]

For Benjamin, surrealist attempts to "politicize" art served as a direct counter to the "aestheticization of politics" which he detected in the fascist movements. Fascism was a culmination of "l'art pour l'art," he argued, which, because of its annihilative uses of technology in defense of the property system, gave a hideous military-political form to the symbolists' aesthetic valorizing of death. Benjamin's studies of nineteenth-century Paris included repeated allusions to the necrophilia of commodity worship, but also linkages between Baudelaire's perverse cult of "satanism" and the bourgeois support for Napoleon III's dictatorship, the model for many later Marxist analyses of fascism. Benjamin quoted Marx on the attitudes of Louis Napoleon's bourgeois supporters: "Only theft can save property, perjury can save religion, bastardy the family and disorder order."[25] At various times, Benjamin related the fascists' "aestheticizing" of death and violence to the symbolists and "decadents" Baudelaire and Stefan George[26], and to actual proto-fascist and aesthetically avant-garde writers such as Ernst Jünger, Filippo Marinetti, and Gabriele D'Annunzio, as well as the French reactionary Maurice Barrès.[27] Ansgar Hillach, who has studied this theme

23. I owe this point to Stephen Klebs, who is working on a doctoral thesis at the University of California, Davis, on French surrealism.
24. Benjamin, *Reflections*, pp. 190–191.
25. Benjamin, *Charles Baudelaire*, p. 23.
26. Benjamin, *Angelus Novus*, pp. 476–481.
27. Ibid., pp. 266, 508–510; "Theories of German Fascism," pp. 121–122; "Work of Art," p. 241; Hillach, "The Aestheticization of Politics," pp. 99–119.

in Benjamin's work, has constructed the following implied historical perspective in his writings: "As Europe moved into the imperialist crisis, the retention of idealistic positions by both the ruling and privileged classes became synonymous with violence, which was turned inward by representatives of the "spirit" and took on heroic features. Their aestheticism, however, becomes politically activated at the moment their privileges (which they defended as prerogatives) are put under massive pressure felt by the entire society. This is the hour of the 'aestheticization of political life' anticipated by d'Annunzio, Marinetti and Barrès." [28] In the "Work of Art" essay, Benjamin also indicted the reactionary potentials of an expressionist aesthetic: he wrote that in Nazi politics "the masses" are given "not their right, but instead a chance to express themselves. The masses have a right to change property relations; Fascism seeks to give them an expression while preserving property." [29] Thus, after his turn toward Marxism, Benjamin sought various means to strip away his own "decadent" aestheticized fascination with death, one of the legacies of his symbolist background.

The "politicized" art which Benjamin held up against fascism included the work of French surrealists, Russian constructivists, and that of his German friend Bertolt Brecht. Through Brecht, Benjamin renewed and strengthened his contact with Russian avant-garde and collectivist art of the 1920s, which he had hailed after returning from Moscow in 1926–27. It is significant that, in analyzing "epic theatre," Benjamin stressed those aspects of discontinuous montage, defamiliarizing estrangement, technological optimism, and aesthetic self-reflexiveness which drew Brecht close to Russian practice of the 1920s (and, more distantly, cubist procedures [30]). In his first public statement on the playwright (June 1930, on German radio), Benjamin described Brecht as providing a vital synthesis between the French avant-garde and Russian political mass art. [31] More than in the case of surrealism, Benjamin found himself in contact in Brecht's plays with the "thinking" of the "masses," particularly the shrewd crudity of their practical sense, [32] and he found this a most useful antidote to his own esoteric her-

28. Hillach, "The Aestheticization of Politics," p. 107.
29. Benjamin, "Work of Art," p. 241. Benjamin wrote that in the "Work of Art" essay he had intended to critique the "principle of expression" and its reactionary functions. See *GS*, I/3, p. 1050.
30. Benjamin, *Understanding Brecht*, pp. 1–26.
31. Witte, *Walter Benjamin*, p. 173.
32. Benjamin, *Understanding Brecht*, p. 16. See also his analysis of Brecht's play "The Mother," pp. 33–36.

meticism. In commenting on his Denmark conversations with Brecht in the late 1930s, he stated: "I felt a power being exercised over me which was equal in strength to the power of fascism—I mean a power that sprang from the depths of history no less deep than the power of the fascists." [33]

Yet, Benjamin was by no means a "disciple." In his interpretation of Brecht's poetry, for example, Benjamin utilized his own unique allegorical understanding in deciphering its social motifs. [34] Moreover, the *Arcades* study, his major project of the 1930s, did not please Brecht very much at all. In an unpublished essay on Baudelaire, Brecht, who had discussed the *Passagenarbeit* with Benjamin, viewed the French poet as unable to give any expression to his historical era, which is suggested by the interpretive gymnastics required to make him "useful." Far from resembling Blanqui, Baudelaire was the "stab in his back": the proletarian defeat in 1848 was his own aesthetic "Pyrrhic victory." [35]

While Brecht did not always approve of Benjamin's literary essays, Benjamin was a careful and sympathetic student of the playwright's work. In the early 1930s, he wrote a number of analyses of epic theatre which showed an acute understanding of Brecht's methods. Connecting some of his own montage techniques with Brecht's, he wrote:

Uncovering (making strange, or alienating) of conditions is brought about by process being interrupted. . . . Interruption is one of the fundamental methods of all form-giving. . . . It is, to mention just one of its aspects, the origin of the quotation. Quoting a text implies interrupting its context. . . . Epic theatre proceeds by fits and starts, in a manner comparable to the images on a film strip. Its basic form is that of the forceful impact on one another of separate, sharply distinct situations in the play. The songs, the captions, the gestural conventions differentiate the scenes. As a result, intervals occur which tend to destroy illusion. These intervals paralyse the audience's readiness for empathy. Their purpose is to enable the spectator to adopt a critical attitude (towards the represented behavior of the play's characters and towards the way in which this behavior is represented). [36]

Benjamin championed Brecht's sensitivity to modern mass urban life and his application to theatre of the principles of construction in film, radio, photography, and the press, [37] the various social and technical

33. Ibid., p. 120.
34. Witte, *Walter Benjamin*, pp. 173–175.
35. Bertolt Brecht, "Die Schönheit in den Gedichten des Baudelaire," *Gesammelte Werke*, Vol. 19, pp. 408–409. See also Brecht's *Arbeitsjournal, 1938–1955*, Vol. 1, p. 16, in which he criticizes Benjamin's interpretation of Baudelaire.
36. Benjamin, *Understanding Brecht*, pp. 18–21.
37. Ibid., pp. 6, 21, 99.

forces which were liquidating the traditional "aura" of art in favor of a potentially liberating political meaning. Thus, Brechtian theatre disclosed a crisis and a redefinition of art which Baudelaire's shocklike poetry revealed in its genre, and which Alfred Döblin, the author of the cubistic novel *Berlin Alexanderplatz* (1928), showed in his.[38] In his Brecht studies, of course, Benjamin was viewing optimistically a process which he surveyed with great ambivalence.

Epic theatre takes account of a circumstance which has received too little attention and which could be described as refilling the orchestra pit. The abyss which separates the actor from the audience like the dead from the living, the abyss whose silence heightens the sublime in drama and whose resonance heightens the intoxication of opera—this abyss which, of all the elements of the stage, bears most indelibly the traces of its sacral origins, has increasingly lost its significance. The stage is elevated. But it no longer rises from an immeasurable depth: it has become a public platform.[39]

Brecht helped Benjamin formulate his own analysis of the liberating potentials of modern reproductive media. As a careful student of French modernism and its Soviet counterparts, Benjamin had often viewed the human imagination on the model of photography or cinema, in which distances in time and space are radically effaced. Before meeting Brecht, in the years 1925–28, he was preoccupied with the "photographic" optical imagery of Proustian memory[40] and surrealist fantasy,[41] on the one hand, and Russian filmic montage, on the other hand. In two 1927 articles on Soviet avant-garde cinema, he sympathetically explored the visual multiperspectivism, mass heroes, and positive views of a collectively controlled technology contained within the work of Eisenstein and others.[42] An article of 1931 on photography was the beginning of his optimistic assessments of the decline of aura. Benjamin described the photograph as making the viewer aware of his "optical unconscious" (e.g., it can disclose the moment a person starts to walk),[43] and he did this in a way which was very similar to his description of "invol-

38. See Benjamin's comments (*Angelus Novus*, pp. 437–443) on Döblin's most important novel, *Berlin Alexanderplatz*, which he compares to Brecht, a novel which Brecht himself much admired. On Benjamin's view of the "crisis of art" in modern poetry, novel and theatre, see Paetzold, "Walter Benjamin's Theory of the End of Art."

39. Benjamin, *Understanding Brecht*, p. 22.

40. On Proustian memory and its relation to photography and cinema, see Shattuck, *Proust's Binoculars*, pp. 3–21, 47–54.

41. The subtitle of the surrealist essay was "The Last Snapshot of the European Intelligentsia." See *Reflections*, p. 177.

42. Benjamin, "Diskussion über russische Filmkunst," and "Zur Lage der russiche Filmkunst," in *Angelus Novus*, pp. 195–199.

43. Benjamin, "A Short History of Photography," *Screen*, 13:1 (Spring 1972), 7.

untary memory" in Proust. "The camera . . . is ever ready to capture transitory and secret pictures which are able to shock the associative mechanisms of the observer to a standstill." [44] But there must be a caption through which the photographer "reads" his own pictures, "literarizes" them, and secures them from commercial purposes. Benjamin emphasized that photography is divided between the kind that has a commodified usage responsive to fashion (" 'the world is beautiful' is its motto") and the kind that pointedly "constructs," and does not romantically "reproduce," the object, thereby liberating it from an anachronistic aura. The most developed forms of the latter kind were contained in Brechtian theatre, Russian cinema, and surrealist literature. [45] Later, Benjamin also included the politically left-wing dadaist photomontage of John Heartfield. [46] In "The Author as Producer" (1934), Benjamin dwelled more fully on commercialized photography, which is capable, for example, of "turning abject poverty itself, by handling it in a modish, technically polished way, into an object of enjoyment." [47]

Besides new optical media, Benjamin also directed his attention to the alteration of the newspaper press, citing the "worker-writer" experiments carried out by Tretjakov and his associates in the 1920s. Benjamin was most excited by the transformation of the passive readers of newspapers into active producers of texts which drew upon their own special areas of technical expertise. To be a "progressive" writer, Benjamin emphasized in "The Author as Producer," is to go beyond the "sterile dichotomy of form and content" and develop and transform the very literary techniques, genres, or media with which one works in a progressive direction. [48] The "worker-writer" experiment was a major example: "Authority to write is no longer founded in a specialist training but in a polytechnical one, and so becomes common property. In a word, the literarization of living conditions becomes a way of surmounting otherwise insoluble antinomies, and the place where the word is most debased—that is to say, the newspaper—becomes the very place where a rescue operation can be mounted." [49]

Such treatments of cinema, photography, and the press represented the utopian side of Benjamin's ambivalent response to the decline of aura and tradition in contemporary society. The other reaction ap-

---

44. Ibid., p. 26.
45. Ibid., pp. 20–25.
46. Benjamin's *Understanding Brecht*, p. 94.
47. Ibid., p. 95. I have altered the translation here to some extent.
48. Ibid., pp. 86–88, 93.
49. Ibid., p. 90.

peared most fully in "Some Motifs in Baudelaire" (1939). But before this time, in the mid-1930s, he wrote a superb study of the decline of narrative art forms in the age of the press, "The Storyteller," which clearly evoked the "new beauty in what is vanishing."[50] To Benjamin, the aura of the storytelling form, the basis of epic, was embedded in a peasant and artisan culture in which tradition was deeply respected and in which the oral transmission of counsel and wisdom, the "epic side of truth," was an important fabric of the community. The rise of the novel signaled the crisis of this narrative art. Developing with the new middle classes, the novel was neither tied to oral tradition nor collectively received; it was born of the "solitary individual who is no longer able to express himself by giving examples of his most important concerns, is himself uncounseled, and cannot counsel others."[51] But both oral and novelistic forms are today being eclipsed by the rise of new information media. The press, in particular, sacrifices transmissible experience and narrative continuity to disparate bits of immediately verifiable current information which must be understandable in themselves. In the age of the newspaper and the assembly line, memory and a usable past are in danger of losing their human functions.[52] In "Some Motifs in Baudelaire," Benjamin continued this line of argument:

If it were the intention of the press to have the reader assimilate the information it supplies as part of his own experience, it would not achieve its purpose. But its intention is just the opposite, and it is achieved: to isolate what happens from the realm in which it could affect the experience of the reader. The principles of journalistic information (freshness of the news, brevity, comprehensibility, and, above all, lack of connection between the individual news items) contribute as much to this as does the make-up of the pages and the paper's style. . . . The replacement of the older narration by information, of information by sensation, reflects the increasing atrophy of experience. In turn, there is a contrast between all these forms and the story, which is one of the oldest forms of communication.[53]

Thematically related to "The Storyteller" and "Some Motifs in Baudelaire" were Benjamin's pieces on Kraus, Proust, and Kafka written in the early 1930s. In his article on Karl Kraus, Benjamin shrewdly examined the Viennese critic's savage attacks upon contemporary journalism, its false claims of "newness" (which are ever-repeated formulae), and its hollowing out of linguistic meaning and cultural tradition.[54] The novels

50. Benjamin, *Illuminations*, p. 87.   51. Ibid.   52. Ibid., pp. 88–98.
53. Benjamin, *Illuminations*, pp. 158–159.
54. Benjamin, *Reflections*, pp. 239–273.

of Proust and Kafka represented, according to Benjamin, different responses to the crisis of experience, tradition, and narrative art. Isolated from collective life, ritual, and community, the individual in Proust's work must seek, through "involuntary memory," to artificially construct his own "tradition" in a way which facilitates the storytelling form under modern conditions.[55] In his reflections on Kafka, Benjamin again viewed the decay of the aura of tradition with elegiac sadness, but within a different context. Through Jewish mystical and folk traditions, the storytelling form and the oral transmission of counsel are possible for Kafka. But in the alienated life of the modern city, such traditions no longer compel belief; they simply live on as empty shells. According to Benjamin, Kafka "sacrificed truth for the sake of clinging to its transmissibility, its haggadic element. . . . This is why, in regard to Kafka, we can no longer speak of wisdom. Only the products of its decay remain."[56] Instead of usable counsels from the past, Kafka shows the disintegration of meaning, but he does so with a collective understanding of the situation faced by millions in the twentieth century: "Kafka's world . . . is the exact complement of his era which is preparing to do away with the inhabitants of this planet on a considerable scale."[57] "In the stories which Kafka left us, narrative art regains the significance it had in the mouth of Scheherazade: to postpone the future."[58]

Having emphasized Benjamin's studied ambiguity concerning the decay of aura and transmissible experience, we should mention that in one possible reading of his major essays of the 1930s a partial resolution emerges. While the aura of tradition is in eclipse as a matter of historical necessity, and one reacts to this development with a sense of "the new beauty in what is passing," the reproductive media of newspaper, radio, film, etc. (and the mass societies to which they cater) contain the potential for a new kind of liberating collective experience and knowledge. Bernd Witte has articulated this very well:

Benjamin . . . experienced newspapers, radio and film as vehicles of mass communication. Unlike Adorno and Horkheimer, however, he does not reject them out of hand as "culture industry." Instead he sees in them a new supra-individual form of communication which will lead to a new collective art if it can be freed from the dominion of capital. This is why Benjamin puts such emphasis on the experiment with writer-workers; for in their communications the individual no longer describes his private fate or that of a fictional hero, rather he communicates social experiences. According to Benjamin, this is a return of the

55. Benjamin, *Illuminations*, pp. 159–160.
56. Ibid., pp. 143–144.   57. Ibid., p. 143.   58. Ibid., p. 129.

story on a higher level, since here it becomes a depository for collective knowledge. In contrast with traditional story-telling this type of writing lacks aura, that is, historical uniqueness. Its supra-individual aspect no longer arises from a natural succession of generations of story-tellers; rather it arises from the universal synchronism brought about by technology, the negative expression of which is the omnipresence of events diffused as information by the mass media.[59]

As far as it goes, this statement seems to be a perceptive clarification of Benjamin's views. It is consistent, moreover, with the forward-looking and utopian directions of Benjamin's "hope in the past." What is missing, however, is how such potential "functional transformations" of the new media do not erase a sense of loss, for Benjamin studiously refused to resolve his own antithetical feelings of melancholy at what was passing and optimistic hope for what the technological future might hold in store, *even if* catastrophe could be averted and a truly socialist society could emerge from the crisis of the bourgeois world.

❖   ❖   ❖

While Benjamin consistently related literature to spatially organized visual arts and reproductive media (especially photography and film), Adorno's treatment of nineteenth- and twentieth-century art was focused upon temporally unfolding music, especially within the Viennese tradition. In the classicism of Haydn, Mozart, and Beethoven, the tendency of Western music (more so than the music of other world cultures) to capitalize upon the passage of time reached a peak.[60] For Adorno, the second Vienna school—Schoenberg, Berg, and Webern—in a very different musical and historical context, showed the erosion of the tradition in a way which was faithful to its original temporal impulse. In so doing, these composers protested the mythically repetitive, nondeveloping social whole. "The Viennese dialectic was the true world-language of music," Adorno wrote, "and what it conveyed was the craftsmanlike tradition of motive-thematic work. This tradition alone seemed to assure music of something like immanent totality, something like the whole, and Vienna was the home of the tradition."[61] But it was not only the discrepancy between coherent temporal development and spatial juxtapositions (strongest in French modernism) that

59. Witte, "Benjamin and Lukács," p. 21.
60. Charles Rosen, *The Classical Style: Haydn, Mozart, Beethoven* (New York, 1972), p. 34. In "Music and Technique," a 1962 article translated in *Telos*, 32 (Summer 1977), Adorno referred to "the development of music in time, the essence of which is the continual production of the new rather than of that which has already been."
61. Adorno, *Introduction to the Sociology of Music* (New York, 1976), p. 162.

set Adorno and Benjamin at odds. Whereas Austro-German music after Haydn and Mozart gave expression to the social reality of individual subjectivity (of which the temporal component was a vital part), visual media directed attention to external objects (or, as in surrealism, toward their images within the psyche). For Adorno, the following were examples of serious aesthetic experience: (1) music-making (whether public or private, for both were a vital form of *praxis* for him); (2) intelligent "structural," as opposed to atomized, listening; and (3) the reflective inner experience of private reading. While reading and structural listening allowed "internalization" and, if the art was worthy, demanded sustained intellectual engagement far more active than mere contemplation,[62] Adorno held (for him a damning judgment) that "visualization in modern mass media makes for externalization, . . . unmistakable optical signs that can be grasped at a glance."[63]

Adorno's concentration upon a "sociology" of music was quite unusual in the history of Marxist aesthetics (which has largely been focused upon the more representational literary or, in some cases, visual forms) and is difficult for Anglo-Saxon readers to understand. The sociology of music is a largely German field, begun seriously by Max Weber, which reflects the extraordinary importance of music in the cultural life of that country.[64] But Adorno's voluminous writings in this domain[65] are unique in their methodology, a multiple analytical approach drawing from Hegel, Marx, Freud, Benjamin, and all the other influences we have traced in earlier chapters. Perhaps most fundamental of all was the dialectic of critical negation and affirmative reconciliation which Adorno found in all "great" music. In the works of Beethoven or Schoenberg, for example, music resisted complicity and "negated" the wider society through its immanent structural logic—thereby providing a "promise of happiness" and utopian hope which all worthy art contains—but it was "not free not to reflect what it reacts against,"[66] the repressive social whole which defeats such promises. Thus, the micro-

62. Adorno, *Philosophy of Modern Music*, pp. 149–150.

63. Adorno, "Television and the Patterns of Mass Culture," in *Mass Culture*, ed. Bernard Rosenberg (New York, 1957), p. 487n.

64. W. V. Blomster, "Sociology of Music: Adorno and Beyond," *Telos*, 28 (Summer 1976), 83–84. In "Ideen zur Musiksoziologie," *Klangfiguren* (Frankfurt a.M., 1959), p. 16, Adorno cited the importance of Weber's pioneering *The Rational and Social Foundations of Music*, first published in 1932, which had focused on the dynamic quality of Western music in relation to changes in societal "rationalization."

65. Vols. 12–23 of the *Gesammelte Schriften* (Frankfurt a.M., 1972–   ) will contain Adorno's massive output of writings on music; only Vols. 13 and 14 have appeared to date.

66. Jameson, *Marxism and Form*, p. 37.

cosm of the musical work contained, in a miniature and highly articulated form, the social contradictions of the age. Yet, these fissures, contrary to the view of Benjamin and Marx, do not promise social transcendence; they structure the process of an endless frustration of hope. If it is truthful, modern music has social value purely as negation, and this occurs only through an isolation from the wider commercial society. Such isolation and highly restricted impact, however, will also "allow this truth to wither" in the general social indifference.[67] While the division between serious and light art, literature, and music is necessary today, as it alone will allow the retention of pockets of resistance, each is a "torn half of an integral freedom," Adorno wrote to Benjamin, "to which however they do not add up." Given the structured contradictions, however—the totally commodified state of the entertainment industry and the social isolation of the best avant-garde work—"it would be romantic to sacrifice one to the other."[68]

Lukács had seen the realist literary culture of the early nineteenth century as a model for twentieth-century writing, basing his aesthetic judgments upon Goethean classicism and Hegelian philosophy. Adorno understood full well that the music of Beethoven, Goethe's and Hegel's contemporary, was historically irretrievable, but Adorno also viewed Beethoven's age as a privileged period of artistic expression against which to judge all earlier and later trends (including those of the "culture industry").[69] Adorno interpreted the emancipation of individual musical "subjects" within compositions of Beethoven's second period ("subjects" whose motivic development over time generates the musical logic of the whole work), as expressions of the revolutionary universalist aspirations of the European bourgeoisie at the point at which they seemed most capable of concrete realization.[70] Particularly in the sonata allegro movements, the objective external structures are largely generated out of the inner logic of the individual motive, the figure of subjective expression, which emphatically reasserts itself in new forms in every "developing variation." As a result, here, more than at any other time in the history of music, the "autonomous" subject exists freely within an objective "totality" that is highly responsive to its actions. In-

67. Adorno, *Philosophy of Modern Music*, pp. 19–20, 105–106.

68. Adorno and Horkheimer, *Dialectic of Enlightenment*, p. 135; Adorno, "Social Situation of Music," pp. 159–161; Adorno to Benjamin, March 18, 1936, *Aesthetics and Politics*, p. 123.

69. This parallel between Lukács and Adorno is discussed by Ferenc Fehér in "Negative Philosophy of Music—Positive Results," *New German Critique*, 4 (Winter 1975), 99–112.

70. Adorno, *Introduction to the Sociology of Music*, pp. 62–63.

stead of externally imposed order, "individual musical productivity re-alizes an objective potential," a characteristic which was only half-developed in the earlier Viennese classicism of Haydn and Mozart.[71] At the same time, "every detail derives its musical sense from the concrete totality of the piece. . . . [In Beethoven's Seventh Symphony], the sec-ond theme gets its true meaning only from the context. Only through the whole does it acquire its particular lyrical and expressive quality." (In popular music of today, in contrast, Adorno charged, the whole is packaged and pre-arranged; each detail, in addition, is detachable and "substitutable" as a "cog in a machine.")[72]

These formulations owe a great deal to the dialectical logic of Hegel (especially the notion of the construction of the object and the subject from out of each other), to which Beethoven's music, according to Adorno, bears a marked affinity.[73] Hegel's radically historical view of becoming, in which each immediacy, each seemingly "natural fact," is overturned in its "abstract" isolation from the developing whole, serves Adorno repeatedly in his social reading of Beethoven. "The developing variation," he writes, "an image of social labor, is definite negation; from what has once been posited it ceaselessly brings forth the new and enhanced by destroying it in its immediacy, its quasi-natural form."[74]

Beethoven culminated the emancipation of musical subjectivity in Viennese classicism; but he also anticipated the dialectical reversals of that tradition in the later Viennese school of Schoenberg. Beethoven's second-period style did not "reflect" social reality. No art does this. It gave voice to historically powerful aspirations for individual self-assertion within a free and equal society which had animated the French revolutionary bourgeoisie and their German philosophical counterparts. Instead of reflecting the social structure, these musical works expressed a widespread critical attitude, a longing to transcend the present order. But in the midst of his second period, and much more toward the end of his life (in the Restoration era after 1815), Beethoven sensed that the promise of unity between individual freedom and social totality was already being buried by a repressive and dehumanizing so-

71. Ibid., p. 217; Rose R. Subotnik, "Adorno's Diagnosis of Beethoven's Late Style," *Journal of the American Musicological Society*, 2 (1976), 244–253; Jameson, *Marxism and Form*, pp. 39–44.

72. Adorno, "On Popular Music," *Studies in Philosophy and Social Science*, 9 (1941), 17–21.

73. Buck-Morss, *Origin of Negative Dialectics*, p. 133, cites an unpublished book-length manuscript of Adorno's (to appear as Vol. 21 of his *Gesammelte Schriften*) which compares Hegelian logic with compositional development in Beethoven's music.

74. Adorno, *Introduction to the Sociology of Music*, p. 290.

cial whole. "The late Beethoven's demand for truth rejects the illusory appearance of the unity of subjective and objective, a concept practically at one with the classicist idea. . . . The subject . . . is no longer secure in the objectivity of the form and cannot produce this form unbroken out of himself. . . . The composition unremittingly controls whatever is to be filled out by the subject under . . . externally dictated stylization principles."[75] In the face of a foreign source of objective authority (Adorno was very vague about the precise historical forms this takes), the musical subject, to retain its integrity, must express itself through the increasingly formalized, fragmentary, and alien character of the music. It must abandon the claim to be able to generate the object world from out of itself. "The subject could use the techniques of music proper to create structures inimical to the expression of subjective freedom or individuality."[76] Thus, in failing to harmonize subject and object, in shattering the classical harmony, the late Beethoven (and Schoenberg after him) is a cognitive success: both Beethoven and Schoenberg protest the suppression of the expressive subject by revealing how it alienates itself in the objects which control it.

While Beethoven's third period evinced a reified subjectivity, the romantic music which succeeded Beethoven disclosed the beginnings of the crisis of temporality. With Schubert and Schumann, the dialectical unfolding of the musical subject in Beethoven's classicism starts to give way to more static and exchangeable units. Instead of motivic evolution and the continual production of the new, individuality concretizes itself into distinct self-contained and detachable "themes" which do not have the authority to generate a course of development out of themselves; instead, they are repeated in what begins to resemble a timeless synchronic form. The process culminates, on the one hand, in the mythic and compulsively recurrent leitmotifs of Wagner (who also subordinates individual reason to brutal and regressive primitive forces and facilitates the use of romantic music by the culture industry), and, on the other hand, in the postromantic abandonment of expressive subjectivity in the impersonal and spatialized impressionism of Debussy.[77] But Adorno was not simply critical of romanticism. The early romantic sub-

75. Adorno, "Alienated Masterpiece: The Missa Solemnis," *Telos*, 28 (Summer 1976), 123.

76. Quoted in Subotnik, "Adorno's Diagnosis of Beethoven's Late Style," p. 256.

77. Adorno, "Fragmente über Wagner," *Zeitschrift für Sozialforschung*, 8 (1939), 1–48; Rose R. Subotnik, "The Historical Structure: Adorno's 'French Model' for the Criticism of Nineteenth Century Music," *Nineteenth Century Music*, 2:1 (July 1978), 39–54.

ject retained an expressive quality whose warmth still performed a critical function and would only later become false and hollow (with Tchaikovsky and Rachmaninoff, for example). "When the detail won its freedom, it became rebellious," Adorno wrote, "and in the period from romanticism to expressionism asserted itself as free expression, as a vehicle of protest against the organization." [78] The point in the twentieth century was not to abandon romantic subjectivity, but to transform it in the act of harnessing it, as, for example, in the emancipation of "ugly" dissonance: to express, through objective musical structures, the anguished experience of the individual feeling subject in a state of advanced liquidation. This was the unparalleled achievement of Schoenberg.

In *Philosophy of Modern Music*, written over the years 1939–48, Adorno synthesized and extended his earlier analyses of Schoenberg and Stravinsky as polar alternatives within the contemporary state of the art. First let us see his treatment of Schoenberg. The analysis is marked by dual approaches which continually intersect. On the one hand, Adorno stresses the breakthrough (in the years 1907–14) of extreme individual suffering and anguish, the expressionist intensification of a romantic subjectivity which must now abandon centering tonality and harmonic consonance in order to give adequate outer form to inner torment. On the other hand, Adorno stresses that such extreme "expression" is made possible only through Schoenberg's objective development of musical form as it was available to him, e.g., the tendency toward the dissolution of a classical tonal center in Wagnerian chromaticism, or the increasingly hollow sound, which is no longer freshly "heard," of late romantic harmony. Adorno's argument proceeds with another dual approach: microscopic analysis of specific details of individual pivotal works, such as the earliest "polytonal" compositions, *Erwartung*, *Piano Pieces*, Op. 11, and *Die Glückliche Hand*; and sweeping theoretical "mediations" of the details through characterizations of the social whole which they alternatively protest and reflect.

Adorno quotes Schoenberg's war against Viennese fin-de-siècle aestheticism: "Music is not to be decorative; it is to be true." He then proceeds to analyze the terrible and discomforting truths which Schoenberg would have us hear:

This knowledge is founded upon the expressive substance of the music itself. What radical music perceives is the untransfigured suffering of man. His impo-

78. Adorno and Horkheimer, *Dialectic of Enlightenment*, p. 125.

tence has increased to the point that it no longer permits illusion and play. The conflicting drives, about whose sexual genesis Schoenberg's music leaves no doubt, have assumed a force in that music which has the character of a case study—a force which prohibits music from offering comforting consolation.[79]

To give full expression to the social material which his works unintentionally disclose, Schoenberg was driven to break through expressionism toward an extreme aesthetic objectivity. This was both because absolute subjectivity and individual autonomy are illusory—they are always objectively mediated by the social process as a whole and by the objective problems of the musical material at hand—and because in the twentieth century the subjective realm is in an advanced state of dissolution. But instead of abandoning the suffering self in the cheerful facades of *Neue Sachlichkeit*, Schoenberg, like Freud, shows the anguishing process of its liquidation:

Society is reflected in the isolation of the Expressionist movement. . . . If the drive towards well-integrated construction is to be called objectivity, then objectivity is not simply a counter-movement to Expressionism. It is the other side of the Expressionistic coin. . . . As soon as the music has clearly and sharply defined what it wished to express—its subjective content—this content becomes rigid under the force of the composition, manifesting precisely that objective quality the existence of which is denied by the purely expressive character of music. . . . With its expressive outbursts the dream of subjectivity explodes. . . . In so doing music does not—like the text—simply drop below the Expressionist level of knowledge, but simultaneously surpasses this level.[80]

Since organic "beauty" tends to deny the suffering and horrors of the existent, making of art a false illusion, Adorno repeatedly emphasized that the "beauty" of modern art must be in its "ugly" refusals to pacify and console. This was the thrust of Schoenberg's war on the complacently "decorative,"[81] and the justification, in effect, for his "emancipation" of the "extreme means of romantic subjectification," dissonance,[82] which had played a subordinate role in classical and romantic harmony. Dissonance was now to be the very form of unresolved tension, the denial of all resolution. In Adorno's interpretation, the cognitive value of modernist "ugliness," which de-aestheticized the artwork from within its technical development, gave expression to the oppressed and resisted the affirmative illusions of current harmony purveyed by

79. Adorno, *Philosophy of Modern Music*, pp. 41–42.
80. Ibid., pp. 48–50.
81. See Schorske, *Fin de Siècle Vienna*, pp. 357–361.
82. Adorno, *Philosophy of Modern Music*, pp. 58–59.

the culture industry.[83] Since "there is no longer beauty or consolation except in the gaze falling on horror," Adorno wrote, beauty that "still flourishes under terror is a mockery and ugliness to itself."[84]

Writing after the bureaucratically rationalized, administrative mass murders of the Jews by the Nazis, Adorno cited Schoenberg's wrenching and painful "Survivor of Warsaw," which refuses all sentimentalizing, as containing an element of that ultimately inexpressible suffering which he held to be most characteristic of our age. Yet, even here, in the farthest reaches of an expressionistic nightmare world which is the actual waking reality, art is inadequate to those who suffer, because, as art, it contains assuaging images and sounds which, "however remotely," still have "the power to elicit enjoyment out of it. . . . Something of its horror is removed. . . . Even the sound of despair pays its tribute to a hideous affirmation."[85] This is what Adorno had in mind when he wrote, in one of his most quoted lines: "To write poetry after Auschwitz is barbaric."[86] Yet, Adorno stressed that such work as Schoenberg's (and, as we shall see, Kafka's and Beckett's) provided some scant hope by its capacity to give even the slightest expression to the horrors of contemporary society. As long as these stridently discordant sounds are still heard with fresh ears, their power is perceived not merely as a reflection of the painful "truths" of the socially existent, but rests upon the "consonant" utopia whose promise they keep alive in their honest acknowledgment of its absence: "Their negativity is true to utopia: it includes within itself the concealed consonance."[87]

Schoenberg's music does more than express the subjective suffering of the disintegrating individual, or offer the promise of a utopian alternative. Through a careful analysis of the evolution of the twelve-tone system from out of Schoenberg's freer "polytonality," Adorno asserts that the music reveals, in its inner structure, the increasing dominance of a repressive, instrumentally rationalized social whole. In striking parallel with the argument of *Dialectic of Enlightenment*, Adorno suggests that the initial freedom of the tone row from a static recurrence of notes and a central tonal authority and hierarchy veers increasingly toward a stultifying system which freezes the structure into a "musical domina-

83. Richard Wolin, "The De-Aestheticization of Art: On Adorno's Aesthetische Theorie," *Telos*, 41 (Fall 1979), 109–116.
84. Adorno, *Minima Moralia*, pp. 25–121.
85. Adorno, "On Commitment," *Aesthetics and Politics*, p. 189.
86. Adorno, *Prisms*, p. 34; "On Commitment," p. 188.
87. Adorno, *Philosophy of Modern Music*, p. 86.

tion of nature." [88] "Beethoven reproduced the meaning of tonality out of subjective freedom. The new ordering of twelve-tone technique virtually extinguishes the subject." [89] In the face of a repressively rationalized social whole, which reappears in the very logic of the music, Schoenberg could only fail in attempting to "emancipate the musical subject." Hence, Adorno writes: "These works are magnificent in their failure. It is not the composer who fails in the work; history, rather, denies the work in itself." [90]

Schoenberg's work shared the artistic project of those expressionists (e.g., Trakl, Heym, Barlach, and Kafka) who sought objective formal means to explore the individual's suffering and experience of impotence and fragmentation. [91] Adorno's indebtedness to this aesthetic of objectified expression was as important in his work as Benjamin's symbolist inspiration was in his.

In Schoenberg the objectification of subjective impulses becomes crucial. . . . Through Schoenberg's polyphony the subjective melodic impulse is dialectically dissolved into its objective multivocal components. . . . The logical consequence of the principle of expression includes the moment of its own negation as that negative form of truth which transforms love into the power of objective protest. [92]

Both Benjamin and Adorno sought to interpret the unintentional social meanings of their contrasting modernisms with the aid of selective Marxian (or other) historical insights. Just as Benjamin came to reject an aestheticized politics anticipated, in his view, by symbolist decadence, so Adorno denied the notion of an absolute subjectivity implicit in the art of the more naive expressionists (e.g., Werfel and Toller). "Art cannot survive when based on a notion of pure expression identical with *Angst*," he wrote. ". . . [But] the expression of suffering and the pleasure taken in dissonance . . . are inextricably interwoven in authentic works of art in the modern age." [93] Adorno stressed that artists' feelings must be given objective external form through work on technical problems within their craft; only through this immanent aesthetic activity will they be able to illuminate wider social conditions within which the subject exists. In an essay on Kafka written during the late

88. Ibid., pp. 51–67.   89. Ibid., pp. 67–69.   90. Ibid., pp. 98–99.
    91. Walter Sokel, *The Writer in Extremis*, pp. 50–51, 106–116, 161–162, only treats literature (with some asides to the visual arts), and neglects Schoenberg, but his superb discussion of expressionist "objectification" helps to clarify Schoenberg's work and, through this, Adorno's relation to expressionism.
    92. Adorno, *Prisms*, pp. 153–159.
    93. Adorno, "Reconciliation Under Duress," *Aesthetics and Politics*, pp. 167–168.

1940s, Adorno stated: "The more the I of Expressionism is thrown back upon itself, the more like the excluded world of things it becomes. . . . Pure subjectivity, being of necessity estranged from itself as well as having become a thing, assumes the dimensions of objectivity which expresses itself through its own estrangement."[94] But in this "completely estranged subjectivity," Kafka "follows the expressionist impulse farther than any but the most radical of the poets. . . . [He] forces Expressionism—the chimerical aspect of which he, more than any of his friends, must have sensed—and to which he nevertheless remained faithful—into the form of a tortuous epic."[95]

Along with Schoenberg's music, according to Adorno, the work of Franz Kafka showed the "capacity to stand up to the worst by making it into language." In his novels, the dream of individuation is shattered in the actual nightmare reality of the contemporary world. Exceeding even Freud in his skepticism toward the notion of an intact ego and psychological autonomy, Kafka presents parabolic images of the guilt and powerlessness of the victim in the face of an utterly reified and impenetrable "rationality" embodied in administrative power. "The social origin of the individual ultimately reveals itself as the power to annihilate him." The full verification of Kafka's method, Adorno emphasized, was accomplished when fascist organization liquidated the last remnants of obsolete "liberal traits," and "advanced" capitalism manufactured "men on the assembly line, mechanically reproduced copies." Subjects who regress into an animal state, as Gregor Samsa does into a bug, show their impotent superfluousness within the unlimited power of monopolistic domination. But Kafka presents this hellish image of slow lingering demise in an unremittingly critical manner. The abandonment of defiance against all-powerful authority indicts a "system" which undermines all resistance except that of alienated art: "Kafka does not glorify the world through subordination; he resists it through nonviolence." Instead of "refining the work outside of history," in an abstract ontology of "existential man," as Kafka himself sometimes allows us to do, we must understand his negativity as deriving its strength from his specific historical milieu, "the literary movement of the decade surrounding the First World War, . . . that of expressionism."[96]

Both Schoenberg and Kafka drove expressionism to its outer limits, "to the point at which the nerve-pictures and the traumata of the latter slowly veer, under the pressure of their own internal logic, into the new

94. Adorno, *Prisms*, p. 262.   95. Ibid.
96. Adorno, *Prisms*, pp. 243–271.

objectivity, the more total order. . . ."[97] It was Adorno's central contention that this "self-estranged objectivity" was an anguished protest against the repressive social forms of the twentieth century, even if in one of its aspects the music reflected the administered world. In the "new objectivity" of Stravinsky, on the other hand, which resembled the *Neue Sachlichkeit* movement of the later Weimar Republic, with its affirmative embrace of machine technology, the individual was being encouraged to adjust joyfully, to conform to the new monolithic environment. Adorno was not pitting pure subject against pure object; he never ceased to mediate one with the other. Rather, he was contrasting two widely different styles of modernist formalization.[98]

To Adorno, "the primacy of breathing over the beat of abstract time contrasts Schoenberg to Stravinsky and all those who, having adjusted better to contemporary existence, fancy themselves more modern than Schoenberg."[99] In the second half of *Philosophy of Modern Music*, Adorno relentlessly polemicized against Stravinsky's anti-romantic abandonment of individual expression, and, in the tradition of the battles between these two schools in the musical life of the Weimar Republic,[100] he contrasted this with Schoenberg's compositional methods.

97. Jameson, *Marxism and Form*, p. 31.
98. In *The Writer in Extremis*, p. 161, Sokel carefully distinguishes expressionist objectification from the later *Neue Sachlichkeit* approach. Speaking of Kafka, Barlach, Heym, Trakl and others, he writes: "All these authors abstract the full concreteness of objective reality from their subjective emphasis, their 'idea' or vision of reality, which alone they seek to express. *Sachlichkeit*, however, is the attempt to present a 'deemphasized' objective reality, i.e., the dispassionate understanding of the external world." Adorno formulated the distinction somewhat differently since he viewed artists such as Schoenberg as expressing their "idea" or "vision" through the formal elaboration and development of technical artistic problems which they had inherited; their work, in addition, unintentionally "expresses" social realities which the critic must illuminate. Yet, although Sokel's discussion is unpolemical, the contrast which he describes is otherwise in keeping with Adorno's central one between Stravinsky and Schoenberg, and through them, between the basic antinomy in *all* modern culture between "negative" and "affirmative" art.
99. Adorno, *Prisms*, p. 152.
100. See Willet, *Art and Politics in the Weimar Period, 1917–1933*, pp. 159–167. Adorno's choice of Schoenberg and Stravinsky as representative of the major currents in modern music was suggestive, but too narrow. One vital force (especially for the best music of Eastern Europe after 1945) was Béla Bartok. Adorno largely disregarded Bartok, though in *Philosophy of Modern Music* he cited Bartok's use of folkloristic elements as having "a power of alienation which places it in the company of the avant garde and not that of nationalistic reaction" (pp. 35n–36n). Yet, in Adorno's view, such attempts to give expression to communal folk cultures (in Bartok's case, Hungarian), were doomed. In 1932 he had written: "There is no longer any 'Folk' whose songs . . . could be taken up and sublimated by art; the opening up of markets and the bourgeois process of rationalization have subordinated all society to bourgeois categories." ("Social Situation of Music," p. 140). In "Negative Philosophy of Music," Ferenc Fehér criticizes Adorno effectively for his revealing neglect of Bartok.

As in his similar attack on jazz, Adorno's assault was monolithic in judgment and, in places, quite farfetched in its sociological interpretations.[101]
The "primitivism" of the Rite of Spring and Petroushka were, according to Adorno, a celebration of sacrifice to the totemic collective,
the regression of the individual and society to a mythic state before the
development of the independent ego. History reverses itself and takes
the form of static images of a brutalized nature seeking revenge on civilization. The shocks of the music cannot be absorbed, since "there is
neither the anticipation of anxiety nor the resisting ego"; the music sub-
mits "to the rhythmic blows dealt it from an external source."[102] As in
his analyses of jazz, a form which much attracted Stravinsky, Adorno
finds a strong sadomasochistic element, an identification with the destructive collective much like the mass psychology induced by fascist
leadership.[103] If the Nazis banned such music as Stravinsky's Rite of
Spring, Adorno claimed, this was because they did not dare to acknowledge so totally the barbarism of their own practice "with its astro-
nomical sacrifice of human beings."[104]

Stravinsky's shift after 1918 toward what was called "neoclassicism"
merely continued the pattern. Now regression took more explicit compositional form as Stravinsky self-consciously abandoned the tradition of "emancipated subjectivity" and temporal unfolding in Western
music since Bach and Mozart, and sought to refurbish an archaic pre-
individualistic musical language. As against the negativity of expressionist dissonance, Stravinsky's musical "restoration" avoided tension
and implicitly affirmed the powers that be: "Every moment of soothing
comfort, of the harmonious, of the displacement of horror in art—the
aesthetic heir of the magic practice, against which all expressionism,
down to the revolutionary works of Schoenberg, protested—this har-
moniousness triumphs in Stravinsky's scornful and cutting tone as the
herald of the Iron Age. He is the Yea-sayer of music."[105]

The easy absorption of Stravinsky's music by the public was made
possible, according to Adorno, by the ready acclimation of that music
to the subjectless administered society of the contemporary world. One
of the essential characteristics of this adjustment was the erosion of in-
wardly felt temporal experience, and its replacement by an externalizing

---

101. For some good criticisms of Adorno's handling of Stravinsky's music, see Robert
Craft, "A Bell for Adorno," Prejudices in Disguise (New York, 1974). Craft, however,
shows little knowledge of Adorno's wider intentions.
102. Adorno, Philosophy of Modern Music, pp. 156–157.
103. Ibid., pp. 143–146, 157–160.
104. Ibid., pp. 145–146.   105. Ibid., p. 170.

obeisance to what exists, all at once, merely in space. "Such suspension of musical time consciousness corresponds to the total consciousness of a bourgeoisie which—in that it no longer sees anything before it—denies the time process itself and finds its utopia in withdrawals into space. . . . One trick characterizes all of Stravinsky's formal endeavors: the effort of his music to portray time as in a circus tableau and to present time complexes as though they were spatial." [106]

In such spatializing, music "abdicated" to "painting" by denying its own meaning as "becoming," [107] Adorno charged. He analyzed the problem by tracing Stravinsky's roots to Russian and, even more so, French music of the late nineteenth century. Stravinsky's music partly derived from the prebourgeois and pre-individualistic elements discernible in Moussorgsky, whose lyricism is "distinguished from the German *Lied* by the absence of any poetic subject." [108] On the other hand, Stravinsky evolves also out of the montage focus and escape from subjective experience in French modernist culture. "He belongs to a type of Western art the highest summit of which lies in the work of Baudelaire, in which the individual—through the force of emotional sensation—enjoys his own annihilation." [109] Stravinsky's music drew heavily from the spatializing "impressionism" of Debussy, Fauré, and Ravel:

The sensual melancholy of Impressionism is the heir to Wagner's philosophical pessimism. In no case does sound go beyond itself in time; it rather vanishes in space. In Wagner, renunciation—the negation of the will to life—was the sustaining metaphysical category; French music, which renounced all metaphysics—even the metaphysics of pessimism—emphasized such renunciation all the more strongly the more it contented itself with a fortune which—as a mere here and now, as absolute transitoriness—is no longer fortune. Such steps of resignation are the pre-forms for the liquidation of the individual that is celebrated by Stravinsky's music. [110]

Unlike the thematic, motivic work of Viennese music from Haydn, through Beethoven and Brahms, to Schoenberg, with its "dialectical spirit of a self-engendering, self-negating . . . whole," the painterly, "coloristic" sounds of Debussy and Ravel have their formal law in the "static juxtaposition of tone levels." [111] The willful abandonment of subjective time, Adorno continued, Stravinsky's music shared with other

106. Ibid., pp. 194–195.   107. Ibid., p. 191.   108. Ibid., p. 144n.
109. Ibid., p. 166.
110. Ibid., p. 190. See also pp. 165–166 and 189.
111. Adorno, *Introduction to the Sociology of Music*, pp. 88–89. For more on Adorno's hostile treatment of French music of 1889–1920, see Subotnik, "The Historical Structure," pp. 54–56.

examples of depersonalized art in the 1920s: the "dream montages which the surrealists constructed out of the residue of the wakeful day"[112]; Brechtian hostility toward humanistic values[113]; and, most significantly, the cubistic montage of Eisenstein's films. (All of these were forms which Benjamin praised.)

> Direct musical material is not developed out of its own driving force. . . . This recalls the statement which Eisenstein once made about film montage: he explained that the general concept . . . proceeded precisely out of . . . juxtaposition as separated, isolated elements. This results, however, in the dissociation of the musical time continuum itself.[114]

Most of the styles to which Adorno compared Stravinsky's music—French surrealism and musical impressionism, filmic montage, and jazz—were either directly within the "affirmative" culture industry or easily appropriated for such use. Each style facilitated, moreover, its still more direct commercial functions in advertising.[115] But just as nonobjective painting was a defense, according to Adorno, against the encroachments of the mechanized art commodity of photography, so Schoenberg and his school "reacted similarly to the commercial depravity of the traditional idiom." They formulated a defensive front which was aided by the relative lateness with which music, the most "nonconceptual and nonobjective" of arts, was pressed into the service of the commodity economy.[116]

In Adorno's infrequent discussions of French modernism, he either attacked precisely those aspects which Benjamin defended, or, as in a few more balanced articles of the 1950s, selectively defended the French aesthetes in a manner that was characteristically different from Benjamin's. Instead of viewing "shocks" in Baudelaire's poetry as explosions of the time continuum, liberating the fleetingly "new" from its mere use as commodity, Adorno viewed these as desperate attempts to avoid lassitude and boredom and create stimulative sensations of whatever kind. Such craving for "convulsive moments of illusory living" would later, in fascism, become the "shocks" about which Goebbels would boast: "At least the National Socialists are not boring." The return of the old in Baudelaire's "correspondences," which Benjamin

---

112. Adorno, *Philosophy of Modern Music*, p. 188.
113. Ibid., p. 170.
114. Ibid., p. 187.
115. Ibid., pp. 170–171, 203; "Über Jazz," *Zeitschrift für Sozialforschung*, pp. 248–250; "Fetish Character of Music," p. 289.
116. Adorno, *Philosophy of Modern Music*, p. 5.

viewed as an anticipation of utopia, Adorno saw as an addictive, compulsive repetition similar to Wagner's.[117] In an article written in 1939–40 on Stefan George and Hugo von Hofmannsthal, the German and Austrian followers of the symbolists, Adorno attacked the "illusory conservation of disintegrating beauty" in the face of industrial society, in contrast with a "renunciation of the beautiful" which "can preserve its idea more powerfully." He showed no sympathy, in particular, for the linguistic strategy of this defensive action, the attempt of all symbolists to "consecrate" themselves to the "thing-world as a sacrifice," precisely what he found so objectionable in Benjamin's writings:

It is not the aim of Symbolism to subordinate all material moments as symbols of an inner sphere. . . . Instead of things yielding as symbols of subjectivity, subjectivity yields as the symbol of things, prepares itself to rigidify ultimately into the thing which society has in any case made of it.[118]

In a celebrated later article, "Lyric Poetry and Society" (1951), Adorno was more sympathetic to the symbolists' efforts. Instead of charging them with a desire to accommodate to the estranged object, he now defended their lyrical poetic submersion in language as a desperately needed attempt to *rescue* personal subjectivity in a reified world, and, in so doing, also preserve language from its commercial misuse. But the central thrust of his interpretation was a championing of the hermetic aestheticism of the symbolists, and other modern poets, in particular the common aim to focus on the "immanent" problems of form within their craft. Adorno contrasted this favorably with all misguided attempts to "politicize" art by subordinating it to heteronomous external activities or intellectually brutalized audiences.[119] Later pieces dealing with Valéry emphasized a similar perspective, both on his language and his aestheticism.[120] Adorno's grounds for the defense of symbolism thus undercut Benjamin's hostility toward subjectivity, as well as his efforts to define a political overcoming of hermetic aestheticism.

Toward surrealism, however, Adorno continued to be as hostile as he had been since the early 1930s. The photographic immediacy of the surrealists' assembled material fragments confirmed these objects in their reified state. Their dream exploration, moreover, "directs itself against the psychological interpretation of the dream" (precisely the feature praised by Benjamin) and "replaces it with objective images," he wrote in 1934. In an article written in 1956, Adorno viewed the discontinuous montage of surrealism as an embrace of dismembered bodily parts conceived as inorganic commodity fetishes: "The subject . . . reveals itself in the face of complete depersonalization as inanimate and virtually dead. . . . Detached breasts, the legs of mannequins in silk stockings in collages—these are reminiscences of those objects of partial drive to which the libido once awoke. The forgotten reveals itself in them, thinglike, dead, as what love really desired and what it wishes to make itself resemble."[121] In *Philosophy of Modern Music*, Adorno had written:

Surrealism is anti-organic and rooted in lifelessness. It destroys the boundary between the body and the world of objects, in order to convert society to a hypostatization of the body. Its form is that of montage. This is totally alien to Schoenberg. With regard to Surrealism, however, the more subjectivity renounces its right over the world of objects, aggressively acknowledging the supremacy of that world, the more willing it is to accept at the same time the traditionally established form of the world of objects.[122]

Adorno found no "profane illumination" here, no utopian "redemption" of "enslaved and enslaving objects," merely a strong reminder— which was at least preferable to the phony optimism of *Neue Sachlichkeit*—of the impossibility of happiness in the "technified world of the present."[123]

Although usually hostile toward French and Russian avant-gardes, Adorno did not only support the work of Austrian or German modernists in the expressionist tradition. By the 1950s, he defended symbolist poets such as Valéry, as we have seen, and included Proust, Gide, Joyce, and Beckett in his wide-ranging sympathetic treatment of the modern novel form.[124] He also occasionally referred approvingly to Picasso's "critical and fragmentary" art.[125] Adorno's defense of such modernists did not merely derive from expressionist premises, even in their objectified forms. His insistence upon a technical self-liquidation of aura within the immanent dialectic of the artwork, and upon the need for formal preoccupations and self-reflexiveness in both art and criticism;

121. Adorno, "Looking Back on Surrealism," *Literary Modernism*, ed. Irving Howe, pp. 220–224.
122. Adorno, *Philosophy of Modern Music*, p. 51n.
123. Adorno, "Looking Back on Surrealism," p. 224.
124. Adorno, "Der Standort des Erzählers im zeitgenossischen Roman," *Noten zur Literatur*, Vol. 1, pp. 61–72.
125. As, for example, in *Philosophy of Modern Music*, p. 51n.

his rejection of classical organic wholeness, romantic subjectivity, or realist "reflection"; and his emphasis upon the fragmentary, transient,
and relativist nature of "truth"—all these were features of many modernist currents. The same could be said concerning his repeated support
of aesthetically avant-garde alienated outsiders, as autonomous as they
managed to be, as opposed to "committed" or "mass" art. Yet, often the
manner in which he supported non-German modernists derived, to a
considerable degree, from a perspective which had been most significant
in expressionism, though best shown in such objectifying artists as
Schoenberg and Kafka. Cubism, for example, was validated through
later bird's-eye photographs of the bombed-out cities of World War II,
according to Adorno.[126] (*Guernica*, we might note, showed Picasso at
his most expressionist.)

Adorno's defense of the modern novel was another case of an analysis which he had developed in relation to expressionist work. Traditional descriptive narrative in the sense of nineteenth-century realism
was no longer historically appropriate, Adorno argued. Only such fragmentation of personality and authorial "standpoint" as occurs in the
novels of Proust, Joyce, or Musil, for example, will adequately disclose
the extent of individual self-estrangement, suffering, and impotence in
our time. To tell a traditional realistic story of individual striving, and
from the vantage of a single narrative voice, would be to falsify the current inhumanity and suggest that the individual still has independent
meaning and impact in the social whole. Modern novelists do well, instead, to disjointedly interrupt narration, present it from multiple perspectives, reveal the power of objects in the unconscious or thoughts of
powerless "characters," and construct the whole through an associa-
tional montage logic—as long as these serve to illuminate, in a potentially critical way, the disintegration of individual subjectivity.[127]
Against Lukács's charge that modernists present an "ontological," time-

126. Adorno, *Prisms*, p. 254.
127. Adorno, "Der Standort des Erzählers," pp. 61–72. Adorno wavered in his judgment of montage as a mode of aesthetic organization, although he was usually quite critical. He attacked the use of montage in surrealism, and in Soviet avant-garde film (as well
as in other examples of mass media); in Benjamin's insufficiently theorized assemblages of
data; and, in his *Aesthetische Theorie* (pp. 232–233), at the end of his life, he viewed
montage as the "inner aesthetic capitulation of art to what is extrinsic to it . . . an unmediated :iominalist utopia." On the other hand, he could acknowledge that if "correctly
done" a montage is "by definition also interpreting" (quoted in Buck-Morss, *Origin of
Negative Dialectics*, p. 296n); and he had some appreciative comments in 1932 on Kurt
Weill's "montage music" of critical "negativity," exposing falsely organic harmonies, particularly in the scores which Weill had composed for Brecht's *Threepenny Opera* and *The
Rise and Fall of the City of Mahagonny* ("The Social Situation of Music," pp. 143–144).

less view of man as an isolated and atomized being, Adorno argued that Joyce, Proust, Beckett, Musil, and others showed how "loneliness is socially mediated and so possesses a significant historical content."[128]

Adorno's bitter expressionist-inspired protest heavily informed his espousal of the one truly outstanding literary figure to emerge, in his eyes, after World War II: Samuel Beckett, whose works readily lent themselves to such an analysis.[129] The Aesthetische Theorie, which remained uncompleted at Adorno's death in 1969, was to have been dedicated to Beckett.[130] In a 1959 essay on Endgame, Adorno viewed Beckett's work as a continuation of Kafka's relentless disclosure of the atrophy of personality in the reified contemporary world; yet, this attrition of selfhood was now more advanced. Beckett's plays and novels are not ahistorically "existential," Adorno warned, but powerful suggestions of the afterlife, or afterdeath, of the historically definable category of individuality. "Instead of excluding the temporal from existence, . . . he subtracts that which time—the historical trend—is in reality preparing to annul. He extends the trajectory of the subject's liquidation to the point where it shrinks to the here-and-now. . . . History is excluded because it has dried up the power of consciousness to conceive history: the power of memory. . . . All that appears of history is its result, its decline. . . ." The parodistic forms of Endgame articulate the epilogue of subjectivity: "All that remains of freedom is the impotent and ridiculous reflex of empty decisions." Heir to the novels of Kafka, Beckett's play employs dramatic constituents—action, exposition, intrigue, peripeteia, and catastrophe—at a later historical stage than Kafka's work; this gives the play the critical thrust of parody. Dead as persons, Hamm and Clov live on as lingering corpses, in a state of rigor mortis, "plagued by the fear of the Flying Dutchman: not to be able to die. The fragment of hope, which means everything, is that perhaps this might change. This movement, or its absence, constitutes the action of the play."[131]

In his widely read attack (published in 1962) on the theory and practice of "committed" literature in the works of Sartre and Brecht, Adorno held up the seemingly "hermetic" Kafka and Beckett as the true exemplars of a critical, socially explosive art. Instead of the prematurely rec-

128. Adorno, "Reconciliation Under Duress," pp. 158–166.
129. Wylie Sypher, for example, has described Beckett's work as a series of studies of the extreme "attrition of personality"; "after the self has shrivelled the human remains . . ." (The Loss of Self in Modern Literature and Art [New York, 1962], pp. 147, 154).
130. Adorno, Aesthetische Theorie, p. 544.
131. Adorno, "Toward an Understanding of Endgame," Twentieth Century Interpretations of Endgame, ed. Gale Chevigny (Englewood Cliffs, N.J., 1969), pp. 82–114.

onciled and affirmative thrust of the directly "political," Beckett's dissonant and "negative" art refuses to be comforted by any forms of current
collective action. Yet, "Kafka's prose and Beckett's plays, or the truly
monstrous novel *The Unnamable*, have an effect by comparison with
which the officially committed works look like pantomimes. . . . By dismantling appearance, they explode from within the art which committed
proclamation subjugates from without, and hence only in appearance.
The inescapability of their work compels the change of attitude which
committed works merely demand."[132] In the spirit of Adorno's perspective, the Polish theatre director Jan Kott wrote, in the 1950s: "We do
Brecht when we want Fantasy. When we want sheer Realism, we do
Waiting for Godot."[133]

❖   ❖   ❖

Adorno's criticism of literary "commitment" contrasted with Benjamin's attempts to "politicize" the art of the modern. To complete this
study of the two thinkers, it is useful to compare their general views of
the relation between art and politics, a major concern for any Marxist
aesthetics. To do so, it is necessary to bring Brecht back once again.
This I shall do by exploring Adorno's critique of Brecht's "committed"
art and Benjamin's seemingly Brechtian notion of the "solidarity" of the
literary "producer" with the industrial proletariat.

In one of his critical letters to Benjamin in the late 1930s, Adorno
wrote that "the further development of the aesthetic debate which you
have so magnificently inaugurated depends essentially on a true ac-
counting of the relationship of the intellectuals to the working class."
This would mean having to liquidate Brechtian motifs, in particular the
cult of technology and "any appeal to the actual consciousness of actual
workers," both of which he saw in Benjamin's writings.[134] Against the
Marxian stress upon labor and Brecht's near identification of literary
and industrial "production," the basis of many of the playwright's strictures upon Lukács's classical and "idealist" postures, Adorno insisted
upon the mediated non-identity of mental and physical work. Culture
draws its strength from this relative autonomy and separation, he argued, even if it also suffers guilt in its dependence upon physical labor
for its very existence. "As long as even the least part of the mind remains

132. Adorno, "On Commitment," pp. 190–191.
133. Quoted in Eric Bentley, "The Theatre of Commitment," in *The Theatre of Commitment and Other Essays on Drama in Our Society* (New York, 1967), p. 203.
134. Adorno, *Aesthetics and Politics*, p. 124.

engaged in the reproduction of life, it is its sworn bondsman," he wrote. "The anti-philistinism of Athens was both the most arrogant contempt of the man who need not soil his hands for the man from whose work he lives, and the preservation of an image of existence beyond the constraint which underlies all work." [135] Thus, the function of art derives from its "purposelessness" in the face of functional and immediate demands for production, profit, or political action. "The Lyric subject . . . owes its existence to special privilege: only the fewest individuals, given the pressures of the necessities of life, are ever allowed to grasp the general truth or shape of things in self-immersion. . . ." [136]

In the essay "On Commitment," Adorno viewed Brecht's plays as fundamentally flawed, both aesthetically and politically, by an instrumentalized political didacticism and oversimplified presentation of the actual realities of the contemporary world. Against Western enthusiasts for Brecht, who sought to disengage Brecht's art from his politics, Adorno argued that, especially in this case, such an attempt at separation was meaningless; Brecht's work stands or falls on our judgment of the political "realism" toward which he aimed. Citing *Saint Joan of the Stockyards*, *Arturo Ui*, and *The Measures Taken*, in particular, Adorno charged, with some justice, that these plays radically reduced the mediated complexities of capitalism, fascism, and communism, respectively.[137] Even more damaging was Brecht's tendencies to "preach to the converted," distort the "real social problems discussed in his epic drama in order to prove a thesis," and thereby construct dramatic implausibilities.[138] The imposition upon his cultivated intelligence of an external discipline in the form of a celebration of the plebeian wisdom of the oppressed, and of the communist movement in whose name it allegedly acted, affected "the very fibre of his poetic art," which was "poisoned by the untruth of his politics":

For what he justified was not simply, as he long sincerely believed, an incomplete socialism, but a coercive domination in which blindly irrational social forces returned to work once again. When Brecht became a panegyrist of its harmony, his lyrical voice had to swallow chalk, and it started to grate. . . . Even Brecht's best work was infected by the deceptions of his commitment. Its language shows how far the underlying poetic subject and its message have moved apart. In an attempt to bridge the gap, Brecht affected the diction of the oppressed. But the doctrine he advocated needs the language of the intellectual.

135. Adorno, *Prisms*, pp. 26–27.
136. Adorno, "Lyric Poetry and Society," p. 63.
137. Adorno, "On Commitment," pp. 182–186.
138. Ibid., pp. 185–197.

The homeliness and simplicity of his tone is thus a fiction. . . . It is a usurpation and almost a contempt for victims to speak like this, as if the author were one of them. All roles may be played, except that of the worker. The gravest charge against commitment is that even right intentions go wrong when they are noticed, and still more so, when they then try to conceal themselves. Something of this remains in Brecht's later plays in the linguistic *gestus* of wisdom, the fiction of the old peasant sated with epic experience as the poetic subject. No one in any country of the world is any longer capable of the earthy experience of South German muzhiks: the ponderous delivery has become a propaganda device to make us believe that the good life is where the Red Army is in control. . . . What his classical predecessors once denounced as the idiocy of rural life, Brecht, like some existential ontologist, treats as ancient truth. His whole oeuvre is a Sisyphean labour to reconcile his highly cultivated and subtle taste with the crudely heteronomous demands which he desperately imposed on himself.[139]

Though penetrating in some of its criticisms, especially of Brecht's communist apologias and role-playing as worker, Adorno's treatment of Brecht was narrow and one-sided. He never seriously engaged the question of the potentiality of Brecht's montage and distancing methods except as they were manifested within the playwright's particular political framework. That they were capable of being used more fruitfully by Brecht than in Adorno's damning examples, or that they might provide a key for other less politically blinded artists, was missing from his account. In attacking polemics, Adorno had turned polemicist. The conclusion of the article followed from his contrast of Brecht with Kafka and Beckett:

An emphasis on autonomous works is itself socio-political in nature. The feigning of a true politics here and now, the freezing of historical relations which nowhere seem ready to melt, oblige the mind to go where it need not degrade itself. . . . It is to works of art that has fallen the burden of wordlessly asserting what is barred to politics. . . . This is not a time for politics, but politics has migrated into autonomous art, and nowhere more so than where it seems to be politically dead. An example is Kafka's allegory of toy-guns, in which an idea of non-violence is fused with a dawning awareness of the approaching paralysis of politics.[140]

While illuminating social meanings latent in the avant-garde work of Schoenberg, Kafka, and Beckett, Adorno never adequately explained his view of intellectual or aesthetic activity as *praxis*, or the value of critical negativity in art, as his closest analyst, Susan Buck-Morss, has recently pointed out. There was also something metaphysical, she con-

139. Ibid., pp. 187–188.
140. Ibid., p. 194.

tinues, in his stress upon "truth." [141] There were democratic elements in his critique of mass culture, separating it from the more common conservative and elitist assaults.[142] But he disparaged *all* art about which it had been claimed that it was "grass-roots," populist, or expressive of a "folk culture"; all, he alleged, were creations of the administered commodity economy or of communist politics. Surely the whole world is not reducible to such monolithic judgments. Adorno also failed to draw adequate conclusions from the tensions between intellectuals and workers which he had realistically emphasized against Brecht's self-deceptions on the matter. Such conflicts need to be acknowledged not merely, as Adorno felt, so that intellectuals and artists might resist the "conformist tendencies" which may be seen in the proletariat,[143] but also so that intellectuals might learn something from workers that they might not themselves know.

In "The Author as Producer" (1934), which he desisted from sending to Adorno, Benjamin explicitly argued some of the very Brechtian theses concerning technology, the proletariat, and communism which Adorno acutely criticized in the essay on "Mechanical Reproduction" two years later. Yet, Benjamin's understanding of the potential "solidarity" of alienated bourgeois intellectuals and workers was more subtle and honest than Brecht's, and, because of that, more effectively countered some of the weaknesses and one-sidedness of Adorno's positions. The essay suffered from an overoptimistic assessment of communist and working-class movements, but was more perceptive concerning the position of the intelligentsia and, through that, the nature of a politically engaged modernism. "Politicized" art, whose definition Benjamin had developed out of surrealist, Brechtian, and constructivist activities, must involve radical changes of aesthetic form, he argued, not the imposition of either party dictates *or* any other political "tendency" or "content." [144] The difference from Adorno lay in Benjamin's Brechtian interest in a progressive literary "refunctioning" of filmic and news media, which Adorno viewed as an extrinsic subordination of the immanent dialectic of avant-garde aesthetic activity. Benjamin's argument was underpinned, however, by the view that the intelligentsia, like the proletariat, does not control its means of production and distribution, and must seek to transform the apparatus which it is employed merely

141. Buck-Morss, *Origin of Negative Dialectics*, pp. 36, 41–42.
142. Jay, *Dialectical Imagination*, pp. 214–218.
143. Ibid., p. 84.
144. Benjamin, *Understanding Brecht*, pp. 86–99.

to supply. But this did not by any means signify that the intelligentsia was identical in its social role with the working class.

The solidarity of the expert with the proletariat . . . can never be other than mediated. . . . Even the proletarianization of the intellectual hardly ever makes him a proletarian. Why? Because the bourgeois class has endowed him with a means of production—in the form of his education—which, on the grounds of educational privilege, creates a bond of solidarity which attaches him to his class, and still more attaches his class to him. Aragon was therefore perfectly right when, in another context, he said: "The revolutionary intellectual appears first of all and above everything else as a traitor to his class of origin."[145]

This notion of the left intelligentsia as tied to, while being at war with, bourgeois culture and class was one of the major themes of Benjamin's journalistic activity from 1925 to the Nazi seizure of power.[146] Whereas Brecht spoke to Benjamin about the "complete proletarianization" of the intellectual, which "establishes his solidarity with the proletariat all along the line,"[147] Benjamin denied this simple identity without falling into the opposite error of claiming the intelligentsia to be "independent" or "free-lance." Ever since the inflation of 1923, Benjamin had argued that intellectuals lead an increasingly commodified existence while experiencing impotence in relation to the means of intellectual production, which they do not control. Yet, he still emphasized that "intellectuals today mimic proletarian existence without in the slightest being bound to the working class."[148] At the same time, he wrote that the "most daring products of the avant-garde—in France and Germany—have only the great bourgeoisie as a public. In this fact lies not a judgment about its value but a sign of the political insecurity which stands behind these manifestations."[149] All this he hoped to help change, of course. But even if avant-garde art were "refunctioned" and "methylated" against absorption as bourgeois entertainment, and even if intellectuals viewed their production in solidarity with that of workers, they would still remain distinct from them, still tied in important ways to the bourgeois class which they rejected.

If intellectuals show a need for revolutionary involvement, Benjamin wrote, this results from their social isolation; in this regard their motives are different from the more directly material ones which galvanize

145. Ibid., p. 102.
146. Witte, *Walter Benjamin*, pp. 145–148, 166–172; see also *Angelus Novus*, pp. 422–428.
147. Benjamin, *Understanding Brecht*, p. 105.
148. Benjamin, *Angelus Novus*, p. 277.
149. Ibid., p. 287.

the masses. They also are more anarchistic, i.e., more interested in revolutionary action than in postrevolutionary social construction, as in the case of the Soviet Union.[150] For Benjamin, the real function of left intellectuals is neither to provide entertaining amusements and consumption for the jaded bourgeoisie—from which perspective he attacked left "independent" publicists such as Walter Mehring and Kurt Tucholsky[151]— nor to provide shock troops for directly proletarian struggles. Their task is to write neither for "snobs" nor for "workers," he emphasized, without explicitly pressing the point against Adorno or Brecht, but to aid in the politicization of the "false consciousness" of their own class, the literary intelligentsia.[152] This includes, most importantly, educating them to an awareness of their dependent economic role as salable commodities within capitalist life, and a sensitivity to the current social functions of the traditional culture which they seek to guard. Benjamin himself sought to move beyond a purely negative role as rebel against his class of origin, to make his "dynamite" serviceable, in however indirect and highly mediated a manner, to the working class. But there was much of a sense of his own social function in one of his descriptions of Baudelaire in the *Arcades* study:

There is little point in trying to include a Baudelaire in the fabric of the most advanced position in mankind's struggle for liberation. From the outset it seems more promising to investigate his machinations where undoubtedly he is at home—in the enemy camp. Very rarely are they a blessing for the opposite side. Baudelaire was a secret agent—an agent of the secret discontent of his class with its own rule.[153]

At the conclusion of our study of encounters between Marxism and modernism, Benjamin's words on Baudelaire suggest a more circumscribed and limited role for the avant-garde than Brecht, perhaps mistakenly, attempted in his direct efforts to educate and be educated by workers. At the same time, Benjamin's description implies (countering Adorno's outlook, in effect) that there are, after all, worthy social struggles *outside* the aesthetic activities of the cultural modernists.

150. Ibid., pp. 287–290.   151. Ibid., pp. 547–561.   152. Ibid., p. 428.
153. Benjamin, *Charles Baudelaire*, p. 104 n. 1.

Conclusion

What general conclusions may we draw concerning Marxism and modernism in view of their encounter in the work of four German writers? First of all, I hope I have demonstrated how the wide-ranging aesthetic and cultural thought of Lukács, Brecht, Benjamin, and Adorno enriched the Marxist tradition in these areas and better equipped it to assess, both sympathetically and critically, the new departures associated with the modernist revolt. As I attempted to show in Chapter 1, Marx's own work contains a wide variety of undeveloped suggestive frameworks, which lead in potentially different directions, for the analysis of twentieth-century advanced culture, especially if we integrate the sparse directly aesthetic observations within his wider historical and social thought. But it was only after the debacle of the German working-class movement in the interwar years and the rise of fascism (which necessitated a rethinking of objectivist and economist Marxism) that such lines of inquiry were elaborated and adequately developed, e.g., the relation between commodity fetishism and modern cultural life, the extension of the concept of material productive activity to the artistic and literary realms, etc. It is, in fact, only with the hindsight of the writings of these four figures, as well as the work of other major "Western Marxist" thinkers of this century such as Korsch and Gramsci, that it was possible to read Marx as we have done in the opening chapter of this book. The confrontation with modernism carried out in the era of Hitler and Stalin by our four writers (this is least of all the case with Lukács) challenged Marxism to finally face the crisis of liberal bourgeois society and values since the 1870s—structures to which classical optimistic Marxism (of the Second International) was much indebted, e.g., in its realist epistemology, trust in automatic progress, etc. Aside from the encounter with modernism, of course, there were other postliberal currents which revitalized the nineteenth-century Marxist tradition in this way, beginning in the 1920s, e.g., Hegelian dialectical philosophy, psychoanalytic theory, and existentialism.[1] But the importance of aesthetic modernism and of related aspects of modern cultural and social life (such as mass media and "popular" culture) for the development of the now influential "Western Marxist" current has not been sufficiently understood.

As for the benefits to modernism of its investigation by aesthetically sensitive Marxists of the caliber of our four thinkers, we might first consider this in the light of its present widely discussed "demise." For approximately three decades now, we have been hearing of the end of the avant-garde; the absorption of modernist techniques into advertising in a consumer society; the rejection of the difficult aesthetic forms of the early twentieth century by many recent writers and artists; or, in general, the exhaustion of the modernist creative impulse. In 1980, Hilton Kramer, the art critic of the *New York Times*, wrote: "It is characteristic of the cultural situation in which we find ourselves that the modern tradition is embraced *as* a tradition and institutionalized as such in the museums, the universities and the mass media—the very agencies of our culture that once opposed the avant-garde so vigorously in its so-called 'heroic' period."[2] In 1972, the late Harold Rosenberg, an astute cultural and social analyst, put the matter in the following way: "The cultural revolution of the past one hundred years has petered out. Only conservatives believe that subversion is still being carried out in the arts and that society is being shaken by it. . . . Exhibitions of art and publications of literature are quite pleased to be absorbed into the teaching and entertainment industries."[3]

Such developments, and the deepening of their hold in the 1970s, after the collapse of the chiliastic hopes of the late 1960s, make Adorno's strictures upon the revolutionary "naivete" of Brecht and

1. On these other currents, in relation to "Western Marxism" since the 1920s, see: Lichtheim, *From Marx to Hegel*; Jay, *The Dialectical Imagination*; Paul Robinson, *The Freudian Left* (New York, 1969); Richard King, *The Party of Eros: Radical Social Thought and the Realm of Freedom* (New York, 1972); and Mark Poster, *Existential Marxism in Post-War France: From Sartre to Althusser* (Princeton, N.J., 1975).

2. Hilton Kramer, "Today's Avant-Garde Artists Have Lost the Power to Shock," *The New York Times*, November 16, 1980.

3. Harold Rosenberg, "The Cultural Situation Today" (1972), reprinted as the introduction to *Discovering the Present: Three Decades in Art, Culture and Politics* (Chicago, 1973), pp. ix–x.

Benjamin look stronger than ever, although flawed by his own monolithic pessimism and left-mandarin outlook. Yet, all four of our writers
analyzed, in different ways, the dialectic of alienation and absorption in
capitalist culture since the 1850s; the problem has become far more
acute, but it is not an entirely new one. The tendency of cultural innovations to be easily embraced as new commodity forms, or to be put to
conservative ideological uses, was a recurrent theme in their writings
(e.g., Benjamin's Baudelaire studies and his whole Paris project revolved
around the commercial Arcades, in which art was placed at the service
of business; while Adorno found the dominating structures of administered postliberal capitalism even in the musical evolution of such a cultural outsider as Schoenberg). All four writers cogently argued, in effect,
that modernism needed to be understood in relation to capitalist economy, society, and culture; and, more broadly, needed to be viewed historically, even if many of its practitioners (in despair at the course of
events) seemed to reject the historical mode of thought. Where Benjamin and Brecht sought, by politically "refunctioning" symbolist metaphor or cubist montage, to illuminate certain realities of capitalism and
point the way beyond it, Adorno tirelessly stressed the emasculation of
revolt through the workings of the fetishistic "culture industry." In this
regard, as in many others, Adorno drew inspiration, as had Benjamin in
his own way, from Lukács's pathbreaking discussion of "reification."
These are but a few examples to illustrate one conclusion: the understanding of modernism, past and present, has much to gain from an extension of Marxist perspectives when wielded imaginatively, and without reductionism, by thinkers such as these four.

In the Soviet orbit, a different pattern obtains from that in the West.
Increasingly deprived of any significant critical function in capitalist society, cultural modernism is at times in Eastern Europe a subversive and
liberating force for democratic social change, or at least for healthy revision of a dogmatic and authoritarian brand of Marxism. After the
Czech "Spring" of 1968, for example, the Stalinist East German Minister of Culture, Dr. Klaus Gysi, attacked the dissident critics Eduard
Goldstücker and Ernst Fischer, who had defended modern literature.
"Such reverence for Kafka," he said, "has been the ideological origin of
all the theories and tendencies of the third way to socialism in Czecho-
slovakia."[4] The exaggeration itself is significant, as is the choice of

4. Quoted in Caute, *The Illusion*, p. 118. The defense of Kafka was in fact an important focus of the Czech intellectual opposition in the years 1963–68. For a good discussion of the Liblice Kafka conference of 1963, in which this pattern first became clear

Kafka as a focus: while in the West the power of a business rationality defuses and neutralizes the critical thrust of modernism, in Communist Eastern Europe Kafka is read (quite plausibly) as a threat to a mystified authoritarian bureaucratic apparatus.

Yet, this book has concentrated upon the "heroic" early phases of modernism from Baudelaire to the 1930s, and not its history since 1945. The former was, of course, the subject to which our four writers addressed themselves, even if they noted the seeds of later absorption in the early decades of modernism. Although the historical (including Marxist) examination of modernist culture may have implications for our understanding of present problems, it is not only for that reason that it is worth pursuing. The question of the overall meaning of cultural modernism—with primary reference to the decades 1880–1930— is a subject of intense interest today on many sides.[5] We are only beginning, however, to compare the various modernist arts and the separate geographical locations of modernist activity. At the same time, very little work has been done on the complex interplay of advanced art with intellectual, social, economic, and political life in this febrile half-century of experimentation.

In this book, I hope I have contributed, even if only in a small way, to the historical understanding of the variety and unity of modernism by tracing a number of quite different Marxist perspectives upon it. That each of these analyses (Lukács's included) is superior to typical Marxist denunciations of the modern arts and insensitivity to formal aesthetic activity, resulted partly from a pattern which I have emphasized in tracing their genesis: all four figures were not Marxists who addressed art so much as they were major aesthetic thinkers who utilized their significant cultural experience when becoming Marxists (often an experience of specific modernist currents) in order to develop their important contributions to a Marxist aesthetics. Thus, while Lukács, with his profound knowledge and love of nineteenth-century culture, helps us to understand the differences between, for example, literary realism and modernism (once we take account of, and criticize, his polemical bias in favor of the former), Brecht, Benjamin, and Adorno bring their sensitivities to cubist, symbolist, and expressionist aesthetics (respectively) to bear upon the more sympathetic Marxist analysis of the arts in this

within a public forum, see Peter Demetz, "Marxist Literary Criticism Today," *Survey*, 82 (Winter, 1972), 63–65.

5. The notes to chapter two provide some indication of the intensity of this current interest in the general significance, and historical meaning, of modernism.

century. Only for this reason is it possible to write of these four as actual "encounters" between Marxism and modernism (with Lukács as a partial exception). We are not dealing here with the crude subordination (as, for example, in socialist realism) of cultural life to a form of Marxism that is blind to aesthetic questions or to the contradictions of the historical process, e.g., the simultaneous resistance to and complicity with the social status quo within the same artistic work.

These are some possible implications for Marxism and modernism which we may draw from this study. We have been concerned here, however, not with these two broad currents *as such*. The discussion of their interrelation has not been staged as a general or theoretical one. Instead, the book has concentrated—after a preliminary survey, in Part One, of those aspects of the two traditions from which the four thinkers drew—upon *specific* and *differing* Marxist-modernist encounters in their work. The structure of the book has been conceived, and its central argument has been developed, so as to explore the rich diversity, debate, and contradiction in their contrasting approaches—in terms of the wide variety of Marxist strands and modernist currents which they reworked, and in terms of their individual responses to the era 1920–50. In the controversies between the four figures, and in the broad comparative analyses which I developed to illuminate them, I have stressed (a central thesis of the book) that different modernist movements were being invoked, revised, or criticized by them, and this contrasting relation to the modernist tradition helps us to understand not only the work of each but the relation between the four.

It is worth recalling how this argument was developed. Emergent from a classical and patrician humanist background, while anxious to exorcise a cultural pessimism about the directions of history, Lukács attacked the "reified" forms of naturalist literature as the prototype of modernist writing. Following naturalist tendencies, modernist avant-garde literature, he charged, failed to continue the progressive humanist perspectives of bourgeois culture in its ascendant phase in the nineteenth century, and simply mirrored and reinforced the reified immediacies of capitalist life: the apparent dissociation of subjective experience and action from objective historical meaning and material structures. To counter this argument, Brecht did not merely present a generalized defense of modernist technical experiment as separable from its present ideological uses, though this was an important part of his response. His contribution to a Marxist aesthetics and analysis of modernism, his dramatic theory, and his confrontation with Lukács all drew particularly on a reformulation of cubist and constructivist methods. The manner in which Brecht sought to "estrange" his audience from the dramatized realities which he did not "represent" but "constructed"; his stress upon nonlinear, discontinuous montage, not only as a mode of apprehending reality but as a means of selectively appropriating cultural tradition; his positive assessment of the end of individual subjectivity in the collectivist age of advanced technology; and his pivotal view of art as a form of material productive activity—all these features of his work, as well as many others, drew heavily from constructivist Moscow and, more indirectly, cubist Paris.

Both the strengths and weaknesses of Brecht's approach may be understood in relation to this specific modernist tradition and his development of it. While overcoming the pervasive influence of increasingly hollow romantic and idealist modes in German culture, which usually tended in a conservative or far-right direction, Brecht, on the other hand, minimized the dangers of his "cold," depersonalized, collectivist outlook and came very close to creating a cult of technological advancement and industrial productivity. Because we have treated Brecht primarily in connection with his valuable critique of Lukács's traditionalism, and have constructed a comparative analysis of the two by using their "debate" as an organizational device and point of reference, such shortcomings of his perspective may not have been emphasized enough; he appears in Part Two of the text in perhaps too favorable a light. While concentrating in Part Three upon the contrast between Benjamin and Adorno, I have sought to rectify this problem somewhat by comparing Brecht with these other two writers, a juxtaposition which more effectively highlights his weaknesses, e.g., his productivist or utilitarian tendencies, his Leninism, and the "proletarian" claims he made for his work.

In the other comparison we have developed, using a "debate" once again as a point of departure and structuring device, a major thread was the contrast between Benjamin's indebtedness to Parisian symbolism and surrealism, and Adorno's defense (fueled by his Viennese experience) of objectified forms of expressionist protest. The divergent patterns of spatial versus temporal orientation, as well as the disparity between Benjamin's dissolving of subjectivity into language and Adorno's concern for the crippled individual personality in the twentieth century—these and other basic differences were not only a matter of philosophic dispute (e.g., the influence of Hegel and Freud upon Adorno) but of modernist direction. Once again, the strengths and weaknesses of each position may be understood in relation to the specific modernist currents from which they drew. Benjamin's strident and salutary attack upon linear, evolutionary complacency drew heavily from the "time-lapse camera" of modern Parisian poetics from Baudelaire to Breton, but so did his obsession with death and his aestheticizing of history and politics. Adorno's sensitivity to the plight of selfhood in the age of administered masses owed much to the literature and music of expressionism, but his one-sidedly defensive attitude towards the social and technical changes of the twentieth century was also very much in that tradition.

I have analyzed the work of these four complex figures in other ways besides concentrating on their differing relations to modernism. Another approach has been the delineation of contrasting strands of the Marxian heritage which each reworked. Brecht tended, for example, toward the French Enlightenment side of Marx's synthesis, while revising this tradition within a twentieth-century framework of greater historical pessimism and a focus on the power of cognitive activity to help construct and reassemble the world of objects. Lukács and Adorno, in differing ways, drew from Marx's background in the age of German idealism. Whereas Lukács used a Marxist reading of Goethe and Hegel to combat the "decay" of twentieth-century Western literature, Adorno championed certain difficult modernist works (such as those of Schoenberg, Kafka, and Beckett) which revealed best how the revolutionary hope expressed in the music of Beethoven was now largely illusory.

I have also studied the response of the four writers to historical developments of the interwar years, especially the crisis of liberal capitalism and the emergence of fascism and Stalinism. Without attempting to review all these findings, I think one general observation is in order which I have not stressed very much up to this point. One of the weaknesses of the historical perspective of all four figures (when viewed with our advantage of hindsight) was the simple dualistic alternative of fascism or "true" socialism which they each saw in their differing ways. (Adorno generally treated the United States and Russia as "totalitarian" societies, in effect, much like Nazi Germany; while Lukács, Brecht, and Benjamin [until 1939], critically supported Soviet "socialism.") Although we may understand this outlook in relation to the great hopes and fears of the interwar years, especially for German intellectuals of the left, it is much clearer to us that these were not the only alternatives for the West. Given the shared apprehension of these writers concerning the strength of fascist forces, and given the continued preoccupation (of the three who survived the war) with the Nazi phenomenon, each failed to take note of another possibility: that liberal capitalist democracy—which was quite different from fascism—might not only survive the depression and world war, but could reconstruct itself on a firmer basis, and that its unique mixture of considerable political freedom and social and economic inequality could continue to muddle through for a long time. Such a perspective on the events of the 1930s makes the apocalyptic dread and utopian hopes of all four thinkers distant from our present vantage point (although who knows what the future may bring?).

A combined outlook of great dread and great hope may, on the other hand, have benefited their writings on cultural life. This dual perspective of Lukács, Brecht, Benjamin, and Adorno was in keeping with the historical expectations of much of the cultural avant-garde in the decades after 1905, when there was an ambiguous sense of living in a "dawn" and "twilight" of humanity, a *Menschheitsdämmerung*. Perhaps it proved of use in their often insightful probings into the meaning of modernism.

Bibliography

The bibliography is arranged as follows:

I. Works Relating to Marx, Marxism, or Marxist Aesthetics

I have included here all materials not specifically focused on Lukács, Brecht, Benjamin, or Adorno.

Anderson, Perry. *Considerations on Western Marxism*. London: New Left Books, 1976.

Arato, Andrew. "Reexamining the Second International." *Telos*, 18 (Winter, 1973–74), 2–52.

Arvon, Henri. *Marxist Esthetics*. Ithaca, N.Y.: Cornell University Press, 1973.

Avineri, Schlomo. "Marx and the Intellectuals." *Journal of the History of Ideas*, 28 (1967).

———. *The Social and Political Thought of Karl Marx*. Cambridge, England: Cambridge University Press, 1968.

Baxandall, Lee, and Stefan Morawski, eds. *Marx and Engels on Literature and Art*. St. Louis: Telos Press, 1973.

Berman, Marshall. "'All That Is Solid Melts Into Air,' or, Marx, Modernism and Modernization." *Dissent*, 25 : 1 (Winter 1978).

Birchall, Ian. "The Total Marx and the Marxist Theory of Literature." In *Situating Marx*, edited by Paul Walton and Stuart Hall. London: Human Context Books, 1972.

Bisztray, George. "Literary Sociology and Marxist Theory: The Literary Work as a Social Document." *Mosaic*, 2 (1971/72), 47–56.

———. *Marxist Models of Literary Realism*. New York: Columbia University Press, 1977.

Buch, Hans Manfred, ed. *Parteilichkeit der Literatur oder Parteiliteratur? Materialien zu einer undogmatischen marxistischen Aesthetik*. Reinbek bei Hamburg: Rowohlt, 1972.

Caute, David. *The Illusion: An Essay on Politics, Theatre and the Novel*. New York: Harper and Row, 1971.

Coletti, Lucio. "The Marxism of the Second International." *Telos*, 8 (Summer 1971).

Coser, L. A. "Marxist Thought in the First Quarter of the Twentieth Century." *American Journal of Sociology*, 78 (July 1972), 173–201.

Demetz, Peter. *Marx, Engels and the Poets*. Chicago: University of Chicago Press, 1967.

————. "Marxist Literary Criticism Today." *Survey*, 82 (Winter 1972).

Dupré, Louis. "Recent Literature on Marx and Marxism." *Journal of the History of Ideas*, 35 : 4 (October–December 1974).

Eagleton, Terry. *Marxism and Literary Criticism*. Berkeley: University of California Press, 1976.

Egbert, Donald Drew. *Social Radicalism and the Arts: Western Europe*. New York: Knopf, 1970.

Ehrmann, Jacques, ed. *Literature and Revolution*. Boston: Beacon Press, 1970.

Enzensberger, Hans Magnus. "The Consciousness Industry: Constituents of a Theory of Media." *New Left Review*, 64 (November–December 1970).

Ermolaev, Hermann. *Soviet Literary Theories, 1917–1939: The Genesis of Socialist Realism*. Berkeley: University of California Press, 1963.

Fetscher, Iring. *Marx and Marxism*. New York: Herder and Herder, 1971.

Fischer, Ernst. *The Necessity of Art: A Marxist Approach*. Baltimore: Penguin, 1963.

Fügen, Hans Norbert. "Literary Criticism and Sociology in Germany: Emphases—Attitudes—Tendencies." In *Literary Criticism and Sociology*, edited by Joseph P. Strelka. University Park, Penn.: Pennsylvania State University Press, 1973.

Gallas, Helga. *Marxistische Literaturtheorie: Kontroversen im Bund proletarischrevolutionärer Schriftsteller*. Neuwied: Luchterhand, 1971.

Gruber, Helmut. *International Communism in the Era of Lenin: A Documentary History*. New York: Fawcett, 1967.

Hinderer, Walter. "Die regressive Universalideologie: Zum Klassikbild der marxistischen Literaturkritik von Franz Mehring bis zu den Weimar Beiträgen." In *Die Klassik-Legende*, edited by Reinhold Grimm and Jost Hermand. Frankfurt a.M.: Athenäum, 1971.

Howard, Dick, and Karl Klare, eds. *The Unknown Dimension: European Marxism Since Lenin*. New York: Basic Books, 1972.

Hyman, Stanley Edgar. *The Tangled Bank: Darwin, Marx, Frazer and Freud as Imaginative Writers*. New York: Atheneum, 1962.

James, C. Vaughn. *Soviet Socialist Realism: Origins and Theory*. London: St. Martin's Press, 1974.

Jameson, Fredric. "Towards Dialectical Criticism." In *Marxism and Form: Twentieth-Century Dialectical Theories of Literature*. Princeton, N.J.: Princeton University Press, 1971.

Jauss, Hans Robert. "The Idealist Embarrassment: Observations on Marxist Aesthetics." *New Literary History*, 7 (Autumn 1975).

Kolakowski, Leszek. *Main Currents of Marxism*. 3 vols. New York: Oxford University Press, 1978.

Korsch, Karl. *Karl Marx*. New York: Russell and Russell, 1963.

————. *Marxism and Philosophy*. New York: Monthly Review Press, 1970.
Lang, Berel, and Forest Williams, eds. *Marxism and Art: Writings in Aesthetics and Criticism*. New York: David McKay, 1972.
Laurenson, Diana, and Alan Swingewood. *The Sociology of Literature*. London: Paladin, 1972.
Levine, Norman. *The Tragic Deception: Marx Contra Engels*. Santa Barbara, Calif.: Clio Books, 1975.
Lichtheim, George. *From Marx to Hegel*. London: Orbach and Chambers, 1971.
————. *Marxism: A Critical and Historical Study*. New York: Praeger, 1961.
Lidtke, Vernon L. "Naturalism and Socialism in Germany." *American Historical Review*, 79 : 1 (Fall 1974), 14–37.
Lifshitz, Mikhail. *The Philosophy of Art of Karl Marx*. London: Pluto Press, 1973.
Marx, Karl. *Capital*. Vol. 1. New York: International Publishers. 1975.
————. *The Grundrisse*. Edited by David McClellan. New York: Harper and Row, 1971.
————. *The Grundrisse: Foundations of the Critique of Political Economy*. New York: Vintage, 1973.
Marx, Karl, and Frederick Engels. *Literature and Art: Selections from Their Writings*. New York: International Publishers, 1947.
————. *Marx and Engels on Literature and Art*. Edited by Lee Baxandall and Stefan Morawski. St. Louis: Telos Press, 1973.
————. *The Marx-Engels Reader*. Edited by Robert C. Tucker. New York: Norton, 1972.
Mayer, Gunther. "Zur Dialektik des musikalischen Materials." *Alternative*, 69 (December 1969).
Mehlman, Jeffrey. *Revolution and Repetition: Marx / Hugo / Balzac*. Berkeley: University of California Press, 1977.
Mészáros, Istvan. *Marx's Theory of Alienation*. London: Merlin, 1970.
Metscher, Thomas. "Aesthetik als Abbildtheorie: Erkenntnistheoretische Grundlagen der materialistischen Kunsttheorie und das Realismusproblem in den Literaturwissenschaften." *Argument*, 77 (December 1972), 919–976.
Miller, James. "Some Implications of Nietzsche's Thought for Marxism." *Telos*, 36 (Summer 1978).
Mitchell, Stanley. "An Extended Note to Ian Birchall's Paper." In *Situating Marx*, edited by Paul Walton and Stuart Hall. London: Human Context Books, 1972.
Ollman, Bertell. *Alienation: Marx's Conception of Man in Capitalist Society*. Cambridge, England: Cambridge University Press, 1971.
Poster, Mark. *Existential Marxism in Post-war France: From Sartre to Althusser*. Princeton, N.J.: Princeton University Press, 1975.
Prawer, S. S. *Marx and World Literature*. Oxford, England: Oxford University Press, 1976.
Raddatz, Fritz, ed. *Marxismus und Literatur*. 3 Vols. Reinbeck bei Hamburg: Rowohlt, 1969.
Rader, Melvin. *Marx's Interpretation of History*. Oxford, England: Oxford University Press, 1978.

Rosenberg, Harold. "Politics as Illusion." In *Liberations: The Humanities in Revolution.* Wesleyan, Conn.: Wesleyan University Press, 1972.

Sander, Hans-Dietrich. *Marxistische Ideologie und allgemeine Kunsttheorie.* Tübingen: Mohr, 1970.

Solomon, Maynard, ed. *Marxism and Art: Essays Classic and Contemporary.* New York: Knopf, 1973.

Tertz, Abram. *The Trial Begins and On Socialist Realism.* New York: Vintage, 1960.

Thomas, Paul. "The Language of Real Life: Jürgen Habermas and the Distortion of Karl Marx." *Discourse: Berkeley Journal of Theoretical Studies in Media and Culture,* 1 (Fall 1979), 59–85.

Trotsky, Leon. *Literature and Revolution.* Ann Arbor: University of Michigan Press, 1960.

Tucker, Robert C. *Philosophy and Myth in Karl Marx.* Cambridge, England: Cambridge University Press, 1961.

Ulam, Adam. *The Unfinished Revolution: An Essay on the Sources of Influence of Marxism and Communism.* New York: Vintage, 1960.

Vassen, Florian. *Marxistische Literaturtheorie und Literatursoziologie.* Düsseldorf: Bertelsmann Universitätsverlag, 1972.

Vázquez, Adolfo Sanchez. *Art and Society: Essays in Marxist Aesthetics.* New York: Monthly Review Press, 1973.

Williams, Raymond. "'Base and Superstructure' in Marxist Cultural Theory." *New Left Review,* 82 (November–December 1973).

———. *Marxism and Literature.* Oxford, England: Oxford University Press, 1977.

Zmegač, Viktor, ed. *Marxistische Literaturkritik.* Bad Homburg: Athenäum, 1970.

II. Works Relating to Modernism in the Arts

Abrams, M.H. *The Mirror and the Lamp: Romantic Theory and the Critical Tradition*. Oxford, England: Oxford University Press, 1953.

———. *Natural Supernaturalism: Tradition and Revolution in Romantic Literature*. New York: Norton, 1973.

Alquié, Ferdinand. *The Philosophy of Surrealism*. Ann Arbor: University of Michigan Press, 1965.

Aragon, Louis. *The Nightwalker* [Le Paysan de Paris]. Translated by Frederick Brown. Englewood Cliffs, N.J.: Prentice-Hall, 1970.

Auerbach, Erich. "The Brown Stocking." In *Mimesis: The Representation of Reality in Western Literature*. New York: Doubleday, 1956.

Bahr, Hermann. "Expressionism." In *Paths to the Present: Aspects of European Thought from Romanticism to Existentialism*, edited by Eugen Weber. New York: Dodd, Mead, 1960.

Balakian, Anna. *Surrealism: The Road to the Absolute*. New York: Dutton, 1970.

———. *The Symbolist Movement: A Critical Appraisal*. New York: Random House. 1967.

Barraclough, Geoffrey. "Art and Literature in the Contemporary World." In *An Introduction to Contemporary History*. Baltimore: Penguin, 1964.

Baudelaire, Charles. *The Flowers of Evil*. New York: Washington Square Press, 1962.

———. "The Painter of Modern Life." In *The Essence of Laughter and Other Essays*. New York: Meridian, 1956.

Beckett, Samuel. *Endgame*. New York: Grove Press, 1958.

———. *Waiting for Godot*. New York: Grove Press, 1954.

Bell, Daniel. *The Cultural Contradictions of Capitalism*. New York: Basic Books, 1976.

Berger, John. *Art and Revolution: Ernst Neizvestny and the Role of the Artist in the USSR*. New York: Pantheon, 1969.

————. *The Moment of Cubism and Other Essays*. New York: Pantheon, 1969.

————. *Selected Essays and Articles: The Look of Things*. New York: Penguin, 1972.

————. *Success and Failure of Picasso*. London: Penguin, 1965.

Boon, James A. *From Symbolism to Structuralism*. Oxford, England: Oxford University Press, 1972.

Bowness, Alan. *Modern European Art*. London: Harcourt Brace Jovanovich, 1972.

Bradbury, Malcolm, and James McFarlane, eds. *Modernism: 1890–1930*. New York: Penguin, 1976.

Breton, André. "First Surrealist Manifesto." In *Surrealism*, by Patrick Waldberg. London: Thames and Hudson, 1965.

Bürger, Peter. *Theorie der Avant-Garde*. Frankfurt a.M.: Suhrkamp, 1972.

Chipp, Herschel B., ed. *Theories of Modern Art*. Berkeley: University of California Press, 1970.

Dickinson, Thorold. *A Discovery of Cinema*. London, England: Oxford University Press, 1971.

Eisenstein, Sergei. *Film Form and Film Sense*. New York: Meridian, 1957.

Eisner, Lotte. *The Haunted Screen: Expressionism in the German Cinema*. Berkeley: University of California Press, 1969.

Engelberg, Edward. "Space, Time and History: Towards the Discrimination of Modernisms." *Modernist Studies*, 1:1 (1974), 7–26.

Flaubert, Gustave. *Madame Bovary*. New York: Mentor, 1964.

————. *Sentimental Education*. New York: Penguin, 1975.

Frank, Joseph. "Spatial Form in Modern Literature." In *The Widening Gyre: Crisis and Mastery in Modern Literature*. New Brunswick, N.J.: Rutgers University Press, 1963.

Frenzel, Ivo. "Utopia and Apocalypse in German Literature." *Social Research*, 39:2 (Summer 1972). Special issue on Weimar culture.

Gay, Peter. *Art and Act: On Causes in History—Manet, Gropius, Mondrian*. New York: Harper and Row, 1976.

————. "Encounters with Modernism: German Jews in German Culture, 1890–1914." In *Freud, Jews and Other Germans: Masters and Victims in Modernist Culture*. New York: Oxford University Press, 1978.

————. *Weimar Culture: The Outsider as Insider*. New York: Harper and Row, 1968.

Gershman, Herbert. *The Surrealist Revolution in France*. Ann Arbor: University of Michigan Press, 1969.

Gleizes, Albert, and Jean Metzinger. "Cubism, 1912." In *Theories of Modern Art*, edited by Herschel B. Chipp. Berkeley: University of California Press, 1970.

Graña, César. *Modernity and Its Discontents: French Society and the French Man of Letters in the Nineteenth Century*. New York: Harper and Row, 1967.

Gray, Camilia. *The Great Experiment: Russian Art, 1863–1922*. London: Abrams, 1962.

Gropius, Walter. "The New Architecture and the Bauhaus." In *Paths to the Present*, edited by Eugen Weber. New York: Dodd, Mead, 1960.

Gruber, Helmut. "The German Writer as Social Critic, 1927 to 1933." *Studi Germanici*, 7:2/3 (1969), 258–286.

———. "The Politics of German Literature, 1914 to 1933: A Study of the Expressionist and Objectivist Movements." Doctoral dissertation, Columbia University, 1962.

Haftmann, Werner. *Painting in the Twentieth Century*. New York: Praeger, 1965.

Hamann, Richard, and Jost Hermand. *Expressionismus: Epochen deutschen Kultur von 1870 bis zur Gegenwart*. Vol. 5. München: Nymphenburger Verlagshandlung, 1976.

Harrison, John. *The Reactionaries: A Study of the Anti-Democratic Intelligentsia*. New York: Schocken, 1967.

Hauser, Arnold. *The Social History of Art*. Vol. 4. New York: Random House, 1958.

Heisenberg, Werner. *Physics and Philosophy*. New York: Harper and Row, 1958.

Hemmings, F. W. J. *Culture and Society in France, 1848–1898: Dissidents and Philistines*. London: Batsford, 1971.

Herbert, Eugenia W. *The Artist and Social Reform: France and Belgium, 1885–1898*. New Haven, Conn.: Yale University Press, 1961.

Howe, Irving, ed. *Literary Modernism*. New York: Fawcett World Library, 1967.

Jacobson, Roman. "Two Aspects of Language: Metaphor and Metonymy." In *European Literary Theory and Practice*, edited by Vernon W. Gras. New York: Dell, 1973.

Jameson, Fredric. "The Vanishing Mediator: Narrative Structure in Max Weber." *New German Critique*, 1 (Winter 1974).

Janik, Allan, and Stephen Toulmin. *Wittgenstein's Vienna*. New York: Simon and Schuster, 1973.

Johnston, William M. *The Austrian Mind: An Intellectual and Social History, 1848–1938*. Berkeley: University of California Press, 1972.

Joyce, James. *Ulysses*. New York: Random House, 1961.

Kafka, Franz. *Letter to His Father*. New York: Schocken, 1966.

———. *Short Stories*. New York: Random House, 1952.

———. *The Trial*. New York: Schocken, 1968.

Kandinsky, Wassily. "Concerning the Spiritual in Art." In *Paths to the Present*, edited by Eugen Weber. New York: Dodd, Mead, 1960.

Kermode, Frank. "The Modern." In *Modern Essays*. London: Fontan, 1971.

Kokoschka, Oskar. "On the Nature of Visions." In *Theories of Modern Art*, edited by Herschel B. Chipp. Berkeley: University of California Press, 1970.

Kramer, Hilton. "Today's Avant-Garde Artists Have Lost the Power to Shock." In *The New York Times*, November 16, 1980.

Kreutzer, Helmut. *Die Boheme: Analyse und Dokumentation der intellektuellen Subkultur vom 19. Jahrhundert bis zum Gegenwart*. Stuttgart: J. B. Metzler, 1971.

Kumar, Shiv K. *Bergson and the Stream of Consciousness Novel*. Glasgow: Blakie and Son, 1962.

Lane, Barbara Miller. *Architecture and Politics in Germany, 1918–1945*. Cambridge, Mass.: Harvard University Press, 1968.

Lehmann, A. G. *The Symbolist Aesthetic in France, 1885–1895*. Oxford, England: Oxford University Press, 1968.

Lewis, Beth Irwin. *George Grosz: Art and Politics in the Weimar Republic*. Madison: University of Wisconsin Press, 1971.

Mallarmé, Stéphane. *Poems*. London: Chatto and Windus, 1936.

Mann, Thomas. *Buddenbrooks*. New York: Vintage, 1961.

———. *Death in Venice and Seven Other Stories*. New York: Vintage, 1954.

———. *The Magic Mountain*. New York: Random House, 1961.

Meyerhold, Vsevolod. *Meyerhold on Theatre*. Edited by Edward Braun. New York: Hill and Wang, 1969.

Miesel, Viktor H., ed. *Voices of German Expressionism*. Englewood Cliffs, N.J.: Prentice-Hall, 1970.

Mitchell, Donald. *The Language of Modern Music*. New York: St. Martin's Press, 1970.

Mitzman, Arthur. "Anarchism, Expressionism and Psychoanalysis." *New German Critique*, 11 (Winter 1977).

Nadeau, Maurice. *The History of Surrealism*. New York: Macmillan, 1965.

Nietzsche, Friedrich. *The Birth of Tragedy and the Genealogy of Morals*. New York: Doubleday, 1958.

———. "On Truth and Lie in an Extra-Moral Sense." In *The Portable Nietzsche*, edited by Walter Kaufmann. New York: Viking, 1954.

Nochlin, Linda. *Realism*. Baltimore: Penguin, 1971.

Ortega y Gasset, José. *The Dehumanization of Art; and Other Essays on Art, Culture and Literature*. Princeton, N.J.: Princeton University Press, 1968.

Pascal, Roy. *From Naturalism to Expressionism: German Literature and Society, 1880–1918*. London: Weidenfeld and Nicolson, 1973.

Poggioli, Renato. *Theory of the Avant-Garde*. Cambridge, Mass.: Harvard University Press, 1968.

Politzer, Heinz. *Franz Kafka: Parable and Paradox*. Ithaca, N.Y.: Cornell University Press, 1966.

Proust, Marcel. *Swann's Way*. New York: Random House, 1928.

Raymond, Marcel. *From Baudelaire to Surrealism*. New York: Wittenborn, Schultz, 1950.

Rimbaud, Arthur. *Complete Works*. New York: Harper and Row, 1976.

Rosen, Charles. *Arnold Schoenberg*. New York: Viking, 1975.

Rosenberg, Harold. "The Cultural Situation Today" [1972]. In *Discovering the Present: Three Decades in Art, Culture and Politics*. Chicago: University of Chicago Press, 1973.

———. *The Tradition of the New*. New York: Grove Press, 1961.

Rühle, Jürgen. *Theater und Revolution*. München: Deutscher Taschenbuch Verlag, 1963.

Sauer, Wolfgang. "Weimar Culture: Experiments in Modernism." *Social Research*, 39:2 (Summer 1972).

Schorske, Carl E. *Fin de Siècle Vienna: Politics and Culture*. New York: Knopf, 1980.

————. "Generational Tension and Cultural Change: Reflections on the Case of Vienna." *Daedalus*, 107 (Fall 1978), 111–122.

————. "The Idea of the City in European Thought." In *The Historian and the City*, edited by Oscar Handlin. Cambridge, Mass.: Harvard University Press, 1963.

Selz, Peter. *German Expressionist Painting*. Berkeley: University of California Press, 1957.

Shattuck, Roger. *The Banquet Years: The Arts in France, 1885–1918*. New York: Doubleday, 1958.

————. *Proust's Binoculars*. New York: Vintage, 1967.

————. "Surrealism Reappraised." In *The History of Surrealism*, by Maurice Nadeau. New York: Macmillan, 1965.

Short, Roger. "The Politics of Surrealism." In *Left-Wing Intellectuals Between the Wars, 1919–39*, edited by Walter Laqueur and George L. Mosse. New York: Harper and Row, 1966.

Simmel, Georg. "The Metropolis and Mental Life." In *The Sociology of Georg Simmel*, edited by Kurt H. Wolff. New York: Free Press, 1950.

Sokel, Walter H. *The Writer in Extremis: Expressionism in Twentieth-Century German Literature*. Palo Alto, Calif.: Stanford University Press, 1959.

————, ed. *An Anthology of German Expressionist Drama: A Prelude to the Absurd*. New York: Doubleday, 1963.

Spender, Stephen. *The Struggle of the Modern*. Berkeley: University of California Press, 1963.

Stromberg, Roland, ed. *Realism, Naturalism and Symbolism: Modes of Thought and Expression in Europe, 1848–1914*. New York: Harper and Row, 1968.

Struve, Gleb. *Russian Literature under Lenin and Stalin, 1917–1953*. Norman: University of Oklahoma Press, 1971.

Stuckenschmidt, H. H. *Twentieth-Century Music*. New York: McGraw-Hill, 1969.

Sypher, Wylie. *From Rococo to Cubism in Art and Literature*. New York: Random House, 1960.

————. *Literature and Technology: The Alien Vision*. New York: Vintage, 1968.

————. *The Loss of the Self in Modern Literature and Art*. New York: Vintage, 1962.

Thomson, Boris. *The Premature Revolution: Russian Literature and Society, 1917–1946*. London: Weidenfeld and Nicolson, 1972.

Toller, Ernst. "Man and the Masses." In *Avant-Garde Drama: Major Plays and Documents, Post–World War One*, edited by Bernard F. Dukore and David C. Gerould. New York: Bantam, 1969.

Tzara, Tristan. "Dada Manifesto." In *Paths to the Present*, edited by Eugen Weber. New York: Dodd, Mead, 1960.

Wellek, René. "Symbolism and Literary History." In *Discriminations: Further Concepts of Criticism*. New Haven, Conn.: Yale University Press, 1970.

Wellek, René, and Austin Warren. *Theory of Literature*. New York: Harcourt Brace, 1956.

Willett, John. *Expressionism*. New York: World University Library, 1970.

————. *Art and Politics in the Weimar Period, 1917–1933: The New Sobriety.* New York: Pantheon, 1978.

Williams, Raymond. *Culture and Society, 1780–1950.* New York: Doubleday, 1960.

Wilson, Edmund. *Axel's Castle: A Study in the Imaginative Literature of 1870–1930.* London: Fontana, 1961.

Ziolkowski, Theodor. *Dimensions of the Modern Novel: German Texts and European Contexts.* Princeton, N.J.: Princeton University Press, 1969.

III. Secondary Works Related to the Debates

A. THE BRECHT-LUKÁCS DEBATE

Anders, Johann-Friedrich, and Elisabeth Klobusicky. "Vorschlag zur Interpretation der Brecht-Lukács Kontroverse: zugleich eine Kritik an Gallas, Mittenzwei und Völker." *Alternative*, 15 (1972), 84–85.

Anderson, Perry, Rodney Livingstone, and Francis Mulhern, eds. "Presentation II." In *Aesthetics and Politics*. London: New Left Books, 1977.

Arvon, Henri. "Bertolt Brecht and Georg Lukács." In *Marxist Esthetics*. Ithaca, N.Y.: Cornell University Press, 1973.

Baier, Lothar. "Streit um den Schwarzen Kasten: Zur sogenannten Brecht-Lukács Debatte." In *Bertolt Brecht I*. Sonderband aus der Reihe Text und Kritik, edited by Heinz Ludwig Arnold. München: Richard Boorberg Verlag, 1972.

Bathrick, David. "Moderne Kunst und Klassenkampf: Der Expressionismus Debatte in der Exilzeitschrift Das Wort." In *Exil und inner Emigration*, edited by Reinhold Grimm and Jost Hermand. Frankfurt a.M.: Athenäum, 1973.

Berghahn, Klaus L. "Volksthümlichkeit und Realismus: Nochmals zur Brecht-Lukács Debatte." *Basis*, 4 (1973), 7–37.

Eagleton, Terry. "German Aesthetic Duels." *New Left Review*, 107 (January–February 1978).

Gaede, Friedrich. "Die marxistische Realismusdebatte. Lukács-Bloch-Brecht." In *Realismus von Brant bis Brecht*. München: Francke, 1972.

Gallas, Helga. *Marxistische Literaturtheorie: Kontroversen im Bund proletarisch-revolutionärer Schriftsteller*. Neuwied und Berlin: Luchterhand, 1971.

Jameson, Fredric. "Reflections in Conclusion." In *Aesthetics and Politics*, edited by Perry Anderson et al. London: New Left Books, 1977.

Lunn, Eugene. "Marxism and Art in the Era of Stalin and Hitler: The Brecht-Lukács Debate." *New German Critique*, 3 (Fall 1974), 12–44.

Mittenzwei, Werner. "Marxismus und Realismus: Die Brecht-Lukács Debatte."
    Das Argument, 46 (March 1968), 12–43. This has been translated in *Pre-
    serve and Create: Essays in Marxist Literary Criticism*, edited by Gaylord C.
    Le Roy and Ursula Beitz. New York: Humanities Press, 1973.
Morel, Jean-Pierre. "A 'Revolutionary' Poetics?" In *Literature and Revolution*,
    edited by Jacques Ehrman. New York: Harper and Row, 1970.
Raddatz, Fritz. "Der Streit mit Brecht." In *Lukács*. Reinbek bei Hamburg:
    Rowohlt, 1972.
Schmitt, Hans-Jürgen. "Einleitung." In *Die Expressionismusdebatte: Materi-
    alien zur eines marxistische Realismus-Konzeption*. Frankfurt a.M.: Suhr-
    kamp, 1973.
Schonauer, Franz. "Expressionismus und Faschismus: Eine Discussion aus dem
    Jahre 1938." *Literatur und Kritik*, 1 : 7–8 (1966).
Vassen, Florian. "Die Expressionismus-Realismus Debatte." In *Methoden der
    Literaturwissenschaften II: Marxistische Literaturtheorie und Literatur-
    soziologie*. Dusseldorf: Bertelsmann Universitätsverlag, 1972.
Völker, Klaus. "Brecht und Lukács: Analyse einer Meinungsverschiedenheit."
    Kursbuch, 7 (1966), 80–101.
Zmegač, Victor. *Kunst und Wirklichkeit: Zur Literaturtheorie bei Brecht, Lu-
    kács und Broch*. Bad Homburg: Gehlen Verlag, 1969.

B. THE BENJAMIN-ADORNO DEBATE

Anderson, Perry, Rodney Livingstone, and Francis Mulhern, eds. "Presentation
    III." In *Aesthetics and Politics*. London: New Left Books, 1977.
Arato, Andrew. "Esthetic Theory and Cultural Criticism." In *The Essential
    Frankfurt School Reader*, edited by Andrew Arato and Eike Gebhart. New
    York: Urizen Books, 1979.
Brenner, Hildegard. "Die Lesbarkeit der Bilder: Skizzen zum Passagenentwurf."
    Alternative, 59/60 (April–June 1968), 48–61.
Buck-Morss, Susan. *The Origin of Negative Dialectics: Theodor W. Adorno,
    Walter Benjamin and the Frankfurt Institute*. New York: Macmillan, 1978.
Eagleton, Terry. "German Aesthetic Duels." *New Left Review*, 107 (Janu-
    ary–February 1978).
Jay, Martin. "Aesthetic Theory and the Critique of Mass Culture." In *The Di-
    alectical Imagination: A History of the Frankfurt School and the Institute for
    Social Research*. Boston: Little, Brown, 1973.
Jones, Michael T. "Frozen Dialectic." In "Constellations of Modernity: The Lit-
    erary Essays of Theodor W. Adorno." Doctoral dissertation, Yale University,
    1978.
Lethen, Helmut. "Zur materialistische Kunsttheorie Benjamins." *Alternative*,
    56/57 (October–December 1967), 228–234.
Lindner, Burckhardt. "Herrschaft als Trauma: Adornos Gesellschaftstheorie
    zwischen Marx und Benjamin." *Text und Kritik*, 56 (1977), 72–91.
"Marxistischer Rabbi." *Der Spiegel*, 22 : 16 (April 15, 1968).
Pfotenhauer, Helmut. *Aesthetische Erfahrung und gesellschaftliche System: Un-
    tersuchungen zum Spätwerk Walter Benjamins*. Stuttgart: Metzler, 1975.

Rose, Gillian. *The Melancholy Science: An Introduction to the Thought of The-odor W. Adorno.* New York: Columbia University Press, 1978.

Slater, Philip. "Historical Materialist Aesthetics." In *The Origin and Significance of the Frankfurt School: A Marxist Perspective.* London: Routledge and Kegan Paul, 1967.

Tiedemann, Rolf. "Zur 'Beschlagnahme' Walter Benjamins, oder wie Mann mit der Philologie Schlitten fährt." *Das Argument,* 10:1–2 (March 1968).

Wawrzyn, Lienhard. "Zu Adornos Benjamin Kritik." In *Walter Benjamins Kunsttheorie: Kritik einer Rezeption.* Darmstadt: Luchterhand, 1973.

IV. Works *by* Adorno, Benjamin, Brecht, and Lukács

The most complete bibliography of Adorno's works is Karl Schultz's "Vorläufige Bibliographie der Schriften Theodor W. Adornos," in *Theodor W. Adorno zum Gedächtnis*, ed. Hermann Schweppenhauser (Frankfurt a.M.: Suhrkamp, 1971), pp. 177–239. The fullest bibliography of Benjamin's works is Rolf Tiedemann's "Bibliographie der Erstdrucke von Benjamins Schriften," in *Zur Aktualität Walter Benjamins*, ed. Siegfried Unseld (Frankfurt a.M.: Suhrkamp, 1972), pp. 225–279. The most complete bibliography of Lukács's writings is in *Georg Lukács—Festschrift zum 80. Geburtstag*, ed. Frank Benseler (Neuwied und Berlin: Luchterhand, 1965).

Adorno, Theodor W. "The Actuality of Philosophy." *Telos*, 31 (Spring 1977).

———. "Alienated Masterpiece: The Missa Solemnis." *Telos*, 28 (Summer 1976).

———. "Der Artist als Statthalter." In *Noten zur Literatur*, Vol. 1. Frankfurt a.M.: Suhrkamp, 1958.

———. *Aesthetische Theorie*. Frankfurt a.M.: Suhrkamp, 1970.

———. "Auf die Frage: was ist deutsch?" In *Stichworte: Kritische Modelle* 2. Frankfurt a.M.: Suhrkamp, 1969.

———. "On Commitment." In *Aesthetics and Politics*, edited by Perry Anderson et al. London: New Left Books, 1977.

———. "Culture Industry Reconsidered." *New German Critique*, 6 (Fall 1975), 12–19.

———. "Expressionismus und künstlerische Wahrhaftigkeit: Zur kritik neuer Dichtung" [1920]. In *Gesammelte Schriften*, Vol. 11. Frankfurt a.M.: Suhrkamp, 1974.

———. "On the Fetish-Character in Music and the Regression of Listening." In *The Essential Frankfurt School Reader*, edited by Andrew Arato and Eike Gebhardt. New York: Urizen Books, 1977.

————. "Fragmente über Wagner." *Zeitschrift für Sozialforschung*, 8 (1939).

————. "Freudian Theory and the Patterns of Fascist Propaganda." In *The Essential Frankfurt School Reader*, edited by Andrew Arato and Eike Gebhardt. New York: Urizen Books, 1977.

————. *Introduction to the Sociology of Music*. New York: Seabury Press, 1976.

————. *Jargon of Authenticity*. London: Routledge and Kegan Paul, 1973.

————. *Klangfiguren*. Frankfurt a.M.: Suhrkamp, 1959.

————. "Letters to Walter Benjamin." In *Aesthetics and Politics*, edited by Perry Anderson et al. London: New Left Books, 1977.

————. "Looking Back on Surrealism." In *Literary Modernism*, edited by Irving Howe. New York: Fawcett World Library, 1967.

————. "Lyric Poetry and Society." *Telos*, 20 (Summer 1974), 56–71.

————. *Minima Moralia*. London: New Left Books, 1974.

————. "Music and Technique." *Telos*, 32 (Spring 1973).

————. *Negative Dialectics*. New York: Seabury Press, 1973.

————. "New Music; Interpretation; Audience." In *Post-War German Culture*, edited by Charles McClellan and Stephen Scher. New York: Dutton, 1974.

————. *The Philosophy of Modern Music*. New York: Seabury Press, 1973.

————. "On Popular Music." *Studies in Philosophy and Social Science*, 9 (1941), 17–48.

————. *Prisms*. London: Spearman, 1967.

————. "Reconciliation Under Duress." In *Aesthetics and Politics*, edited by Perry Anderson et al. London: New Left Books, 1977.

————. "Scientific Experiences of a European Scholar in America." In *The Intellectual Migration: Europe and America, 1930–1960*, edited by Donald Fleming and Bernard Bailyn. Cambridge, Mass.: Harvard University Press, 1969.

————. "A Social Critique of Radio Music." *Kenyon Review*, 7:2 (Spring 1945), 208–217.

————. "On the Social Situation of Music." *Telos*, 35 (Spring 1978), 128–164.

————. "Society." *Salmagundi*, 10–11 (Fall 1969–Winter 1970), 144–151.

————. "Sociology and Psychology." *New Left Review*, 46 (November–December 1967), 67–80; and 47 (January–February 1968), 79–97.

————. "Der Standort des Erzählers im zeitgenössischen Roman." In *Noten zur Literatur*, Vol. 1. Frankfurt a.M.: Suhrkamp, 1958.

————. "Television and the Patterns of Mass Culture." In *Mass Culture*, edited by Bernard Rosenberg and David Manning White. New York: Free Press, 1957.

————. "Towards an Understanding of *Endgame*." In *Twentieth-Century Interpretations of Endgame*, edited by Gale Chevigny. Englewood Cliffs, N.J.: Prentice-Hall, 1969.

————. "Über Jazz." *Zeitschrift für Sozialforschung*, 5:2 (1936).

————. "Über Jazz." In *Moments Musicaux*. Frankfurt a.M.: Suhrkamp, 1964. (Pages 119–120 contain a 1937 supplement to the 1936 article not previously published.)

————. *Über Walter Benjamin.* Frankfurt a.M.: Suhrkamp, 1970.

————. "Valérys Abweichungen." In *Noten zur Literatur*, Vol. 2. Frankfurt a.M.: Suhrkamp, 1961.

————, and Max Horkheimer. *Dialectic of Enlightenment.* New York: Herder and Herder, 1972.

Benjamin, Walter. *Angelus Novus: Ausgewählte Schriften 2.* Frankfurt a.M.: Suhrkamp, 1966.

————. *Charles Baudelaire: A Lyric Poet in the Era of High Capitalism.* London: New Left Books, 1973.

————. *Briefe.* 2 vols. Edited by Theodor W. Adorno and Gershom Scholem. Frankfurt a.M.: Suhrkamp, 1966.

————. "Diskussion über russische Filmkunst und kollektivische Kunst überhaupt" [1927]. *Alternative*, 56/57 (October–December 1967).

————. "Doctrine of the Similar." *New German Critique*, 17 (Spring 1979), 65–69.

————. "Eduard Fuchs: Collector and Historian." *New German Critique*, 5 (Spring 1975), 27–58.

————. "Einbahnstrasse." In *Gesammelte Schriften*, IV/1. Frankfurt a.M.: Suhrkamp, 1972.

————. "Erfahrung und Armut." In *Illuminationen.* Frankfurt a.M.: Suhrkamp, 1961.

————. *Gesammelte Schriften*, I/3. Frankfurt a.M.: Suhrkamp, 1974.

————. *Illuminations.* Edited by Hannah Arendt. New York: Schocken, 1969.

————. *The Origins of German Tragic Drama.* London: New Left Books, 1977.

————. "Probleme der Sprachwissenschaft: Ein Sammelreferat." *Zeitschrift für Sozialforschung*, 4 (1935), 246–268.

————. *Reflections.* Edited by Peter Demetz. New York: Harcourt Brace Jovanovich, 1978.

————. "A Reply." In *Aesthetics and Politics*, edited by Perry Anderson et al. London: New Left Books, 1977.

————. "A Short History of Photography." *Screen*, 13:1 (Spring 1972).

————. "Theories of German Fascism." *New German Critique*, 17 (Spring 1979), 120–128.

————. *Understanding Brecht.* London: New Left Books, 1973.

————. "Zentralpark." In *Gesammelte Schriften*, I/2. Frankfurt a.M.: Suhrkamp, 1974.

Brecht, Bertolt. *Arbeitsjournal, 1938–1955.* 2 vols. Frankfurt a.M.: Suhrkamp, 1973.

————. "Aufsätze über den Faschismus." In *Gesammelte Werke*, Vol. 20. Frankfurt a.M.: Suhrkamp, 1967.

————. "Aufsätze zur Literatur." In *Gesammelte Werke*, Vol. 19. Frankfurt a.M.: Suhrkamp, 1967.

————. "Baal." In *An Anthology of German Expressionist Drama*, edited by Walter H. Sokel. New York: Doubleday, 1963.

————. "Bemerkungen zu einem Aufsatz." In *Gesammelte Werke*, Vol. 19. Frankfurt a.M.: Suhrkamp, 1967.

————. "Bemerkungen zum Formalismus." In *Gesammelte Werke*, Vol. 19. Frankfurt a.M.: Suhrkamp, 1967.

————. Bertolt Brecht to Karl Korsch. Letters held at the International Institute of Social History, Amsterdam.

————. *Brecht on Theatre: The Development of an Aesthetic*. Edited by John Willett. New York: Hill and Wang, 1964.

————. *The Caucasian Chalk Circle and The Good Woman of Setzuan*. New York: Grove Press, 1957.

————. "Die Dreigroschenprozess." In *Gesammelte Werke*, Vol. 18. Frankfurt a.M.: Suhrkamp, 1967.

————. "Die Expressionismus Debatte." In *Gesammelte Werke*, Vol. 19. Frankfurt a.M.: Suhrkamp, 1967.

————. *Galileo*. New York: Grove Press, 1966.

————. "Kunst und Politik, 1933–1938." In *Gesammelte Werke*, Vol. 18. Frankfurt a.M.: Suhrkamp, 1967.

————. "Mann ist Mann." In *Gesammelte Werke*, Vol. 1. Frankfurt a.M.: Suhrkamp, 1967.

————. *The Manual of Piety. Die Hauspostille*. New York: Grove Press, 1967.

————. "Marxistische Studien." In *Gesammelte Werke*, Vol. 20. Frankfurt a.M.: Suhrkamp, 1967.

————. "The Measures Taken." In *The Jewish Wife and Other Short Plays*. New York: Grove Press, 1965.

————. *The Messingkauf Dialogues*. London: Methuen, 1965.

————. "Me-ti. Buch der Wendungen." In *Gesammelte Werke*, Vol. 12. Frankfurt a.M.: Suhrkamp, 1967.

————. "Mother Courage and Her Children." In *The Modern Theatre*, Vol. 2, edited by Eric Bentley. New York: Doubleday, 1955.

————. "Notizen über realistische Schreibweise." In *Gesammelte Werke*, Vol. 19. Frankfurt a.M.: Suhrkamp, 1967.

————. "On Non-Objective Painting." In *Marxism and Art: Writings in Aesthetics and Criticism*, edited by Berel Lang and Forest Williams. New York: David McKay, 1972.

————. "Praktisches zur Expressionismus." In *Gesammelte Werke*, Vol. 19. Frankfurt a.M.: Suhrkamp, 1967.

————. "Radiotheorie, 1927–1932." In *Gesammelte Werke*, Vol. 17. Frankfurt a.M.: Suhrkamp, 1967.

————. "Der Rundfunk als Kommunikationsapparat." In *Gesammelte Werke*, Vol. 18. Frankfurt a.M.: Suhrkamp, 1967.

————. "Die Schönheit in den Gedichten des Baudelaire." In *Gesammelte Werke*, Vol. 19. Frankfurt a.M.: Suhrkamp, 1967.

————. *Selected Poems of Bertolt Brecht*. New York: Grove Press, 1959.

————. "Sowjettheater und proletarisches Theater." In *Gesammelte Werke*, Vol. 15. Frankfurt a.M.: Suhrkamp, 1967.

————. "Svendborger Gedichte." In *Gesammelte Werke*, Vol. 9. Frankfurt a.M.: Suhrkamp, 1967.

————. *The Threepenny Opera*. New York: Grove Press, 1964.

————. "Über Dialektik." In *Gesammelte Werke*, Vol. 20. Frankfurt a.M.: Suhrkamp, 1967.

————. "Über den formalistischen Charakter der Realismustheorie." In *Gesammelte Werke*, Vol. 19. Frankfurt a.M.: Suhrkamp, 1967.

————. "Über den Realismus, 1934–1941." In *Gesammelte Werke*, Vol. 19. Frankfurt a.M.: Suhrkamp, 1967.

————. "Übergang vom bürgerlichen zum sozialistischen Realismus." In *Gesammelte Werke*, Vol. 19. Frankfurt a.M.: Suhrkamp, 1967.

————. "Volksthümlichkeit und Realismus." In *Gesammelte Werke*, Vol. 19. Frankfurt a.M.: Suhrkamp, 1967.

————. "Vorrede zu 'Mann ist Mann', April, 1927." In *Gesammelte Werke*, Vol. 17. Frankfurt a.M.: Suhrkamp, 1967.

————. "Vorschläge für den Frieden." In *Gesammelte Werke*, Vol. 20. Frankfurt a.M.: Suhrkamp, 1967.

————. "Weite und Vielfalt der realistischen Schreibweise." In *Gesammelte Werke*, Vol. 19. Frankfurt a.M.: Suhrkamp, 1967.

————. "Writing the Truth: Five Difficulties." In *Galileo*. New York: Grove Press, 1966.

Lukács, Georg. *Aesthetik*, 2 vols. Neuwied und Berlin: Luchterhand, 1963.

————. "Aus der Not eine Tugend." In *Marxismus und Literatur*, Vol. 2. Edited by Fritz Raddatz. Reinbek bei Hamburg: Rowohlt, 1969.

————. "On Bertolt Brecht." *New Left Review*, 110 (July–August 1978), 88–92.

————. "Ein Briefwechsel zwischen Anna Seghers und Georg Lukács." In *Marxismus und Literatur*, Vol. 2. Edited by Fritz Raddatz. Reinbek bei Hamburg: Rowohlt, 1969.

————. "Es geht um den Realismus." In *Marxismus und Literatur*, Vol. 2. Edited by Fritz Raddatz. Reinbek bei Hamburg: Rowohlt, 1969.

————. *Essays on Realism*. Cambridge, Mass.: MIT Press, 1981.

————. *Essays on Thomas Mann*. New York: Grosset and Dunlap, 1965.

————. *Goethe and His Age*. New York: Grosset and Dunlap, 1969.

————. "'Grösse und Verfall' des Expressionismus." In *Marxismus und Literatur*, Vol. 2. Edited by Fritz Raddatz. Reinbek bei Hamburg: Rowohlt, 1969.

————. *The Historical Novel*. Boston: Beacon Press, 1962.

————. *History and Class Consciousness: Studies in Marxist Dialectics*. Cambridge, Mass.: MIT Press, 1971.

————. "The Ideal of the Harmonious Man in Bourgeois Aesthetics." In *Marxism and Human Liberation*. Edited by E. San Juan, Jr. New York: Dell, 1971.

————. "The Intellectual Physiognomy of Literary Characters." In *Radical Perspectives in the Arts*, edited by Lee Baxandall. Baltimore: Penguin, 1972.

————. *Der junge Hegel*. Zürich: Europa, 1948.

————. *Lenin: A Study of the Unity of Thought*. London: New Left Books, 1970.

————. "Marx und das Problem des ideologischen Verfalls." *International Literatur*, 7 (1938).

————. "Marx and Engels on Aesthetics." In *Writer and Critic and Other Essays*. Edited by Arthur D. Kahn. New York: Universal Library, 1971.

————. *Marxism and Human Liberation*. Edited by E. San Juan, Jr. New York: Dell, 1973.

———. "Mein Weg zu Marx." In *Georg Lukács zum siebzigsten Geburtstag*. East Berlin: Aufbau Verlag, 1955.

———. "Narrate or Describe?" In *Writer and Critic and Other Essays*. Edited by Arthur D. Kahn. New York: Universal Library, 1971.

———. "The Old Culture and the New Culture." In *Marxism and Human Liberation*. Edited by E. San Juan, Jr. New York: Dell, 1973.

———. *Political Writings, 1919–1929*. London: New Left Books, 1972.

———. *Realism in Our Time: Literature and the Class Struggle*. New York: Harper and Row, 1971.

———. "Reportage oder Gestaltung? Kritische Bemerkungen anlässlich eines Romans von Ottwalt." In *Marxismus und Literatur*, Vol. 2. Edited by Fritz Raddatz. Reinbek bei Hamburg: Rowohlt, 1969.

———. *Schriften zur Literatursoziologie*. Edited by Peter Ludz. Neuwied und Berlin: Luchterhand, 1963.

———. "The Sociology of Modern Drama." In *The Theory of the Modern Stage*, edited by Eric Bentley. Baltimore: Penguin, 1965.

———. *Soul and Form*. Cambridge, Mass.: MIT Press, 1978.

———. *Studies in European Realism*. New York: Universal Library, 1964.

———. "Tendenz oder Parteilichkeit?" In *Marxismus und Literatur*, Vol. 2. Edited by Fritz Raddatz. Reinbek bei Hamburg: Rowohlt, 1969.

———. *The Theory of the Novel*. Cambridge, Mass.: MIT Press, 1971.

———. "An Unofficial Interview." *New Left Review*, 68 (July–August 1971), 49–58.

———. "On Walter Benjamin." *New Left Review*, 110 (July–August 1978), 83–88.

———. *Writer and Critic and Other Essays*. Edited by Arthur D. Kahn. New York: Universal Library, 1971.

———. *Die Zerstörung der Vernunft*. East Berlin: Aufbau Verlag, 1954.

V. Works *on* Adorno, Benjamin, Brecht, and Lukács

WORKS ON ADORNO

Barnouw, Dagmar. "'Beute der Pragmatisierung': Adorno und Amerika." In *Die USA und Deutschland: Wechselseitige Spielungen in der Literatur der Gegenwart*, edited by Wolfgang Paulsen. Bern and München: Francke, 1976.

Benjamin, Jessica. "The End of Internalization: Adorno's Social Psychology." *Telos*, 32 (Spring 1977).

Blomster, W. V. "Sociology of Music: Adorno and Beyond." *Telos*, 28 (Summer 1976), 81–112.

Buck-Morss, Susan. "The Dialectic of T. W. Adorno." *Telos*, 17 (Fall 1973).

———. *The Origin of Negative Dialectics: Theodor W. Adorno, Walter Benjamin and the Frankfurt Institute*. New York: Macmillan, 1977.

———. "T. W. Adorno and the Dilemma of Bourgeois Philosophy." *Salmagundi*, 38 (Winter 1977), 76–98.

Connerton, Paul. *The Tragedy of Enlightenment: An Essay on the Frankfurt School*. Cambridge, England: Cambridge University Press, 1980.

Craft, Robert. "A Bell for Adorno." In *Prejudices in Disguise*. New York: Random House, 1974.

Fehér, Ferenc. "Negative Philosophy of Music—Positive Results." *New German Critique*, 4 (Winter 1975), 99–112.

Friedman, George. *The Political Philosophy of the Frankfurt School*. Ithaca, N.Y.: Cornell University Press, 1981.

Held, David. *Introduction to Critical Theory: Horkheimer to Habermas*. Berkeley: University of California Press, 1980.

Jacoby, Russell. "Marxism and the Critical School." *Theory and Society*, 1 (1974).

———. "Towards a Critique of Automatic Marxism: The Politics of Philosophy from Lukács to the Frankfurt School." *Telos*, 10 (Winter 1972), 119–140.

Jameson, Fredric. "T. W. Adorno; or, Historical Tropes." In *Marxism and Form:*

Twentieth-Century Dialectical Theories of Literature. Princeton, N.J.: Princeton University Press, 1971.

Jay, Martin. *The Dialectical Imagination: A History of the Frankfurt School and the Institute for Social Research.* Boston: Little, Brown, 1973.

———. "The Frankfurt Schools Critique of Marxist Humanism." *Social Research*, 39:2 (Summer 1972).

———. "The Permanent Exile of Theodor Adorno." *Midstream*, 15:10 (December 1969).

Jones, Michael T. "Constellations of Modernity: The Literary Essays of Theodor W. Adorno." Doctoral dissertation, Yale University, 1978.

Kaiser, Gerhard. *Benjamin Adorno: Zwei Studien.* Frankfurt a.M.: Athenäum, 1974.

Krahl, Hans-Jürgen. "The Political Contradictions in Adorno's Critical Theory." *Telos*, 21 (Fall 1974).

Lichtheim, George. "Adorno." In *From Marx to Hegel.* New York: Herder and Herder, 1971.

Lindner, Burckhardt, and W. Martin Lüdke, eds. *Materialien zur ästhetischen Theorie Theodor W. Adornos.* Frankfurt a.M.: Suhrkamp, 1979.

Lyotard, Jean-François. "Adorno and the Devil." *Telos*, 19 (Spring 1974).

Petazzi, Carlo. "Studien zu Leben und Werk Adorno." *Text und Kritik*, 56 (1977).

Rose, Gillian. *The Melancholy Science: An Introduction to the Thought of Theodor W. Adorno.* New York: Columbia University Press, 1978.

Slater, Phil. *The Origin and Significance of the Frankfurt School: A Marxist Perspective.* London: Routledge and Kegan Paul, 1977.

Subotnik, Rose. "Adorno's Diagnosis of Beethoven's Late Style." *Journal of the American Musicological Society*, 2 (1976), 242–275.

———. "The Historical Structure: Adorno's 'French Model' for Nineteenth-Century Music." *Nineteenth-Century Music*, 2:1 (July, 1978), 36–60.

Therborn, Göran. "The Frankfurt School." *New Left Review*, 63 (September–October 1970).

Weitzman, Ronald. "An Introduction to Adorno's Music and Social Criticism." *Music and Letters*, 52:3 (July 1971), 287–298.

Wolin, Richard. "The De-Aestheticization of Art: On Adorno's *Aesthetische Theorie.*" *Telos*, 41 (Fall 1979).

WORKS ON BENJAMIN

The most up-to-date bibliography is Gary Smith's "A Bibliography of Secondary Literature," in a special Walter Benjamin issue of *New German Critique*, 17 (Spring 1979), 189–208.

Adorno, Theodor W. "A Portrait of Walter Benjamin." In *Prisms.* London: Spearman, 1967.

———. *Über Walter Benjamin.* Frankfurt a.M.: Suhrkamp, 1970.

Arendt, Hannah. "Introduction." In *Illuminations.* New York: Schocken, 1969.

Bathrick, David. "Reading Benjamin from West to East." *Colloquia Germanica* 12:3 (1979).

Brewster, Philip, and Carl Howard Buchner. "Language and Critique: Jürgen Habermas on Walter Benjamin." *New German Critique*, 17 (Spring 1979), 15–29.

Bürger, Peter. "Zur Diskussion der Kunsttheorie Benjamins" and "Der Allegoriebegriff Benjamins." In *Theorie der Avant-Garde.* Frankfurt a.M.: Suhrkamp, 1974.

Fekete, John. "Benjamin's Ambivalence." *Telos,* 35 (Spring 1978).

Fuld, Werner. *Walter Benjamin: Zwischen den Stühlen.* München: Hauser, 1979.

Günther, Henning. *Walter Benjamin: Zwischen Marxismus und Theologie.* Olten, Switzerland: Walter, 1974.

Habermas, Jürgen. "Consciousness Raising or Redemptive Criticism." *New German Critique*, 17 (Spring 1979), 30–59.

Heise, Rosemarie. "Der Benjamin Nachlass." *Alternative,* 56/57 (October–December 1967).

Hering, Christoph. *Der Intellektuelle als Revolutionar: Walter Benjamins Analyse intellektueller Praxis.* München: W. Fink, 1979.

Hillach, Ansgar. "'The Aestheticization of Politics': Walter Benjamin's Theories of German Fascism." *New German Critique,* 17 (Spring 1979), 99–119.

Holz, Hans Heinz. "Prismatisches Denken." In *Über Walter Benjamin.* Frankfurt a.M.: Suhrkamp, 1968.

Jacobs, Carol. *The Dissimulating Harmony: The Image of Interpretation in Nietzsche, Rilke, Artaud and Benjamin.* Baltimore: Johns Hopkins University Press, 1978.

Jameson, Fredric. "Walter Benjamin; or, Nostalgia." In *Marxism and Form: Twentieth-Century Dialectical Theories of Literature.* Princeton, N.J.: Princeton University Press, 1971.

Kaiser, Gerhard. *Benjamin Adorno: Zwei Studien.* Frankfurt a.M.: Athenäum, 1974.

Lacis, Asja. *Revolutionär im Beruf: Berichte über proletarianisches Theater, über Meyerhold, Brecht, Benjamin und Piscator.* München: Rogner und Bernhard, 1972.

Lindner, Burckhardt. "'Links hatte noch alles sich zu enträtseln.'" In *Benjamin im Kontext,* edited by Burckhardt Lindner. Frankfurt a.M.: Syndikat, 1978.

Lukács, Georg. "On Walter Benjamin." *New Left Review,* 110 (July–August 1978).

Materialien zur Benjamins Thesen über den Begriff der Geschichte. Edited by Peter Bulthaup. Frankfurt a.M.: Suhrkamp, 1978.

Mitchell, Stanley. "Introduction to Benjamin and Brecht." *New Left Review,* 77 (January–February 1973).

Paetzold, Heinz. "Walter Benjamin's Theory of the End of Art." *International Journal of Sociology,* 7 (1977), 25–75.

Pfotenhauer, Helmut. *Aesthetische Erfahrung und gesellschaftliche System: Untersuchungen zum Spätwerk Walter Benjamins.* Stuttgart: J.B. Metzler, 1975.

Rabinbach, Anson. "Critique and Commentary; Alchemy and Chemistry; Some Remarks on Walter Benjamin and This Issue." *New German Critique,* 17 (Spring 1979), 3–14.

Radnoti, Sandor. "Benjamin's Politics." *Telos,* 36 (Summer 1978), 63–81.

Rosen, Charles. "The Origins of Walter Benjamin." *New York Review of Books*, November 10, 1977.

————. "The Ruins of Walter Benjamin." *New York Review of Books*, October 27, 1977.

Rudbeck, Carl. "The Literary Criticism of Walter Benjamin." Doctoral dissertation, State University of New York at Binghamton, 1976.

Scholem, Gershom. "Walter Benjamin." *Leo Baeck Yearbook*, 10 (1965), 117–136.

————. "Walter Benjamin and His Angel." In *On Jews and Judaism in Crisis*. New York: Schocken, 1976.

————. *Walter Benjamin—Geschichte einer Freundschaft*. Frankfurt a.M.: Suhrkamp, 1975.

Sontag, Susan. "The Last Intellectual." *New York Review of Books*, October 12, 1978.

Szondi, Peter. "Hope in the Past: Walter Benjamin." *Critical Inquiry*, 4:3 (Spring 1978).

Tiedemann, Rolf. "Historischer Materialismus oder politischer Messianismus?" In *Materialien zur Benjamins Thesen über den Begriff der Geschichte*, edited by Peter Bulthaup. Frankfurt a.M.: Suhrkamp, 1978.

————. "Nachwort." In *Charles Baudelaire: Ein Lyriker im Zeitalter des Hochkapitalismus*. Frankfurt a.M.: Suhrkamp, 1967.

————. "Nachwort." In *Versuche über Brecht*. Frankfurt a.M.: Suhrkamp, 1966.

————. *Studien zur Philosophie Walter Benjamins*. Frankfurt a.M.: Europäische Verlagsanstalt, 1965.

Über Walter Benjamin. Frankfurt a.M.: Suhrkamp, 1968.

Unger, Peter. *Walter Benjamin als Rezensent: Die Reflexion eines Intellektuellen auf die zeitgeschichtliche Situation*. Bern and Frankfurt a.M.: Peter Lang, 1978.

Unseld, Siegfried, ed. *Zur Aktualität Walter Benjamins*. Frankfurt a.M.: Suhrkamp, 1972.

"Walter Benjamin: Towards a Philosophy of Language." *Times Literary Supplement* (London), August 22, 1968.

Wawrzyn, Lienhard. *Walter Benjamins Kunsttheorie: Kritik einer Rezeption*. Darmstadt: Luchterhand, 1973.

Weber, Shierry M. "Walter Benjamin: Commodity Fetishism, the Modern and the Experience of History." In *The Unknown Dimension: European Marxism Since Lenin*. New York: Basic Books, 1972.

Wellek, René. "The Early Literary Criticism of Walter Benjamin." *Rice University Studies*, 57 (1971), 123–134.

————. "Walter Benjamin's Literary Criticism in His Marxist Phase." In *The Personality of the Critic*, edited by Joseph P. Strelka. University Park: Pennsylvania State University Press, 1973.

"Werkbiographie." *Text und Kritik*, 31/32 (1971).

Wiesenthal. Lieselotte. *Zur Wissenschaftstheorie Walter Benjamins: Über einige Zusammenhange von Erkenntnis-, Sprach- und Wissenschaftstheorie im Frühwerk Walter Benjamins*. Frankfurt a.M.: Athenäum, 1973.

Witte, Bernd. "Benjamin and Lukács: Historical Notes on the Relationship Between Their Political and Aesthetic Theories." *New German Critique*, 5 (Spring 1975), 3–26.

————. "Krise und Kritik: Zur Zusammenarbeit Benjamins mit Brecht in den Jahren 1929 bis 1933." In *Walter Benjamin—Zeitgenosse der Moderne*, edited by Peter Gebhardt et el. Kronberg: Scriptor Verlag, 1976.

————. *Walter Benjamin—Der Intellektuelle als Kritiker: Untersuchungen zu seinem Frühwerk*. Stuttgart: J. B. Metzler, 1976.

Wohlfahrt, Irving. "No-Man's Land: On Walter Benjamin's 'Destructive Character.'" *Diacritics*, 8 : 2 (Summer 1978), 47–65.

————. "'The Smallest Guarantee, the Straw at Which the Drowning Man Clutches': On the Messianic Structure of Walter Benjamin's Last Reflections." *Glyph*, 3 (1978), 148–212.

Wolin, Richard. "An Aesthetic of Redemption: Benjamin's Path to *Trauerspiel*." *Telos*, 43 (Spring 1980), 61–90.

WORKS ON BRECHT

Adorno, Theodor W. "On Commitment." In *Aesthetics and Politics*, edited by Perry Anderson et al. London: New Left Books, 1977.

Arendt, Hannah. "Bert Brecht, 1898–1956." In *Men in Dark Times*. New York: Harcourt, Brace and World, 1968.

Bathrick, David. "Affirmative and Negative Culture: The Avant-Garde Under 'Actually Existing Socialism'—The Case of the *GDR*." *Social Research*, 47 : 1 (Spring 1980), 166–187.

————. "Brecht's Marxism and America." In *Essays on Brecht: Theatre and Politics*, edited by Siegfried Mews and Herbert Knust. Chapel Hill: University of North Carolina Press, 1974.

————. "The Dialectics of Legitimation: Brecht in the *GDR*." *New German Critique*, 2 (Spring 1974).

Benjamin, Walter. *Understanding Brecht*. London: New Left Books, 1973.

Bentley, Eric. "The Theatre of Commitment." In *The Theatre of Commitment and Other Essays on Drama in Our Society*. New York: Atheneum, 1967.

Berckman, Edward K. "The Function of Hope in Brecht's Pre-Revolutionary Theater." *Brecht Heute*, 1 (1971), 11–26.

Bloch, Ernst. "Entfremdung, Verfremdung: Alienation, Estrangement." In *Brecht*, edited by Erika Munk. New York: Bantam Books, 1972.

Bormans, Peter. "Brecht und der Stalinismus." In *Brecht Jahrbuch 1974*. Frankfurt a.M.: Suhrkamp, 1975.

"The Brecht Explosion." In *Essays and Reviews from the Times Literary Supplement*. London: Oxford University Press, 1968.

Brüggemann, Heinz. "Bert Brecht und Karl Korsch: Fragen nach Lebendige and Toten in Marxismus." In *Über Karl Korsch*, edited by Claudio Pozzoli. Frankfurt a.M.: Fischer Verlag, 1973.

————. *Literarische Technik und soziale Revolution. Versuche über das Verhältnis von Kunstproduktion, Marxismus und literarische Tradition in den theoretischen Schriften Bertolt Brechts*. Reinbek bei Hamburg: Rowohlt, 1973.

Buck, Theo. *Brecht und Diderot: Über Schwierigkeiten der Rationalität in Deutschland*. Tübingen: M. Niemeyer, 1971.

Dahmer, Helmut. "Bertolt Brecht and Stalinism." *Telos*, 22 (Winter 1974–75).

Dickson, Keith. *Towards Utopia: A Study of Brecht*. Oxford, England: Oxford University Press, 1980.

Esslin, Martin. *Brecht: The Man and His Work*. 2nd edition. New York: Doubleday, 1971.

Ewen, Frederic. *Bertolt Brecht: His Life, His Art and His Times*. New York: Citadel Press, 1967.

Fetscher, Iring. "Bertolt Brecht and America." *Salmagundi*, 10–11 (Fall 1969–Winter 1970).

Friedrich, Rainer. "Brecht and Eisenstein." *Telos*, 31 (Spring 1977).

Fuegi, John. "The Soviet Union and Brecht: The Exile's Choice." In *Brecht Heute*, 2 (1972).

Gray, Ronald. *Bertolt Brecht*. New York: Grove Press, 1961.

Groth, Peter, and Manfred Voigts. "Die Entwicklung der Brechtschen Radiotheorie, 1927–1932." In *Brecht Jahrbuch 1976*. Frankfurt a.M.: Suhrkamp, 1977.

Hoover, Marjorie L. "Brecht's Soviet Connection, Tretjakov." *Brecht Heute*, 3 (1973), 39–56.

Kopelew, Lew. "Brecht und die Russische Theaterrevolution." *Brecht Heute*, 3 (1973), 19–38.

Lacis, Asja. *Revolutionär im Beruf: Berichte über proletarisches Theater, Meyerhold, Brecht, Benjamin und Piscator*. München: Rogner und Bernhard, 1972.

Lethen, Helmut. *Neue Sachlichkeit, 1924–1932: Studien zur Literatur des Weissen Sozialismus*. Stuttgart: J.B. Metzler, 1970.

Lindner, Burckhardt. "Brecht/Benjamin/Adorno—über Veränderungen der Kunstproduktion im wissenschaftlich-technischen Zeitalter." *Text und Kritik*, 1 (1972), 14–36. (Special issue on Brecht.)

Mayer, Hans. "Bertolt Brecht and the Tradition." In *Steppenwolf and Everyman: Outsiders and Conformists in Contemporary Literature*. New York: Crowell, 1971.

———. "Bertolt Brecht oder die plebejische Tradition." In *Literatur der Übergangszeit: Essays*. Wiesbaden: Limes Verlag, n.d. (though probably 1949).

———. *Brecht in der Geschichte*. Frankfurt a.M.: Suhrkamp, 1971.

Mennemeier, Franz Norbert. "Bertolt Brechts Faschismus-Theorie und einige Folgen für die literarische Praxis." In *Literaturwissenschaft und Geschichtsphilosophie: Festschrift für Wilhelm Emrich*, edited by Helmut Arnzten et al. Berlin: de Gruyter, 1975.

Metscher, T.W.H. "Brecht and Marxist Dialectics." *Oxford German Studies*, 6 (1971–72), 132–144.

Mitchell, Stanley. "From Shklovsky to Brecht: Some Preliminary Remarks Towards a History of the Politicization of Russian Formalism." *Screen*, 15:2 (Summer 1974), 74–80.

———. "Introduction to Benjamin and Brecht." *New Left Review*, 77 (Jan.–Feb. 1973).

Müller, Klaus-Detlev. "Brechts Me-Ti und die Auseinandersetzung mit dem Lehrer Karl Korsch." *Brecht Jahrbuch 1976*. Frankfurt a.M.: Suhrkamp, 1977.

————. *Die Funktion der Geschichte im Werk Bertolt Brechts: Studien zum Verhältnis von Marxismus und Aesthetik*. Tübingen: Max Niemeyer, 1967.

Qureshi, Qayum. *Pessimismus und Fortschrittsglaube bei Brecht: Beiträge zum Verstandnis seines dramatischen Werkes*. Köln: Bohlau Verlag, 1971.

Rasch, Wolfdietrich. "Bertolt Brechts Marxistischer Lehrer." *Merkur*, 17 (1963), 996–1003.

Ryan, Lawrence. "Bertolt Brecht: A Marxist Dramatist?" *Aspects of Drama and the Theatre*. London: Methuen, 1965.

Sokel, Walter H. "Brechts marxistischer Weg zur Klassik." In *Klassik-Legende*, edited by Reinhold Grimm and Jost Hermand. Frankfurt a.M.: Athenäum, 1971.

————. "Brecht's Split Characters and His Sense of the Tragic." In *Brecht: A Collection of Critical Essays*, edited by Peter Demetz. Englewood Cliffs, N.J.: Prentice-Hall, 1962.

————. "Brecht und Expressionismus." In *Die sogenannten Zwanziger Jahre*, edited by Reinhold Grimm and Jost Hermand. Frankfurt a.M.: Athenäum, 1970.

Sternberg, Fritz. *Der Dichter und die Ratio: Erinnerungen an Bertolt Brecht*. Göttingen: Sachse und Pohl, 1963.

Suvin, Darko. "The Mirror and the Dynamo: On Brecht's Aesthetic Point of View." In *Radical Perspectives in the Arts*, edited by Lee Baxandall. Baltimore, Md.: Penguin, 1972.

Völker, Klaus. *Bertolt Brecht: Eine Biographie*. München: Hanser Verlag, 1976. (This was published in an English translation in 1978 by Seabury Press, New York.)

Willett, John. *The Theatre of Bertolt Brecht*. New York: New Directions, 1968.

Witt, Hubert, ed. *Brecht as They Knew Him*. New York: International Publishers, 1974.

Zimmerman, Mark. "Brecht's Aesthetics of Production." *Praxis*, 3 (1976), 115–137.

WORKS ON LUKÁCS

A good bibliography of secondary literature on Lukács is in *Text und Kritik*, 39/40 (October 1973), 86–88.

Adorno, Theodor W. "Reconciliation under Duress." In *Aesthetics and Politics*, edited by Perry Anderson et al. London: New Left Books, 1977.

Arato, Andrew. "Georg Lukács: The Search for a Revolutionary Subject." In *The Unknown Dimension: European Marxism Since Lenin*. New York: Basic Books, 1972.

————. "Lukács' Path to Marxism, 1910–1923." *Telos*, 7 (Spring 1971).

————. "Lukács' Theory of Reification." *Telos*, 11 (Spring 1972), 25–66.

————. "Notes on History and Class Consciousness." *Philosophical Forum*, 3:3–4 (Spring–Summer 1972). (Special issue on Lukács.)

————, and Paul Breines. *The Young Lukács and the Origins of Western Marxism*. New York: Seabury Press, 1979.

Berman, Russell. "Lukács' Critique of Bredel and Ottwalt: A Political Account of an Aesthetic Debate of 1931–32." *New German Critique*, 10 (Winter 1977).

Breines, Paul. "Lukács, Revolution and Marxism, 1885–1918." *Philosophical Forum*, 3:3–4 (Spring–Summer 1972).

———. "Marxism, Romanticism and the Case of Georg Lukács: Notes on Some Recent Sources and Situations." *Studies in Romanticism*, (Fall 1977).

———. "Praxis and Its Theorists: The Impact of Lukács and Korsch in the 1920s." *Telos*, 11 (Spring 1972).

———. "Young Lukács, Old Lukács, New Lukács: A Review Essay." *Journal of Modern History* 51:3 (September 1979), 533–546.

Congden, Lee. "The Unexpected Revolutionary: Lukács' Road to Marx." *Survey*, 91/92 (Spring–Summer 1974).

Deutscher, Isaac, "Georg Lukács and Critical Realism." In *Marxism in Our Time*. Berkeley: University of California Press, 1972.

Federici, Silvia. "Notes on Lukács' Aesthetics." *Telos*, 11 (Spring 1972).

Fehér, Ferenc. "The Last Phase of Romantic Anti-Capitalism: Lukács' Response to the War." *New German Critique*, 10 (Winter 1977), 139–154.

Illés, L. "Die Freiheit der künstlerischen Richtungen und das Zeitgemässe." In *Littérature et Réalité*, edited by B. Köpeczi and P. Juhász. Budapest: Akadémiai Kiadó, 1966.

Jameson, Fredric. "The Case for Georg Lukács." In *Marxism and Form: Twentieth-Century Dialectical Theories of Literature*. Princeton, N.J.: Princeton University Press, 1971.

Jones, Gareth Stedman. "The Marxism of the Early Lukács." *New Left Review*, 70 (November–December 1971).

Kettler, David. "Culture and Revolution: Lukács in the Hungarian Revolution of 1918." *Telos*, 10 (Winter 1971–72).

Királyfalvi, Béla. *The Aesthetics of György Lukács*. Princeton, N.J.: Princeton University Press, 1975.

Lichtheim, George. *Georg Lukács*. New York: Viking Press, 1970.

Löwy, Michael. *Georg Lukács: From Romanticism to Bolshevism*. London: New Left Books, 1979.

———. "Lukács and Stalinism." *New Left Review*, 91 (May–June 1975).

Ludz, Peter. "Der Begriff der 'demokratischen Diktatur' in der politischen Philosophie von Georg Lukács." In *Festschrift zum achtzigsten Geburtstag von Georg Lukács*, edited by Frank Benseler. Neuwied and Berlin: Luchterhand, 1965.

Markus, György. "The Soul and Life: The Young Lukács and the Problem of Culture." *Telos*, 32 (Summer 1977), 95–116.

Mészarós, Istvan. *Lukács' Concept of Dialectic*. London: Merlin Press, 1972.

———, ed. *Aspects of History and Class Consciousness*. London: Routledge and Kegan Paul, 1971.

Miles, David H. "Portrait of the Marxist as a Young Hegelian: Lukács' *Theory of the Novel*." *PMLA*, 94:1 (1979), 22–35.

Parkinson, G.H.R. *Georg Lukács*. London: Routledge and Kegan Paul, 1977.

———, ed. *Georg Lukács: The Man, His Work, His Ideas*. New York: Random House, 1970.

Plotke, David. "Marxism, Sociology and Crisis: Lukács' Critique of Weber." *Berkeley Journal of Sociology*, 20 (1975–76).

Raddatz, Fritz. *Lukács*. Reinbek bei Hamburg: Rowohlt, 1972.

Radnoti, Sandor. "Bloch and Lukács: Two Radical Critics in a 'God-Forsaken' World." *Telos*, 24 (Summer 1975).

Rosenberg, Harold. "The Third Dimension of Georg Lukács." *Dissent*, 11:4 (Fall 1964), 404–414.

Sander, Hans-Dietrich. *Marxistische Ideologie und allgemeine Kunsttheorie.* Tübingen: J. D. B. Mohr, 1970.

Sontag, Susan. "The Literary Criticism of Georg Lukács." In *Against Interpretation and Other Essays.* New York: Dell, 1969.

Steiner, George. "George Lukács and His Devil's Pact." In *Language and Silence: Essays, 1958–1966.* Middlesex, England: Penguin, 1969.

Tökei, F. "Lukács and Hungarian Culture." *New Hungarian Quarterly*, 13:47 (Autumn 1972), 108–128.

Watnick, Morris. "Georg Lukács: or Aesthetics and Communism." *Survey*, 23 (January–March 1958), 60–66; 24 (April–June 1958), 51–57; 25 (July–September 1958), 61–68; and 27 (January–March 1959), 75–81.

VI. Works on German and European Social, Political, and Cultural History, and Miscellaneous

Arato, Andrew. "The Neo-Idealist Defense of Subjectivity." *Telos*, 21 (Fall 1974), 108–161.

Biale, David. *Gershom Scholem: Kabbalah and Counter-History*. Cambridge, Mass.: Harvard University Press, 1979.

Bloch, Ernst. "Diskussionen über Expressionismus." In *Marxismus und Literatur*, Vol. 2. Edited by Fritz Raddatz. Reinbek bei Hamburg: Rowohlt, 1969.

———. *Erbschaft dieser Zeit*. Frankfurt a.M.: Suhrkamp, 1962.

———, and Hans Eisler. "Die Kunst zu erben." In *Marxismus und Literatur*, Vol. 2. Edited by Fritz Raddatz. Reinbek bei Hamburg: Rowohlt, 1969.

Bracher, Karl Dietrich. *The German Dictatorship*. New York: Praeger, 1970.

Brady, Robert. *The Rationalization Movement in German Industry: A Study in the Evolution of Economic Planning*. New York: Howard Fertig, 1970.

Brunschwig, Henri. *Enlightenment and Romanticism in Eighteenth-Century Prussia*. Chicago: University of Chicago Press, 1974.

Butler, E. M. *The Tyranny of Greece over Germany*. Cambridge, England: Cambridge University Press, 1935.

Childs, David. *Germany Since 1918*. New York: Harper and Row, 1970.

Coates, Wilson, and Haydn White. *An Intellectual History of Western Europe*. Vol. 2: *The Ordeal of Liberal Humanism*. New York: McGraw-Hill, 1970.

Coser, Lewis. *Men of Ideas: A Sociologist's View*. New York: Free Press, 1965.

Cuddihy, John Murray. *The Ordeal of Civility: Freud, Marx, Lévi-Strauss and the Jewish Struggle with Modernity*. New York: Basic Books, 1974.

Deak, Istvan. *Weimar Germany's Left-Wing Intellectuals: A Political History of the Weltbühne and Its Circle*. Berkeley: University of California Press, 1968.

Deutscher, Isaac. *Stalin: A Political Biography*. New York: Vintage, 1960.

Gilbert, Felix. "Intellectual History: Its Aims and Methods." *Daedalus*, 100:1 (Winter 1971), 80–97.

Gillis, John R. *The Development of European Society, 1770–1870*. Boston: Houghton Mifflin, 1977.

Grunfeld, Frederic. *Prophets Without Honour: A Background to Freud, Kafka, Einstein and Their World.* New York: Holt, Rinehart and Winston, 1980.

Habermas, Jürgen. *Knowledge and Human Interests.* Boston: Beacon, 1971.

———. *Philosophe-Politische Profile.* Frankfurt a.M.: Suhrkamp, 1971.

———. *Theory and Practice.* Boston: Beacon, 1973.

Halliday, Fred. "Karl Korsch: An Introduction." In Karl Korsch, *Marxism and Philosophy.* New York: Monthly Review Press, 1970.

Handlin, Oscar. "The Jews in the Culture of Middle Europe." In *Studies of the Leo Baeck Institute.* Edited by Max Kreutzberger. New York: Frederick Ungar, 1967.

Hawkes, Terence. *Structuralism and Semiotics.* Berkeley: University of California Press, 1977.

Hawthorn, Geoffrey. *Enlightenment and Despair: A History of Sociology.* Cambridge, England: Cambridge University Press, 1976.

Hobsbawm, Eric. *The Age of Capital, 1848–1875.* New York: Mentor, 1975.

Hofstadter, Richard. *Anti-Intellectualism in American Life.* New York: Vintage, 1962.

Horkheimer, Max. *Critical Theory: Selected Essays.* New York: Seabury, 1972.

———. *Eclipse of Reason.* New York: Seabury, 1973.

Hughes, H. Stuart. *Consciousness and Society: The Reconstruction of European Social Thought, 1890–1930.* New York: Vintage, 1961.

———. *Contemporary Europe: A History.* Englewood Cliffs, N.J.: Prentice-Hall, 1961.

Iggers, Georg G. *The German Conception of History: The National Tradition of Historical Thought from Herder to the Present.* Middletown, Conn.: Wesleyan University Press, 1968.

Jacoby, Russell. *Social Amnesia: A Critique of Contemporary Psychology.* Boston: Beacon, 1975.

Jay, Martin. "The Extraterritorial Life of Siegfried Kracauer." *Salmagundi,* 31/32 (Fall 1975–Winter 1976), 49–106.

———. "The Jews and the Frankfurt School: Critical Theory's Analysis of Anti-Semitism." *New German Critique,* 19 (Winter 1980), 137–150.

———. "Some Recent Developments in Critical Theory." *Berkeley Journal of Sociology,* 18 (1973–74), 27–44.

Kelly, George Armstrong. *Politics, Idealism and History: Sources of Hegelian Thought.* London: Cambridge University Press, 1969.

King, Richard. *The Party of Eros: Radical Social Thought and the Realm of Freedom.* New York: Dell, 1972.

Knütter, Hans Helmuth. *Die Juden und die deutsche Linke in der Weimarer Republik.* Düsseldorf: Drost Verlag, 1971.

Kolakowski, Leszek. *Positivist Philosophy from Hume to the Vienna Circle.* Middlesex, England: Penguin, 1972.

Kracauer, Siegfried. *From Caligari to Hitler: A Psychological History of the German Film.* Princeton, N.J.: Princeton University Press, 1960.

———. "The Mass Ornament." *New German Critique,* 5 (Spring 1975), 67–76.

Landes, David. *The Unbound Prometheus: Technological Change and Indus-*

trial Development in Western Europe from 1750 to the Present. Cambridge, England: Cambridge University Press, 1969.

Laqueur, Walter. *Weimar: A Cultural History*. New York: Capricorn, 1973.

Lebovics, Hermann. *Social Conservatism and the German Middle Classes, 1914–1933*. Princeton, N.J.: Princeton University Press, 1968.

The Legacy of the German Refugee Intellectuals. Special issue of *Salmagundi*, 10–11 (Fall 1969–Winter 1970).

Lethen, Helmut. *Neue Sachlichkeit, 1924–1932: Studien zur Literatur des "Weissen Sozialismus."* Stuttgart: J.B. Metzler, 1970.

Lichtheim, George. *Europe in the Twentieth Century*. New York: Praeger, 1972.

Löwy, Michael. "Jewish Messianism and Libertarian Utopia in Central Europe." *New German Critique*, 20 (Spring/Summer 1980), 105–116.

Marcuse, Herbert. *One-Dimensional Man: Studies in the Ideology of Advanced Industrial Society*. Boston: Beacon Press, 1964.

———. *Reason and Revolution: Hegel and the Rise of Social Theory*. Boston: Beacon, 1960.

Medvedev, Roy. *Let History Judge: The Origins and Consequences of Stalinism*. New York: Vintage, 1971.

Mitzman, Arthur. "Anti-Progress: A Study in the Romantic Roots of German Sociology." *Social Research*, 33:1 (Spring 1966).

———. *The Iron Cage: An Interpretation of Max Weber*. New York: Universal Library, 1969.

Mosse, George L. *The Crisis of German Ideology: The Intellectual Origins of National Socialism*. New York: Grosset and Dunlap, 1964.

———. *The Culture of Western Europe*. 2nd edition. New York: Rand McNally, 1974.

———. *Germans and Jews: The Left, The Right and the Search for a "Third Force" in Pre-Nazi Germany*. New York: Grosset and Dunlap, 1970.

Niewyk, Donald W. "The Economic and Cultural Role of the Jews in the Weimar Republic." *Leo Baeck Institute Yearbook*, 16 (1971).

Paxton, Robert. *Europe in the Twentieth Century*. New York: Harcourt Brace Jovanovich, 1975.

Pells, Richard. *Radical Visions and American Dreams: Culture and Social Thought in the Depression Years*. New York: Harper and Row, 1973.

Pinkney, David H. *Napoleon III and the Rebuilding of Paris*. Princeton, N.J.: Princeton University Press, 1958.

Pulzer, Peter G.J. *The Rise of Political Anti-Semitism in Germany and Austria*. New York: John Wiley, 1964.

Ringer, Fritz. *The Decline of the German Mandarins: The German Academic Community, 1890–1933*. Cambridge, Mass.: Harvard University Press, 1969.

Robinson, Paul. *The Freudian Left*. New York: Harper and Row, 1969.

Rosen, Charles. *The Classical Style: Haydn, Mozart, Beethoven*. New York: Norton, 1972.

Roth, Cecil. *A History of the Jews*. New York: Schocken, 1970.

Rothman, Stanley, and Philip Isenberg. "Sigmund Freud and the Politics of Marginality." *Central European History*. 7:1 (March 1974), 58–78.

Sachar, Howard. *The Course of Modern Jewish History.* New York: Dell, 1958.

Schoenbaum, David. *Hitler's Social Revolution.* New York: Doubleday, 1966.

Scholem, Gershom. *Major Trends in Jewish Mysticism.* New York: Schocken, 1946.

———. *The Messianic Idea in Judaism and Other Essays on Jewish Spirituality.* New York: Schocken, 1971.

Shils, Edward. "Daydreams and Nightmares: Reflections on the Critique of Mass Culture." *Sewanee Review,* 65 (1957).

———. "The Theory of Mass Society." In *Center and Periphery: Essays in Macrosociology.* Chicago: University of Chicago Press, 1975.

Simmel, Georg. *The Philosophy of Money,* translated by Tom Bottomore and David Frisby. London: Routledge and Kegan Paul, 1978.

Skinner, Quentin. "Meaning and Understanding in the History of Ideas." *History and Theory,* 8:1 (1969).

Stern, Fritz. "The Political Consequences of the Unpolitical German." In *The Failure of Illiberalism.* New York: Knopf, 1972.

———. *The Politics of Cultural Despair: A Study in the Rise of the Germanic Ideology.* Berkeley: University of California Press, 1961.

Taylor, Charles. *Hegel.* Cambridge, England: Cambridge University Press, 1975.

Thompson, E. P. "Time, Work Discipline and Industrial Capitalism." *Past and Present,* 51 (1967).

White, Hayden. *Metahistory: The Historical Imagination in Nineteenth-Century Europe.* Baltimore: Johns Hopkins University Press, 1974.

Wieseltier, Leon. "Gershom Scholem and the Fate of the Jews." *New York Review of Books,* April 14, 1977.

———. "The Revolt of Gershom Scholem." *New York Review of Books,* March 31, 1977.

Index

Boldface page numbers indicate major discussions.